Sick from Freedom

Sick from Freedom

*African-American Illness and Suffering during
the Civil War and Reconstruction*

JIM DOWNS

OXFORD
UNIVERSITY PRESS

OXFORD

UNIVERSITY PRESS

Oxford University Press is a department of the University of Oxford.
It furthers the University's objective of excellence in research, scholarship,
and education by publishing worldwide.

Oxford   New York

Auckland   Cape Town   Dar es Salaam   Hong Kong   Karachi
Kuala Lumpur   Madrid   Melbourne   Mexico City   Nairobi
New Delhi   Shanghai   Taipei   Toronto

With offices in

Argentina   Austria   Brazil   Chile   Czech Republic   France   Greece
Guatemala   Hungary   Italy   Japan   Poland   Portugal   Singapore
South Korea   Switzerland   Thailand   Turkey   Ukraine   Vietnam

Oxford is a registered trade mark of Oxford University Press
in the UK and certain other countries.

Published in the United States of America by
Oxford University Press
198 Madison Avenue, New York, NY 10016

Library of Congress Cataloging-in-Publication Data
Downs, Jim.
Sick from freedom : African-American illness and suffering during the Civil War and reconstruction / Jim Downs.
p. cm.
Incl--udes bibliographical references and index.-
ISBN 978-0-19-975872-2 (hardback); 978-0-19-021826-3 (paperback)
1. African Americans—Health and hygiene—History. 2. Slaves—Emancipation—Health aspects—United States.
3. Freedmen—Diseases—United States. 4. United States—History--Civil War, 1861-1865—Health aspects. I. Title.
RA448.5.N4D69 2012
613.089'96073—dc23   2012004181

For all those who were emancipated but never made it to freedom

CONTENTS

ACKNOWLEDGMENTS

This book has a long history that can be traced to the University of Pennsylvania and the fateful semester when I opted to abandon my childhood dream of becoming an actor and instead decided to become an academic. My undergraduate teachers inspired me in ways that I find difficult to recount but made sense to a 21-year-old who believed that getting a PhD was the most exciting prospect in the world. While the term "inspired" has become cliché in book acknowledgments, I employ it here, if only to evoke its Latin origins, meaning "to breathe." And for that, I am truly indebted to my college teachers at Penn: Herman Beavers, Nancy Bentley, Stephanie M. H. Camp, Ellie DiLapi, Drew Gilpin Faust, David Fox, Robert Gregg, Farah Jasmine Griffin, Dana Philips, Martin Orzeck, and most adoringly the late Lynda Hart, whose deep passion and unwavering commitment to ideas continues to enable me to breathe.

Because of my college professors' advice, I did not rush into graduate school but instead spent many years teaching at the middle school and secondary level. In my final years of teaching, I pursued an MA in American Studies at Columbia. There, I met an electrifying group of scholars, who helped me to focus my academic interests and encouraged me to pursue a degree in history. I am most grateful to Ann Douglas, Eric Foner, Winston James, and Anne McClintock. The summer after I completed my MA, I had the good fortune to earn an NEH fellowship for teachers and work at the National Archives, where I first was introduced to the Freedmen's Bureau. Leslie Rowland amazed me with her encyclopedic knowledge of the period and the sources, and encouraged me to continue to work with the records. The following year Jean Fagan Yellin hired me as a research assistant for the Harriet Jacobs Papers, which provided the basis for this project. Her ardent commitment to the study of the past made me believe in the possibilities of archival research.

Two years later, I entered Columbia's PhD program in history. Betsy Blackmar and Alice Kessler-Harris taught me how to think and to write like a historian, while Barbara J. Fields posed many questions that I still wrestle with in my teaching and writing. Herb Sloan, Casey Blake, Andrew Delbanco, and most especially, Maura Spiegel created important intellectual spaces that made graduate school rewarding. Among the U.S. graduate cohort, I have developed many meaningful and important friendships that have stood the test of time and of Fayerweather Hall. For their intellectual companionship, I am grateful to Jennifer Fronc, Shannan Clark, Monica Gisolfi, Jung Pak, Nancy Banks, Ashli White, Zaheer Ali, Reiko Hillyer, Jeffrey Trask, Sara Gregg, Betsy Herbin, Nancy Kwak, Natasha Korgaonkar, Adrienne Clay, Lisa Ramos, Dave Eisenbach, and Janice Traflet.

My greatest debt at Columbia is to my adviser Eric Foner, whose unwavering support is the main reason why I am a historian today. While he is certainly the leading historian of Reconstruction, he is also an excellent teacher and supportive mentor. He carefully read every word of my dissertation and continued to read various iterations of this manuscript, always offering sharp and critical feedback. I am lucky to have had the chance to work with him. Kathleen M. Brown picked up where Foner left off. She helped to transform the book from an institutional biography of the Medical Division of the Freedmen's Bureau to a broader analysis of emancipation, health, and the changing role of the federal government. Not only did she read various drafts of the manuscript, but she also continually served as a sounding board on a number of issues from my questions about eighteenth- and nineteenth-century medicine to more structural questions on how to organize various chapters. She is someone whose work I have long admired; the fact that she helped me so much on this project means more to me than she knows, or I wish to tally. At a conference that Kathy organized at Penn, I first met Catherine Clinton. Over the years, she has championed my work, supported this project, and published the first article that came out of my dissertation. Her scholarship on the South provided a necessary framework for this project and her deep knowledge of the nineteenth century helped me fill in the plot of this book. She consistently encouraged me to be mindful of the narrative quality of my writing, and her many books have served as models in this regard.

I am incredibly fortunate to have received support from a number of institutions that enabled me to complete this book; their assistance provided not only financial help but also encouragement for me to continue with this project. For supporting the research at the dissertation stage, I would like to thank the John Hope Franklin Travel Grant at Duke University, Helfand Medical Fellowship, Library Company of Philadelphia, Virginia Historical Society's 2003 Andrew Mellon Research Fellowship, and the Gilder Lehrman Institute Research Fellowship, New York Historical Society. At Columbia University, I am grateful to the Office of the Dean of the Graduate School of Arts and Sciences, which provided a scholarship during my first year, summer funding in my second year, and research funds in my final year. I am particularly grateful to Margaret Edsall. The Department of History provided teaching fellowships in the years in between. The Public Policy Research Fellowship at the School of Public Policy and International Affairs provided funding in my fourth year. The American Studies program offered me a teaching fellowship in my final year that enabled me to finish the dissertation in the fall and teach in the spring. After I graduated from Columbia, Princeton University's Committee on Research in the Humanities and Social Sciences Grant provided funding in 2006 to return to the archives. At Connecticut College, the Judith Opatrny Junior Faculty Fellowship, Meredith Anders Award for Junior Faculty, RF Johnson grants, and Hodgkin Funds enabled me to conduct research and to write, as did the pre-tenure sabbatical for junior faculty. I would also like to extend a warm thanks to Dean Roger Brooks who awarded me with a second research sabbatical in my fifth year at the College that enabled me to complete a large chunk of the manuscript. During my sabbaticals, I also received additional research funding from the Gilder Lehrman Center at Yale University, the Andrew W. Mellon Fellowship at the Massachusetts Historical Society, and the Mayers Fellowship at the Huntington Library.

This project began to take shape in David Rothman's History of Medicine seminar and continued to develop in many conversations I had with David Rosner, who served on the dissertation committee. Samuel Roberts's course on Racism and Public Health was fundamental to this book as were his comments at the dissertation prospectus stage. Betsy Blackmar helped me to conceptualize the analytical frame for the dissertation; her broad intellectual range and critical imagination helped me throughout the writing of the project in graduate school. Maura Spiegel meticulously read the dissertation and offered brilliant and creative ways to read the sources. Nancy Stepan served on the dissertation committee and provided valuable feedback that guided the early stages of revision. Farah Jasmine Griffin was my undergraduate teacher and moved to Columbia when I was in graduate school. She served on the dissertation committee and advised me throughout graduate school. At a very early stage of my training, she taught me to understand that people's lives do not fit neatly into archival records, and she encouraged me to probe the fissures and silences in the evidence. Margaret Humphreys and Todd Savitt both read the dissertation and offered invaluable suggestions on how to turn the dissertation into a book.

Over the years, a number of faculty and colleagues have helped me develop this project and have supported my work. Glenda Gilmore disrupted my intellectual balance in a number of conversations that helped me to think in more depth about Southern lives. Carla Peterson's infectious curiosity emboldened me to move forward. Clarence Walker warned me not to fall into the pitfalls of academic trends and continually supported the objectives of this project. Anthony Kaye has enthusiastically supported this book and offered wise advice at a crucial turning point. Christopher Capozzola served as a sounding board on my many trips to the archives in Boston, and helped me think about creative ways to read the sources. Christine Stansell's elegant prose set a high standard for how to write history. I have emulated her books over the years; the fact that she has read parts of this book and supported this project means a great deal to me. I first met Thavolia Glymph many years ago when I was a teacher at an NEH Institute on the Freedmen's Bureau; her knowledge of the South awed me then and continues to amaze me now. She has helped me think through a number of the conceptual problems of this period, and her scholarship and keen knowledge of the South has profoundly influenced this book. Stephanie M. H. Camp was my teacher in college. Although she tells me that we have outgrown that relationship, I continue to learn so much from her. At critical junctures, Seth Rockman helped me to elucidate my argument, and, at the bottom of the ninth, his astute comments helped me sharpen my analysis.

Bill Deverell, Steven Hahn, Anne Kornhauser, and Catherine McNicol Stock encouraged me to end the book on the West. Cathy and Anne read drafts on this subject and helped me to think through this period and place more carefully. At conferences and various meetings, I have been fortunate to have a number of leading scholars comment on the work. I would like to thank Sharla Fett, Keith Wailoo, Martha Hodes, Susan L. Smith, Kate Masur, Heather Cox Richardson, Stephanie M. H. Camp, Sara Gregg, and Conevery Bolton Valencius. I have also been very lucky to meet and to collaborate with a number of junior scholars, including Carole Emberton, Hannah Rosen, Susan O'Donovan, Melissa Stein, Brian Connolly, Allyson Hobbs, and Freddie LaFeminia, who compelled me to think about this project from new and exciting angles. Special thanks to Brandi Brimmer who has helped me navigate my way through the Pension Records, and in the process became a friend. Greg Downs professes no relation, but I am inclined to think that our intellectual camaraderie counts for something. He has discussed with me many of the ideas in this book and has been a great friend. Nicholas Syrett is one of my favorite historians and has guided me through the writing of this book. Jennifer Fronc and Monica Gisolfi have been talking to me about this project since graduate school and continue to offer fresh interpretations. Since we were undergraduates, Jennifer Manion has not only been one of my closest friends but also one of the fiercest intellectuals that I have ever encountered. She has always understood the political, intellectual, and personal roots of this project, and when I needed it the most, she has pushed me to dare more.

At Connecticut College, Eileen Kane has helped me the most with this book. Her ability to deliver forceful and persuasive prose is second to none; she has also helped me think through the broader relevance of the study. Ann Marie Davis's knowledge of medical history has pointed me in the right direction on a number of occasions. Monique Bedasse has always understood that this project is about "the people," which has been the most important form of encouragement. Sarah Queen has been an enormous supporter of my work since I arrived at the college. Mab Segrest has shared her new research on the history of mental health in the South and has been a wonderful colleague and friend. Cathy Stock has been a great mentor and enthusiastically supported my work over the years. Nancy Lewandowski has provided herculean administrative support during the writing (and photocopying) of this book. Finally, my most important debt is to the past and present members of the untenured faculty of color alliance, whose commitment to equality and understanding of how race works have provided an important refuge. I am especially grateful to Sandy Grande, Cherise Harris, Jennifer Domino Rudolph, Courtney Baker, Dave Canton, Sunil Bhatia, Christina Lee, and most of all, Aida Heredia—whose office has been an oasis.

While writing can be a solitary endeavor, I have been blessed to have the support of many friends who have been willing to discuss this book with me. T. K. Hunter has helped me with this book since she first discovered me sobbing in Butler Library after I got comments back from Foner on chapter 3. She got me back on my feet then and continues to help me think through the main arguments of the book now. Her ability to rattle off historical details from the eighteenth and nineteenth centuries and seamlessly weave them into a conversation reminds me why I came to history in the first place. Many of the ideas in this book began with conversations with Anne Kornhauser. Her ability to hone in on the limitations of a particular argument or to identify the possibilities of an analytical position make her one of the smartest historians whom I have ever met and one of the best editors of my work. Susane Colasanti and I have made seasonal pacts, which have ensured that this book would be done. Since college, Todd Anten has been my first reader and the first person I turn to for advice.

I decided to publish with Oxford University Press because of Susan Ferber, which had little to do with being stranded with her and two other colleagues at a motel at the Mall of America on a trip home from a conference. Susan is hands-down a phenomenal editor. She meticulously read the manuscript and offered incisive comments on how to sharpen the argument. This is a better book because of her intelligence, her alacrity, and her hard work. I would also like to thank Joellyn Ausanka at OUP for her patience and help during the production stages of this book.

My family and nonacademic friends have been most supportive during this project. Joe Figini consistently opened his home to me while I was on research jaunts to the National Archives in Washington, DC and has been an enthusiastic supporter of my work. Daniel McLaughlin let me stay with him in LA while I was at the Huntington Library and did not fail to find the humor in any given day. Nick Davilas wholeheartedly supported my work on this project since it was a dissertation, but he cannot understand why it was not done after I defended.

When I was a teacher at Rumson Country Day School in New Jersey, I had the auspicious opportunity to lead a group of mothers in a monthly book club. What began 13 years ago as a part-time job has become one of the most enjoyable intellectual endeavors of my life. For that, I am grateful to Nena Bernard, Joanne Clark, Sally Anne French, Shelley Gordon, Sharon Lee, Lore MacDonald, Yolanda Penny, Stella Ryan, and the late Wendy Glass, who first invited me to lead the group. My history book group in West Philly, comprised of Kathy Brown, Lori Ginzberg, Jennifer Manion, and Scott Wilds, has been my intellectual home for years. My New York City friends, affectionately referred to as "The BFFs," have been most supportive of me during the writing of this book, I am lucky to have such a wonderful community of friends that include Christopher Stadler, Christi Helsel, Shay Gipson, Geoff Lewis, Mike Montone, and the lowercases: Blake Sedberry, Brad Goetz, Stephen Barrow Barlow, Caroline Krueger, John Bantivoglio, Ross Leimberg, Jennifer Pomeranz, Michael Wisz, Natalie Tirado, and Daniel Kiashek. Andrea and Harley Dalimonte have been family since 206 Bloomfield. A major shout out to the crew at Grounded in the West Village, where I wrote most of this book.

My family reminds me of the importance of this book. My Uncle Joe continued to ask me questions at holiday events about the status of the project and consistently shared with me his curiosity of the past. My Aunt Lynn has urged me, if nothing else, to "keep it real" when writing this book. My cousins, Michael Ferrara and Karen O'Neill Mullane, inspire me with their commitment and passion to teach. My brother and sister have reminded me that family matters above everything else, while my grandparents reminded me of my connections to the past. At each of my graduations, my father always turned to me and said, "No one can take that away from you." For a people that have had so much taken away from them, or as my Dad likes to remind me, "have been oppressed for nine hundred years," the mere publication of this book is an act of defiance. In ways that I find difficult to articulate, my Mother has influenced me the most in the way that I have read the sources, her ability to immediately identify the emotional composition of a person or of an experience has shaped this project from the start. Finally, this book is dedicated to those who did not survive emancipation. Their plight reminded me of the value of life and the reality of my own freedom. Above all they have, in ways that only people from across time and place can, given me purpose.

Sick from Freedom

Introduction

How does one rewrite the chronicle of a death foretold and anticipated,
as a collective biography of dead subjects, as a counter-history of the
human, as the practice of freedom?
 —Saidiya Hartman, *"Venus in Two Acts," Small Axe (2008)*

He was a casualty of war. Yet, he did not fall victim to a gunshot wound, nor was he stampeded by the thunderous march of troops, who ran toward enemy lines. He did not succumb to dysentery, pneumonia, or smallpox, which plagued Union and Confederate camps. Nor was he even a victim of one of the most lethal incubators of disease during the war: military prisons—where measles, rats, and lice proliferated among the emaciated bodies of soldiers. By strict definition, he was not even a casualty because he deserted the army, no longer able to stomach a war that pitted brother against brother.

It is difficult even to define him as a casualty, because the war had a much more triumphant and glorious consequence for him. It freed him and his mother, father, five siblings, and the roughly four million other slaves held against their will. The war offered him and his family "freedom," a chance to escape from the barbarity of a system that had transformed his body into a commodity, but the limits of his humanity were soon retested in a nation at war. After escaping from slavery, he and his siblings made it to a Union camp where an official diagnosed them as "nearly starved, their limbs are frozen." After taking a closer look at his condition, the Union officer noted that he was "likely to lose both feet."[1]

Due to the fact that the war had ultimately freed them from the institution of slavery, it became almost linguistically impossible to articulate his family's suffering. Instead, a whole new vocabulary developed that enshrined the revolutionary destruction of slavery and anticipated the transformative coming of freedom. Military officials, federal authorities, Northern journalists, and even their main allies, abolitionists, did not classify freed slaves as casualties or count them among the soldiers who died, but defined them as "fugitives," "contraband,"

3

"refugees," and ultimately as "freedmen." Casualties referred only to white soldiers, whose deaths, as horrific and unfortunate as they were, were described as
the ultimate sacrifice for a greater political cause. Their demise, in turn, became
commemorated as part of a larger cultural discourse known as the "good death."[2]
Bondspeople who fled from plantation slavery during and after the war, and
embraced their freedom with hope and optimism did not expect that it would
lead to sickness, disease, suffering, and death. The Civil War, however, produced
the largest biological crisis of the nineteenth century, claiming more soldiers'
lives and resulting in more casualties than battle or warfare and wreaking havoc
on the population of the newly freed.[3] The causes of the high rates of illness
and mortality during the Civil War resulted from various factors, including the
unsanitary conditions of army camps, polluted waterways, unburied bodies of
animals and soldiers, overcrowding, dislocation, and the medical profession's
uncertainty about how to respond to the massive epidemics that plagued the
South, among other issues. Disease and sickness had a more devastating and
fatal effects on emancipated slaves than on soldiers, since ex-slaves often lacked
the basic necessities to survive. Emancipation liberated bondspeople from slavery, but they often lacked clean clothing, adequate shelter, proper food, and access to medicine in their escape toward Union lines. Many freed slaves died once
they secured refuge behind Union camps. Even after the war ended, they continually struggled to survive in a region torn apart by disease and destruction.

Our unnamed freedman, however, managed to survive, along with his five
siblings. His father enlisted in the army based on a federal agreement that his
military service would provide his wife and children with protection from Confederate guerrillas, who often lurked around the perimeters of Union camps. Yet,
his family's arrival at a Union camp in Chattanooga, where roughly 2,500 other
emancipated slaves had fled after Union occupation of the city in 1863, did not
guarantee them the safety and stability they sought.[4] Instead, the military ordered
the family relocated to Nashville. In general, Union commanders saw the presence of newly emancipated slaves, who formed makeshift communities just outside Union barracks, as a distraction from larger military objectives. Struggling
to survive, freedpeople frequently begged for scraps of uneaten food, worn-out
boots, and unused tents. Since military officials did not provide ex-slaves with
the necessities to survive, army leaders regularly ordered them to be moved from
one camp to another. Yet, keeping freedpeople on the move and thereby preventing them from settling often had devastating consequences on their health.

He and his family were moved from Chattanooga to Nashville and then back
to Chattanooga without their mother. She had died in Nashville, more than
likely from the undocumented illnesses that claimed the lives of so many emancipated slaves.[5] He and his siblings were certainly casualties of war. Their starvation and illness compounded by the death of their mother defines them as

casualties, but since their dislocation unfolded in the context of liberation, they were, and still are, defined in terms of their newly freed status.

In the Union-occupied city of Chattanooga in the winter of the 1865, his unhealthy condition could easily be overlooked. Battle left a more indelible imprint on the region than his liberation. Several hundred tons of ammunition and "two thousand pieces of artillery" replaced the city that was once known for its proximity to the Tennessee River.[6] Church bells no longer rang on Sundays alerting people to the commencement of services, because the Presbyterian church had been turned into a hospital for white sick, injured soldiers.[7] A hill located in the southeast part of the town had been transformed into a burial ground for the hundreds of Union troops that perished in the Battle of Chattanooga.[8] The war also ushered in a smallpox epidemic that threatened the city's residents. Fear of the epidemic did not prevent members of the Thayer and Noyal Company from following through with their plans to hold a circus. Yet before the event concluded, a storm blew in, causing the tent to collapse, and within minutes crowds of people were soaked with mud.[9] In the midst of all this calamity and chaos, our nameless young freedman nevertheless remains an anomaly. While there were efforts to turn churches into hospitals and earmark a resting ground for fallen soldiers, caring for emancipated slaves was not a primary goal or concern of the military.

It is difficult to imagine how badly someone's feet must be frozen that an Army official had thought that the best solution would be amputation. It is at these moments that the historian's tools seem unable to convey the magnitude of the situation.[10] A mere sentence scratched on a page from a century ago about a child escaped from slavery, separated from his father, mourning the loss of his mother, watching his siblings starve to death, and confronted with having his frozen feet amputated is only a tragic outline that barely captures the full story of his plight. How long did he suffer before he caught the attention of the military? How many days, weeks, or even months had he gone without shoes before the rain, cold, and ice made it too painful to walk? Had he escaped from slavery during the summer and lived in a place where most slaves walked around barefoot? Or does his lack of shoes reflect the mistreatment he endured during slavery? Perhaps his owner did not provide shoes to his labor force, or maybe he lost his shoes, or they were stolen.

It is almost impossible to answer these questions, partly because the child enters the historical record anonymously. No record of his name, birthplace, or destination appears in the Union officer's report. But telling the story, in a few sentences, of a child whose feet had frozen and faced impending amputation helps us to understand the challenges that emancipation posed and paints a more complex picture of the Civil War's meaning for freedpeople. Amidst the traditional stories of Northern and Southern white families whose fathers and sons were separated from their homes during the war are many stories of former enslaved families for whom freedom brought dispersal, an inability to secure shelter and food, and fatal illness. In most accounts of the Civil War, sick and dying freedpeople rarely appear.

The few and scattered references of freedpeople suffering from the challenges of emancipation have been overlooked because these episodes do not fit into the patriotic narratives of the Civil War. Frozen feet and starvation complicate accounts dominated by heroic black soldiers or freedwomen in Union camps, caring for both freed slaves and Northern troops. These carefully cast representations of freedpeople were often created by white authors in the late nineteenth century who strove to highlight the happy outcomes brought by emancipation.[11] Recounting the hardships endured by former slaves during emancipation risked sending the erroneous message that the institution of slavery was not wholly cruel—inadvertently supporting the argument of antebellum, proslavery advocates in response to the abolitionist movement. White Southerners defended slavery as a more humane institution that protected the interests of black families compared with the fate of the working poor in the burgeoning industrial cities of the North, where families were torn apart by poverty, alcoholism, and immorality.

The experience of sick freedpeople was often pushed aside in favor of a liberation narrative that heroically described the abolition of slavery, or it was chalked up as a natural outcome of the war, which caused massive carnage and produced an enormous death toll among soldiers. Consequently, agents of the federal government did not tell the stories of the tens of thousands of emancipated slaves who suffered and died during the Civil War from the explosive outbreak of epidemic disease. The names and experiences of these freedpeople were too politically problematic to be recorded.[12] Generations later, historians have certainly documented freedpeople's struggles, but they often define hardship as freedpeople's fight for suffrage, equal wages, and land ownership. They conclude these studies by revealing how freedpeople either overcame the adversity that stood in their way toward freedom, or they explain that even when freedpeople failed, these episodes serve as powerful examples of black people's indefatigable determination and invincible autonomy.[13] This book reveals the obstacles that freedpeople faced that could not have been defeated no matter how willing or independent they may have been. The outbreak of epidemics and sickness compounded by the inability to secure clothing, shelter, and food left many freedpeople dead and caused inordinate suffering among those who survived.

Freedpeople suffered from sickness and poverty, and struggled to have their voices heard by contemporary officials, who were hell-bent on portraying the South as rebuilt, and later by historians, who were in search of heroic icons to shatter racist stereotypes. The destruction of slavery left little rhetorical room for freedpeople to articulate how emancipation was a glorious achievement but one that brought new struggles that threatened their survival. While some journalists and federal officials certainly exposed and even exaggerated the problems of the postwar period, those who supported federal intervention in the South carefully orchestrated depictions of progress in the Reconstruction South. In general, federal officials avoided documenting freedpeople's suffering, because they wanted to promote an image of the Reconstruction South as prosperous. They often praised the military in their efforts to rebuild the South and described freedpeople as healthy and robust, suggesting that the federal government could terminate its efforts in the South.

The mere reference to freedpeople's health spurred debate that reflected Americans' ideological position on the polemical subject of emancipation rather than insight into freedpeople's actual health and well-being. Proslavery advocates pounced on any sign of freedpeople's illness as proof that the antebellum parable was true: that without white people's instruction, bondspeople would suffer and die. Former abolitionists, bondspeople's most sympathetic allies, did document freedpeople's health conditions but it is unclear in their depictions of suffering if what they were seeing were the medical problems caused by emancipation or if they were coming face-to-face with the harsh realities of slavery; or, if their descriptions reflected more about their own Victorian-inflected notions of health and cleanliness than freedpeople's actual health conditions.

Based on a careful analysis of a broad range of sources from government documents to newspaper reports to medical records, *Sick from Freedom* reveals that tens of thousands of freed slaves became sick and died due to the unexpected problems caused by the exigencies of war and the massive dislocation triggered by emancipation. The distress and medical crises that freed slaves experienced were a hidden cost of war and an unintended outcome of emancipation. While sickness and epidemics certainly existed in the South before, the Civil War, like many major wars throughout the nineteenth century, gave rise to explosive epidemic outbreaks and inordinate mortality and suffering. Contemporary wars such as the Crimean War fought between England and Russia in the mid-nineteenth century resulted in high mortality rates due to the biological crises that erupted. When Cuba revolted against Spain in 1895–98, enteric fever, smallpox, and yellow fever broke out in proportions; and during the Russo-Turkish War of 1877–78, typhus spread beyond the battlefields to nearby cities and towns.[14]

Military officials on both sides of the Mason-Dixon Line scrambled to develop effective medical corps and sanitary commissions, but the rapid spread of disease compounded by the lack of understanding of microbiology and germ theory during the mid-nineteenth century often thwarted their efforts. Furthermore, the destruction of slavery and the gradual erosion of the plantation economy, combined with the federal government's initial ambivalence and often ambiguous plans on how to rebuild the South, left former slaves without an institutional structure to help them survive the biological crises that the war generated. The ending of slavery led to the abrupt dismantling of antebellum systems of medical care (both those organized by enslaved people and by individual slaveholders on local plantations), and it exhausted the networks of support provided by municipal almshouses and state hospitals.

This created an institutional vacuum that left ex-slaves defenseless against disease outbreaks, which was further exacerbated by freedpeople's nebulous political and economic status. Emancipated slaves did not have a clear political status during and after the war. While the ratification of the Fourteenth Amendment in 1868 granted former enslaved people the right to be recognized as citizens and the ratification of the Fifteenth Amendment enabled freedmen to vote in 1870, it took a great deal of time for these transformations to occur. In the context of political history, 1862 to 1870 represents a short time frame, but when viewed from a medical perspective, eight years is a rather long time to struggle with inadequate food, clothing, shelter, and medical treatment.[15]

Economically, freedpeople's health was often connected to their employment status. Without gainful employment, many freed slaves became sick during the early transition to the free labor economy. Military officials rigorously evaluated freedpeople's bodies, determining who could work and in what capacity. Before the war, slaveholders and auctioneers developed the maxim of "soundness" to describe an enslaved person's economic value in terms of their physical health.[16] During the war, the military replaced this term with the formulation "able-bodied," which evaluated freedpeople's bodies and health based on their ability to work. Unlike slaveholders, the military privileged the employment of men, which left thousands of freedwomen, elderly, orphaned, and disabled freed slaves without formal opportunities to earn incomes. Living under such uncertain economic conditions left many freedpeople vulnerable physically as well as economically. Compounding matters, both during and after the war, freedpeople suffered from limited employment opportunities in agriculture, the industry for which the government considered them most suitable. The war destroyed much of the land for cultivation, while drought and the crop failures of 1866–67 further devastated large parts of the South—leaving thousands of emancipated slaves penniless. The onset of famine in 1867 led to chilling mortality rates among newly freed slaves.

Due to the massive epidemics, suffering, and poverty that inundated the South, health increasingly became a political issue. While health had been a political issue during slavery, Reconstruction was an empty promise without some semblance of reasonable health.[17] Freedpeople needed to be somewhat healthy to participate in the political campaigns for citizenship and suffrage or even to pursue any other benefits associated with the coming of rights, namely education, marriage, and land ownership. Freedpeople petitioned military officials for

Secret goal of the medical division of
the Freedmans *Introduction* bureau was to make

food, clothing, shelter, medicine, and proper burials for their families, which
represented their first efforts to gain political rights. By requesting federal medical intervention, freedpeople expanded the notion of political rights.

[handwritten margin note: freed people healthy enough to replace the labor force must municipality help disband]

The federal government responded to these appeals by arguing that state and
municipal authorities in the South should assume responsibility for freedpeople's
health. These institutions, which had historically offered universal support to the
poor and dispossessed, began to claim that they would only assist "citizens," who,
according to their definition, referred to white Southerners; they summarily
refused to provide assistance to formerly enslaved people. The federal government thus created the Freedmen's Bureau to serve as a temporary institution to
facilitate freedpeople's quests for access to the benefits of citizenship. Under the
auspices of the War Department, the federal government created the Medical Division of the Freedmen's Bureau, which included the construction of more than
40 hospitals and almshouses, and the employment of over 100 doctors and countless nurses, stewards, and aides to provide medical treatment to over one million
freed slaves.[18] The overarching, often unspoken, mission of the Medical Division
was to facilitate the creation of a healthy labor force. By establishing hospitals and
hiring doctors to provide medical treatment to emancipated slaves, the federal
government aimed to temporarily fill the void that civil authorities and slaveholders left in the wake of the war and emancipation. The creation of the Medical
Division facilitated the development of a free labor economy in the postwar South
by systematically dividing the population of freedpeople into those that the government and military defined as "able-bodied" and those marked as "dependent."
These hospitals, in turn, served more as shelters and almshouses than as institutions devoted to comprehensive medical care. Doctors often supplied freedpeople with clothing, food, and shelter, and provided only scant reports to federal
officials about the actual diseases or sicknesses that infected freedpeople.

It was a struggle for doctors to administer even this basic care and protect
freedpeople from illnesses. On a practical level, federal officials failed to develop
a workable administrative structure that effectively distributed supplies to the
South and provided doctors with the necessary money to hire staff. On an ideological level, many federal officials feared that providing ample support would
encourage freedpeople to become dependent on the government for food, shelter, and clothing; as a result, many federal administrators limited the amount of
support that hospitals received. Ironically, the government initially created the
Medical Division, in part, to facilitate the creation of a healthy labor force, but the
inefficiencies of the hospital system, combined with many federal officials' reluc-
tance to support this form of federal intervention, left hospitals unprepared to
respond to the sickness and epidemics that broke out across the postwar South.

Compounding matters, the Bureau's system of documenting illnesses led to
an incomplete and inaccurate portrait of health conditions in the South. When

Bureau physicians narrated illness, they either summarized the general health conditions of their jurisdiction in very broad and often terse terms, or they tallied mortality rates and the numbers of sick freedpeople using statistical reports, which represented new global trends in late-nineteenth century medicine. The Bureau uniformly adopted nosological reports from English and French doctors, in which they classified, quantified, and documented the diseases they diagnosed among freedpeople. Similar to the ways in which these reports were deployed throughout England, continental Europe, and parts of Asia, the Bureau's use of quantitative data helped to solidify medical authority during Reconstruction.[19]

While Bureau doctors relied on this form of disease classification to chart freedpeople's health, the data that they obtained from these statistical reports did not offer them a clear explanation or understanding of disease causation or transmission. The discovery of the microbe as the cause of a number of bacterial diseases, such as tuberculosis, diphtheria, and cholera, did not take place until the late nineteenth century. In the decades leading up to these revolutionary changes, physicians and hygienists on the ground began to move away from an understanding of disease that emphasized morality, social standing, and personal appearance as the central culprits for disease causation and began to investigate how the conditions of the physical world contributed to the spread of sickness and disease.[20] While the lack of understanding of microbiology certainly meant that doctors and scientists did not have a cure or even an etiological awareness of the behavior of diseases, it did not leave them entirely helpless against the spread of disease. In general, the recognition of the physical environment as a component of disease causation mobilized reformers on both sides of the Atlantic to organize sanitary reform efforts. In the United States, these efforts began locally, but as the Civil War produced an alarming amount of unexpected bloodshed and illness, reformers created the U.S. Sanitary Commission, modeled after the British Sanitary Commission, to promote healthier environments.

Additionally, the efforts of some Bureau physicians to create a sanitary environment unfolded within a broader, albeit more polemical, context about the role of the physician as either healer or scientist, which animated debates within the medical community throughout the early to mid-nineteenth century. At the beginning of the nineteenth century, American society questioned the efficacy of "regular" physicians as healers who employed aggressive forms of treatment, which included bloodletting, purging, and vomiting, and turned to "irregular" physicians or sectarians who practiced less aggressive forms of medical care, such as hydrotherapy and homeopathy.[21] By the 1830s, a number of American physicians began to travel to France for medical education. There they learned to investigate the causes of illness and value science in medical diagnosis and treatment. When they returned to the United States, older generations of physicians were impressed with their scientific knowledge, but questioned their efficacy as healers. Consequently, a divide developed between doctors who valued the practical, experiential methods of healing and those who were formally trained and emphasized scientifically based medical treatment.[22]

Despite this intense debate, the architects of the Medical Division of the Freedmen's Bureau did not take a direct stand on this issue; they neither committed themselves to a scientific approach that investigated the cause of illness and relied on new ideas about science to treat freedpeople nor did they identify themselves with healers while seeking to cure freedpeople from the many diseases that plagued them in the postwar years. Instead, Bureau doctors stationed throughout the South often provided treatment based on their own assessments, training, and understandings of medicine. Some Bureau physicians did attempt to investigate how the placement of privies led to outbreaks of dysentery among the freedpeople, while some hoped to prevent smallpox among freedpeople with rudimentary forms of vaccination. By and large, however, the majority of Bureau physicians simply responded to emergency medical crises and provided former slaves with basic necessities, such as food, clothing, and shelter. The distribution of these supplies indirectly suggests that Bureau doctors understood disease causation as rooted in the physical world, yet the Medical Division's administration never formally issued a detailed protocol on medical treatment that Bureau physicians should follow. The common practice that unified Bureau doctors across the South was their use of nosological reports, which they sent to their supervisors in Washington, DC.

That said, many Bureau physicians seemed to harbor beliefs that black people were inherently inferior and susceptible to certain illnesses and immune to others.[23] Compounding matters, Freedmen's Bureau doctors also interpreted freedpeople's health through the highly charged ideological prism of the South as a distinct region with its own peculiar etiology.[24] Consequently, their diagnoses often reflected stereotypes about the South and black people.[25]

By late 1869, the federal government turned responsibility for freedpeople's health over to state authorities, which had been their plan since arriving in the postwar South. Many military officials did not return home to the North, but were assigned to the Western territories, where they facilitated Native Americans' transition from so-called nomadic life to federally organized reservations. The infrastructure that developed during Reconstruction for new black citizens was transplanted in the West and became a national strategy for Native Americans. Reformers who worked as teachers for the freedpeople also traveled west and established schools for Native Americans.

The restructuring of this region, like the postwar South, was not as seamless as federal officials may have hoped. The federal government's inability to deliver supplies, resources, and food to Native Americans often exacerbated sickness and disease. As in the Reconstruction South, waiting for the crops to grow often led to devastating periods of starvation and sickness among Indians in the West. Comparing the West and the Reconstruction South illustrates that illness was often a byproduct of the federal government's efforts—including their reloca-tion of populations and reallocation of labor—to rebuild a region.

This book, therefore, is not only a study of disease and death as consequences of emancipation but of the expansion of federal power during the mid- to the late nineteenth century. Long before the late twentieth century debates about health care, military officials, erstwhile abolitionists, and former slaves articulated the need for the federal government to create a system of medical care that would respond to the dire health conditions of freedpeople during and in the imme-diate aftermath of the Civil War. The establishment of the Medical Division marks a watershed in the history of federal power. By assigning doctors to pro-vide medical support to black people throughout the urban and rural South, the Medical Division placed federal officials for the first time in U.S. history in direct and intimate contact with the bodies of ordinary people.[26]

The federal government's creation of the Medical Division of the Freedmen's Bureau unfolded within a broader international context when many national governments became intimately involved in matters of health and medicine. The outbreak of the Crimean War between England and Russia produced enormous health crises that led to the establishment of the British Sanitary Commission. Additionally, British imperial powers stationed across Asia in the nineteenth century triggered the Chinese and Japanese governments to become more actively involved in sanitary and public health reforms. In general, the pandemic outbreak of Asiatic cholera in the nineteenth century caused European govern-ments to take a more active role in matters of health and medicine. The United States' establishment of the Medical Division of the Freedmen's Bureau coin-cided with these larger international transformations.[27]

Amidst evidence of the expansion of the federal government and the creation of the Medical Division, there is a lack of first person testimony by freedpeople about their health conditions. The format of the Medical Division's records did not capture freedpeople's narrations of their health problems. There was not a protocol in the medical records, which consisted mostly of quantitative reports, for doctors to document freedpeople's description of their medical conditions. In other divisions of the Freedmen's Bureau, freedpeople's voices appear in the shape of affidavits, contract disputes, and passionate requests for schools to be built. Their voices have been preserved because Freedmen's Bureau agents and Northern teachers recognized the value of recording freedpeople's desire to learn, to earn a fair wage, or to own land. These groups often wanted to showcase to their Northern contemporaries and sponsoring organizations that their efforts were leading to the successful reconstruction of the South. A similar impulse did not exist among these groups to officially document freedpeople's pain, suffering, and illness. The lack of direct statements by freedpeople about their health conditions sharply contrasts with the preponderance of their voices in other records. These copious documents resulted less from the bureaucratic workings of the educational, labor, and legal administrative structures and more from the ways in which freedpeople, Bureau agents, and Northern reformers wanted to present a positive image of the Reconstruction South to the federal government and the rest of the nation.

The effort to excavate freedpeople's voices regarding their health conditions requires imagining the context in which medical treatment transpired. When Bureau doctors made requests to their supervising officials in Washington for more blankets, clothing, food, and medicine for former slaves, their demands did not simply result from their observations, but likely occurred because freedpeople asked for their help. As Bureau doctors entered hospitals, walked by freedpeople's living quarters, or passed families on their way to the fields, conversations surely took place between these individuals that did not get systematically documented. There was no need for Bureau doctors to offer a transcript to their commanding officers in D.C. about their brief conversations with freedpeople, so none were provided. It is also necessary to consider that freedpeople may have been reluctant to report their health conditions to army officials or to Bureau doctors in first place. From the perspective of many nineteenth-century Americans, black and white, rich and poor, hospitals were shelters for the dispossessed that carried a social stigma. Reporting a health problem would have also led white doctors to scrutinize, touch, and evaluate freedpeople's bodies in potentially uncomfortable and invasive ways.

Diagnosing Freedom

Charting the history of sickness, suffering, and death reveals the complicated legacy of freedom for many former slaves, and it reveals how emancipation functioned as a long, protracted process rather than as a shotgun moment of liberation. The phrase "from slavery to freedom," frequently used to describe the transformation of slaves into free people, eclipses emancipation as a process and fails to attend to the specificities of time and place. This problem is also discursive. "From slavery to freedom" posits a dichotomy. Yet, even when freedom is not explicitly defined as the opposite of slavery, but merely staged as a distinct moment separate from it, these episodes can be misleadingly seen as antithetical. These two distinctly separate events have different historical processes that need to be treated and investigated on their own terms, not as polar opposites.[28]

Within the broader context of the history of slavery in the Caribbean and Latin America, historians often use the term "the process of emancipation" to explain the complicated legal, political, economic, and social transitions that slaves confronted along their road toward freedom. In places such as Cuba and Guadeloupe, the ending of slavery was a protracted process, which at times inched toward liberation with the passage of various laws and the reformulation of economic contracts, but then other laws or policies retracted these earlier accessions and mandated a return to chattel slavery.[29] So, if historians were mathematicians, they might use a sine curve to represent graphically the ebbs and flows of emancipation followed in other parts of the Atlantic world. In the United States, historians have operated under the false presumption that the Civil War created a sudden halt to slavery, unlike the gradual process that characterized the emancipation of enslaved communities in the Caribbean and Latin America.[30] Taking a closer look at the health conditions of emancipated slaves and examining how and why freed slaves suffered and died suggests that the "process of emancipation" would be a more apt way to describe their experiences.

To that end, chapter 1 investigates the process of emancipation in the United States by paying particular attention to freedpeople's nebulous political status, the ambiguous military policies addressing emancipation, and the unhealthy environments in which they were forced to live. The chapter subsequently argues how these factors led to high mortality rates and epidemic outbreaks. It also uncovers how the military, federal government, the Office of Surgeon General, sanitary reformers, the medical profession, and even freed slaves were unprepared for the medical catastrophes produced by war and proved unable to stop the spread of illness and disease. Chapter 2 further examines why disease broke out among emancipated slaves by revealing how the federal government's inability to develop a free labor economy in the postwar South left thousands of former slaves unemployed and subsequently susceptible to disease outbreaks. It then traces how the Medical Division of the Freedmen's Bureau developed in response to the medical crises that plagued the Reconstruction South. Federal and army officials' concerns about freedpeople's medical condition were rooted in developing a healthy labor force, which contradicted former abolitionists and sanitary reformers' call for federal intervention based on a benevolent concern for freedpeople's health and well-being.

Chapter 3 outlines both the bureaucratic structure and administrative hierarchy of the Medical Division and moves toward the interior of Freedmen's Hospitals. Modeled on nineteenth-century Northern asylums, these hospitals were makeshift institutions that provided access to basic necessities, such as shelter, clothing, and food. The chapter explains how Freedmen's Hospitals were not systematically constructed throughout the South, but often established in response to a specific medical emergency.

[handwritten top margin:] even though the government had the necessary knowledge to stop the epidemic, they treated it as a

The most devastating medical crisis that erupted throughout the postwar South was the smallpox epidemic, which is at the center of chapter 4. This traumatic episode claimed the lives of thousands of freed slaves from 1862 to 1868. The epidemic resulted in large part from the inefficiencies of Freedmen's Hospitals to establish effective quarantines and conduct vaccinations as well as the federal government's neglect of freedpeople's health. Although medical and municipal authorities understood how to contain outbreaks of smallpox since the late eighteenth century, when the epidemic first appeared among emancipated slaves in 1862, federal officials, Southern planters, and both the Northern and Southern press began to interpret the high mortality rates among freedpeople as signs of the extinction of the black race. By turning a biological crisis into a discourse about racial survival, the federal government consequently did very little to address the explosion of the virus throughout the South.

Chapter 5 investigates who among the population of freed slaves were most affected by the outbreak of sickness and disease, which further underscores the relationship between freedpeople's economic status and their health conditions. The abrupt and often chaotic organization of the labor force excluded women, the elderly, the physically disabled, and children from opportunities to participate in the burgeoning labor economy. In fact, there were often not enough labor opportunities available to employ able-bodied freedmen. The war had destroyed much of the land available for cotton cultivation, which was then exacerbated by a crop failure in 1866–67 that led to a widespread famine.

Chapter 6 charts the eventual demise of the Medical Division of the Freedmen's Bureau when Bureau doctors and officials transferred authority of freedpeople's health to civil authorities. Since the Bureau's arrival in the Reconstruction South, its authorities desperately attempted to negotiate with municipal and state officials to take charge of freedpeople left by the void of Southern planters and the destruction of the plantation economy. The passage of the Civil Rights Act of 1866, combined with the creation of new state governments in the South, led civil authorities to allow emancipated slaves to enroll in municipal and state institutions. The chapter also explores how the political fervor of the period enabled freedpeople to voice their health concerns to local and state governments, and how these institutions of power ultimately heeded their petitions. Focusing on how the Reconstruction period inspired freedpeople to make claims about their health matters to the state, the chapter then turns to the national level and examines how the expansion of the pension system allowed black veterans and their dependents to articulate their health conditions to the federal government in hope of receiving financial assistance for their medical problems.

The Epilogue follows Bureau officials on their journey from the Reconstruction South to the West, where they, along with former abolitionists and military

[handwritten left margin:] war destruction / crop failure / women / Leon

[handwritten right margin:] discourse and didn't explain their knowledge because may get the extinction was natural and inevitable

personnel, worked to facilitate Native Americans' transition to reservations. Using the Reconstruction South as a model, these officials encouraged Native Americans to develop a system of agricultural production similar to the postwar plantation South. Consequently, illness broke out among Native Americans as government officials attempted to create a system of free labor in the service of Native American resettlement. Many of the same problems that developed in the South reemerged in the West. Federal officials lacked an understanding of the environmental challenges of transforming large plots of land into an agrarian economy. Moreover, government and army officials orchestrated mass, forced migrations of Native peoples that often led to outbreaks of sickness and disease.

The 1860s ushered in a number of changes that profoundly transformed the nation. While the emancipation of enslaved people and the increased resettlement of Native Americans represent critical turning points in the political, legal, social, and economic history of the United States, these transformations produced devastating and unanticipated consequences. When soldiers in the North reached for the rifles that hung above the mantles of their front doors and marched off to war, they did so in the name of ending slavery. But in the effort to dismantle the institution of slavery, very few considered how ex-slaves would survive the war and emancipation. An abstract idea about freedom became a flesh-and-blood reality in which epidemic outbreaks, poverty, and suffering threatened former bondspeople as they abandoned slavery and made their way toward freedom.

The process of emancipation had the potential to take many different directions. Some freedpeople would make it to the newly built schools that stood defiantly in the shadow of the former Confederate theater. Others would finally get their chance to own land and to earn a fair wage. Even more would take their place in line at voting booths and for the first time participate in the political franchise that would indelibly transform the meaning of citizenship for generations to come. Beyond the political, economic, legal, and social promises that the end of the Civil War would bring, some would find hope in a world where bondage no longer tied them to the land, and others would find love and finally gain state recognition for their marriages.

Some would never enjoy any of these rights and privileges of the free. They became sick, suffered, and even died. Those who survived starvation, abject destitution, and epidemic outbreaks lived with the haunting memories of having witnessed the deaths of their kin and contemporaries. More than likely they also saw a larger transformation begin to take shape. During the Civil War years, the military would slowly develop a policy that addressed their health concerns; thousands of benevolent workers would travel on train and horseback to deliver supplies and treatment; leaders in Washington would read the letters written by enlisted black soldiers condemning the conditions that their families were forced to endure. The federal government, in an unprecedented move, would draw the blueprints for a national system of medical care in the South to respond to the health conditions of emancipated slaves. Yet, this system ultimately failed to adequately respond to freedpeople's health problems and often unwittingly exacerbated the medical crises that plagued the postwar South.

when maybe the government drew up a blueprint for post-war healthcare for emancipated people, it ultimately failed

Dying to Be Free

The Unexpected Medical Crises of War and Emancipation

In health there is freedom. Health is the first of all liberties.
—Henri Frederic Amiel, *The Journal of Henri Frederic Amiel* (1891)

[handwritten annotation: Camp Nelson: Union-post that served as a refuge for emancipated slaves in Kentucky]

Winter came early to Kentucky in 1864. By November, the temperature had already dropped to below freezing, turning the morning dew that had settled on the once rolling pastures into frost. But the rainstorm that blew in by the end of the month with chilling winds and frigid temperatures made life difficult for the Union army soldiers who had settled on the roughly 4,000 acres that lay 20 miles south of Lexington. Known as Camp Nelson, the Union fortress housed roughly 3,000 to 8,000 Union soldiers and served mostly as a commissary and quartermaster depot, providing livestock, supplies, and rations for the Army of Ohio.[1] During the Civil War, Camp Nelson also became a refuge for newly emancipated slaves whose wartime mobility transformed the Civil War into one of modern history's most significant episodes of human migration.

In other parts of the South, enslaved people had begun to escape captivity from Southern plantations as early as 1861. Thousands of bondspeople hearing of Northern victories emancipated themselves from chattel slavery and fled to federal lines for protection. In 1863, President Lincoln enacted the Emancipation Proclamation, which legally freed enslaved people throughout the Confederate theater. But for bondspeople who lived in the border states, like Kentucky, the institution of slavery remained intact. For them, freedom depended upon the advances of the Union army or the knowledge of a Union camp that could serve as a refuge. Camp Nelson's location made it a particularly popular refuge for those who remained enslaved in Kentucky and in neighboring eastern Tennessee. By November of 1864, an estimated 500 emancipated slaves had fled to the Union post and transformed it into a village for freedpeople, which even included a training ground for newly enlisted black recruits.

*army — Emancipated slaves who fled to union
rts made the deal [giving something] for the union
army in exchange for food, shelter, and*

Joseph Miller, a slave, and his wife and four children were among the hundreds *Safety for their family* of families that made it to the camp hoping to find protection from Confederate forces and a chance to gain their freedom. The Union army allowed the Millers to enter the camp on one condition: Miller must enlist in the Union army in order for his family to be provided with shelter and food. Miller agreed. Throughout the Civil War South, this deal was made for enslaved families whose able-bodied men would either serve as soldiers or as manual laborers in the Union army.

Yet, on the morning of November 22, 1864, Brigadier General Speed S. Pry broke this promise. He ordered white Union soldiers to evacuate all freedpeople from the Union fortress. As the wind picked up and the rain began, Union soldiers mounted their horses and galloped toward the outskirts of the camp, where the freedpeople had created a provisional village. Hundreds of tents had been pitched around the perimeter of Camp Nelson; the black soldiers had taken the tents the army had given to them and turned them into living quarters for their families. Many of the families were asleep as the army officials entered into the freedpeople's community and demanded that the ex-slaves leave at once. Some freedpeople busily collected whatever clothing and personal items they had secured on their flight from slavery, while others remained confused by the sight of soldiers dressed in blue but behaving like the enemy. Frustrated that some of the ex-slaves were taking too long to leave the camp, many of the soldiers began ripping down the tents and tearing up the living areas while freedpeople were still inside.[2]

A mounted guard abruptly woke the Miller family and demanded that they leave Camp Nelson immediately. Joseph pleaded with the guard, asking that his family be allowed to stay because his seven-year-old son had been sick and was recovering slowly. The Union officer ignored the request, but Miller retorted, "I told the man in charge of the guard that it would be the death of my boy. I told him that my wife and children had no place to go. I told him that I was a soldier of the United States."[3] Nevertheless, the guard responded that if his family did not "get up in the wagon he would shoot the last one of them." The Millers reluctantly left the tent.

The Miller family had neither a place to live nor a reliable source of food. *taken from the elements* Many former slaves like the Millers often escaped from chattel slavery with only the clothes on their backs and had little to protect themselves from severe weather. Once they became sick, they often got sicker and many died.[4] Any folk remedies or cures they may have developed while enslaved were impossible while they were on the move—running from slave masters, Confederate guards, and even untrustworthy Union soldiers.[5]

While the Emancipation Proclamation officially freed the slaves in the Confederacy, it contained no provisions for how they would survive in the midst of the war. For those in the border states, like the Millers, the situation was especially precarious, since the Emancipation Proclamation only applied to the "states under rebellion."[6] The Millers thus remained legally enslaved. Despite escaping from their owner, the Millers were defined by the federal government and the Union army as "fugitives." So, when the military officials at Camp Nelson ordered Miller's wife, Isabella, and their four children, ranging from four to ten years old, to immediately vacate the protected Union camp and venture out into the unknown Kentucky territory, they had to leave.[7]

As his family climbed into the army wagon, Miller stood by helplessly as armed Union soldiers drove them out of the camp. About six or eight wagons full of freedwomen and children were expelled from the camp that morning. As the families left, Union soldiers destroyed the remaining huts and traces of their life there.[8] As one Union official later noted, "The weather at the time was the coldest of the season. The wind was blowing quite sharp and the women and children were thinly clad and mostly without shoes."[9] Miller followed his wife and children as far as the end of the Union lines, unsure where they were being taken or when he would see them again.

Later that night, after he completed his work for the day, Joseph left the Union camp in search of his wife and children. After walking for over six miles he came upon "an old boarding house belonging to the colored people" in Nicholasville, Kentucky. As he walked inside the building, he was struck by how cold it was. A crowd of former slaves gathered around the only fire in the house, as the Union guard watched over them. In a corner, on the other side of the room, he spotted his family, "shivering with cold and famished with hunger." They had not been given "a morsel of food the whole day." He quickly learned that his ill son had died earlier that afternoon; he froze to death as he was being transported in the wagon from Camp Nelson to the boarding house.[10] Unfortunately, Miller could not spend the night with his family, because he was under strict orders to return to the Union camp.

Alone on the walk back to Camp Nelson, Miller was free, without the fear that a slave catcher or a vengeful master would be on his trail. In the far distance he could see the outline of the campsite where, weeks before, the site of Union troops and blazing bonfires represented freedom for the Miller family. The next morning Miller walked back to Nicholasville. At this point, he had walked more than 18 miles in less than 24 hours. No doubt exhausted, he dug a grave by himself and "buried his own child." Once again, he left his family behind and returned to Union headquarters, not knowing if his wife or children would be given food, not knowing if they would manage to secure a place by the fire, and not knowing how they would survive.

About six months later, news of the Miller family's condition and whereabouts did surface. A sexton, employed in the vicinity of Camp Nelson, recorded that roughly three weeks after Miller's son died, his wife Isabella and his son Joseph Jr. died. Ten days later, his daughter, Maria, died. Then a day after the New Year, Miller's only remaining child, Calvin, passed away.[11]

The grief must have been unbearable for Miller. His family survived slavery, managed to escape from the plantation together, and made it safely to a Union camp. Miller gave his labor and his life for the Union cause to protect his family and to ensure that they would be given food, shelter, and clothing, which is what the federal government promised for his service as an enlisted soldier. But the policy ultimately failed them. While the Miller family was no longer enslaved, they were obligated to follow military instructions, which determined the tragic course of their freedom.

The Miller family did not die from complicated medical ailments or unknown diseases; they died because they did not have basic necessities.[12] The environment that Isabella Miller and her children were forced to live in made them vulnerable to illness, which was only compounded by their nebulous political status; they were no longer enslaved but still unable to be independently mobile and to make their own choices. They were refugees and forced to live in unhealthy environments. During the war years, the military did not create a policy that responded to their medical needs or a program that provided them with resources; the only support promised was not realized.

As an enlisted soldier, Joseph Miller was given food, clothing, and shelter. The amount of rations, the quality of his uniform and boots, and the condition of his tent may not have been ideal or even comparable to what was allotted to white regiments, but it was more than what was provided to nonenlisted freedpeople. Yet, he suffered nonetheless. According to the sexton's records, Joseph Miller died on January 6, 1865, just a few days after the death of his youngest son, Calvin.[13] He certainly could have been infected by the diseases that took the lives of his wife and children or weakened from the exertion of his efforts to look after them—or perhaps he died from a broken heart.

The Miller family did not experience liberation from chattel slavery as a jubilee, but rather as a continuous process of displacement, deprivation, and ultimately death. Far more common than previously thought, the deaths befalling these refugees convey the astounding vulnerabilities of slaves in heroic pursuit of freedom during the war. The Millers' flight to Union lines fit squarely in the standard historical accounts of slaves' self-emancipation, but their deaths scarcely lend themselves to celebratory accounts of liberation. Instead, their experience reveals the unintended and unexpected consequences of war and emancipation.

Illness: The Unexpected Enemy

Sickness and disease immediately threatened the lives of the roughly 500,000 freed slaves who had escaped from slavery during the Civil War and later the 3.5 million more who were freed when the Civil War ended.[14] Both the Confederacy and Union had anticipated that the war would quickly end. As a result,

they were unprepared for the problems of a protracted war—massive dislocation, widespread poverty, prolonged starvation, and, most of all, the dramatic
outbreak of sickness and disease.[15] These were the predictable outcomes of warfare throughout human history, as was the birth of a substantial refugee population that would make claims upon the resources of one or both of the belligerents.
In the case of the Civil War, the nebulous political status of most of the
substantial refugee population served to exacerbate the likelihood that the bulk
of suffering would take place far from the battlefield.

When members of Congress and the president considered the possibility that
the war would lead to emancipation, they discussed it in terms of the economic,
legal, political, and social consequences—paying very little, if any, attention to
the human consequences of emancipation. Where were slaves to live? How
would they find adequate food or clean drinking water? What would happen if
they became sick or injured? Thus, when former slaves began to escape from
plantations across the Confederate South and came into direct contact with
Union military officials, the human reality of emancipation shocked federal
leaders. As O. O. Howard, the leader of the Freedmen's Bureau, explained, "The
sudden collapse of the rebellion, making emancipation an actual, universal fact,
was like an earthquake. It shook and shattered the whole previously existing
social system."[16] Describing what emancipation looked like, Howard wrote years
later, "Many thousands of blacks of all ages, clad in rags, with no possessions
except the nondescript bundles of all sizes which the adults carried on their
backs, had come together at Norfolk, Hampton, Alexandria, and Washington.
Sickness, want of food and shelter, sometimes resulting in crime, appealed to the
sympathies of every feeling heart."[17]

When slaves ran away from Southern plantations, they ran toward a war.
Union camps at first represented a safe haven, but, as former slaves quickly
learned, life behind Union lines proved to be toxic. With no more than the
clothes on their backs, thousands of slaves ran to Union lines throughout the
Civil War. "You saw them, of both sexes, of all ages, in every stage of health,
disease, and decrepitude, often nearly naked their flesh torn in escaping," wrote
John Eaton in the summer of 1864 in response to the flight of ex-slaves from
Southern plantations to federal lines.[18] As Maria Mann, a teacher serving in
Helena, Arkansas, described in 1863, freed slaves "arrived to the Union camp
with swellings, open sores, and eaten up with vermin . . . Their mortality," she
explained, "greatly increased."[19]

When slaves escaped from the plantation, they often had to travel for days,
weeks, and sometimes months before making it to safety. Living on their own
without adequate shelter, clothing, and food often resulted in sickness.[20] For
example, it took months for one family to finally make it to Camp Nelson, the
same Union barracks where Joseph Miller and his family briefly resided. During

common narratives of emancipation and emphasize the thrill of freedom and don't touch on how long it must have taken to reach safety and how temporary that safety was

this anonymous family's escape from plantation slavery, Confederate soldiers captured the father of the family and dragged him off to Virginia. When the mother arrived at the Union barracks, officials there described her as "hungry and sick." Weeks later, her husband managed to escape from Confederate forces and discovered that his family had been taken to Camp Nelson. On learning about his family's whereabouts, he "sprang up with a cry of joy." He made the long trek to Kentucky, only to find that his wife had died. The journey to the Union camp had been too difficult for her, and, according to military records, she died of exposure, never knowing her husband was on his way.[21]

When historians narrate the transition from slavery to freedom, they often emphasize the thrill of freedom and the success of escaping from slavery, which has the unintended effect of diminishing the grueling process that was actually emancipation. In particular, it overlooks the time it took for ex-slaves to make it to safety. A South Carolinian physician understood the medical impact that emancipation had on ex-slaves. He explained, "It might be well here to inquire into any changes in hygienic condition they may have undergone in their sudden transition from a state of slavery to that of freedom, which may have produced such unfavorable results."[22] While this physician may have been a defender of slavery and his motivation for commenting on the health consequences of emancipation are problematic, his statement reveals the health hazards that liberation unintentionally caused.

Throughout the war, ex-slaves were constantly on the run; this sudden and severe dislocation often gave rise to illness. Observing the arrival of ex-slaves to Washington, DC, during the Civil War, Elizabeth Keckley, an enslaved woman and Mary Lincoln's seamstress, commented on the abrupt change wrought by emancipation: "Poor dusky children of slavery, men and women of my own race—the transition from slavery to freedom was too sudden for you!"[23] To better understand the suffering that Keckley witnessed, it is necessary to redraw the timeline that charts emancipation. The chronology of emancipation began with slaves' escape from slavery as early as 1862, which then culminated in the Emancipation Proclamation of 1863, and then in 1865, the passing of the Thirteenth Amendment, which formally abolished the institution of slavery. Despite these radical transformations, former bondspeople struggled to survive day after day, week after week, month after month, while confronting harsh climate changes, from sweltering heat to snow to nonstop rain and cold winds, in a devastated landscape. In an interview conducted many years after the war ended, Matilda Hatchett, a former slave, recalled how the flight from slavery led to sickness and death, "We was freed and went to a place that was full of people. We had to stay in a church with about twenty other people and two of the babies died there on account of the exposure. Two of my aunts died, too, on account of exposure then."[24]

[Handwritten annotations at top: "folk healing + plantation medicine could not help [emancipated] SICK [freed] FR because it couldn't [address epidemic] outbreaks and they weren't in one place long enough to cultivate plants"]

The folk remedies that enslaved people had developed during the antebellum period for minor aches and pains, noncontagious illnesses, and childbirth proved inadequate to combat the onslaught of contagious illness and epidemic outbreaks.[25] Furthermore, plantation healing depended upon the vegetables and herbs that healers cultivated in their gardens and knowledge of the surrounding area, which were lost when they were displaced from familiar surroundings. During slavery, both slaves and slaveholders had created quarantine strategies, from constructing "sick houses" to ensuring that healthy people had access to clean clothing and bedding to avoid infection. Being forced to live in overcrowded environments put former bondspeople at an increased risk of contracting a contagious illness.

[Handwritten annotation in left margin: "separated from kin who would have acted as their caregivers"]

The collapse of the plantation economy and the breakdown of the enslaved community created broader social transformations that left bondspeople defenseless against sickness. The exigencies of war and emancipation separated black families and triggered an abrupt breakdown of kin networks, which resulted in freedpeople not having the systems of support that sustained them during slavery.[26] This had a practical consequence: family and kin were most likely to provide the nursing care that might give a person their best chance of survival in an age before germ theory.

They also developed knowledge of slaveholders and overseers and knew who could be trusted; during the war and early years of Reconstruction, they encountered a whole new cast of personalities from Union soldiers to Northern female reformers, and needed to assess their motives. While the war had promised freedom and an opportunity for families to reunite, in reality families were splintered. As A. L. Mitchell, lieutenant colonel in the Union army and superintendent of the Freedmen, noted in 1864, "The colored soldiers have complained most bitterly about the way they have been treated, by their wives being taken away from them and sent they knew not to what camp or plantation."[27]

Without the support of family and kin networks to secure adequate shelter, food, clothing, and basic medical care, enslaved people became increasingly vulnerable to illness. In January of 1862, *Harper's Weekly* reported that more than 1,500 former slaves arrived at Fort Monroe in Virginia of whom roughly 600 were women and children without clothing.[28] Drawing from the soldiers' worn and unwanted uniforms, the military provided coats, shoes, and hats for some of the formerly enslaved men, but lacked clothing for *all* the women and children. Similarly, the *Freedmen's Record* reported: "Clothing is their most pressing need, especially for women and children, who cannot wear the cast-off garments of soldiers."[29] Government reports, correspondence, and letters tell of the hundreds of freedwomen who did not qualify for labor and begged for rations. Some mothers congregated around Bureau offices and hospitals hoping to gain a cup of beans, pork (if they were lucky), and, at least, a blanket or a pair of shoes to keep warm.[30]

The aggressive recruitment of freedmen first as laborers, then as soldiers in the Union army, left their families without a source of income and support, which inadvertently contributed to many freedpeople becoming sick. The problem was that the Union army preferred making formal employment contracts with freedmen. The military brokered an agreement with enlisted black men that either their salaries would be sent to their families or their families would be able to reside within the camps that employed them. Yet, as in the case of Joseph Miller and his family, this promise was not always kept. Waiting for their husbands' salaries to arrive or hoping that the Union army would provide them with basic necessities led to tens of thousands of formerly enslaved women and their children suffering.[31] Two weeks after the Miller family's expulsion from the camp, E. D. Townsend, the assistant adjutant general at Camp Nelson, wrote to the quartermaster general in Washington, DC, telling of the "large number of colored women and children that accumulated at Camp Nelson." He explained that many of them were the wives of the "colored soldiers and that there will be much suffering among them this winter unless shelters are built and rations issued to them."[32]

As the war progressed, this type of suffering and desperation escalated. Not only did the military often fail to pay black soldiers, or paid them less than promised, but also the army was often on the go, which made it more difficult for a freedwoman to have a claim for rations validated once her husband, father, or son moved away. Additionally, the army did not have boundless opportunities for paid employment; some freedmen therefore migrated searching for work, leaving their wives and children in a Union camp. Living on the Roseland Plantation in Louisiana in 1865, a freedwoman wrote to her husband in the army that she had "no money of any account" and was "not able to get enough to pay so much rent." Compounding matters, she told her husband that their daughter had been very sick with a fever for over two weeks, and she did not have money to pay for a doctor to visit. By the time she wrote this letter in July of 1865, her master had returned to the plantation and informed all enslaved people living there that they must now pay eight dollars a month in rent or they would be evicted.[33] Many families had to contend with the reordering of economic relations, the introduction of a cash economy, and the challenges of being left without the support of an able-bodied laborer. Families were often forced to remain on the same plantations where they were enslaved and became sick without the means of procuring treatment or cures.[34]

Many enlisted men were concerned that emancipation left their wives and children stuck on plantations without the support and help to survive. In

Hampton, Virginia, during the winter of 1864–65, an enlisted black solider wrote from a hospital bed to his wife, hundreds of miles away in Kentucky, about her condition. While he did receive letters from his wife, he was suspicious that she did not compose them, but that the master wrote the letters in order to manipulate him to return to the plantation. In the first of the two letters, his wife's voice seems to come through: she describes having another child and comments that his sisters are doing well. She then ends the letter on a loving note, "I must conclude my short letter by saying that I send my love to you all and keep the Best part for your self so no more till death." The slave owner, Jerry Smith, signed the second letter. Writing on behalf of the soldier's wife, he explained how a family of emancipated slaves, who had moved away from the plantation and settled in Cincinnati, "starved to death," and "two of the youngest had ate flesh of their fingers."[35] This graphic description may be true or an exaggeration employed by the slaveholder to warn the husband that encouraging his wife and children to abandon the plantation while he was employed in the Union army would lead to more harm than good.

The fact remains that women and children were left vulnerable to sickness and disease, manipulative slaveholders, and even apathetic Union officers during the Civil War. While historians interpreted the enlistment of black soldiers as an illustration of the patriotic commitment of former slaves to take on the Confederate enemy and to dismantle the institution of slavery, this depiction overlooks the disastrous and fatal effects on the women and children left behind.[36] The enlistment of black men in the Union army as soldiers and laborers in Vicksburg, Mississippi, for instance, left more than 10,000 women and children without the means to survive. In the summer of 1863, Union forces led by General Grant had finally taken control of the Confederate stronghold after many failed attempts, but the siege of Vicksburg was a pyrrhic victory for freed slaves. Union forces were in need of male bodies to fill the ranks once occupied by white soldiers who perished, so they turned to formerly enslaved men as suitable replacements. As Union army soldiers proudly hoisted the American flag and marched off triumphantly, freedwomen and their children were left in the burnt ashes of the Northern Mississippi Valley region without the means to survive.

Freedwomen were in a difficult position. They could not leave the Confederate theater and migrate to the North. They were at risk of being captured by Confederate troops and sent back into slavery.[37] They had no access to food. The prospect of the scraps left by the Union army offered a more stable supply of food than the unknown prospects of leaving the refugee camps entirely.[38] During slavery, many enslaved women cultivated their own vegetable gardens as either the primary or a supplementary source of food for their diets, but this was impossible for those constantly forced to move. Moreover, they may have had the skills to hunt, fish, or gather, but they may not have had the tools needed.

A few weeks after the Battle of Vicksburg, Union officials sent a medical inspector to survey the conditions of the black troops in the area, because the federal government was developing a concern about the health and well-being of their new recruits. But it was the condition of their families that captured the attention of the medical inspector and formed the subject of his report. More than 10,000 freedwomen and children had unofficially congregated on the outskirts of the Union camp, according to Dr. James Bryan. Freedpeople had settled close to the black troops for protection, but living along the shores of Sherman's Landing and within proximity to Milken's Bend and Goodrich's Landing offered little in the way of support. Children suffered from exposure and other diseases. When Bryan described their condition, he did not emphasize their plight or health condition but underscored their capacity for "modern employment."[39]

According to the logic of many federal officials in the Civil War era, employment was often seen as the solution for curing health problems. If employment were available, the freed children could work to earn rations and clothing. To prove this point, Bryan explained that children in the North were able to work their way out of poverty and avoid getting sick by earning wages that provided them with the basic necessities to survive. Unlike many of his contemporaries, Bryan's comments suggest that he did not subscribe to the popular nineteenth-century theory that black people were inherently inferior and thus more prone to illness than white people. Instead, by claiming that poor white children in the North were in a similar situation indicates that Bryan understood sickness as the product of certain social factors that could be controlled and avoided. The problem, however, was that in the ravaged plantations of northern Louisiana, employment was not a possibility, thus many of the children fell victim to exposure and other diseases.[40]

The suffering experienced by children and families torn apart by emancipation was not unique to the Mississippi Valley. In Chattanooga, Tennessee, in January of 1865, a military official reported that former enslaved people were "dying by scores—that sometimes thirty per day die & are carried out by wagon loads, without coffins, and thrown promiscuously, like brutes, into a trench." Similarly, in Helene, Arkansas, Maria Mann reported that bodies of emancipated slaves were placed in the same carts with carcasses of mules and horses to be buried in the same pit.[41]

The mere fact that the dead bodies could be collected without the use of a coffin powerfully reveals that even Northerners, allegedly fighting for the freedom and dignity of those subjected to human bondage, were transporting black people like animals.[42] The adverb "promiscuously" is also telling. This term was used to refer to the unacceptable comingling of men and women or black people associating with white people in the same space. The author of this report was clearly offended by the ways in which the white Northern soldiers disrespected the then-nineteenth century social norm not to separate black men from women and aptly portrays this incident as a violation of the human dignity of emancipated slaves. It is not a surprise, given their disrespect for the dead as well as lack of proper care for their bodies, that the living would be treated poorly by the Union army and thus not receive the necessary support they needed to survive.

Unprepared to Battle Illness

Illness invariably develops whenever a population undergoes a major transformation, including the movement of people from one geographic region to another or the introduction of a large group of people to an already densely populated area, both of which occurred during the Civil War. Thousands of Northerners dressed in Union blue flooded the South, bringing with them established disease patterns and pathogens, while bands of white Southern men marched from the Deep and Low Country South to join the Confederate army in Richmond. Soldiers set up temporary privies and unregulated cisterns, which disrupted the ecosystem and created unhygienic conditions. Added to this were ex-slaves fleeing the plantation South. The fact that these groups interacted with each other and congregated in the same areas, where they were each deprived of basic necessities, accelerated the spread of disease.[43] Historian Paul E. Steiner further argues that "army traffic and military activities commonly created mosquito breeding sites by disrupting drainage systems; they also caused the accumulation of animal offal, garbage, and human excreta, and attracted diseased camp followers, and often required of the soldier exposure to the elements—heat, cold, mud, rain."[44] Emancipated slaves and soldiers also came in contact with diseased animals, from the horses and hogs that they were ultimately forced to eat to the rats that lived among them.[45]

Of course, the idea that population movement brought about medical crises was not new to nineteenth-century Americans, but they understood these shifts as often regionally bound and falling under the jurisdiction of local physicians, reformers, and concerned citizens. When the slave trade brought people from the Caribbean and Africa to seaports along the Atlantic coast, it changed the health composition of plantations in the Low Country South and the Mississippi Valley. Slaveholders, in turn, hired doctors and constructed sick houses on their plantations, while enslaved people drew on cultural remedies and cures to ward off disease. When potato blight destroyed Ireland's main crop and forced thousands of Irish immigrants to cross the Atlantic Ocean, radically transforming the medical demography of Northern cities from Boston to Philadelphia, benevolent associations provided charitable relief. When epidemic outbreaks of contagious diseases devastated communities of newly arrived immigrants and neighborhoods of rural migrants displaced by the erosion of the agrarian economy, physicians working with local governments called for mandatory vaccinations. Meanwhile, even merchants in the East and fur traders in the West got involved in the battle against sickness by cleaning up towns and ports, fearing that an imposition of quarantine would cut off their business with neighboring vendors and markets.[46]

Despite the success of these local and regional efforts, the outbreak of the Civil War called for a centralized administrative structure that documented these medical crises and disseminated protocol on how to stop the spread of disease. Because such an institution did not exist, local physicians as well as Union and Confederate military doctors were often unable to prevent the continued outbreak of illness among regiments, and, especially, among emancipated slaves. By the end of the war, this would change. The Union army, through the Office of the Surgeon General, had collected a great deal of data from surgeons and doctors serving in the field and began investigating how overpopulated areas became infected with dysentery, camp measles, epidemic mumps, inflammatory diseases of the respiratory organs, malaria, and pneumonia.[47] While some Civil War doctors may have been aware of antebellum medical practices to guard against the spread of disease (such as quarantine), changing migratory patterns and the constant problem of overpopulation thwarted individual efforts. Without a federally organized structure to formally codify health regulations and to establish preventive measures for the entire country (which was impossible because the war divided the nation in half), individual efforts could not slow or stop illness from spreading across political borders.[48] By 1866, a year after the war ended, the federal government managed to develop a national protocol to prevent the fatal spread of Asiatic cholera in the United States, but during the war illness skyrocketed.

In large part, no one was equipped for the outbreak of sickness at such a high rate during the Civil War. Both Union and Confederate officials often thought about the war in terms of political and economic gain, paying little attention to the health of former slaves. The federal government discussed the war mostly in terms of military strategy, the recruitment of troops, and the morale of the citizenry. Additionally, military officials on both sides of the Mason-Dixon Line consistently strategized to end the war and did very little to prepare for a prolonged conflict in which illness materialized as a constant enemy. "We are encamped in low, wet ground, and the heavy rain keep much of it overflowed," reported Alfred Castleman, a Union soldier, stationed between Yorktown and Jamestown. "Sickness among the troops rapidly increasing. Remittent fever, diarrhea, and dysentery prevail." Sickness and disease devastated

Union camps so badly that many officers, like Castleman, feared they would be unable to lead successful military campaigns. The federal government lacked the money, resources, and infrastructure to respond to the medical crises that erupted throughout the war.[49]

The Army Medical Department was full of men who had assumed their posts based on seniority, "and the lack of retirement for age or disability kept the upper ranks full of old men, who, all their lives had been engaged in small things," according to an early twentieth-century army medical historian.[50] In regard to the surgeon general's preparation for a medical crisis, Captain Louis C. Duncan explained, "The Surgeon General of the Army was no doubt a worthy gentleman, he was about as much prepared for war as were the people of San Francisco for an earthquake."[51] Ashburn further explains that there were no general hospitals when the war began, and "hospitals had to be improvised, in hotels, halls, and other unsuitable buildings."[52]

Thus when the first major battle of the American Civil War, commonly known as the Battle of Bull Run, was fought on the outskirts of Manassas, Virginia, on July 21, 1861, no one was prepared to treat the hundreds of soldiers who were severely wounded, nor were they prepared to bury the dead bodies. Terrified by the sight of mangled, bloody bodies, Union recruits fled. Meanwhile, unable to move, hundreds of wounded soldiers lay on the ash-burnt grass and dirt among dead bodies and injured animals. Some soldiers suffocated on their own blood and vomit, while others were paralyzed by gunshot wounds. Horribly, the military lacked the infrastructure and manpower necessary to rescue many of the dying and wounded and were in need of hospitals to treat the injured soldiers.[53]

Learning of the disastrous results of the Battle of Bull Run and, more important, recognizing the limitations of the federal government, physicians and women reformers gathered in New York City to create a centralized governing body that would be able to respond to the war's medical catastrophes. Beginning in the first decades of the nineteenth century, health reformers had increasingly advocated for municipal governments to adopt measures that promoted cleaner and healthier environments. When the Civil War commenced, these local sanitary organizations expanded their efforts to aid the war effort and piloted a number of programs from fundraising fairs to societies that knitted mittens and socks for army regiments. By the late summer of 1861, elected members of the New York–based Sanitary Commission traveled to Washington and received approval from the president, secretary of war, and the surgeon general to organize a national corps of citizens who would provide medical support and relief to the Union army.[54]

Modeled after the British Sanitary Commission (which was formed during the Crimean War to reduce the spread of illness), the U.S. Sanitary Commission dispatched reformers throughout the Confederate theater to inspect the conditions of Union camps and to attend to wounded soldiers. Sanitation reformers were most concerned with the dangers of improper ventilation, the problems of overcrowding, and the health risks of dirty clothing. Composed mostly of women, the Sanitary Commission sought to provide a "strictly preventive service" to the army, "consisting in a thorough investigation of the causes of preventable diseases."[55] To that end, it provided military officers with information on how to maintain cleaner and healthier environments. The civilian physicians working in the Commission provided army surgeons with "concise treatises" that provided "the latest results of medical investigations, concerning those diseases which experience has proved always prevail in large armies."[56] The Sanitary Commission distributed a total of nineteen of these so-called monographs throughout the war to army doctors.[57]

Despite the manpower and resources that these doctors and medical reformers provided, the Sanitary Commission could not prevent the explosive outbreak of illness throughout Union camps. In the few existing army hospitals, patients often became sicker and died due to unsanitary conditions. Untreated wounds led to gangrene, incorrectly administered vaccinations manifested into "foul" ulcers, and unhygienic conditions led to dysentery, the war's most lethal disease.[58] Meanwhile, overcrowded environments remained an unavoidable consequence of emancipation, war, and the movement of troops, all of which further facilitated the spread of illness.

Adding to these conditions was the hazardous condition of the water supply during the war. Some physicians claimed that soldiers were forced to drink water "containing saline or organic impurities."[59] Meanwhile, rivers, lakes, and streams often became the dumping grounds for the bodies of dead horses and for the trash and human excrement left by a military regiment on the run.[60] At Camp Barker in Washington, DC, in 1863, for example, former slaves suffered from a lack of fresh and clean water. "The water inside the camp appears to produce diarrhea, and the wells in the neighborhood where we received our supply from, are drying up," wrote Surgeon Alexander T. Augusta, a member of the black infantry. Augusta also asked his supervising officials for a new water system to be developed, "as there is a great danger should a fire take place" and destroy the property.[61]

Sanitary reformers blamed their inability to stop disease from spreading on the poor quality of the army barracks. Military camps, by their very nature, were temporary stations constructed along the battle trail, built out of makeshift tents and inadequate materials.[62] Jacob Gilbert Forman of the Western Sanitary Commission described the barracks as "rough buildings, with many open cracks, and floors without any space beneath, were far from comfortable, and the regimental hospitals were not well warmed, nor kept at an even temperature, nor properly ventilated." The consequence, he noted, "was that many of the measles patients were afterwards attacked with pneumonia and died."[63] In general, members of the Sanitary Commissions stationed throughout Union camps launched searing attacks on the army's handling of health regulations. In his capacity as the executive secretary of the Sanitary Commission, Frederick Law Olmstead, the social critic and journalist, condemned Clement L. Finley, the surgeon general of the army, as "vain and incompetent."[64]

Doctors: Unprepared to Battle Illness during the Civil War

Nineteenth-century doctors were also at a loss about how to prevent the further spread of sickness and disease. Most, if not at all, Union doctors had no experience in treating scores of patients in a given day or dealing with mass outbreaks of pneumonia and intestinal viruses. As Major-General Benjamin Butler remarked in response to the yellow fever epidemic that tore through New Orleans in 1862, "No surgeon in my army ever saw a case of yellow fever or had any instruction in meeting this hideous foe."[65] Many Civil War doctors had no training in developing health measures for a regiment of a hundred troops. As P. M. Ashburn, historian of the Medical Corps, explained, "A great defect in the Medical Department provision for the personnel was the complete lack of training. Officers learned through their mistakes."[66] Nor did they have experience in setting up the safety measures or preventive mechanisms to stop a virus once it spread among a population of people living in close quarters. Although the American War for Independence and the Mexican-American War actually provided Civil War doctors with historical precedents on how to handle the outbreak of illness during a war, many physicians in the nineteenth century refused to heed the lessons learned from earlier epochs.[67] Few, if any, Civil War doctors had prior military experience, which would have prepared them for the medical problems that they were to witness.[68] More to the point, many of the Union physicians came from small private practices, others had worked in charitable hospitals treating the poor, while the remaining doctors were still in the midst of their medical training. These apprentices worked in almshouses, where they cared for the dispossessed, hoping to gain experience. When the war broke out they volunteered their efforts to treat the soldiers. In many of these cases, the magnitude of the Civil War and the number of patients would have been a challenge and shock to these doctors.[69]

The confusion surrounding medical practice was due in large part to the fact that, by the mid-nineteenth century, there were conflicting interpretations about how disease spread as well as debates regarding medical treatment. Some medical reformers subscribed to the then-new understanding of sanitation, which posited how the conditions of a physical environment contributed to the outbreak of disease. Therefore, they worked tirelessly to build sewers, to remove dead animal bodies from populated areas, and to whitewash streets with lime. Meanwhile, doctors also debated the efficacy of physicians as healers versus scientists. Known as "heroic medicine," some doctors followed an approach of treatment that intervened and modified the symptoms of the patient, such as normalizing secretions; extracting blood; and promoting perspiration, urination, or defecation, so that the body could return to its normal balance.[70] A number of these doctors often administered mercury to treat illness, which actually worsened symptoms and resulted in the deaths of many patients. Physicians, who approached medical treatment from a more scientific perspective, followed the lead of their European contemporaries and began to employ a more academic approach to the study of disease, which attempted to understand the symptomology, causes, and course that a particular illness took.[71] The medical profession was divided in its approach to how medicine should be practiced. In fact, the founding of the American Medical Association in 1846 hoped to resolve this dilemma by establishing a unified coalition of medical professionals, but the founding mission of the AMA would not be realized until the late nineteenth century.

The lack of a unified understanding of medical practice and knowledge only made it that much more difficult for federal officials and Union doctors to assess the health conditions of the South. Not until the forced resignation of Surgeon General Finley and Lincoln's appointment of William Alexander Hammond as surgeon general, did Union doctors began to systematically report illness and disease. Before then, there was no clear protocol for doctors to report on the medical conditions of the South to federal leaders in Washington. Hammond began to require doctors in the field to keep records of "the sick and wounded" and then to report on "fractures, gunshot wounds, amputations, exsections, fevers, diarrhoeas and dysentery, scorbutic diseases, respiratory diseases," and "similar remarks on other preventable diseases."[72] He also established an Army Medical Museum to mass unique specimens from doctors. The result of these endeavors eventually led to the publication of the *Medical and Surgical History of the War of the Rebellion*.

Despite this encyclopedic record of health conditions, these reports may reveal little accurate information about conditions in the South. Hammond may have created a system for physicians to tally the number of cases of a particular disease, but doctors often reported only those illnesses that they could recognize and likely shoehorned unfamiliar symptoms into known diagnoses. Furthermore, Northern physicians often described the South as a distinct region with a different climate and landscape that both created different patterns of disease transmission and gave rise to certain illnesses that remained endemic to the area.[73] In fact, after the war ended, federal officials published a comprehensive study based on Civil War doctors' reports, which charted the spread of disease based on regional difference. The study even included an inserted pull-out map that illustrated the spread of disease state by state.[74] In a widely disseminated report circulated among Union officials about differences between Northern and Southern climates, army commissioners explained that the "Southern climate suits" freedpeople "far better than" the North.[75]

These etiological distinctions further complicated treatment. For example, malaria was often associated with Southern climates. Thus, Union doctors throughout the Civil War often claimed that malaria and yellow fever remained a constant problem for Union troops (and often treated those infected with malaria with quinine), but it is unclear how many people were actually infected with these so-called Southern illnesses.[76] Many physicians subscribed to the then accepted belief that freed blacks had developed immunity against malaria. As E. P. Buckner, a Union army physician stationed in Kentucky, noted, black men were the ideal soldiers to guard Southern forts, "as neither hot climate nor malarial fevers affect them in any material degree."[77] In 1826, Dr. Philip Tidyman, a South Carolina physician and planter, published an article in the *Philadelphia Journal of the Medical Physical Sciences* about how "negroes who reside on the large rice plantations and in other places in the vicinity of stagnant water" remained unaffected by intermittent fever, which is "so hostile to the white inhabitants." The Southern doctor went on to explain to his Northern readers that if infected, blacks require "little medicine to rid him of this insidious enemy."[78] Obviously, malaria did in fact infect African Americans. The medical knowledge of the day often took precedence over the actual symptoms, and black people were thus not treated for malaria.[79] As a result, malaria claimed higher mortality rates among black troops than their white counterparts.[80]

Throughout the nineteenth century, various members of the medical profession not only made claims about the distinctiveness of the Southern landscape but also published widely disseminated articles that postulated physiological differences between races. As J. W. Compton, a physician from Kentucky, explained in a report to the U.S. surgeon general in May, 1865, that surgeons who were "appointed from States in which there were no negros . . . are wholly unacquainted with the idiosyncrasies of the negro, a perfect knowledge of which could only be acquired by years of practice among the sick of this race, with frequent opportunities of observing their peculiarities and habits during sickness and health." Dr. Compton further argued that black people differ from white people "as widely from the white man physiologically, as does his skin or hair; hence the importance of understanding his peculiarities."[81] Immediately following the war, Dr. Benjamin Apthorp Gould published a comprehensive comparative analysis of the health and physical differences between white and black troops.[82] The publication of articles, like these, that propagated the idea that black people required less treatment than white people infected with intermittent fever undoubtedly informed and shaped how Union doctors approached the rapid outbreak of illness in the South and could also explain why efforts to develop preventive measures to stop the violent spread of intermittent fever, which plagued freedpeople in the Civil War South, were not quickly adopted by Union officials.[83]

When Union doctors arrived in the South and treated Union soldiers in the Confederate theater and eventually confronted sick freedpeople throughout the South, they assumed regional and racial differences based on a complicated mix of prewar propaganda and medical fiction, all of which made the task of assessing the health conditions of the South, diagnosing illness, and treating afflicted former slaves more difficult.[84] Military officials and doctors made a number of claims about black people's physiology, from arguments that black men were innately invulnerable to fever and thereby better suited to be stationed in the swampy climes of Louisiana to the false notion that black men fell victim to dysentery because of their dietary habits from slavery.[85] Convinced of the differences between the races, some Union doctors refused to touch sick black people. A physician in Arkansas, employed by the federal government to provide medical treatment to the troops, would not "put his ear to the chest" of a black patient to see if he had pneumonia.[86] The physician's failure to examine the black patient caught the attention of a supervising official, who reported the case to higher authorities. That said, there were thousands of freed slaves throughout the Civil War South whom physicians were under no formal obligation to treat. In the few instances when Union doctors were ordered to provide a preliminary diagnosis of freedpeople's health conditions, they could easily avoid touching their bodies. Many physicians also had no experience treating African-American patients and approached black patients based on a medical fiction that black patients were physiologically different from white patients and thereby required different treatment. As a black soldier remarked in response to a white Union physician's treatment of smallpox, "the doctor ... has acknowledged his ignorance of the true character of the disease, alleging that he never saw black folks with small-pox, and consequently is unable to decide upon the treatment."[87]

Despite the mid-nineteenth century turn in medical diagnosis that emphasized a scientific understanding of disease causation over social appearance and morality as the root of illness, many doctors continued to diagnose freedpeople based on what they were trained to see or assumed they would see in black patients.[88] Civil War doctors more commonly viewed African-Americans as suffering from contagious illnesses than from health problems that did not pose a risk to the larger community. Throughout the war, freed slaves consistently became marked as carriers of smallpox, dysentery, and yellow fever when in fact just as many were dying from exposure and starvation. Therefore, African-Americans mostly, if not exclusively, entered the medical records as suffering from contagious diseases and illnesses, while other medical problems remained unreported. Infant mortality among African-Americans, for example, remains undocumented for this period.[89]

It is also important to consider factors that nineteenth-century reformers and physicians could not imagine. Germs attacked, despite medical practitioners' fastidious efforts to whitewash homes and streets with lime. Since an understanding of bacteriology did not develop until the end of the nineteenth century, germs invisibly and silently attacked army regiments and emancipated slaves, as did mosquitoes.[90] Physicians continuously complained about malaria outbreaks but did not know that mosquitoes carried and spread the disease.[91]

Federal Government: Unprepared to Battle Illness during the Civil War

Despite the alarming rates of mortality and illness, the government did not address the health and medical crises that confronted slaves as they made it to freedom. Congressmen understood emancipation as a probable outcome of the war without understanding what the human costs of emancipation would be. They may have discussed the political implications of emancipation in terms of the economic, social, and legal status of soon-to-be-freed slaves, and they may have also rightly predicted that the war would indeed lead to the ending of slavery. But the questions about where ex-bondspeople were to live, what they were to eat, and how they would find suitable work had not been asked, nor did they form a central piece of Congress's or the president's deliberations on the pending collapse of the institution of slavery. Witnessing the arrival of emancipated slaves in New Orleans from as far as Mobile, Alabama, to the Mississippi Valley, John Eaton, a Union army official and chaplain, realized that the immediate question for the federal government was not simply, "How was the slave to be transformed into a freedman?" But, rather, "How was he to be fed and clad and sheltered?"[92]

Even the abolitionists, the long-term activists behind ending slavery, debated the end result of emancipation but failed to consider how this process would unfold. Some abolitionists claimed that if freed, those of African descent should be sent back to Africa, while others embraced the idea that slaves should be able to pursue free lives in the United States as had occurred with the gradual manumission laws in the early nineteenth-century North.[93] Either scenario, however, failed to consider the day-to-day reality of how emancipation would unfold. Where would ex-slaves go, for example, while they waited to be transported to Africa? What would they eat and where would they live as they searched for employment and new homes after being freed from chattel slavery? The relative ease in which gradual emancipation unfolded in the North during the early nineteenth century could have deceived Northerners into thinking that emancipation could progress seamlessly.[94]

Nevertheless, Eaton's question fell on deaf ears during the early years of the war. Little was done to improve the quality of life within the refugee camps or provide ex-slaves with the requirements of survival, in large part because federal leaders thought about wartime emancipation only in terms of the political consequences. Freed slaves, however, transformed the meaning of emancipation from an abstract concept to a practical and political reality. At first, Union officials were shocked and quite disturbed by the presence of former slaves trying to enter their camps. Unsure of how to respond to ex-slaves approaching Union lines, military leaders referred to ex-slaves as "fugitives" and turned many of them away and, in some cases, returned them to slaveholders. When a fugitive enslaved woman and her child appeared at a Union camp in Virginia in 1861, General Oliver Otis Howard, who was nicknamed the "Christian General" and would later become the head of the Freedmen's Bureau, followed strict military protocol and returned them to the plantation mistress, who had tracked them to the Union camp. Although Howard sympathized with the fugitive woman's situation and described her favorably in his autobiography years later, he remained beholden to the military's "stringent orders not to harbor any slave property." When the mistress asked Howard for a guard to escort the fugitive woman and her child back to the plantation—since she feared that the enslaved woman would overpower her and run away—Howard refused, arguing that he would "never use bayonets to drive a poor girl and child back into bondage."[95] While Howard refused to use military force to enslave the woman, his decision not to give her safe refuge behind Union lines caused two visitors from Maine who were staying in the camp to admonish Howard for his actions.[96]

Not all Union officials were as strict in following military orders as Howard. Determined to win the war, some saw value in the additional manpower that former enslaved men could offer as laborers. As one military pamphleteer wrote, "In the heart of the Rebel States there exist four millions of an oppressed race, who would gladly aid us in the war we are carrying on, but from regard to the feelings and interests of our enemies we have hitherto refused their assistance." In an effort to persuade Union officials, the writer went on to argue that both presidents Washington and Jackson "did not hesitate to solicit, to employ, and to reward the military services of Negroes."[97] Other military leaders unofficially declared enslaved people free when they entered federal lines. General J. W. Phelps, who was stationed in Ship Island, in 1861–62 issued an "emancipation pronunciamento." Similarly, in Hilton Head, General David Hunter, in May 1862, proclaimed "that persons heretofore held as slaves are therefore declared forever free." Both instances caught the attention of the Northern press, who rebuked Phelps's actions, and President Lincoln, who reprimanded Hunter for making a decision above his station.[98]

In the Yorktown Peninsula of the state of Virginia, General Benjamin Butler strategically devised a way that would emancipate enslaved people from Southern plantations without unsettling slave owners in the border states, who were carefully watching to see if Lincoln could continue to claim to save the Union without outlawing the institution of slavery throughout the South. "The question is whether they shall be used for or against the Government of The United States. I shall hold these negroes as *contraband* of war."[99] This statement set into motion a policy that Union officials throughout the Confederate theater would follow. Despite Butler's declaration to free the slaves as contraband, he viewed emancipated slaves in terms of their monetary value. Describing the arrival of freed slaves to federal lines, Butler wrote, "The negroes came pouring in day by day, and the third day from that I reported the fact that more than $60,000 worth of them had come in."[100]

The term "contraband" did not necessarily mean free.[101] The military continued to capitalize on this uncertainty by admitting emancipated slaves to overcrowded and unsanitary camps, depriving them not only of economic and political independence but also of adequate clothing, food, and shelter. According to Butler's plan, freed slaves were to be given basic necessities in exchange for their labor in Union camps, but the army often did not uphold their part of the bargain—despite the fact that ex-slaves continued to work. Freed slaves were left as hostages in Union camps throughout the South. As "contraband," they were stuck, and they could not leave Union lines even if they wanted to. They were promised support, but had little hope of actually receiving it. Placed under such tight restrictions, they were forced to live in unsanitary and overcrowded living environments in which they became increasingly vulnerable to camp diseases.[102]

Even when emancipation was legalized by the Emancipation Proclamation in 1863, it could not protect formerly enslaved people from health threats. Lincoln designed the Emancipation Proclamation to bolster the Union army's manpower, while simultaneously depleting the Southern labor force. It was not a policy or document that addressed how the overthrow of slavery would shape the lives of slaves. Some nineteenth-century observers understood this. In a letter to prominent religious leader and abolitionist, Levi Coffin, John Eaton summed it up best when he stated, "Some among us, and some in England, have considered this emancipation a farce; because it was proclaimed by President Lincoln as a military necessity, and not on the ground of humanity and justice." Eaton went on to explain the complicated nature of emancipation, "Others declare emancipation inhuman, because it has been attended with so much suffering; overlooking the fact that the war itself would have produced as much without any attempt at emancipation; and that the distress then would have been without the alleviation afforded by the joys of freedom."[103]

In 1864, when Eaton wrote this comment, he explained the suffering that freedpeople endured was an unavoidable consequence of the war and that the larger "joys of freedom" had trumped any pain or problems that freedpeople experienced. A year later, in 1865, when reporting on the conditions of the freedpeople, his opinion had changed: "Having had the unusual opportunities for observation during the past 3 years," Eaton wrote, "I could not fail to notice particularly the condition of the race which has undoubtedly been the cause of the rebellion, followed by the carnage, sorrow and desolation of civil war."[104] Having worked firsthand with the freedpeople for three years, Eaton came to understand the deadly consequences of emancipation. He no longer referred to emancipation as "the joys of freedom" but as the "sorrow and desolation of the civil war."

Propaganda and Emancipation

Reports that detailed the effects of emancipation often reflected the author's opinion of emancipation rather than freedpeople's health conditions. Prior to the war, there was no policy established or program in place for the emancipation of over four million slaves. Any talk that developed about emancipation functioned purely on a theoretical level. "It is easy to talk of emancipation," William Aikman, a religious leader, penned in the midst of the war in 1862:

> But he has thought loosely and ill who sees no great difficulties in bringing it to a happy issue; who has not questions arise in his mind to give him pause when he contemplates a social change so vast in the state of a race of twelve millions of men. Let not the reader suppose a mistake in the figures, we mean twelve millions and not four; there are four millions of slaves to be made free, but a change is to be wrought in the social state of the eight millions of whites, which is only less than that of the blacks. To alter radically, to remodel the whole social fabric of a great and numerous people, to shift the foundation stones, remove them, and place others in their places, without racking the edifice or tumbling it in a hideous ruin, is the work of no inexperienced or careless architect.[105]

The publication of Aikman's pamphlet, "The Future of the Colored Race in America," in 1862 accurately predicted the social upheaval that emancipation would cause, and, more important, in the document, he astutely noted that it was "easy to talk" of emancipation during the early years of the war but much harder to actually design a plan that would respond to the enormous structural changes that liberation would involve.

When emancipation began, many Northern journalists did not initially discuss the high mortality rates among former slaves and instead focused their attention on the destruction in the South; they spread word of destroyed bridges, homes burned to the ground, and cities in shambles. Meanwhile, Southern journalists exaggerated the health problems that emancipation ignited, pointing to the sick and dying condition of ex-slaves as salient proof that the proslavery parable came true: that if freed, slaves would go "extinct." Southern (and even, at times, Northern) officials understood the deadly consequences of the war as natural outcomes of emancipation.[106] The *Richmond Dispatch* argued that the health problems that emancipation engendered proved that black people were better off in slavery. "During the present war thousands of negroes have been released from servitude to their masters, but we say unhesitatingly that in nine cases out of ten, if not in a far greater ratio, the change has been positively injurious to their condition, morally and physically. How many of the contrabands are better provided for than they were in slavery? How many are more useful to society? How many are happier?" The newspaper then referred to the Union camps where the former slaves lived as "little else than pens of idleness, squalor and disease." The reporter for the *Richmond Dispatch* wrote, "We shudder to think of the scores of hundreds, of black men, women and children whose miserable deaths are attributable solely to the change in their condition produced by the war—to their own helplessness, and to the neglect and indifference of those whom they in their ignorant and strange faith, looked upon as their benefactors and friends."[107]

Drawing attention to the fact that freed slaves were dying in their flight from slavery only buttressed white Southerners' claim that ex-slaves could not lead independent lives and would go extinct. The high rates of sickness and death that defined life in the contraband camps became powerful ammunition for proslavery advocates to use against abolitionists, who for decades had accused slaveholders of mistreating enslaved people. As the *Richmond Dispatch* reporter pointed out, former slaves' "benefactors and friends" could not adequately take care of them.

O. O. Howard explained how proslavery advocates misunderstood the cause of illness and suffering among freedpeople when he wrote:

> Looking at the great numbers of indigent freedmen, old men and women and helpless children, in every Southern State, I have not wondered that the old slaveholder should pour into my ear the glowing accounts of the

blessedness of slavery in its prosperous and patriarchal days, and that he should heap curses on that freedom which he believes to be the occasion of so much restlessness and suffering. But you and I know that the real cause of the desolation and suffering is war, brought on and continued in the interest of and from the love of slavery.[108]

Final Diagnosis

The disease, death, and suffering that plagued freedpeople during the Civil War years resulted from the simple fact that no one predicted that military engagement and the subsequent emancipation would lead to the largest biological war of the nineteenth century. Physicians could not cure the fatal infections contracted nor could the army of medical civilians that formed the Sanitary Commission prevent the arresting spread of disease. The federal government could offer little assistance. Former slaves escaped to Union lines, but struggled to survive in an environment devastated by war and plagued with sickness. The illnesses that likely caused many former slaves to become sick and to die were not unknown during the nineteenth century. Many army physicians would have likely seen pneumonia and dysentery in their private practices or read about smallpox and yellow fever during their medical education. Yet, the Civil War radically transformed nineteenth-century medical knowledge and practice. It increased the number of patients that doctors treated and enlarged the scale and context in which illness erupted. Outbreaks that were typically confined to local cities and towns blew up into epidemics that plagued entire regions and crossed state lines. Ideas about the distinctiveness of the South as a region that had its own etiology could be found in medical journals and in the popular medical discourse; the start of the war turned these ideas into governing maxims that guided policies on how to treat and prevent the spread of disease. Similarly, throughout the eighteenth and early nineteenth centuries, many physicians learned about the health "of the Negro" as a separate race or they may have developed ideas about race based on common assumptions and propaganda that circulated throughout the antebellum North. The Civil War morphed these ideas into practices that influenced how army doctors treated, touched, and probed black bodies, and in other instances these ideas served as the justification for neglect. The most significant factor that led to the widespread outbreak of disease was the massive dislocation that the war and emancipation caused. The failure to anticipate thousands of mobile people who congregated in places without an infrastructure to support them led to disease outbreaks and death.

2

The Anatomy of Emancipation

The Creation of a Healthy Labor Force

The first wealth is health.
  —Ralph Waldo Emerson, *"Power," The Conduct of Life (1860)*

A freedwoman clung to the body of her eight-year-old son in a Union camp in southern Illinois. She had managed to escape from slavery and to navigate her way safely to the camp, but during her flight from a Southern plantation she was separated from her husband. Her eight-year-old son was the only family she had left. Before the war started, she watched helplessly as her three other children were torn from her side and sold to a plantation somewhere in the Deep South. Now, she was helpless again; this time, she could not protect her son from an unknown illness that was making him sicker by the hour. The freedwoman approached the captain in charge of the camp for help, but he brushed off her appeal.

Next, the freedwoman approached a white woman who was working in the camp, distributing supplies to soldiers and emancipated slaves. Laura Haviland, a suffragist and a key player in the Underground Railroad, had arrived in southern Illinois as a benevolent reformer. The formerly enslaved woman thought that she would have better luck if Haviland petitioned the captain on her behalf. Much to Haviland's surprise, when she explained to the captain the freedwoman's predicament, he responded, "I don't know whether it is so or not; they get up all sorts of excuses."[1] Hours later, the woman's child died.

The freedwoman's troubles did not end with the tragic and sudden death of her son. A boat was waiting at the dock to take the freedpeople to an unknown location. Without having time to mourn her son, the freedwoman was ordered to pack her belongings and board the boat. She approached Haviland a second time for help. Years later, Haviland recalled in her diary what the freedwoman said to her (using the mother's dialect): "Oh, Missus, it 'pears like I can't leave him so; they leave him here tonight, an' dess wharf-rats are awful. Da eat one dead chile's face all one side off, an' one of its feet was gnawed off. I don't want to leave my chile on di bare groun.'"[2]

Fearing that the government would not properly bury the dead child, Haviland went back to the captain. "What is the difference," responded the Captain, "if that child shouldn't be buried this afternoon, or whether wharf-rats eat it or not?" Infuriated by the captain's attitude, Haviland stated: "You promised to have it buried this afternoon . . . and I told the poor woman that it was done . . . I see no other way to hold you to that promise, for I shall meet her on the island, I must report to her."

For abolitionists who spent decades tirelessly fighting for the end of slavery, the predicament of former slaves during the Civil War elicited their immediate concern. In their view, former slaves managed to escape the violent grip of the slavocracy, but were offered little support from military officials. Benevolent reformers, therefore, worked assiduously to persuade the military and the federal government to create a policy to respond to the freedpeople's needs.[3]

For military officials, emancipation was an obstacle to their larger strategic and militaristic objectives. Moreover, they had no guidelines or instructions on how to respond to the problems that freedpeople endured. There was no policy on how the military would treat infected emancipated slaves, nor was there a protocol to follow when slaves died, needed coffins, and required proper burials.[4] The military understood sickness as a byproduct of war. As the captain later explained to Haviland, "You won't allow such things as these to break your heart, after being in the army a little while and seeing our soldiers buried in a ditch, with no other than a coffin or winding sheet than the soldier's dress." The military's callous position only invigorated benevolent associations' claims that they needed to be in the South and serve the freedpeople.

In many ways, the captain's complaint that numerous soldiers had only the clothes on their backs to cover their bodies in death was a justified reaction in the face of the unexpectedly high death toll that he and his contemporaries confronted. That said, the federal government and the military were, nonetheless, planning ways to bury the dead soldiers.[5] But, nothing was done on the federal level to respond to the deaths that afflicted the population of liberated slaves; federal officials did not even take an accurate count of how many liberated slaves died during the war, let alone create cemeteries and burial grounds for them.[6]

In spite of the lack of provisions provided for freedpeople, we should not lose sight of the freedwoman: she tried to have her voice heard when it seemed as if no one was listening. The military officer wasn't listening—he complained that "they" always come up with "excuses." Excuses for what? Sickness? A plea for assistance? Is that meant to refer to the pain, terror, or the sounds of a dying baby crying as a mother runs after a Union man seeking help?

For the freedwoman, Laura Haviland was likely just another face in the crowd—a woman who may have ladled out a small bowl of meatless soup for her the day before or broken off a chunk of hard tack. But as the freedwoman ran toward Haviland, her child cried. She panicked and begged. When she finally caught the attention of this benevolent woman—who came in the name of Christ and redemption to the Civil War South—the abolitionist was mesmerized by her. Why else would the Northern woman remember her words verbatim? Why would she recall in her diary, years later, the mispronunciation, the accent, the vernacular? Most likely, the gruesome picture of rats gnawing on lifeless children propelled her to action and was scorched in her memory. Despite her efforts, the child cried, and, finally, his body contorted in death.

Maybe the historian, here, falls into the same trap as Laura Haviland—emotionally hooked by the drama of death and dying. But how else can we tell of what could have been and how it all went down? Cries of suffering were not entered into the official, historical record. Fear was not catalogued in a database under "freedom." Dead children's names did not appear on bronze memorial plaques in city halls after the war ended. So, what shall we do? Let the freedwoman linger in the accented and abbreviated language of a diary?

The freedwoman tried to push though the military protocol that did not recognize her child's sickness; when that failed, she turned to a kind stranger, who did not even ask her name. But the freedwoman stands there now, staring back at us, her pain, persistence, and suffering burst forth from a few pages in a diary. How will we describe her? She cannot be counted among the freedwomen who sang in jubilee and danced in praise of the Union army; nor can she be counted among the freedwomen who withdrew from the gang labor force and devoted their energies to being mothers and wives as their husbands pursued careers as sharecroppers. She cannot be defined as a mother of the next generation of women who would join the club movement and fight against Jim Crow segregation. Nor can she take her place a generation earlier among the women who risked everything and ran away from slavery, hid in attics, or dressed as men to find their way out of the South. Instead, she appears in the records during "freedom," but her fate contradicts historians' generalizations about that time of great triumph in the lives of former slaves.

We will never know what happened to her or where her son's body was buried. Throughout the Civil War, thousands of freedwomen had similar experiences; their presence would become a nuisance to the military and even to former abolitionists. As historian Barbara J. Fields powerfully explained:

> Freed slaves made a nuisance for the army and they also made an issue that the army had to deal with. And if the army had to deal with it, the War Department had to deal with it. If the War Department had to deal

Congress made Freedmen's Bureau in response to managing slave population rising problem

with it, Congress had to deal with it. That means that every fugitive slave who made a nuisance of himself to the local commander eventually made a figure of himself to the Congress of the United States.[7]

By 1865, Congress eventually responded to the predicament of freed slaves by passing legislation that led to the creation of the Freedmen's Bureau—an agency that grew out of the War Department that was designed to help former slaves adjust to the social, economic, legal, educational, political, and medical challenges that emancipation posed. The Freedmen's Bureau consisted of four main parts that often overlapped: a Land Division that distributed abandoned and confiscated land to freed slaves; an Educational Division that worked with former abolitionists to establish schools throughout the South; a Legal Division that mediated disputes between former slaveholders and slaves and negotiated employment contracts; and a Medical Division devoted entirely to the health needs of formerly enslaved people.[8]

The roots of the Medical Division and the Freedmen's Bureau, more generally, can be traced to the early federal policy surrounding emancipation, as it provided a blueprint for the legislation that federal officials drafted after the Civil War. During the war, many military officials and federal authorities understood emancipation in terms of the labor power that former bondspeople could offer to the military, government, and national economy. The freedwoman and her son, and the many thousands of others like them throughout the Civil War South, were seen purely as a nuisance to the army's broader objectives, because they did not fit into the military's profile of a burgeoning plantation labor force. Former abolitionists, like Haviland, soon realized the limitations of their benevolent interventions and began to call on the federal government to introduce legislation to address the problems that resulted from the collapse of plantation slavery and the destruction caused by the war.

The key players who would shape Reconstruction policy and develop the blueprints for the first federal system of medical care emerged during the war. Former abolitionists went South and became advocates for freedpeople's medical predicaments.[9] Military officials remained invested in freedpeople's labor and made provisions for their living and health conditions, but only when it related to their employment in the army as manual laborers and eventually as soldiers. The federal government's policies regarding the sudden and unexpected nature of emancipation followed the military's cue and viewed emancipation not as a revolutionary transformation for freed slaves, but as a consequence of war that often got in the way of the larger issues facing the nation.

The government became interested in the health conditions of freed slaves because it wanted to create a healthy labor force. Federal attention did not develop organically nor did it result from official observations, but transpired as a result of the claims made by former slaves, benevolent reformers, and even a handful of concerned military officers. When the federal government eventually responded by creating the Freedmen's Bureau in 1865 and subsequently developing a system of medical care for former slaves throughout the South, ideas about freedpeople's labor power shaped the terms of the policy. When emancipated slaves reached Union lines, military authorities evaluated their status based on their ability to contribute to the Union army's war effort. If army officials deemed ex-slaves unable to work for the Union cause, they were locked up in contraband camps.

The notion that emancipation depended on one's ability to work can be seen most clearly in the federal government's initiative to re-create the plantation labor force and to replant profitable cottonseed during the Civil War.[10] In the plantation islands that dotted the South Carolina and Georgia coasts, four main actors gathered in what would become the "Rehearsal for Reconstruction" at Port Royal. The federal government took over the role of the slaveholders and assumed ownership of the land; military authorities served as overseers, controlling the labor force and monitoring their behavior. New to the Sea Islands, Northern abolitionists arrived as teachers. Freedpeople were recast in a familiar role; they were forced to return to the plantation as field laborers. Reporting on the conditions at Port Royal, the *Liberator*, the Northern abolitionist newspaper, explained in February of 1862 that "all the fugitives are kept under equally strict *surveillance*." The newspaper further stated that the freedpeople at Fortress Monroe, located in northern Virginia, were in a similar position, "every one of the two thousand fugitives is restrained of his freedom just as he was on his rebel master's plantation."[11] Many former slaves protested the forced return to the plantation and were reluctant to plant what they defined as the "slave crop," despite the meager financial incentives the government offered.[12] As a result, these various experiments were not as successful as the federal government had hoped.[13]

Freedpeople's labor during the Civil War did not offer them autonomy, a fair wage, or mobility, benefits that would become possible after the war ended. Instead, freedpeople labored for the profit and benefit of the Union army, and their only reward was the shaky and unguaranteed promise of protection from Confederate forces and vengeful slaveholders.[14] As one Union official straightforwardly declared, "To entice the slave from his plantation by calling him to freedom, without teaching him that freedom means labor, is cheating and deceiving him and the results will be those of deception."[15] The forgetting of the political and economic interplay "freedom means labor" has inadvertently downplayed the military's economic investment in formerly enslaved people's labor power and the fact that freedpeople had no other choice but to work for the Union army if they wanted to escape chattel slavery.[16] Not until after the war ended did former slaves' autonomy not depend on their ability to work and could an unencumbered notion of "freedom" be achieved. Even when labor did not seem to be the preoccupying concern of federal government authorities, it nevertheless played an integral role. For instance, one of the major reasons the government supported former abolitionists' efforts to build schools for freedpeople throughout the South was to ultimately provide an industrial, free labor economy with more sophisticated workers. The creation of the schools was also, according to O. O. Howard, the leader of the Freedmen's Bureau, an effort to stave off "beggary and dependence."[17]

If employment was not readily available, former slaves were placed in contraband camps. These camps not only served as a refuge for emancipated slaves who fled to Union lines for protection, but they also were used by federal authorities as a holding ground for enslaved people until their labor could be deployed. In a camp near Baton Rouge in March 1863, a brigadier general wrote to a lieutenant colonel asking "to be allotted from among the contrabands at this post—fifty able-bodied negroes for labor in the Quartermaster and Commissary Departments of this Brigade." He further added, "I desire that that these negroes be permanently attached to the Brigade and I shall see that they are properly commanded and directed so that their labor shall be efficient."[18] In 1864 in Vicksburg, 3,700 freed slaves were allowed to leave the contraband camp because they agreed to work on a plantation. Similarly in Helene, Arkansas, over 2,000 former slaves were released from a contraband camp to become part of a plantation labor force.[19]

In many ways, the contraband camps performed a similar function to antebellum slave pens where auctioneers held people before they were sold on the market.[20] These pens were not torn down or even closed off during the war but were used for emancipated slaves until the federal government could work out plans to establish a labor force to be sent to the Mississippi Valley and the Lower South. The placement of freedpeople in former slave pens calls into question the liberation rhetoric that often surrounds the notion of emancipation. A Northern newspaper described the conditions of ex-slaves in a northern Virginia slave pen: "They have been stowed away in narrow, dark, filthy sheds, old houses, cellars—any sort of places—with scarcely rags enough to cover their persons, or straw enough to sleep upon. Many are lodged in the old slave-pens." Forced to live in such unhealthy environments, freedpeople suffered from malnutrition, starvation, and exposure, while others came down with smallpox, dysentery, and yellow fever and died.[21] Contraband camps and slave pens sadly represented for many former slaves their first encounter with "freedom."

Slave emancipation in the United States was a piecemeal process. For many, this process ranged from being put straight to work in the army to being locked in a contraband camp to being placed under strict military surveillance on

ally occupied plantations. This series of events was similar to what un-
d in various enslaved economies throughout the Atlantic world, where the
institution of slavery slowly eroded with the passing of various laws, creation of
labor contracts, and military conscription.[22]

The misunderstanding that emancipation led directly to "freedom" can be
traced to the military commander who first granted fugitive slaves asylum in
Union camps during the war, Major-General Benjamin F. Butler. There is a
disconnect between Butler's initial drafting of the contraband policy, which
mandated that freedpeople work in order to guarantee their freedom, and his
later autobiographical recollections in which he celebrated the contraband
policy as a prelude to the Emancipation Proclamation, making no reference to
the fact that freedpeople needed to work to be free.[23] Like much of Union army
policy, Butler's initiatives developed in response to crises that required immediate
attention. Butler's willingness to allow escaped enslaved people to enter Union
lines in Virginia in the early years of the war, despite the Fugitive Slave Law of
1850, which warranted their return to their masters, should not be viewed as a
prelude to the Emancipation Proclamation. It was purely an act of military
necessity that developed in response to the question of political refugees, and,
more important, an effort to capitalize on the labor power that fugitive slaves
could provide. It was not a sympathetic gesture toward fugitive slaves. In fact,
when one fugitive slave made it to federal lines in Louisiana, Butler's subordinate
offered him refuge in the Union camp. Butler told his subordinate, "If I have any
use for the services of such a boy, I employ him without any scruple If I have not
I do not harbor him."[24] In another instance, Butler was concerned about the
work remaining undone by the thousands of freed slaves fleeing from plantation
districts throughout Louisiana to New Orleans.[25] As he explained to a leading
Union official, "Crops of sugar are left standing to waste which would make
millions of dollars."[26]

Butler did not emphasize the contraband policy or the subject of emancipation
in his private letters and professional correspondence from the 1860s, which
suggests that these policies formed a rather insignificant part of his larger military
career. Throughout his letters, Butler mostly details the challenges he faced as the
Union army took over New Orleans, making few references to the thousands of
emancipated slaves who fled to the Crescent City. Many of his letters were written
to military leaders and government officials in Washington about the need to evacuate Baton Rouge and the special orders delivered to the people of New Orleans
about the liquidation of the city's banks. Spliced throughout this correspondence
are letters to his wife, but he does not, like antebellum abolitionists writers, draw
comparisons between his family and the suffering that enslaved families endured.[27]

When Butler penned his autobiography in the early 1890s, the subject of
emancipation and the contraband policy appears more prominently, although, it

is still not a major theme. He described the contraband policy in a single chapter and mentioned it in the conclusion in a summary of his achievements that ranged from his successful capture of Annapolis to recruiting over 6,000 soldiers for the war effort.[28]

By 1892, when Butler's autobiography was published, public attention had turned to the uncertain position of emancipated slaves in post-Reconstruction decades. White Southerners had overturned the political and economic advances that the Radical Republicans had established throughout the South and had begun to impose legal, political, and economic restrictions on former slaves. These political developments, combined with the presence of black Southerners in the North and South, more than likely prompted Butler to reflect a bit more about the contraband policy. Two decades after formulating this policy, Butler began to claim credit for paving the way for Lincoln's Emancipation Proclamation. As he noted in his autobiography, "I first declared the legal principles by which, under military law, slaves could be free, and thereby made the President's proclamation of emancipation possible."[29]

Like Lincoln's Emancipation Proclamation, Butler understood emancipation as part of a military necessity, as did others in positions of power during the Civil War.[30] "It was a time of great depression at the North," wrote Charles A. Humphreys, chaplain of the Second Massachusetts Cavalry Volunteers. "The Emancipation Proclamation," he claimed, "had not begun to give any effective aid to our arms."[31] In a worried letter written to the editor of the black newspaper, the *Weekly Anglo African*, in March 1862, J. V. Givens focused on the economic ramifications of slave liberation when he explained how some freedpeople escaped from slavery to Washington, DC, hoping to find their freedom, but once they arrived "the poor slave is compelled to go and serve some farmer sixty miles in the country."[32]

If there was any political element embedded within these early federal initiatives that responded to emancipation it was certainly not a concern about black suffrage, civil rights, or citizenship. The passage of the Second Confiscation Act on July 17, 1862, which legalized Butler's contraband policy, for instance, made no claims to basic civil rights or freedoms, but instead emphasized how the president is authorized to "employ as many persons of African descent as he may deem necessary and proper for the suppression of this rebellion, and for this purpose he may organize and use them in such manner as he may judge best for the public welfare." The latter part of the phrase allowed those in positions of authority to use freedpeople's labor in any way they saw fit, which effectively regulated and subordinated freedpeople's autonomy.

Moreover, the act stipulated that people of African descent were to be colonized "in some tropical country beyond the limits of the United States." The extent to which the federal response to emancipation did not anticipate political suffrage or express concern for the well-being of emancipated slaves is captured in this declaration that former slaves would not even be living in the United States. The fact that the plan for colonization continued well into the summer of 1862, just a few months prior to the Emancipation Proclamation, further illustrates the government's concern with freedpeople's labor and its lack of an investment in their political future. While the Second Confiscation Act was formal legislation on emancipation rather than an impromptu initiative enacted by military authorities, it nonetheless failed to address the unhealthy conditions that plagued former slaves throughout the South.

As the number of freed slaves increased, military officials looked to the federal government for guidance, but federal policies on emancipation responded only to freedpeople's legal status. As Ulysses S. Grant recalled, "There was no special authority for feeding them unless they were employed as teamsters, cooks, and pioneers with the army; but only able-bodied men were suitable for such work."[33] In Alexandria, Virginia, General Heintzelman expressed frustration in response to the growing number of former slaves arriving in 1862, "What shall be done with these people, beyond temporary expedients, I have not the time to consider?"[34] Further south in the Mississippi Valley, General Stephen A. Hulbert expressed similar concern, referring to the 5,000 ex-slaves that arrived in the region as a "weight and incumbrance." Despite not having approval to issue them rations, Hulbert nevertheless drew on army provisions to feed the ex-slave population but worried about the roughly 2,000 others who were in Memphis without support and who were bound to face "disease and death."[35]

While Union officers in the Civil War South wrestled with the mounting number of dead bodies and the emotional turmoil that the death toll inflicted, military and federal leaders in Washington, DC, offered little help. Ideas about suffrage and citizenship did not gain momentum until slavery was abolished and freed slaves along with Radical Republicans began to articulate the meaning of freedom once the war ended. During the war, federal policy developed erratically and paid little attention to either the slaves' political rights or to their health and well-being.

One of the reasons federal authorities in Washington and many army officials stationed throughout the South did not offer assistance to former slaves or were not sympathetic to their plight was that they viewed former slaves as refugees. Few federal and military authorities had firsthand experience with refugees in war.[36] While some certainly fought in the Mexican War, for most, the Civil War was the first time that they experienced combat and witnessed the effects of war. Consequently, their ideas about war came from studying European wars and conflicts.[37] In their studies of European war at West Point or college, if they attended either, Union officers regarded refugees as part of the backdrop that valorized the victorious army's honor and celebrated its courage. As a result, when Union soldiers came face-to-face with freedpeople—who were starving, living on desecrated plantations, or crying over the bodies of dead children—they tended to walk away, because they were taught to keep their eye on the battle and to recognize that civilian suffering was a normal part of war. Additionally, many Union soldiers previously had very little contact with, or ever seen, large numbers of black people, and thus, they barely recognized dark-skinned refugees as people.

Simply calling former slaves "refugees" indicates how Union military commanders failed to recognize the revolutionary status of freed slaves. It was not until after the war that military officials, government leaders, and the Northern press designated former slaves as "freedmen" and used the term "refugee" to refer to displaced white Southerners. But during the war, the label "refugees," or Butler's term "contraband," was applied to ex-slaves. Neither of these terms connoted any degree of freedom, rights, or liberty; in fact, they implied restriction and forced subordination.

Former abolitionists, however, began to define ex-slaves as "freedmen" earlier. This change in terminology recognized ex-slaves' potential political status and gestured toward welcoming slaves into the polity. "Let them be called Colored Refugees," penned a journalist from the popular abolitionist newspaper the *Liberator* in 1862, "until we can obtain for them a recognized freedom and citizenship."[38] A reporter for the *Weekly Anglo African* echoed this sentiment, describing the evolution in the terms used to describe former slaves that began with Butler's use of the word "contraband," which was then replaced with General Wool's "ungracious" label "vagrants," which in turn was summarily dismissed by the abolitionists who devised the term "freedmen." "The terminology applied to slaves," the reporter explained, "indicates a daily advancing state of public sentiment."[39] Former abolitionist groups throughout the North and the Midwest also changed their name to "Freedmen's Societies" and established periodicals and fundraising efforts, which used some version of the term "freedmen."

Nevertheless, since the federal government and the military defined former slaves as "refugees," they did not feel responsible for their condition. A reporter for the *Atlantic Monthly* astutely noted, in 1861, in response to a question of who should provide medical assistance to newly emancipated slaves: "Here was a new question, and a grave one, on which the government had as yet not developed a policy."[40] The reporter for the *Atlantic Monthly* rightly identified the lack of a policy or mechanism within the federal government to extend its power and authority to assist emancipated slaves during the war years. So for freedpeople living in a world where they lacked political capital and where the federal government did not see its role as offering relief even to its citizens, and certainly not to those it considered "refugees," the chances of receiving much-needed government assistance were limited.

Abolitionists as Health Advocates

Given the federal government's principal interest in freedpeople's labor power, former abolitionists throughout the Civil War focused their attention on freedpeople's health and well-being. Initially, abolitionists recognized that once slaves were freed, they would require an education, so they planned schools throughout the South to teach former slaves how to read and to write; but after arriving in the South, they quickly realized that they needed to turn their attention to freedpeople's suffering and illness. Some of these groups proselytized religious doctrine to emancipated slaves, while others encouraged cleanliness and taught "manners." Leaving aside the polemical nature of some of this work, former abolitionists, nevertheless, recognized the federal government was not in a position to help freed slaves and that charitable associations must do the work. As one Northern benevolent group proclaimed, "The Government does what it can for them, and employs some of the able-bodied as laborers and soldiers, and will do more and more for them as its policy takes form; but the masses are and must be for a time, to a great extent dependent upon charity."[41]

As early as February of 1862, former abolitionists formed the National Freedmen's Relief Association in New York City at the Cooper Institute in order to respond to the dire conditions of former enslaved people in the Civil War South. The National Freedmen's Association established committees in all "cities, villages, and towns" to provide relief and resources for newly emancipated slaves.[42] The Emancipation League, for example, formed in Massachusetts, while Quakers in New York and Pennsylvania organized similar groups of reformers.

Armed with Bibles and books, these leagues and associations marched into the South with noble expectations of teaching former slaves, but their educational goals were derailed once they came in contact with the freedpeople. The suffering described in *Uncle Tom's Cabin* and the poignant speeches delivered by Frederick Douglass about the lives of bondspeople could not have prepared them for the dire conditions of former slaves. A. F. Pillsbury, a Northern reformer, described for the readers of *Freedmen's Record* a formerly enslaved woman whom she encountered in a contraband camp. She wrote:

> Mary, a middle-aged woman with a bad cough, and other diseases, which had become almost chronic, arose from her ragged covering and straw on the floor, with a face beautiful from suffering and resignation, simply standing, without asking for any thing. If I could have led Mary

before you in Boston, as she looked then, your hearts would have ached for many a day. I promised her clothing and medicine, told she would get well, and I would not forget her.[43]

Northern reformers devoted their energies to helping to ameliorate suffering from exposure; nameless diseases; hunger and malnutrition; and lack of shelter, clothing, and blankets. They started by writing to their sponsoring organizations, families, and friends about the dreadful conditions that confronted freed slaves, tapping into the efficacious abolitionist networks that had raised money and communicated important information expeditiously during the heated political battles of the 1830s and 1850s. As J. C. Maxwell explained to his readers in 1862 in the *Christian Recorder*, a black abolitionist newspaper, freedpeople "demand in unmistakable language, our immediate concern."[44] He further explained, "There are thousands of them at Fortress Monroe, Hilton Head, Cairo, and other places; and although the Government supplies them with food, they are in want of other necessities that sustain life. Winter is hard by, and they must have blankets and comfortable clothing, or they will perish and die to our utter shame."[45] Advertisements calling for volunteers to travel to the South to help newly emancipated slaves appeared in politically progressive newspapers, like the *Weekly Anglo African* and the *Liberator*; while the New England Freedmen's Aid Societies and more religiously oriented groups, such as the Quakers, published stories and advertisements in their monthly bulletins.[46] Stories of the agents' experience in the South were also told in churches, political meetings, and lyceums to audiences filled mostly with abolitionists and reformers.

Reading and learning about the conditions of formerly enslaved women was of particular interest and concern to white women reformers, who had read Stowe's *Uncle Tom's Cabin* and Harriet Jacobs's *Incidents in the Life of a Slave Girl*—narratives that underscored the human connection between enslaved mothers and their children. The abolitionist movement impelled many Northern white women to act on behalf of enslaved women in the South who were in jeopardy of losing their children to the domestic slave trade. The struggles that emancipation posed became the sequel for Northern women to provide aid to freedwomen who remained at risk of losing their children due to the exigencies of war and emancipation. The trope of motherhood that formed the backbone of both of these political campaigns mobilized white women across the North to use the domestic skills and experience they gained before the war, working in churches and other charitable relief organizations, to support freedwomen in the South.[47] For example, Sarah Gage attended a meeting in Philadelphia, hosted by the Quaker Friends, where she learned about the suffering of freedwomen and children in the South. She returned to her home in Lambertville, New Jersey, and founded the Freedmen's Home Relief Association of Lambertville.

After a few months of fundraising, Gage left her small town and traveled to Beaufort, South Carolina, to establish a school and assist the freedpeople.[48]

Once these reformers arrived in the South, much of the despair and death they reported on surely resulted from the mass devastation the war caused and the chaos of emancipation, but were also the result of slavery. Many slaveholders cared very little about the health and well-being of their labor force, so many enslaved people entered the war already sick and suffering. Therefore, it is virtually impossible to determine if ex-slaves' suffering and sickness were the direct result of the war or the result of slavery. It is also unclear if the Northern benevolent workers' reports were distorted because of their Victorian notions of cleanliness and purity that they brought with them to the South.[49] Nonetheless, the details they provided illustrate the horrible conditions. As one benevolent reformer portrayed the situation:

> No one North would believe that our land held such scenes within her borders. Three young men, sick, lay on the floor with nothing but a filthy blanket. No straw, no pillow! One emaciated form had neither coat or blanket—had been struggling with life for 6 or 7 weeks, till now his voice had no strength to make replies. A half loaf of dry bread, and a little boiled rice in a tin can was waiting on the floor by each head.[50]

Benevolent reformers began to use whatever political acumen they gained in the prewar decades to help improve the lives of emancipated slaves. An agent for the New York Rochester Ladies Anti-Slavery Society, Julia Wilbur, arrived in Alexandria, Virginia, in the fall of 1862, in which the city had been transformed into a hospital station for Union soldiers. After visiting a former bank that had been converted to a sick ward, Wilbur then made her way near the "Old Capitol Prison," where former slaves, criminals, and vagrants were kept. Overwhelmed by the devastation and sickness she witnessed, she wrote in her diary that evening: "What a place I have found. How can I stay here? It is too uncomfortable to sit and write."[51] Yet, Wilbur did stay. Unlike military officials in Alexandria, who not only neglected former enslaved women and children but also refused to enter their living quarters, Wilbur did not shy away from the overcrowded, disease-ridden places that could "prove contagious and fatal." "I went in to the oldest tenement, I saw," she wrote in her diary in November 1862. She found "3 women and 13 children . . . Old women lying in damp places." Turning to one of her fellow reformers, she pled that they must bring bedding to the women "to keep them from sleeping on the ground." Later that day, she returned to the "slave pen."[52] There, "in one room with one window," she discovered "20 women and children, some of them sick." Lying on the bare damp floor, "only few could get near the small fire . . . I had to leave . . . It was horrible! I went to the other room until I felt sick. I had to leave."[53]

After Wilbur left the slave pen, she did not allow the images she observed to quickly fade from view. Though a newcomer to Alexandria, she wrote a letter that evening to the provost marshal of Alexandria asking for barracks to be built for the contraband. "Women and children are sick and dying, not for want of necessary food, but for want of suitable shelter from this cold storm," Wilbur explained in 1862. "Could barracks be built for them at once so that we could have them move together & a physician and medical stores be provided for them, I think we can get supplies of clothing and bedding from the North, & they can be made comparatively comfortable for the winter."[54] Wilbur's call for adequate shelter was in line with new developments in nineteenth-century medicine that stressed the relationship between overcrowded living spaces and illness. Physicians and medical authorities attempted to cure health crises by improving the physical environment in which afflicted people lived, from creating proper ventilation to white-washing rooms with lime to encouraging proper hygiene.[55] Yet, as mentioned previously, the majority of Union physicians and military officers during the Civil War viewed sickness among emancipated slaves as the result of their physiological inferiority and inherent vulnerability to disease.[56]

Wilbur reminded the provost marshal, the leading government official in Alexandria, that army generals gave her the right "to act as a matron, visitor, advisor, and instructor to these poor women." She then chided him for having done nothing to assist the women and children since she had informally told him of their suffering. "And, as a result," she wrote, "on this wintry morning, I have presumed to appeal to the President of the U.S. on behalf of suffering humanity."[57] This triggered the provost marshal, who had ignored her earlier requests for the construction of new barracks, to forward Wilbur's request to the military governor of Alexandria. Although the provost marshal agreed to the construction of barracks because of the "increasing population" of contraband in the town, he only gave authority "to build cheap barracks," in order for the contraband to be "subjected to the necessary supervision and control."[58]

General Heintzelman, who ultimately received these requests, refused to build even temporary barracks because he feared that such places would make the former slaves dependent on the government for support. He argued: "If we build temporary barracks they will soon be filled. Now there are a number of Contrabands in this vicinity, who are supporting themselves. When they learn that the government will feed and shelter them, they will flock to Alexandria."[59] He further stated that the freedmen "would spend their wages, and leave the women and children a tax on the government." In the end, military and government fears of dependency meant no relief for homeless freedwomen and children.

The fear of dependency ran like a cancer throughout the rhetoric of Union officials in the Civil War South. Both federal leaders in Washington and local military officers in camps feared that any gesture of help or support would encourage former bondspeople to become dependent on federal aid and assistance.[60] Underlying this fear was the long-held belief that black people required white supervision to work or they would be indolent and unproductive. Thus, according to the logic of Union officials, building homes or providing support for destitute freedwomen and their children would remove the need for freedpeople to work for their own livelihood. As the *Weekly Anglo African,* a popular abolitionist newspaper, reported, the federal government attempted to "get rid of the poor fugitives," who fled to Washington, DC, and northern Virginia for support, in fear that they would become dependent on the government for assistance.[61] Fears of dependency did not begin with the emancipation of the slaves but can be traced back to antebellum discussions of Northern municipal governments that reluctantly established temporary shelters for unemployed workers. The architects of these institutions feared that those who resided in such almshouses would take advantage of that assistance and not be able to work independently.[62]

For military officials throughout the Confederate theater, employment became the way to stave off or prevent dependency from escalating. In fact, early federal policy in response to emancipation focused on removing former enslaved people from contraband camps and Union fortresses and returning them to abandoned and confiscated plantations to work.[63] In the spring of 1862 when Union forces occupied New Orleans, the city was on the brink of complete destruction. The devastation caused by the battle displaced white residents, forcing them to leave their burned-down homes and live on the streets. The vibrant free black community in the Crescent City was under siege: Northern soldiers did not make strict distinctions between those who were slaves and those who were free before the war or, for that matter, those who the war had recently freed. Hearing of Union victory in New Orleans, enslaved people from plantations down the Mississippi River in the Natchez district journeyed to that city, hoping to find freedom but instead encountered devastation. Southern white women mocked and ridiculed Union soldiers and resisted the Yankee takeover by engaging in individual acts of defiance. Meanwhile, a yellow fever epidemic tore through the region, infecting hundreds of people, both black and white. Given that the city lacked an established system of privies and a quarantined area, people turned to the city's streets when they became ill, which were soon filled with black vomit, which is symptomatic of yellow fever infections.[64]

With fears of dependency hanging over the newly occupied Union city, Butler reformulated his contraband policy to employ not only freed slaves within the city's limits but also poor white residents.[65] In his letter to the military commandant and City Council of New Orleans asking for their assistance, Butler explained: "Painful necessity compels some action in relation to the unemployed and starving poor of New Orleans. Men willing to work can not get work by which to support themselves and families, are suffering for food."[66] According to Butler's logic, if the residents of New Orleans were unemployed they would be susceptible to the "epidemic so earnestly prayed for by the wicked," but if they were employed they would not be destitute, and therefore "not in harm's way."[67] Butler's campaign attempted to solve two problems: men would clean the city streets and squares, reducing the spread of dirt and disease, and they would then be able to draw military rations, comparable to a day's service in the army, without becoming dependent on government aid.

Despite this plan, however, Butler did not employ all the poor people who were within Union lines. He gave preference to "white men," leaving hundreds of starving former slaves on the outskirts of New Orleans.[68] Learning about fugitive slaves' suffering, Secretary of War Edwin Stanton questioned the effectiveness of Butler's new plan. "It is a physical impossibility to take all," Butler explained in May 1862 in response to the accusations that he ignored fugitive slaves. "I cannot even feed the white men within my lines."[69] In the midst of Confederate women spitting on Union soldiers, white Southerners going hungry, and a military scrambling to develop an effective strategy to occupy a city, former slaves were left without any support or direction from the federal government. Even when federal authorities were notified about the dire and destitute conditions former slaves confronted, military officials often privileged white people as more worthy recipients of support.

Origins of the Freedmen's Bureau

The health of newly freed slaves in New Orleans and throughout the Civil War South entered political debates about the government's responsibility for its citizens, at least in part, because freedpeople themselves understood chronic and unremitting illness compromised their ability to exercise their rights. Although the federal government's initial forays into providing freed slaves with assistance can be traced to the few and scattered military reports from officials in the South about the freedpeople's health predicament, government response can also be traced to the countless and often undocumented ways that freedpeople themselves informed military and federal officials about the suffering they endured and the illnesses that plagued their families. Formally, some black Union soldiers used their newly enlisted status to advocate for better conditions for their families. Informally, freedpeople petitioned Northern benevolent reformers and teachers, working in the South, to ask military officials on their behalf for medical support and relief. As a result of freedpeople's articulations and the military's documentation of their conditions, two important institutional responses developed: the American Freedmen's Inquiry Commission and the Department of Negro Affairs.

The American Freedmen's Inquiry Commission (AFIC) grew out of the War Department under the leadership of Secretary Edwin Stanton.[70] Local officers, stationed throughout the Confederate theater, first reported on the arrival of freed slaves to Union lines. These reports eventually made their way to supervising officials in the army and then ultimately to federal authorities in Washington. Stanton in turn sent three federal officials, Robert Dale Owen, James McKay, and Samuel G. Howe, to survey the South and to investigate employment opportunities available to freedpeople and to suggest ways to improve existing forms of employment.

Stanton needed healthy workers. In fact, the initial report that members of the AFIC submitted in May of 1863 after their tour of various Southern locales, including the Carolinas, Florida, and Washington, DC, among other places, concentrated on the questions of former slaves' ability to work and the system of labor that should be developed in the South.[71] In their final report in 1864, questions of labor remained paramount in their assessment of the freedpeople, but after having lived among and observed the freedpeople for the better part of a year, the AFIC concluded by recommending that the federal government "offer the freedmen temporary aid and counsel until they become a little accustomed to their new sphere of life."[72]

Reports on the predicament of emancipated slaves made their way through the Union army's bureaucracy and eventually to other federal offices in Washington, DC, beyond the War Department. Because the military occupied abandoned and confiscated Confederate lands, some of the reports were routed to the Treasury Department, overseen by Salmon P. Chase, the 1850s architect of the Republican Party. How to deal with these lands invariably involved questions about the freedpeople, who inhabited the lands after fleeing from chattel slavery. A law established on March 3, 1863, led Chase to appoint federal agents to seize the abandoned properties. The government planned to have federal agents convert confiscated land into working plantations. By September 11, 1863, Chase divided the Confederate South into five districts and intended to have freed slaves work the land as part of a gang labor force.[73]

Like the War Department, the Treasury Department had a similar investment in former bondspeople's labor, which led Chase to create the Department of Negro Affairs—developed in direct response to freedpeople's living conditions and needs. Unlike the War Department, which relied solely on military officials to learn about the conditions in the Civil War South, the Treasury Department drew on reports filed by abolitionists serving in Freedmen's Aid Societies, as well as by some military officers who were sympathetic to freedpeople's plight and attentive to their health conditions. The Department of Negro Affairs became a mouthpiece for radical members of Congress as well as for Northern reporters to convey their disapproval about the suffering of former slaves throughout the South. Charles Sumner, the Republican congressman from Massachusetts, actively endorsed the work of the Treasury Department; while reformers like James E. Yeatman, who spearheaded the Western Sanitary Commission, filed reports about freedpeople's health predicaments. After touring through the South, Yeatman harshly criticized the War Department's organization of freed slaves into a labor force. He wrote to Lincoln and passionately explained, "No language can describe the suffering, destitution and neglect which prevail in some of their 'camps.' The sick and dying are left uncared for, in many instances, and the dead unburied. It would seem, now, that one-half are doomed to die in the process of freeing the rest."[74] Lincoln directed Yeatman to meet with Chase, who was in a better position to help him.

Due to longstanding tensions between benevolent reformers and military officials, though, Yeatman's reports only widened the bureaucratic rift between the War Department (American Freedmen's Inquiry Commission) and the Treasury Department (Department of Negro Affairs). Each agency firmly believed that their response to emancipation was more successful. The War Department had developed a contract-lease system that aggressively removed emancipated slaves from contraband camps and put them back to work as plantation hands. Yeatman had argued that this system was unjust and that freedpeople were poorly treated and forced to assume a "state of involuntary servitude, worse than that from which they have escaped."[75] Yeatman further stated that "The poor negroes are everywhere greatly depressed at their condition . . . They do not realize . . . that they are free men."[76]

Throughout 1863 and 1864, Yeatman and various military reformers, especially General Lorenzo Thomas, battled over how to best organize the labor force.[77] The military's employment contracts centered exclusively on former slaves being returned to Southern plantations; whereas, benevolent reformers argued that freedpeople became sick and often died when they were forced to return to the plantation in the service of the federal government. Yeatman designed a new plan that met the military's objective to produce a labor force but also took into consideration the needs of the freedpeople. In short, the plan was to offer freedpeople more autonomy in their decision to return to the plantation South rather than compel them to return to the cotton fields. Chase approved the plan and authorized Yeatman and others to implement it throughout the South. Chase and Yeatman soon realized that while their proposal was theoretically sound, they were unable to inspire emancipated slaves to leave Union camps and return to plantations as workers. The Treasury Department's plan failed because it lacked the War Department's manpower to physically force former bondspeople back to work. The War Department thus reasserted control over the creation of the labor force, but the Treasury Department remained involved in discussions about freedpeople's health, living, and working conditions.

While federal officials struggled to develop the plans to create an efficacious labor force, benevolent reformers continued to report to their sponsoring organizations. Unlike the federal agencies, benevolent Freedmen's Aid Societies provided an organized and systematic method of reporting on the health conditions of the former slaves. Agents sent monthly reports to their sponsoring associations, describing in great detail the physical conditions of the freedpeople. This institutional mechanism provided a framework to begin a discussion about freedpeople's health. When military officials described the unhealthy conditions that freedpeople confronted, they did so to illustrate the havoc of emancipation, the destruction of the war-ravaged South, and the fear of contagion—not with a concern for the health and well-being of former slaves.

In contrast, when Northern reformers discussed former slaves' raggedy clothes and sickly conditions, they did so to call attention to the medical crisis. They strongly believed in freedmen's ability to adjust to the challenges of free labor, promoting their readiness to work and till their own land. As Harriet Jacobs noted in 1862 after visiting a contraband camp in Alexandria, Virginia, "All expressed a willingness to work, and were anxious to know what was to be done with them after the work was done."[78] Benevolent reformers also enthusiastically described the freedpeople's eagerness to attend school.[79] As a report from the American Freedmen's Union Commission explained, "the eagerness of the negroes to learn can scarcely be overstated. The school houses are crowded, and the people are clamorous for more."[80]

In short, the benevolent organizations, which were mostly comprised of female reformers, better documented the conditions of the freedpeople and provided a more coherent narrative of their health than the federal agencies or the military.[81] As reports from benevolent workers in the field continued to come in, benevolent organizations slowly began to realize they were unable to solve the larger problems confronting freedpeople on their own. Organized by ideological, religious, and regional affiliations, benevolent associations in various parts of the country decided to band together. Between December of 1863 and July of 1864, these unified Freedmen's Aid Societies petitioned Congress to pass legislation that would provide emancipated slaves with medical support, rations, and shelter. In 1864, Freedmen's Aid Societies in the Midwest gathered at a convention in Indianapolis where they plotted to elicit the help of the federal government to support sick emancipated slaves. Voicing their concerns about the conditions of freed slaves in the border states and about the strife between Northern teachers and the Union army, they collectively vowed to appeal to Lincoln to send them a "Supervising Agent" with the military power and authority to assist them in their work.

In January 1863, the Emancipation League in Massachusetts sent a petition to Congress for a "Bureau of Emancipation."[82] Thomas D. Eliot, U.S. representative from Massachusetts, first brought the issue of an emancipation bill to Congress that month, but committee members immediately dismissed it. In December of the same year, he brought a second bill, which was referred to a select committee that proposed giving the Commissioner of the Freedmen's Affairs full responsibility for all the laws and regulations that related to the freedmen. For his role, the commissioner was able to appoint assistants, organize departments, and, most important, protect the rights of freedpeople. All military and civil officers would report to him.[83]

Those in favor of the Freedmen's Bill legislation argued that the overthrow of slavery devastated the lives of former slaves so thoroughly that the federal intervention needed would simply be a continuation of the Second Confiscation Act established during the war. Eliot stated: "The liberation of millions of slaves without federal protection would have constituted a crime against humanity."[84] Despite Eliot's plea, his bill drew criticism from members of Congress, who opposed federal intervention and argued that federal support of the freed slaves was unconstitutional. Samuel Cox, an Illinois Democrat, stated:

> [I]t is argued, something must be done for the poor blacks. They are perishing by thousands. We must look the great fact of anti-slavery and its millions of enfranchised victims in the face and legislate for their relief... Something should be done. The humanity which so long pitied the plumage should not forget the dying bird. But what can be done without violating the Constitution of the United States, or without entrenching upon a domain never granted by the States or the people in their written charter of powers? What can be done? Oh! ye, honey tongued humanitarians of New England ... I would beseech you to go into the camps of the contraband, who are starving and pining for their old homes, and lift them out of the mire into which your improvident and premature schemes have dragged them.[85]

Cox laid the burden of responsibility on New England benevolent groups since they were the leading supporters of abolition. Leaving aside Cox's opposition to the federal government providing "charity" to emancipated slaves, he went a step further and condemned "no government farming system, no charitable black scheme, can wash out the color of the negro, change his inferior nature, or save him from his inevitable fate."[86]

For Cox, like others who had opposed the end of slavery, the illness of freedpeople was clear evidence of the error of emancipation. The health of freedmen was indeed a political issue. Cox used the reports circulated by military officials and the benevolent organizations that detailed the suffering and sick condition of the freedpeople as evidence that black people were inherently unfit for the challenges of freedom and would naturally "perish." By supporting former slaves, advocates of the Freedmen's Bill legislation condoned "amalgamation and miscegenation."[87] Since congressmen were uncertain of the outcome of emancipation, the fear of amalgamation became the justification for leaving former slaves to suffer and die.

Despite Cox's criticisms, the House passed the Freedmen's Bill with a slight margin of two votes on March 4, 1864. Yet, the bill still needed to be passed in the Senate. Since it originally began as a temporary measure to establish the American Freedmen's Inquiry Commission, the War Department insisted that, if passed, it would house the Freedmen's Bureau and, by extension, the Bureau would be a temporary institution. The struggle between the War Department and Treasury Department resurfaced when the bill made it to the Senate floor. Charles Sumner, a long-time supporter of the Treasury Department, held the bill so that it could be housed in the Treasury Department, despite prodding from members of his own party that this tactic could fail and lead to the total loss of the Freedmen's Bureau. While Sumner's motives remain unclear, it seems that the Treasury Department had been more receptive to the concerns of abolitionists. Moreover, Sumner determined that federal assistance should be permanent, since the benevolent organizations lacked the manpower and resources to provide long-term support for the freedpeople. Therefore, it seems possible that Sumner may have thought the Bureau would have a longer tenure if it was housed in a permanent wing of the federal government.[88]

Ultimately, Congress passed Sumner's bill in June 28, 1864.[89] By March 3, 1865, President Lincoln signed the act to establish the Bureau of Refugees, Freedmen, and Abandoned Lands, commonly known as the Freedmen's Bureau. The "Bureau" status indicated that federal intervention would be temporary, and it would not be considered a "department" or permanent agency. Nonetheless, the major objective of the bill was achieved: the architects of the Freedmen's Bill—along with the benevolent associations—successfully compelled Congress to seriously address the problems that emancipation engendered. The Freedmen's Bureau was granted a provisional charter for a year to begin the process of organizing a labor force, managing abandoned land, and establishing schools throughout much of the postwar South. President Andrew Johnson—based on President Lincoln's previous recommendation—appointed Maj. Gen. Oliver Otis Howard, the "Christian General" as he was often called, to serve as the leader of the agency.

That the first pieces of legislation developed by the federal government in response to emancipation were not about "freedom," "rights," or "citizenship," but rather about labor sharply undermines the triumphant notion of emancipation.

It also questions the commonly held idea that freed slaves used their wartime labor service as a way to shape their entrance into a free labor economy.[90] Even when former abolitionists began the "Rehearsal for Reconstruction," in Port Royal in order for emancipated slaves' to gain the tools to eventually enter a free labor economy, their plans failed. Northern reformers were ultimately not allowed to play an official role in assisting freed slaves in this adjustment to a free labor economy nor were their plans to economically rebuild the South considered workable, as Yeatman's proposition revealed.

Examining freedpeople's labor within the context of the war—not with an eye toward Reconstruction—reveals that freed slaves' labor power became the only way that the federal government would recognize and engage with their liberation. This is not to argue that freedpeople did not gain insight about the workings of a free labor economy based on their wartime experiences; but that the line between the Civil War years and the Reconstruction decade has become blurred by historians who, following the agenda of government sources too closely, overemphasize the ways in which wartime labor provided the foundation for later employment. These were two separate periods in which questions of labor were handled very differently.[91] In the former, the federal government callously employed former slaves for the shortsighted benefit of the Union cause; subsequently, military and federal officials, in the shape of Freedmen's Bureau agents, continued to emphasize freedpeople's labor as central to the federal government's involvement in the South—but at least the government began to consider freedpeople's future. These agents took a more active role in creating, mediating, and negotiating contracts between former slaveholders and slaves, which was not a hallmark of labor relations during the Civil War.

Yet, the Freedmen's Bureau still inherited the assumption that freedpeople's labor power would serve as the basis for federal interaction and legislation that involved the future of freed slaves. In fact, the federal government justified its expansion of power into the South based on the prospect of freedpeople returning to the South as plantation laborers. The Freedmen's Bureau's four main divisions were all directly and indirectly connected to labor issues. The Land and Labor divisions mediated contracts between former slaveholders and former slaves, and settled disputes when arguments broke out about salaries, mistreatment, and unfilled promises. Bureau authorities also distributed land and managed confiscated and abandoned territories to be later used for agricultural production. Recognizing benevolent societies' claims that freed slaves needed certain skills to adjust to a free labor economy, the Education Division established schools whose curricula emphasized basic skills that would expand former slaves' employment opportunities beyond agricultural production. Finally, the Medical Division of the Bureau was also deeply tied to labor issues. Freedmen's Hospitals became the refuge for freedpeople who could not work, forcibly separating the sick, aged, and orphaned from those deemed "able-bodied." While this system of medical care did respond to the high rates of sickness and mortality that plagued the South, the government had a financial investment in ensuring that freedpeople were, in fact, healthy and able-bodied.

The federal government's obsession with freedpeople's labor nevertheless circumscribed how freedpeople's health would be defined and who would define it. The active role that former abolitionists played in military camps as advocates for freedpeople's health conditions ended with the creation of the Freedmen's Bureau. Although former abolitionists continued to work with the freedpeople in Bureau-sponsored schools as teachers and reported on health conditions in their letters to their sponsoring agencies in the North, Bureau agents and military officers often disregarded their comments and criticisms.[92] Very little room was left even for freedpeople to define their own medical needs. Benevolent reports that provided illustrative documentation of health conditions were replaced by statistical, purposely empirical Bureau reports of the overall number of freedpeople who were sick and dying. Such tabulations of the number of sick and dying helped the federal government calculate who could work. While the organization of the Freedmen's Bureau and the Medical Division, in particular, represented an unprecedented move for the federal government, the fact that this enterprise remained tethered to questions of freedpeople's labor power suggests that "freedom" depended upon one's ability to work.

3

Freedmen's Hospitals

The Medical Division of the Freedmen's Bureau

He who has health, has hope. And he who has hope, has everything.
—Arabian Proverb

Let us begin with the basics. Nineteenth-century hospitals were deplorably dirty by modern standards. The number of unattended patients was often matched by the number of rats that scurried through the halls and appeared on the kitchen floors at nightfall. One representation of hospitals in a popular magazine of the time depicted rats climbing up a bedpost and onto the body of a female patient in the middle of the night.[1] Medical advice books warned of the dangers that hospitals produced regarding "carbolic acid poisoning," which, in the age before the current understanding of ventilation, was nineteenth-century parlance that referred to the hazards of breathing contaminated air.[2]

It is no wonder that in Charleston in 1868, Lizzie Vanderwhost refused to be admitted to a Freedmen's Hospital despite a physician's claim that she required medical assistance. Vanderwhost's friends petitioned local authorities and wrote letters stating that they would find a physician to take care of her. Vanderwhost was admitted to Freedmen's Hospital, which before the war was known as Roper's Hospital—a municipal asylum for the poor and sick. The Medical Division subsequently took over Roper's Hospital, yet the stigma of it as an asylum for the poor prompted Vanderwhost's friends to hire a private doctor to treat her. Like many nineteenth-century Americans—black and white, rich and poor, newly emancipated and freeborn—Vanderwhost resisted the idea of being placed into an institution that housed the poor and dispossessed.

Many nineteenth-century Americans marked patients in hospitals as aberrant due to their lack of kin connections and their subsequent dependence on charity. Hospitals in this period oscillated between serving the basic medical needs of those who did not have families to care for them and providing shelter, clothing, and support to the indigent. Given a hospital's dual objectives, an institution often treated hundreds of patients. In some cases, the ratio of patients to doctors could be roughly 200:1, and in institutions that treated patients with mental disabilities, the ratio, at times, could be 1000:1.[3] These discrepancies existed because, throughout the nineteenth century, there was minimal variation between institutions that provided shelter to the poor and to prostitutes and those that attempted to offer medical care and comfort to the sick and suffering. Hospitals, asylums, dispensaries, and almshouses all provided some form of relief and refuge for those who—unlike their middle- and upper-class contemporaries—could not afford to be treated by doctors in their own homes.[4]

Due to her friends' pledges to provide care for her, Vanderwhost managed to avoid being admitted to the hospital.[5] Yet, for many emancipated slaves in the immediate aftermath of the war, Freedmen's Hospitals, despite their horrendous conditions, represented their only chance to survive the sickness, disease, and poverty that plagued the postwar South. They offered freedpeople the fundamentals: clean clothing, shelter, food, and basic medicine. In fact, so many freedpeople sought relief and medical care that the hospitals lacked the resources to provide support for all those who asked for it, let alone develop measures to search the postwar South for freedpeople who needed medical help. Further, the federal government did not have the capability to require emancipated slaves to be admitted.

The fact that the physician argued that Vanderwhost required assistance suggests that she may have been elderly or severely disabled, not simply sick. Sick ex-slaves were often provided with temporary medical assistance and then encouraged to recover on their own, usually with the help of family members, so that they could rejoin the labor force. Nineteenth-century doctors and federal officials carefully guarded against people taking advantage of the federal government's "charity" and developed rigid guidelines for who qualified for federal assistance. Bureau officers and physicians placed elderly or disabled former slaves in a different category. Their age or disability marked them as unable to join the labor force and thereby worthy of institutional support. Since Vanderwhost's discharge was based on her friends' promise that they would find a doctor for her suggests that perhaps she could not find one on her own.

Lizzie Vanderwhost's experience nevertheless reflects the broader history of almshouse and hospitals in nineteenth-century America, as well as the symbiotic, if vexed, relationship between labor and charity. From the late eighteenth century to the outbreak of the Civil War in 1861, municipal authorities supported the organization of these hospitals and almshouses since they facilitated the creation of a free labor economy. Early in the nineteenth century, as the rise of industrialization led to the collapse of individual proprietorship, many people who could not find employment in the burgeoning mills and workshops cropping up throughout the northeastern United States were left penniless.

Almshouses offered temporary charitable relief to these individuals as they attempted to find adequate work. Finding steady employment was not as easy as the administrations at these institutions had hoped. Superintendents became frustrated as the lines of people requesting relief grew longer and the number of patients at hospitals increased exponentially. Underlying the superintendents' frustration were fears that dependency jeopardized the prospect of a free labor economy, threatened the success of industrialization, and contradicted the widely embraced American notion of "individualism."[6] Nonetheless, because the operation of these institutions developed in response to the changing organization of a labor force and the overall functioning of the economy, many nineteenth-century Americans tolerated almshouses and hospitals as temporary institutions that would ultimately improve the quality and character of American workers. Nineteenth-century hospitals, at least in theory, exemplified the efforts of many Northern reformers to offer charitable relief to those displaced by the unexpected disruptions of industrialization.

Unhelpful Charity

The arrival of former slaves on the doorsteps of almshouses and hospitals called into question the practices of these humanitarian institutions. Inundated with requests from poor white Southerners since the beginning of the war, many of these institutions, at first, did not have the resources to extend their services to former slaves.[7] Moreover, among the dozens of dispensaries and almshouses in the postwar South that could potentially offer relief, these institutions explicitly denied freedpeople assistance. In Louisiana, the chief medical surgeon observed in October 1865: "In this city [Shreveport] the Civil Authorities made no provision whatsoever to relieve sick and destitute freedmen. They are not admitted to the Charity Hospital unless it is some exceptional cases of more than usual interest to the Medical profession. The same feeling is exhibited throughout the State generally."[8]

Bureau officials assumed that since local governments had previously gathered afflicted white people from the rural parts of the state and then sent them to the state hospitals, freedpeople would also be admitted to these state-run hospitals under similar provisions. In Charleston, South Carolina, Bureau leaders demanded an explanation from the administration of Stewart City Hospital for the "delay and neglect" in removing black patients from rural areas to the Pest House in the outer regions of the town, but the local authorities argued that they never agreed to admit infected freedpeople.[9] Physicians in Savannah, Georgia, claimed that there were no sick people in the city ward, and in response to the growing number of black patients, particularly among the migrants in the surrounding area, Bureau doctors asserted in 1866, "Those colored people that followed Sherman's Army should be the responsibility of the City of Savannah."[10]

Most almshouses refused admission to freedpeople because state and local governments failed to recognize newly emancipated slaves as citizens. State and local authorities further claimed that municipal officials designed asylums as temporary refuges for those who suffered from economic loss—in essence arguing that freed slaves were not former workers but indolent and unworthy dependents. Bureau officers initially challenged local governments' refusals to assist freedpeople and attempted to coerce these institutions into extending relief to newly emancipated slaves. In the fall of 1866, a Bureau agent in Mobile, Alabama, appealed to the city, after the local government denied freedpeople admittance to an almshouse, by arguing that freedpeople were, in fact, entitled to aid because they were denied wages from their own labor. "I can only repeat that these people are the county poor and measures for their support and medicines must be their responsibility," he wrote. "If you say they are not from households they are still destitute, simply because those have taken from them the net proceeds of their labor."[11] Beyond Mobile, civil authorities refused to provide medical assistance to freedpeople throughout the South in 1865–66.[12]

Compounding matters, when the war ended, there were fewer than six army medical units that provided assistance to former slaves. Treatment depended largely upon the availability of resources, the size of the ex-slave population in a Union camp, and the informal and often capricious decisions made by military officials in charge of a jurisdiction.[13] As early as 1862, both Robert Reyburn, a Union surgeon in Washington, DC, and John Eaton, Union chaplain in the Mississippi Valley, allowed ex-slaves access to their camps and provided medical aid to them.[14] Yet, in order to qualify for any form of assistance, freedpeople had to be willing to contribute their labor power to the federal government.

The few remaining military camps in the South offered the only institutional source of medical support for freedpeople after the war ended, which left hundreds of thousands of newly emancipated slaves without medical care.[15] As the military folded their operations in parts of the postwar South, the wartime policy, which once afforded former slaves rations, clothing, and medicine, ended. Describing the fallout of this program, one military agent explained that "the great ingathering of freedmen at the first centres of military occupation, and the resultant outbreaks of disease, compelled immediate provision." But, he continued, "Once these accumulations were dispelled, the number of patients was not so equally reduced . . . Victims of criminal assault, of accident and of disease continually came in as having plainly nowhere else to go, and often in moribund condition."[16] Arriving in North Carolina in the spring of 1865, a Bureau agent pointed to a specific case of freedpeople "left almost entirely without any medical care" for five months.[17]

When the military had abandoned the freedpeople in the final months of the war at a Union camp in North Carolina in 1865, sickness and disease escalated; the military left no personnel or medical assistance for unemployed former slaves. According to the chief surgeon in North Carolina, General Sherman sent about 10,000 freedpeople "down the Cape Fear River to Wilmington" and established a camp for them at Fort Anderson on Cape Fear. However, sickness plagued this camp. The several doctors present could not prevent the rampant spread of disease. The chief surgeon in the camp claimed his subordinates, the acting surgeons, who worked in the jurisdiction "paid very little attention to the sick."[18] According to the chief surgeon's report, an estimated 2,000 freedpeople died at Fort Anderson on Cape Fear between March 17 and May 31, 1865—an average of 30 ex-slaves a day. He concluded his report to a federal official in Washington by stating, "It is impossible to account for the cause or causes of this terrible mortality, as no record was ever kept of the camp, nor any report made of the sickness or death. There was no hospital accommodation at this camp."[19]

There are things that we will never be able to recover or reconstruct. Who counted the dead? Was it the shocking discovery of their bodies or the questions of where they would be buried that led to this estimate? Since there was not, as the chief surgeon asserted, a hospital to care for them or even a mechanism to report on their sickness, there likely was no infrastructure in place to bury them. Why would there be? Their migration to Cape Fear resulted from Sherman's order not from any formal plan for the emancipation of four million people.

What happened to those who lived? What did survival mean to people who endured slavery but witnessed the death of 30 people a day? Family members gone, parents buried, and children never given the chance to grow up as free. Indeed, the surgeon was right when he stated, "it is impossible to account for this terrible mortality," but it is equally impossible to account for how the others survived.

Before the Civil War, many slaveholders provided medical assistance and even, in some cases, built hospitals for enslaved people on their plantations. After the war, they argued that it was the responsibility of the federal government to assume health expenses because the government freed the slaves. As one Louisiana planter crudely explained, "When I owned niggers, I used to pay medical bills and take care of them; I do not think I shall trouble myself much now."[20] A Bureau doctor from South Carolina, wrote, "We take care of those in the vicinity of towns and employers provide medical aid to those working on plantations."[21] Planters in northern Virginia refused to provide medical treatment and actually sent newly employed freedpeople who became infected with smallpox back to Washington, DC. The dispute between Bureau officials and planters escalated in Strawberry's Ferry, South Carolina, when smallpox reappeared along the Cooper River in December 1865. "If planters vaccinated former slaves the first time smallpox entered the region," a physician argued, "many people would have been saved"; instead, "many have died."[22]

On some plantations, former slaveholders and ex-slaves began the slow process of introducing the subject of health care as part of their contractual agreements in response to the epidemic outbreak of disease.[23] Yet planters consistently deemed it the responsibility of the freedpeople to pay their own medical expenses. Similar to antebellum slaveholders, who hired out enslaved people to other plantations and shifted responsibility for medical care to those who were renting, postwar planters willingly contracted to provide former slaves with living arrangements but shifted the burden of medical expenses to those laborers.[24] In his agreement with freedpeople on his plantation in Abbeville, South Carolina, in July 1865, Charles J. Haskell agreed to furnish food, clothing, and the usual supplies—including food to raise hogs and time off to cultivate gardens—but stipulated that freedpeople must pay for medicine and doctor's visits.[25]

Many emancipated slaves, however, lacked the money to pay for medical expenses. Moreover, these agreements only applied to those who actually secured employment. Of course, many freedpeople, who avoided former slaveholders as employers and attempted to work independently, had no such arrangement. "We went begging," remembered a former slave, about the days and weeks following his family's emancipation. Only "finding berries to eat," he lacked clothing and medical treatment to protect his wife and children from exposure.[26]

The Medical Fallout of Presidential Reconstruction

The creation of the Freedmen's Bureau was an attempt to respond to the vacuum left by slaveholders, yet the Freedmen's Bureau's efforts were immediately thwarted. The federal government denied responsibility for ex-slaves' medical care at the highest level. Andrew Johnson claimed that there was no precedent for establishing medical care in the South and that such a measure would violate his constitutional authority as president.[27] As Radical Republicans, who served as the architects of the Bureau, developed plans for the operations of the Freedmen's Bureau on Capitol Hill, blocks away at the White House, President Johnson attempted to derail the efforts of his own party by returning power to the planter elite. A firm believer in states' rights, Johnson vigorously opposed the Freedmen's Bureau as the institution that would rebuild the South. Johnson denounced the Bureau as unnecessary and expensive; he argued that former slaveholders could better reconstruct the South if given the necessary financial support and governmental authority. He contended that before the Civil War there were four million slaves and 320,000 slaveholders; after the Civil War, there were four million slaves that cost the federal government 12 million dollars. In response to Johnson's position on the Bureau, Republican Senator Lyman Trumbull of Illinois approached Johnson in the fall of 1865 to reach a compromise, explaining that asylums, among other forms of support, were desperately needed to assist former slaves in their transition to free labor.[28]

According to the Johnson administration, providing physicians, medicine, and hospitals for the freedpeople would only incite dependency. As a result, his policy limited the operations of the Freedmen's Bureau and prevented military and Bureau officials on the ground from providing medical relief and support. While Johnson's plan to rebuild the South has been judged an abysmal failure because he pardoned Confederate slaveholders and limited federal aid to reconstruct the South, his policies are even a greater failure when judged by their fatal health consequences for the freedpeople. By returning power to Confederate slaveholders and in essence prioritizing their demands over those of emancipated slaves, he prevented the creation of an infrastructure to stop the spread of disease or to address the abject poverty and prolonged starvation that beleaguered the South.

As Johnson and members of Congress continued to debate the objective of the Freedmen's Bureau, the emancipated slaves' situation continued to deteriorate. Hungry, sick, and homeless, they rummaged through evacuated Union camps and salvaged worn, discarded uniforms, donned hats and scarves, and accepted, if available, blankets and food from Northern charitable groups. Meanwhile, former slaveholders, whom Johnson assumed would rebuild the South, ignored the thousands of newly emancipated slaves dying from exposure, malnutrition, and fever. As Bureau officials slowly arrived in Louisiana, southern Virginia, and the Carolinas in June of 1865, they discovered the bodies of dead freedpeople in the streets and learned of others left to die in the countryside— but only when townspeople complained about the stench. Bureau agents found elderly and feeble freedpeople in barns and hovels without food or clothing; on deserted plantations, they found scores of sick ex-slaves, huddling for warmth around fires.[29] And in cities, military officials found emancipated slaves crowded in empty lots, begging for assistance outside of churches, and taking refuge in former Confederate prisons and slave pens.[30] As one military official observed, the freedpeople "were crowded together, sickly, disheartened, dying on the streets . . . no physicians, no medicines, no hospitals." Such scenes, he wrote, "were calculated to make one doubt the policy of emancipation."[31]

As leader of the Bureau, O. O. Howard refused to wait for Congress to legislate an initiative to provide medical assistance. Howard created the Medical Division of the Freedmen's Bureau on June 1, 1865. He explained, "Soon after taking charge of the Bureau, I found it necessary to regulate hospitals and asylums . . . and to extend medical aid as far as practicable to the refugees and freedmen who became sick and were unprovided for by any local supply from a private source."[32] Asserting that the establishment of hospitals throughout the South would reduce mortality rates among former slaves, Howard cited the success of hospitals in Washington, DC, under Robert Reyburn, and the Freedmen's Hospital in the Mississippi Valley, supervised by John Eaton, where medical intervention led to mortality rates dropping from 30 percent to 4 percent.[33]

Using these hospitals as models, Howard developed the blueprints for hospitals throughout the South.[34] On June 16, 1865, he appointed former Union surgeon Caleb Horner as the chief medical surgeon, who, along with a handful of doctors in the nation's capital, began to design the organizational and bureaucratic structure of the Medical Division.[35] In each state where the Freedmen's Bureau established headquarters, an assistant commissioner oversaw the responsibilities of the various divisions and reported back to the main headquarters in Washington. Horner appointed a chief medical surgeon in each state to be in charge of the hospitals and physicians, to report any severe outbreaks of contagious disease, and to assess the overall health conditions in the state. Further down the bureaucratic ladder were assistant surgeons, who were in charge of particular regions and were required to make weekly and monthly reports to the assistant commissioner in charge of the state, who then made an annual report to the chief medical surgeon in Washington.

The establishment of Freedmen's Hospitals was accompanied by fears that able-bodied individuals would become dependent on the government for support. This anxiety shaped every decision that federal authorities made about the construction, organization, and the management of medical care in the Reconstruction South. Freedmen's Hospitals were not purely devoted to the comprehensive health and well-being of emancipated slaves but rather functioned as institutions that provided temporary care—namely, shelter, clothing, food, and basic medical treatment—to freed slaves so that they could join the labor force.

While the blueprints for the Medical Division seemed workable, the execution of these plans unfolded rather haphazardly because of conflicting economic and political agendas. Howard developed a medical system not only to lower the mortality rates of the ex-slave population but also to facilitate the creation of a free labor economy on Southern plantations. Each day, Howard received hundreds of reports from Bureau agents in the South about the struggles to create a labor force; to cultivate the land; and, in essence, to build an economy from the ground up. As he recalled years later in his autobiography, "The supervision and management of all subjects relating to refugees and freedmen gave a broad scope for planning and multitudinous duties. When I stepped into my office and began to examine the almost endless communication heaped on my desk, I was at first appalled."[36] "My first decision was that labor must be settled," Howard wrote, "if we would avoid anarchy and starvation what we do must be done immediately."[37]

Similar to almshouses that isolated the sick in an effort to create social order in antebellum cities and towns, Howard devised the plans to create a medical system in the South in order to avoid "anarchy."[38] Sickness created chaos in the postwar South and jeopardized the building of an effective labor force. Constructing a hospital system, therefore, was Howard's effort to create order. His creation of the system did not result purely from a benevolent concern about the health and well-being of former slaves but was firmly rooted in his broader campaign to establish social order.

Howard's statement that "labor must be settled" evokes the formative wartime policies surrounding emancipation, which emphasized freedpeople's labor power as contingent upon their emancipation. In the first circular that he authored as the leader of the Freedmen's Bureau, which was widely published throughout the country, he wrote, "The negro should understand that he is really free but on no account, if able to work, should he harbor the thought that the Government will support him in idleness."[39] Here, Howard foregrounds his concern about the necessity of former slaves working. Moreover, like wartime army officials, Howard did not shy away from the idea that military compulsion would be needed in order to return former bondspeople to postbellum plantations. The mere suggestion of compulsory labor however caused the Northern press to rile against Howard's proposal, charging that "that the negro had merely changed masters from the Southern slave owners to the United States."[40]

In response of the Northern press's allegations, Howard defended himself as a staunch proponent of free labor and a firm protector of the government's charitable relief programs. That said, he later confessed in his *Autobiography* that he raised the issue of military compulsion to stave off the criticism of the Bureau as an institution that "would simply 'feed niggers in idleness,' as they expressed it . . . I wished to start right." To prove that the Bureau would not encourage dependency, Howard furnished statistical proof to members of Congress that government relief would be temporary and limited. He posited that the number of freedpeople in Washington, DC, and "in different parts of the South" requesting relief from June to August 1865 grew from 144,000 to 148,120. Yet, once he tightened restrictions for those who qualified for aid by September of 1865, he proudly boasted, the number of those receiving relief dropped significantly, to 74,951.[41]

Much of the rationale behind the operations of Freedmen's Hospitals can be gleaned from Howard's statements. To begin with, Howard's boastful proclamation that the number of people receiving relief declined rapidly reveals the federal government's goal of reducing aid. This does not mean that the conditions in the South improved, that mortality rates decreased, or that ex-slaves were no longer hungry or sick. It simply means that the government had determined that the South no longer warranted federal intervention. It is unclear how officials reached this decision or how Howard calculated the reduced number of people worthy of relief.

Howard's statements further posit the temporary nature of federal intervention, and by temporary, he meant a nearly immediate cessation of support. The
statistics for the distribution of aid from June to August were barely printed
before Howard managed to halve the amount of relief. That the number of
people requesting relief increased signaled to him that the ex-slave population
was becoming permanently dependent on the federal government for relief.
What this assessment fails to consider is that the ex-slave population in a particular region was not stagnant; in fact, freedpeople were constantly on the move—
in search for food, lost family members, and employment. All of these factors led
to changing population patterns and differences in the number of people in need
of relief. More to the point, Howard does not provide specific geographic regions
where people sought relief but vaguely states that dependency was increasing in
"different parts of the South." His failure to offer a more precise analysis exposes
the often loose and imprecise language that federal leaders employed in their
descriptions of the postwar South as well as the vagueness that characterized the
prospect of rebuilding the South.

The Anatomy of Freedmen's Hospitals

The project of creating a national system of medical care throughout the Reconstruction South did not attend to the specificities and variations of particular
places, nor did it offer federal agents, stationed throughout the South, the tex-
tual space in reports to articulate nuance or variation of the medical problems
that they confronted. Instead, federal reports generalized conditions, broadly
summarized problems, and, most important, often kept an eye open for any sign
of improvement to justify the federal government's eventual withdrawal from
the South. As Howard explained, "We were laboring hard to reduce the number
of freedmen's courts, hospitals, asylums," as well as the charitable-relief efforts
provided by the federal government.[42]

This ethos ultimately led to the mismanagement of Freedmen's Hospitals and
undermined the operations of the first-ever federal health care program. By
working under the assumption that Freedmen's Hospitals were temporary institutions, federal leaders failed to create a clear administrative protocol on how
these institutions would run. Moreover, Bureau physicians stationed throughout
the South, whose job was to treat the sick, struggled to do so, as they faced
extreme pressures by federal leaders to reduce relief and medical aid. Without
support to run functioning hospitals, Bureau doctors found it that much more
difficult to stop the spread of disease or to address the consequences of poverty.

Given this predicament, Freedmen's Hospitals functioned less effectively than
Northern almshouses, which were dilapidated and poorly organized institutions.

Superintendents of Northern institutions at least recognized that almshouses would probably be permanent fixtures in the North, which facilitated their broader missions. Since the federal government was always looking for ways to cut medical aid, Freedmen's Hospitals struggled against presumptions of their temporary status to operate effectively.

Moreover, federal authorities did not systematically construct hospitals throughout the South, the way they did schools or labor offices. Since most federal agents and military officials lacked medical experience or training, they built hospitals and contracted physicians only in response to need, usually presented in the form of a report to the Freedman's Bureau that an area was "unhealthy" or where "mortality rates increased." As the leader of the Bureau in Alabama explained, "The hospital system of the bureau is the result rather of past necessities than of a plan to furnish medical attendance to refugees and freedmen as a class."[43] This was also true beyond the Bureau; physicians often lamented that hospitals were constructed in response to demand, rather than established as permanent institutions that could prevent medical disasters. Many doctors across the country advocated for the state to take a more preventive approach to the treatment of disease and the construction of hospitals.[44]

The problem with establishing hospitals only in response to demand was that, in much of the rural South, no one was responsible for documenting health conditions and notifying federal authorities about the need for medical support. Rev. A. S. Fiske, a Bureau agent in the Mississippi, recommended to leaders in Washington that a doctor should be assigned to each area in the South where former slaves lived. "The proper care of the sick, and charge of sanitary affairs," he explained, "requires that each provost-marshal district should have a medical officer, who should be in control of all sanitary affairs on the plantation."[45] In the fall of 1865, there were roughly 80 doctors and only a dozen hospitals in operation to treat well over four million slaves.

The lack of clear protocol on how to establish a hospital in a given region led to the federal government loosely assigning doctors to various Southern towns and cities where they assumed former slaves congregated after the war. Once arriving at these locations, Bureau doctors, who had little contact with treating black patients and had not been trained for the challenges of a postwar crisis, needed to assess the medical conditions. What they encountered and how they perceived the conditions of the South remains unclear, since the government did not solicit their impressions or observations.

Some Bureau doctors served in the military during the war, and others worked in private practices in the North or South before becoming employed by the federal government during the early years of Reconstruction. For other physicians, Freedmen's Hospitals served as their training ground for the medical profession. Like Northern carpetbaggers who fled to the postwar South for tical advancement, some novice doctors recognized the opportunity to experience, treating scores of sick freedpeople.[46] It is unclear how these doctors met their first patients or how they identified their mission to ex-slaves. Nor is it clear how freedpeople described their health to these mostly white men, some of whom wore military garb and other clothing similar to what their former masters wore. There were some doctors who traveled to the South with the best intentions of helping freed slaves. Committed to learning more about the medical problems that confronted freedwomen and their newborn babies, Dr. Rebecca Crumpler, one of the few African-American women physicians employed by the Bureau, traveled from Massachusetts to Richmond, Virginia, to have the opportunity to work with freedpeople. "I was enabled, through the agency of the Bureau under Gen. Brown, to have access each day to a very large number of indigent, and others of different classes, in a population of over 30,000 colored," Crumpler stated.[47]

Once they arrived in their assigned jurisdictions, Bureau doctors' first objective was to set up a hospital. This depended on assessing the medical condition of the freedpeople. Doctors had to determine whether the hospital would serve as a quarantine facility for those infected with a contagious viruses, like smallpox, or if it would function as a shelter for those that were homeless and vulnerable to exposure.[48] Matters were more complicated when one institution had to serve both objectives.

In the midst of confronting these questions, physicians also devised the actual blueprints to construct hospitals. Due to their limited budgets and the temporary nature of Freedmen's Hospitals, they converted schools, hotels, municipal buildings, and almshouses into hospitals. None of these plans could be formally executed until doctors received permission from leaders in Washington.[49] One local doctor asked Bureau officials for permission to use a recently constructed school building as a hospital. "It is absolutely necessary," he explained in September 1865, "that some provision be made at once for these people, as they are sure suffering very much and the shanties at present occupied are utterly unfit for human beings."[50] Bureau doctors in Savannah, Georgia, consequently turned "the city poorhouse" into a hospital that was also used as a school.[51]

The type of medical care that hospitals could offer freedpeople and the number of patients that they could treat depended upon the availability and resources that federal authorities provided local Bureau doctors. "We have labored under great inconvenience for a suitable building for a hospital purposes which the sick could be suitably nursed and cared for as well as a suitable place to bestow and care for the old and the infirm," explained a doctor on the outskirts of Washington, DC, in 1865.[52] Freedmen's Hospitals in Washington, DC, New Orleans, and Charleston housed as many as two hundred beds in one hospital, treating those infected with typhoid fever as well as offering shelter to the orphans and elderly. But the vast majority of Freedmen's Hospitals, like those in rural parts of North Carolina and Georgia, could treat no more than twenty patients, due to lack of funding.[53]

Additionally, Bureau doctors struggled to find available land to construct hospitals. Johnson's return of land to former slaveholders thwarted the efforts of those who attempted to establish hospitals on abandoned land or plots of land the Union army had used as campgrounds and refugee places for newly emancipated slaves. In Orangeburg, South Carolina, Bureau doctors turned a former quartermaster store for the Union army into a supplies post for the Freedmen's Hospital, but a local townsman demanded its return and the doctors were ultimately forced to give up the land and the hospital on it.[54] Similarly, in Roanoke, North Carolina, the government ordered Bureau officials to move the hundreds of freed slaves who migrated to the island during the war to another location, so that the land could "be restored to its original owners."[55] As Southern slaveholders scrambled to reclaim their property lost in the war, the land available for Bureau doctors' use shrank. Bureau physicians required land for a number of functions from providing shelter to those, who Harriet Jacobs described, as "living with nothing but the bushes over their heads" to offering refuge for those afflicted with chronic dysentery and were subsequently unable to work.[56]

Freedmen's Cemeteries

Bureau doctors required plots of land to bury the freedpeople who died during and after the war. In their haste to cut the Bureau's funding in the winter of 1866, the Johnson administration failed to consider the cost of coffins and the need for cemeteries to bury dead freedpeople. When Bureau physicians first alerted federal officials of the need for burial grounds, they commanded the Bureau doctors to work out arrangements with local governments.[57]

Local authorities, in turn, often rejected such requests, opposing the mere suggestion that freedpeople be buried near the same lot used for white Southern residents. In Raleigh, North Carolina, sparks flew when municipal officials informed Bureau agents in April 1866 that "the cemetery is a resting for those remains of Union soldiers and not an indiscriminate burying ground for freedmen." Bureau officials responded by asking for an appropriate place to bury the freedpeople, but municipal authorities failed to provide an adequate solution, all the while demanding that the bodies be removed.[58] Debates about where to bury freedpeople reignited the issue of who was in charge of the Reconstruction South: the federal government or local authorities.

On an emotional level, the turmoil of not being able to properly bury loved ones must have been unbearable for former slaves. On a public health level, the lack of cemeteries for freedpeople created dangerous health problems. In April 1865 in Charleston, South Carolina, freedpeople infected with typhoid fever were left to die in isolation and not properly buried. As a city official there explained, "The health of this institution and the city requires that dead bodies by typhoid fever should be removed with as little delay as possible."[59]

Without a sanctioned area for burial, the bodies of many dead freedpeople were left exposed. If the local medical staff could secure an ambulance, they could transport some of the bodies of freedpeople to remote locations in the country-side.[60] But ambulances were a new invention and few existed around the South. The idea of transporting dead bodies from one location to the next via an ambu-lance gained momentum after the Battle of Bull Run, but such a program demanded funding, manpower, and, most of all, a designated area to bring the bodies—which ultimately made this relatively easy task difficult to accomplish. In many parts of the South, the failure of both the federal and local governments to create cemeteries rendered such transportation moot. As a result, members of the local medical school in Montgomery, Alabama, scavenged the town for the bodies of dead freedpeople to be used—without the permission of family members—for medical experimentation. Reports from freedpeople in Washington, DC, and other parts of the South, told of similar situations in which medical practitioners snatched the bodies of dead former slaves for experiments.[61] Bureau doctors fran-tically wrote to officials in Washington for allotments to their budgets to stop these practices from continuing and for the money to pay local carpenters to build coffins. "I need three coffins immediately," wrote a doctor in Charleston, South Carolina, in 1868; "I have no time to make a special requisition."[62] But like other requests placed by local doctors, these orders were left unanswered.

Help Wanted

As Bureau doctors struggled to acquire land and funding, they were also over-whelmed by running a bureaucracy. Paperwork piled up on physicians' desks: weekly and monthly medical reports, pharmacy inventories, employee con-tracts, and various other administrative forms competed with actually treating patients. After waiting months for officials in Washington to respond to a call for medical assistance for over 3,000 freedpeople in Roanoke, North Carolina, a Freedmen's Bureau agent, in September of 1865, wrote again, explaining that, "much suffering will endure if supplies are not provided."[63] As an institution re-liant entirely upon federal administrators for funding, supplies, and manpower, each Bureau doctor needed to have a steward on staff to maintain accurate records and to handle the correspondence between local doctors and federal administrators.[64]

Bureau doctors, however, struggled to find competent stewards to assist them with hospital management. Local military authorities assigned Union soldiers, who were still stationed in the South, to serve as hospital stewards. While this provided a temporary solution to the problem, as more Union camps folded their operations and soldiers left the South, the number of available soldiers that could read and write dramatically decreased.[65] When the Union army left Memphis, Tennessee, in September 1865, a local Bureau doctor panicked for fear of not having an assistant who could handle the overwhelming paperwork that the hospital amassed. He wrote, "I feel that I cannot overstate or exaggerate our wants in this particular hospital . . . in a hospital with over 100 patients, where the convalescents are alike ignorant and untaught or rather inteachable, the service of a good steward are indispensable . . . all the white troops here are being mustered out."[66]

Initially, Howard planned to simply extend Union army stewards' and physicians' contracts. In an order from General Tillson in Georgia, for instance, army surgeons were required to continue to stay in the region and "to treat those in need" until sickness and disease dissipated.[67] But Georgia was the exception; many soldiers refused to stay on duty. "We are now needing additional help of that kind," wrote a Bureau doctor to his supervising officer in September 1865.[68] Like many members of the army, medical personnel also refused to remain in the South after the war, and, consequently, many former slaves suffered because of lack of medical treatment.[69] As one Union physician described the situation in September 1865, "There are upwards of three hundred sick and but two surgeons to minister to them; and the result is that the former are overworked and yet the latter have not the care that humanity demands."[70] Thus numerous doctors simply left the South, refusing to provide medical care, even if it meant breaking the Hippocratic oath. As John Eaton, stationed in the Mississippi Valley, later explained in his autobiography, "the soldiers in the Army were a good deal opposed to serving the Negro in any matter."[71]

Without consistent and reliable support from the Medical Division, Bureau doctors had no choice but to turn to local, white Southern physicians for assistance—often to no avail. As former slaves migrated from the sugar and cotton plantations of Louisiana to Shreveport and New Orleans for employment and medical assistance, local white doctors—despite prodding from the Bureau—declined to provide treatment to the migrants.[72] Similarly, in Greensboro, North Carolina, a local doctor unapologetically refused to provide medical treatment to a group of sickly freed slaves.[73]

Although some white doctors agreed to assist Bureau physicians, federal authorities only permitted such hires on a short-term basis. In many cases, the Bureau would only hire a physician for three to six months, refusing to extend beyond a nine-month period. Short-term doctors' contracts made it difficult for chief surgeons to run a hospital; as soon as an assistant physician was trained to treat patients and carry out administrative duties, his contract would expire. That said, many doctors were unwilling to stay on staff beyond the initial three-month period. The long hours, combined with the responsibilities of managing the hospital, resulted in many physicians declining to extend their contract. A Bureau official in Mississippi remarked in 1866, "When any of these gentlemen do not renew contracts, much inconvenience, to say the least, is the result, and generally there is danger that patients will suffer before a new contract will be accepted."[74]

On the other hand, when local doctors did agree to renew their contracts, Bureau leaders doubted their intentions. As the assistant surgeon in charge of medical operations in South Carolina said in December 1865, it was very difficult to find Southern white physicians who were "faithful friends to the colored race."[75] Bureau officials on the ground suspected eager doctors who were willing to open Bureau hospitals of being charlatans, only interested in treating freedpeople to gain experience, a common practice among novice doctors in the nineteenth century.[76] As one Bureau official lamented in October 1865, "It's too difficult to find a honest, good doctor that won't abuse the poor."[77] In an attempt to prevent disingenuous physicians from filling their ranks, the Bureau required applicants to provide verification of their medical training and experience, as well as letters of recommendation testifying to their sincere commitment to providing medical care to the freedpeople. But sometimes due to freedpeople's immediate need for medical care, this process was not carried out. In some cases, local doctors, who did not have contracts with the Bureau, provided immediate, free medical assistance to former slaves but later charged the Bureau for their services—which created problems for Bureau administrators, who did not have the funds or authority to pay these doctors.[78]

In addition to hiring additional Bureau doctors, local physicians also struggled to hire competent and committed nurses, attendees, and cooks to staff Freedmen's Hospitals. Federal restrictions, however, often thwarted these efforts. Federal authorities required Bureau doctors to wait until they received permission from the national Bureau office before they initiated employment contracts with hospital staff.[79] But Bureau doctors immediately and desperately needed nurses to distribute rations, change sheets, wrap bandages, and bathe the patients. Physicians also needed cooks to prepare the meals, and, even—in some hospitals—guards to protect the rations and supplies.

After physicians, attendees proved to be the second most challenging and important positions to fill. Attendees were responsible for ensuring that hospitals were sanitary to guard against sickness. Beginning in the late eighteenth-century, several military leaders, doctors, and ordinary citizens began to theorize about how dirt caused the spread of disease. Bureau doctors desperately needed attendees to sweep and mop floors, wash tables, desks, and walls with lime; and launder clothes to keep toxic smells away.[80] In some cases, attendees also provided medicine to patients. At the Freedmen's Hospital in Arlington, Virginia, in 1867, the supervising physician complained to federal authorities that attendees had given patients the wrong medicine. The doctor blamed the attendees' "blunder" on the cramped conditions of the hospital and claimed that if attendees could properly number each bed, such mistakes would be prevented in the future. The doctor also emphasized the role of attendees to maintain "more perfect cleanliness," which, he argued, could be achieved by proper inspection and preservation of the bedding.[81]

But without funds allotted from the federal government to hire the proper personnel, Bureau medical officials were unable to maintain efficient hospitals. Although federal officials eventually approved contracts to hire hospital staff and allowed Bureau agents to contract local physicians to serve in the hospital, they did not provide the necessary funds to pay the medical staff. As one frustrated doctor dryly remarked in September 1865, "The Bureau seems to me imperfect as it provides for the employment of surgeons but makes not appropriations for their pay."[82] Throughout the South, Bureau offices and medical authorities could not consistently pay their staff, to the point that many employees often quit and the Bureau could not replace them.

Freedmen's Hospitals Bureaucracy

Within the broader framework of the Freedmen's Bureau, the communication to the federal level came at a greater cost to the Medical Division than to other divisions of the Bureau. Officials who supervised schools, legal matters, and employment contracts also needed to funnel their requests through a federal bureaucracy, but the time that elapsed waiting for a response about hiring another teacher, approving the terms of an employment contract, or resolving a legal conflict did not have the same repercussions for doctors, forced to wait for medical queries to be answered. As a result of the slowness of federal bureaucracy health conditions worsened, and, in many situations, freedpeople died while waiting for treatment. Throughout North Carolina, from Raleigh to Wilmington, agents and doctors produced reports about the dire and unhealthy conditions of the state in 1865, but calls for assistance were not answered. By January 1866, physicians stationed in various districts were still waiting for additional doctors to arrive and supplies to be delivered. Not surprisingly, a physician in Salisbury reported on January 24, 1866, "that several had died from want of great attention."[83] Not until March, six months after the initial requests were made, were doctors' calls for more assistance finally answered.

Despite the dire situation, Bureau doctors were required to follow the bureau-cratic regulations. In order for Bureau physicians to receive supplies—whether it was secondhand tents, clothing, or medicine—the chief medical surgeon of the Bureau required local doctors to provide comprehensive reports ranging from the number of patients treated to detailed accounts of inventories. If they did not follow the prescribed guidelines, they would not be provided with funding, sup-plies, or staff. Bureau doctors struggled to comply with these federal mandates.[84] In less than a three-month period in 1866 in South Carolina, for example, local Bureau doctors throughout the state were unable to provide reports to the chief medical surgeon. Their reasons for failing to do so ranged from being sick them-selves to a sudden outbreak of fever that turned their "district into a hospital," which left no time for sending reports.[85] A doctor serving in the outskirts of South Carolina waited months to receive his shipment and when he did get part of the requested material it was "broken and spoiled."[86] Supervising officials jus-tified such a tedious process because they claimed some doctors stole supplies and embezzled money.[87]

Those doctors who attempted to abide by the headquarters' command often found themselves in a bureaucratic mess. Obtaining the correct request forms or knowing how to calculate number of patients seen versus the number of patients remaining under their care from the previous week posed problems for Bureau physicians. Once they filled out the correct reports, they invariably did not know to whom the request should be sent. A doctor in Georgia wondered if the form should be dispatched to the Commissary office, since that office dealt with clothing, or sent to the Medical Purveyor, who dealt largely with the freed-people's relief.[88] A similarly flummoxed physician, who was stationed at the Freedmen's Hospital in Shreveport, Louisiana, made repeated requests for ban-dages but "heard nothing" from the main headquarters. "I have to use bandages every day and it is impossible for me to procure them, there was no one to even get them in any other way," he wrote in September 1865. Not only did this doctor struggle with the lack of supplies, he also lacked the correct forms to make his requests and had to use "army blanks" instead. A doctor stationed in Louisiana expressed a similar frustration about how to organize the federal forms in September 1865, "I have no date from which to make correct weekly reports for the whole time I have been in charge."[89]

The directives established by the Bureau in Washington made sense to a group of former military leaders, but to doctors, many of whom did not serve in the Union army and worked in private practices, the constant change of orders, issuance of circulars, and delivery of memos was simply confusing. "Enclosed are your monthly reports AGAIN for corrections, separate monthly reports from consolidated reports," wrote a Bureau supervisor to a doctor in New Berne, North Carolina, in 1866.[90] "Your statements of funds due at the Freedmen's

Hospital," wrote one supervising official in 1867, "is returned for your signature. Your attention is directed to form 57, p. 95 of the Officer's Manual."[91]

Uncertainty over how to file the correct federal reports was a particular problem for doctors in rural regions, who had a difficult time accurately assessing the number of patients they would visit at a freedmen's camp or on a plantation. Traveling on horseback through the outskirts of South Carolina, Dr. Smith informed his supervising officer in October 1865 that it was impossible for him to provide weekly reports of the sick and wounded for the past three months, since he was unable to follow-up on his "outdoor patients." Unlike local doctors in hospitals who had the opportunity to check on a patient's daily progress and provide status updates in weekly reports, doctors in rural regions were unable to keep accurate accounts, which hindered them from getting the necessary medical supplies, or providing an accurate representation of health conditions in the Reconstruction South.[92]

The likelihood of getting their requests answered, or even received, partly depended upon doctors' proximity to the nation's capital. Those in Alexandria, Virginia, found it easier to send word to officials about the health conditions of the freedpeople in the region; also, there were over eight hospitals in a 20-mile radius of the small suburban town, so the ratio of doctors to patients was relatively low.[93] In the Deep South, it was more difficult to manage a reliable and effective correspondence to the national headquarters, and there were, as a result, fewer hospitals. Those that were in operation in this part of the country were often understaffed and without ample supplies.[94] When cholera began to appear among newly emancipated slaves in the summer of 1866, a physician in Georgia wrote to the quartermaster for supplies but was then sent on a wild goose chase, contacting various officials in the Bureau before ultimately being denied the medicine. "I inquired of the Quartermaster about the middle of last month," he wrote, "if he could assume a bill for medicines that I had contracted in the emergency of the Cholera breaking out. He said he could but subsequently informed me that according to General Howard's field order 4, he cannot pay for the medicine without an order from General Tillson." In the two months the doctor waited for an order of quinine, bismuth, and chloroform, many patients succumbed to the cholera.[95]

Situations like this erupted throughout the South largely because of the complicated bureaucracy that Bureau doctors needed to follow in reporting health issues. Even when Bureau officials received doctors' reports, bureaucratic problems nonetheless surfaced. On a weekly and monthly basis, Bureau physicians often sent medical reports to assistant commissioners, who were the liaisons to federal authorities, detailing the number of sick patients under their charge and the fluctuations in mortality rates. Bureau doctors had hoped that such statistical reports would lead to additional resources and support. Yet, when assistant commissioners gathered this information from various doctors in a given state, they often did not include notes about the medical condition in the state under their supervision and instead focused on economic issues relating to the distribution of abandoned land, contract disputes between former slaves and planters, or the progress of the Education Division.[96]

If assistant commissioners did discuss health conditions, they often stated "that health was improving" or "death rates decreased" over the past month, ignoring the comprehensive evidence presented by physicians on the ground.[97] In Georgia, for example, the assistant commissioner described the success of the Bureau's efforts in a number of areas but failed to emphasize the dire health needs of the former slaves. After not receiving a response from the national headquarters regarding their immediate request for medical assistance, local freedpeople in Savannah, Georgia, took matters into their own hands in the fall of 1865. The freedpeople in Savannah approached several "prominent citizens" and asked them to write letters to the Freedmen's Bureau on their behalf. Even after this intervention, the Bureau did not respond. Not until a group of "colored patrons" approached a local physician, Dr. Caulfield, did the freedpeople receive medical treatment. Although Caulfield was willing to treat them, he was uncertain how to establish a suitable hospital for them. He wrote to officials in Washington several times for instruction, but his letters went unanswered.[98] Throughout the postwar South, freedpeople frequently sought medical care independently, but their experiences were often not included in the Bureau's documentation, because it was not required that the Bureau record on all freedpeople's health, just those who they directly supported.[99]

Freedmen's Hospitals as Almshouses

As freedpeople, local doctors, and Bureau agents struggled to negotiate the tangled web of federal bureaucracy in the Reconstruction South, President Johnson vetoed a bill in February 1866 that would have increased funding to the Medical Division.[100] This funding was not requested for expensive medications or to hire experienced doctors, but rather to cover the rudimentary expenses of the hospitals to keep them in operation. In view of the fact that many hospitals simply operated as almshouses, Bureau doctors only needed Congress to provide meager financial support in order for medical staffs to afford basic necessities, such as candles, kerosene, soap, fresh beef, bread, squash, molasses, and other staple foods.[101] Many local physicians requested funding for large kitchens, stoves, and sleeping areas to accommodate the destitute and sick freedpeople. In Savannah, for example, the Freedmen's Hospital included "three large coal stoves for each of the five largest wards and two for each of the smaller, and for the kitchen it required to coal cooking stoves." In this particular hospital, there was also a laundry and a stove used for heating the iron in case of a "long wet spell."[102] In Alabama, Bureau doctors requested a "kitchen to accommodate over 200 freedpeople . . . to ensure that only cooked rations should be issued," and "to provide comfort for those who cannot cook for themselves."[103]

The need for kitchens was of particular importance, since Bureau physicians understood proper nutrition as the cure for illness. A proper diet, medical officials contended, not only staved off the symptoms of dysentery but also improved the freedpeople's general health. By providing freedpeople with fresh vegetables and well-cooked meat, medical staffs attempted to wean newly emancipated slaves off the allegedly poor diets that they had grown accustomed to during slavery and which, Bureau officials claimed, was the cause of the alarming death rates among them. Describing the need for adequate nutrition, the chief medical officer in Louisiana explained in 1866, "Great difficulty has been experienced in the hospital from inability to furnish a proper diet for the sick, and a fair proportion of the deaths reported can be readily traced to a lack of proper nourishment." To remedy this problem, he recommended "an addition to and increase of the hospital stores in the shape of farinaceous articles of diet, would be of great benefit to the sick, reduce the mortuary report of the hospitals, and greatly assist the medical officers in the treatment of patients under their charge."[104]

In addition to proper nourishment, doctors also requested clean clothing and bedding to protect freedpeople from exposure. By providing freedpeople with proper nutrition, adequate bedding, clean clothing, and suitable shelter, they had a good chance of defending freedpeople against an onslaught of disease and sickness. Many of the illnesses that infected freedpeople—intestinal viruses and smallpox—resulted from the mere fact that they were forced to live in crowded, unsanitary conditions, where they lacked access to the basic necessities.

One of the ways that doctors hoped to create healthier environments was to construct hospitals that had proper ventilation. Providing adequate ventilation in hospitals, in large part due to the influence of the U.S. Sanitary Commission's efforts to reform army medicine, was one of the crowning achievements of Civil War medicine. Medical army historians boasted to their European contemporaries that U.S. Army doctors had managed to limit the amount of sickness and disease during the war by establishing proper ventilation measures. Therefore, some Bureau physicians paid particular attention to the architecture and design of Freedmen's Hospitals, noting the need for open windows and less crowded spaces. In Arlington, Virginia, in 1867, the doctor in charge of the hospital advocated "tearing down the partitions" between the private rooms so that the "whole building can be more thoroughly warmed in the cold weather and better ventilation can be obtained in warm weather."[105]

Yet on the Bureau's constrained budgets, constructing or even renting buildings that offered proper ventilation proved difficult. Understanding the necessity of fresh air and principles of ventilation, Bureau doctors improvised and used former army tents to house patients. Modeled after the Indian tepee, the Sibley tent, invented by a U.S. Army official, had a circular opening at the top that facilitated ventilation. While tents may not have provided the most ideal shelter for emancipated slaves, doctors were, nevertheless, able to use them for quarantined patients and to house overflow patients when hospitals were full.[106]

The Cost of Medical Care

One of the major problems that Bureau doctors faced was the question of payment. Should federal authorities provide free medical aid to formerly enslaved people? Or should former slaveholders in their new role as employers be responsible for medical expenses? Or should freedpeople themselves pay for doctor's visits? These questions were not just about medical care but reflected the power struggle over who was responsible for reconstructing the South. As a result, there were no direct and easy answers. Problems like these continued to crop up in the Education and Labor divisions, but when these conundrums surfaced in the Medical Division the consequences were much more severe. As a Bureau physician in North Carolina explained, "The majority of the freedpeople who are overtaken by disease are in most cases totally unable to pay the smallest charge for medical attention and unless public charity is extended to them, they die in some excluded place uncared for."[107]

Far removed from the suffering, many federal officials easily dismissed doctors' requests for increases in their budget to pay the staff by writing back that freedpeople should be charged for medical services. Bureau doctors boldly rejected such suggestions because they realized that freedpeople were in no position to pay for medical treatment. The federal government's proposition fundamentally contradicted the entire purpose of the Medical Division as an almshouse for freedpeople that provided free medical care.[108]

Even if freed slaves may have wanted to pay for such expenses, they usually could not afford to do so, due to the financial problems they confronted as the South slowly and clumsily transitioned from a slave to a free labor economy. On many plantations freedpeople were denied their wages. In his report on the condition of freedmen in the Mississippi Valley, James Yeatman, president of the Western Sanitary Commission, noted, "The poor Negroes are everywhere greatly depressed at their condition. They all testify that if they were only paid their little wages as they earn them, so that they could purchase clothing, and were furnished with the provisions promised they could stand it; but to work and get poorly paid, poorly fed, and not doctored when sick, is more than they can endure."[109]

Federal authorities continued to ignore these requests for medical aid because President Johnson, as well as many of his staff, opposed the Bureau and wanted the operations of the Medical Division to be terminated immediately.[110] In a circular issued to assistant commissioners on May 30, 1865, Howard stated, "Relief establishments will be discontinued as speedily as the cessation of hostilities and the return of industrial pursuits will permit. Great discrimination will be observed in administering relief, so as to include none that are not absolutely necessitous and destitute."[111] Increasing funds for the Medical Division only, according to federal authorities, encouraged freedpeople to be dependent on the national government for their livelihood. These officials continued to contend, "that the charity of the government must be guarded."[112]

For many federal authorities, the answer to doctors' pleas for medical support often was either to simply find employment for those freedpeople out of work or to transport afflicted freed slaves to another location. Members of Johnson's administration rejected requests for increased medical assistance by arguing that those in need of support should be removed to areas in need of laborers. The rationale that employment could prevent and even cure sickness grew out of the wartime policies that insisted on freedpeople returning to the South as plantation laborers. After touring plantations throughout the South to check on the status of the Bureau, two U.S. army generals argued, "A majority of the freedmen to whom this subsistence has been furnished are undoubtedly able to earn a living if they were removed to localities where labor could be procured."[113] Once freedmen were gainfully employed, federal officials speculated, they would not be destitute and, therefore, not vulnerable to sickness and disease. In Washington, DC, in 1865–66, the federal government offered free transportation to ex-slaves to enable them to move to areas in need of workers. The problem, of course, was that freed slaves had migrated to the Upper South during and after the war in order to escape from the suffering, disorder, and disease of the Deep South.[114]

According to the Johnson administration, federally sponsored hospitals were not a necessary and critical part of rehabilitating the postwar South. They served as a constant reminder that the freedpeople relied on the government for support. Leaders of the Bureau stationed in Texas assured the Johnson administration in October 1865 that they had done everything "to prevent the necessity of establishing hospitals."[115] The hospital constructed in Houston, the assistant commissioner further explained, would only be temporary. For this Bureau agent, and many others like him, hospitals represented failure and had the potential to lead to "systemized pauperism."[116]

While the Bureau's leader, O. O. Howard, expressed similar fears when the government first began the process of disseminating relief and establishing hospitals in 1865, by 1867, many local and federal Bureau officers grew increasingly intolerant of freedpeople's needs and repeatedly denied them assistance. The goodwill that they had reluctantly bestowed upon the freedpeople in the immediate aftermath of war dissipated and was replaced with the pitiless conviction that federal relief invariably produced dependency. After surveying a freedmen's community in Washington, DC, in the spring of 1867, a military agent recognized the suffering condition of the newly emancipated slaves. Yet when the question of constructing a hospital to protect freedpeople from disease was raised, he advised "the colored people to be persuaded to leave" since a hospital "attracts a community of dependents."[117]

Unlike federal leaders, Bureau doctors viewed hospitals as important and necessary sites of medical intervention. Without Freedmen's Hospitals, wrote a physician from Montgomery, Alabama, in January 1865, many freedpeople "would have greatly suffered, perhaps perished."[118] Beginning as early as the summer of 1866, Bureau doctors along with a handful of sympathetic federal agents fought to keep their hospitals in operation, despite aggressive federal efforts to shut down these institutions.[119] Bureau doctors responded to staff shortages by ignoring federal regulations and independently employing local freedpeople to work as attendees, cooks, and nurses. As the assistant commissioner in North Carolina explained, "If medical attendance cannot be procured without [contracts] I will take the responsibility of making such contracts."[120] Without federal support, Bureau doctors, in many cases, paid these employees in food rations.

As a way to reduce the hospitals expenses, Bureau doctors also adopted a popular practice commonly used in Northern almshouses, assigning menial tasks to patients rather than hire attendees. "We must at all times have some of the labor in the hospitals done by convalescents," explained a Bureau official to a doctor in North Carolina in the winter of 1866.[121] In Louisiana, the chief medical officer reported that patients assisted nurses since "paid help has been reduced to the minimum."[122] These efforts served a dual purpose: they helped reduce the hospitals' expenses, and they facilitated the broader goal of free labor. Similar to those who ran Northern almshouses, Bureau doctors believed that asylums could provide freed slaves with basic training to enter the workforce, with the byproduct of lowering the operating costs of their hospitals.[123]

Hiring local freedpeople and patients and paying them in rations offered one way of lowering a hospitals' expenses; but as Alexander Augusta, an assistant surgeon in Savannah, Georgia, and one of the few black doctors employed by the Bureau, explained in May 1867, even with patients assisting the laundress with the washing, his hospital still required an increase in the monthly budget.[124]

The cost of rations, in particular, drained a hospital's monthly budgets since the prices for fresh vegetables, chicken, and meat varied according to the market. "Prices are double the cost of the Raleigh Market," asserted a doctor in New Bern, North Carolina. "Eight chickens bought at the rate of sixty-cents each and four bushels of sweet potatoes at $1.25 a bushel" was far too expensive for the hospital to afford, he reported in January 1867.[125]

Bureau physicians found the answer to their financial worries in their own backyards. Instead of waiting for shipments of rations to arrive or worrying if they had enough money to buy supplies, they converted plots of land at the outer perimeters of their hospitals into vegetable gardens. Growing corn, squash, and beans provided doctors in Arkansas, Georgia, and Louisiana with nourishment for the sick. Creating their own vegetable gardens also enabled Bureau doctors to lower the expenses of the hospital by assigning patients to sell and barter the vegetables to members of the surrounding community. In his annual report to federal authorities in 1866, the assistant commissioner in Little Rock, Arkansas, boasted about the success of his vegetable garden. "It has not only paid for the rent of the land and other expenses, but the estimated value of the products over all expenses is $108.25. To say nothing of the sanitary effect upon the hospital and asylum," he continued, "it has enabled the hospital to save and accumulate a fund of $160.81 for use during the winter when the garden will not be available."[126]

When federal leaders learned that a cadre of local doctors had discovered their green thumbs, O. O. Howard, to the chagrin of most doctors, required all medical staff to plant vegetable gardens to lower their hospitals' expenses.[127] While in theory this seemed feasible, it nonetheless created even more problems and work for hospital staffs. Some doctors waited for seed; others lacked fertile land.[128] Dr. Augusta, the assistant surgeon who spearheaded the garden project in Georgia, actually faced a number of obstacles at harvest time. After planting his seeds and not seeing results, he discovered that Sherman's army had occupied the land and had left it in a condition that made it unfavorable for growing vegetables. Compounding matters, a herd of cattle decided to graze on the field. The physician's requests for fences to prevent the cattle from destroying his garden were left unanswered.[129]

Benevolent Assistance

The continual neglect by the federal government to provide Bureau doctors with adequate support prompted many physicians in the postwar South to approach benevolent associations for assistance. Since many Northern benevolent groups who were stationed in the South from the war had begun the process of providing relief and support to freedpeople, mostly in regard to education efforts, these organizations willingly formed alliances with Bureau officials. After being commissioned to Augusta, Georgia, the supervising Bureau agent told the local doctor that he should obtain the assistance of the teachers there to help provide clothing and in organizing the hospital.[130] Despite ideological conflicts between the benevolent organizations and the Freedmen's Bureau, in many places, these associations helped to lower the expenses at the hospital.[131]

The Western Sanitary Commission and the North Western Freedmen's Aid Commission provided supplies to hospitals in Arkansas and Mississippi, while the National Freedmen's Aid Society contributed $1,000 to the construction of a hospital in Tennessee. In Alabama, the Cleveland Freedmen's Union Commission, along with the North Western Freedmen's Aid Society, provided much-needed support and clothing to freedpeople in Mobile and the surrounding area.[132] In Washington, DC, the citizens in Georgetown organized the National Association for the Relief of Destitute Colored Women and Children.[133] Meanwhile, the members of the New England Freedmen's Aid Society, the American Missionary Association, and the New York Society of Friends supported Bureau doctors in the Carolinas, Georgia, and northern Virginia.[134]

Of particular support to the Freedmen's Hospitals were the "Colored Benevolent Societies." In fact, one physician suggested to Caleb Horner, the Surgeon-in-Chief in Washington, that his work with the "Colored Benevolent Societies" was so successful that he recommended Bureau officials encourage local physicians to approach these organizations. He wrote in September 1865 of a strategy "that I have adopted, which works well and you might find worth suggesting to other surgeons. In all these large towns are Colored Benevolent Societies. I have talked with committees and in some cases gone before the meetings to explain my mission and purpose and have them to contribute . . . we work together and I have a pledge of $75–$2100 or more a month for the hospital."[135] With the help of Northern free black women, Harriet Jacobs organized a "fancy fair" in order to raise money for the hospitals in Alexandria.[136]

While benevolent associations provided a formal network of relief, there were also a number of other informal responses to the predicament of sick freedpeople that did not get captured in traditional archival documentation. There were invariably thousands of freedpeople who suffered from sickness or were impoverished but never appeared before a Bureau doctor or requested relief from a federal asylum. Based on the expansive notion of what constituted kin within the postwar black community, there were surely freedpeople who offered a member of their community temporary shelter, food, and clothing.[137] When a reformer in Beaufort asked a "young man who broke his leg a month ago" and was "lying destitute and helpless" why he did not go to the Bureau doctor for assistance for his leg, he replied, "I have learned by experience that it is direct

cruelty to the race for the government to assist the people with ratio
form, and in this I am happy to state I am sustained by the best frien
freedmen in this place."[138] This particular incident reveals the extent t
many freedpeople purposely did not turn to the federal government for   ,
since it could have, according to this freedman, have negative consequences for
freedpeople to seek federal charity. Yet, receiving assistance from "the best
friends of the freedmen," that is the Northern reformers who published the
report, endorses the claim that former abolitionists should serve in the postwar
South. This was part of the rationale for publishing such intimate stories in the
Northern press: to garner more financial support for the critical work, which
reformers performed. Freedpeople may have received a combination of relief—
some drawn from federal sources and other support provided by kin networks.
In sum, there is no single algorithm to calculate how relief was disseminated
during this period or who provided it.

That said, Northern teachers, who lived and worked within freedpeople's
communities, witnessed the extent to which kin networks provided fellow
emancipated slaves with medical assistance and support. C. E. McKay, a Northern teacher stationed in Baltimore, Maryland, discovered a boardinghouse operated by a freedwoman in 1868, "when a young colored boy" approached her,
announcing that "Miss Downs wants you to come see her." Located in an alley
in a deserted part of the city, Downs opened her home to destitute children
and freedwomen. She also rented out rooms in her home to local boarders and
used the money, along with some cash she earned as a washerwoman, to buy
medicine for the orphans in need. After visiting the boardinghouse, McKay
wrote to her Northern association urging it to send funds to support Downs's
efforts. "A part of this [Downs's income] has to be expended in medicines for
one of the little orphans, who is dropsical, her head and neck swelled to an
unnatural size, and her arms and legs slender as pipes."[139] Downs's boardinghouse represents one of the many efforts within the black community to provide support and medical assistance for those in need, even if their ailments
were not contagious.

The Bureau recognized these kin connections within freedpeople's communities, which is the reason why military officials throughout the postwar South
advocated for families to take over the responsibilities of caring for those who
were sick or impoverished. Moreover, by late 1866, some groups of freedpeople
had been able to regain their footing and were, as a result, able to establish board-
inghouses, like the one Downs started in Baltimore, or were in a position to
establish colored benevolent societies. Given that Northern middle- and upper-
class black people in places like Philadelphia and New York provided charitable
relief to manumitted and poorer blacks in the decades before the war, it is likely
that these groups either directly provided relief to emancipated slaves or pooled

their resources and donated money, clothing, and food through the organizational efforts arranged by Northern Freedmen's Aid Societies.[140]

This piecemeal relief signaled to federal officials that they could reduce the amount of aid allotted to freedpeople despite the fact that sick freed slaves' continued to need assistance. Even with the Republicans' control of Congress in 1867 and the efforts made by many in the House and Senate to extend the Bureau's contract until 1868, the guidelines set forth by officials during Johnson's administration to terminate the Bureau after a few years remained intact. When Johnson first began to evaluate the Bureau's operations in the South, he assigned former military officials to serve as inspectors. Basing their reports on cleanliness, the health conditions of the patients, and the staff, they determined whether hospitals should remain open.[141]

On one level, assigning officials to inspect hospitals built on wartime practices, initiated by the Sanitary Commission, to ensure that hospitals were healthy, clean environments that could adequately treat patients and prevent the spread of disease. On another level, the deployment of inspectors throughout the postwar South became a way for Johnson and other federal critics of the Bureau to marshal evidence about the conditions in the South that justified their decision to reduce federal aid. In the overwhelming majority of the reports, the inspectors unanimously determined to close down hospitals. Either the health conditions in the region were, according to their estimation, "improving" and therefore, no longer required federal intervention, or the hospital was in abysmal condition and thus needed to be closed since it was unable to provide adequate medical care. There was rarely, if ever, any middle ground or a call to keep the hospital in operation. In many of the inspectors' reports, contradictory and ambiguous descriptions of health conditions of the community were recorded, which reflected the tensions between doctors, who fought to maintain hospitals, and Bureau agents and inspectors, who attempted to disband them. When the local doctor in St. John's Parish, Louisiana, in September of 1866 reported that cholera "was raging fearfully" in his region, the supervising officer claimed that the doctor "exaggerated the violence" that the disease inflicted.[142]

The difference of opinion between Bureau doctors and federal leaders regarding the health conditions in the postwar South partly resulted from the failure of both groups to provide a clear definition of sickness. Instead, they continually relied on adjectives such as "suffering," "sickly," and "destitute" to describe the medical conditions of newly emancipated slaves. Or in their assessment of freedmen's communities, they described the general, overall health status as "dependent," "idle," or, "self supporting."[143] While, on the surface, the terms and their meanings varied, concerns about labor underpinned each of these definitions. The meaning of sickness among federal leaders and Bureau agents was intimately tied with concerns relating to freedpeople's labor power.

In Plymouth, North Carolina, in 1866, for example, a local doctor offered to provide medical services free of charge to newly emancipated slaves in response to their ill health and lack of medical treatment. When military officials contacted authorities in Washington in July 1866, so that this doctor could be compensated and "that some plan could be adopted" to provide permanent medical care to the former slaves, government leaders in Washington sent an inspector to the region. After he "conversed with a number of citizens of the places as to the condition of the freedmen in that subdistrict," he concluded that he saw "no reason why any action should be taken to procure medical aid as they are generally self supporting."[144] The inspector's choice of the term "self supporting" ignores the freedpeople's poor health conditions that prompted the unsolicited assistance of the local doctor and instead evaluates freedpeople's health status within a labor context. Self-supporting connotes economic independence and self-reliance and has nothing do with health. Moreover, the use of this term contains a judgment about freedpeople's labor power not their medical needs.

Furthermore, Radical Republicans and members of Johnson's administration— who otherwise disagreed on the objectives of the Bureau—shared a view of ill-health as it related to one's ability to perform arduous field labor. In their view, sickness was avoidable, and employment would protect freedpeople from sickness. In the proposed bill that attempted to extend the duration of the Freedmen's Bill to 1866, the Radical Republicans took a rather Johnsonian stance and claimed that afflicted freedpeople who qualified for employment would be ineligible for medical assistance or relief. They posited "that no person shall be deemed 'destitute,' 'suffering,' or 'dependent upon the Government for support,' within the meaning of this act, who, being able to find employment, could by proper industry and exertion avoid such destitution, suffering or dependence."[145] According to the bill, if freedpeople were capable of "being able to find employment," the government would not provide medical assistance to them if they became sick—revealing the extent to which federal officials and Bureau authorities, regardless of party affiliation, understood health in relation to labor.[146]

The understanding that one's employment opportunities determined access to medical relief impelled assistant commissioners and planters to enforce regulations that would cut off medical services to those who could work. In North Carolina, the assistant commissioner, after touring much of the state, reprimanded the doctors in his jurisdiction for providing medical assistance to freed slaves who could easily be employed. Meanwhile, in Shreveport, Louisiana, in 1866, the assistant commissioner ordered the hospital closed because of the great demand for laborers.[147]

The failure of the Medical Division to provide adequate medical assistance resulted from the federal government's understanding that ill-health was connected to freedpeople's alleged unwillingness to work. According to Johnson and his staff, the more money, resources, and funds that federal officials pumped into the fledgling Bureau hospitals, the more dependence would increase in the South. And according to their logic, such dependence would prevent former slaves from returning to the plantation as laborers. Johnson and his administration continued, as a result, to ignore the ways in which the effects of the war and dislocation exacerbated the spread of sickness, particularly the explosive spread of smallpox among former slaves in 1865–1866.

Reconstructing an Epidemic

Smallpox among Former Slaves, 1862–1868

That was the end of the optimism epidemic.
—Salman Rushdie, *Midnight's Children* (1981)

"You must provide buildings or tents to meet the emergency at once," wrote the Chief Medical Officer in North Carolina to a Bureau doctor stationed in New Bern, North Carolina. "You must go out vigorously with vaccination and if necessary make applications with other physicians," he exclaimed. Smallpox had threatened the black residents of the small coastal town, and the only Bureau doctor remaining in New Bern stood defenseless as he read orders from Bureau headquarters. The Freedmen's Hospital that had been built a few months ago had since been disbanded due to federal regulations to reduce the number of hospitals in the South. Due to the massive migrations of people in and out of New Bern, smallpox entered the town, and to compound matters, Bureau administrators feared an impending outbreak of cholera.[1] At the same time, former Union surgeon Dr. Thomas Knox discovered "smallpox in almost every dwelling" that he visited in South Carolina and the surrounding area. The incessant presence of the virus overwhelmed Northern teachers, who instead of reporting to their benevolent agencies about their work with freed children, consistently documented the harm and "terrible havoc" that the virus inflicted among newly emancipated slaves.[2] "We should soon have a pitted or pock aristocracy," penned a Southern journalist in New Orleans in 1865. "It is almost unfashionable," he quipped, "not to have about on the face the scars and blotches of that most loathsome disorder . . . Wherever we go, on the street, in the cars, in the market, at the places of amusement and at church—everywhere and at all times we meet with the irrepressible pock."[3]

These are the scattered pieces of evidence referring to communities of freedpeople falling victim to a smallpox epidemic that began in Washington, DC, in the winter of 1862, spread to the Upper South in 1863–64, culminated in the Lower South and Mississippi Valley in 1865, and eventually seeped into the Western territories in 1867–68, infecting Native Americans. Physicians did not record freedpeople's names or details about their condition, but tallied their illness under the heading "number infected." In the millions of documents that chronicle the battles of the Civil War and the coming of Reconstruction, there is not one photograph of those suffering from a smallpox epidemic. Instead, the dominant images of Reconstruction show hard-fought political battles won: large groups gathering under a banner of citizenship, and freedwomen singing liberty. There are virtually no sources that describe what the epidemic meant for freedpeople during emancipation.[4]

On the federally occupied plantations and in the so-called freedmen's villages, where the federal government boasted about their experiment with free labor, how did freedpeople cope with the outbreak of the epidemic? When did they recognize that they were infected with what some nineteenth-century doctors referred to as a "pestilence" or the "deadly scourge"? Did they awaken at night with a hot sweat and a fever, the first symptoms of the virus? How did they react when their skin broke with tiny pustules erupting on their face, arms, and chest? Had they witnessed the effects of smallpox on the body of a friend or family member before the war or had they seen a case among the Union troops?[5]

Freedpeople, like many other nineteenth-century Americans, may have purposely hidden those infected with smallpox from public view. Akin to those with leprosy, people infected with smallpox may have been ostracized, exiled to the remote corners of a town, forced to live out their lives in a rural, unknown place, quarantined by local authorities to prevent the spread of disease. Even if they managed to survive the virus, the scars that it left on their bodies would invariably serve as a reminder that they were once carriers of the "deadly scourge." Moreover, in nineteenth-century America, evidence of a past infection of smallpox on one's body could have connoted immorality, poverty, and/or promiscuity.[6] Any of these reasons would have further marginalized those infected with the virus.[7]

Even though there were medical reasons to justify isolating afflicted freedpeople, the economic, political, and social pressures more than likely codified these practices. Bodies covered with a sickness that produced pustules should not be seen by Northern journalists touring the South, who wanted to write about the "South that will rise again." Radical Republicans may have reconsidered their campaign to expand their party's base in the postwar South if they were forced to shake hands with someone infected with "the pox."[8] Southern planters, who were already reluctant to engage in contract negotiations with people they considered their property, certainly did not want to see the effects of an epidemic that could potentially decimate their labor force.

Maybe those suffering with smallpox were also hidden because freedpeople feared that Northern and Southern doctors would visit sick former slaves in the name of a so-called cure, but were actually motivated by a prurient fascination to observe how smallpox erupted on black skin. While former abolitionists wrapped the bodies of those infected with smallpox in clean blankets and then wrote passionate letters to their sponsoring organizations for money and resources to combat the epidemic, some of those reformers may have questioned whether their Southern adversaries were right—that the "negroes would go extinct." Finally, religion may have figured into freedpeople's calculations for hiding those infected with smallpox. Nineteenth-century Americans often understood catastrophes that claimed the lives of so many people as rooted in spiritual causes—God's will or demonic power—not as the result of physical, natural, or medical causes. No freed person would have wanted to provide a white observer with possible evidence of God's disapproval of emancipation.[9]

This absence of evidence of freedpeople's feelings as they cared for and lost loved ones in this epidemic is not a mere coincidence but reflects a larger effort by many in the Freedmen's Bureau and in Congress to conceal an episode that, if fully exposed, could have jeopardized the rebuilding of a region that before the war was deemed by many in the North as "backwards" and "peculiar."[10] Only signs of progress or hope could be displayed to the rest of the country in order for them to economically invest in the South. Only visions of free labor and landownership could be propagandized to apprehensive Northerners and white Southerners whose support of Reconstruction was essential to achieve national reunion.

All of this was exacerbated by how the military defined smallpox, how the federal government responded to the outbreak, how doctors treated it, and how the press reported on it. When smallpox first broke out in 1862, military and federal officials in the North followed health protocols to stop the spread of the virus among soldiers, but justified the outbreak among freedpeople as a "natural outcome" of emancipation. The outbreak reinforced theories that newly freed black people were on the verge of extinction, which provided little incentive for federal agents to try to stop its spread. Additionally, even when various doctors and federal officials rejected that theory and committed themselves to stopping the spread of the virus, the massive dislocation that emancipation caused thwarted their efforts: smallpox spread with the formerly enslaved people and the armies that moved throughout the South. Freedmen's Hospitals also proved unable to defend freedpeople from attacks of the virus, because doctors lacked the resources, personnel, and support to establish adequate quarantines and conduct inoculations and vaccinations. In contrast, when cholera broke out in 1866, the federal government established efficacious health regulations and measures that prevented the expansion of that epidemic. Believing that cholera threatened the entire population, federal officials employed efficient measures to stop the disease. During the nineteenth century, cholera produced enormous fear among federal officials because it was a relatively new epidemic and local governments and doctors had little experience treating it, yet federal officials managed to disseminate protocols to local governments on how to prevent the spread of the bacteria. Ironically, smallpox was a virus that local governments and doctors had battled since the eighteenth century, yet when it broke out among emancipated slaves, federal officials failed to follow the protocols and procedures that doctors and communities had implemented for decades. Instead, these officials propagated a medical fiction that smallpox was a disease limited to former slaves—despite advances in nineteenth-century medicine that underscored environmental factors as the cause of the virus's transmission.[11]

Known for centuries as a fatal virus, smallpox attacked communities around the globe. It struck both Union and Confederate camps during the Civil War and turned battlegrounds into makeshift hospital stations.[12] After both sides laid down their weapons, the virus continued its assault on freedpeople.[13] Military authorities often responded to the outbreak of smallpox in their camps by placing afflicted soldiers in pest houses to isolate the virus, or vaccinating and sometimes revaccinating vulnerable troops. Due to the unsanitary conditions of the camps and the constant movement of soldiers and prisoners, the military's efforts at preventing the virus from spreading often failed.[14] The two viruses that cause smallpox can be spread by inhaling the expelled air of an infected person or through contact with contaminated bedding or clothing.

Former slaves who entered Union camps during the war were susceptible to both strains of the virus and were disproportionately infected.[15] Once infected, they developed slight fevers. By the second week, flat reddish spots erupted on their faces, which then spread to their arms, chest, back, and legs. After a few days, the fever intensified and the reddish spots turned into pimples and then blisters.[16] Depending on the severity of the infection, patients either survived or succumbed to the virus. If they could survive the fever for two weeks, they had a good chance of living.

Both during and after the war, the military and the Medical Division of the Freedmen's Bureau struggled to protect freedpeople from smallpox despite policies that encouraged ex-slaves to be in motion. When smallpox exploded in the South, the migratory patterns of former slaves traveling to plantations in search of work worsened the spread of the virus. The federal government did not stop or redirect freed slaves from returning to plantations, but instead increased the number of ex-slaves descending on a particular region or restricted them to over-crowded and unsanitary refugee camps.[17]

The Initial Outbreak

At the same time that freed slaves arrived at the nation's capital in 1862, smallpox broke out in the city.[18] Horse-and-buggies were converted into ambulances to transport afflicted soldiers from one camp to the next. While wealthy Washingtonians were vaccinated two to three times in fear of being infected with the full-blown deadly virus, city officials scrambled to develop a procedure to vaccinate school-age children. Some freed slaves dosed their bodies with tar to ward off possible infections.[19] Newspapers reported incidents of hysteria that ensued after the mere mention of the "distemper." Letter-writers from the capital warned travelers and passersby to avoid the area at all costs, and yellow flags were hung throughout the city to signal the presence of the "deadly scourge."[20]

One Washingtonian diarist recorded in January 1862 "that smallpox prevailed among the Negroes."[21] The metropolitan police requested that the army remove the bodies of former slaves who died of smallpox and were left on city streets.[22] As the virus spread throughout city, military and municipal officials, as well as city residents and newspaper reporters, blamed the virus on the arrival of freedpeople to the area. After visiting the Old Capitol Prison in Washington, DC, where he saw many "Negroes confined there as contraband," Brigade Surgeon Stewart informed his subordinate, B. B. French, that in every case in which "small pox had come under his notice it originated among the Negroes." He then ordered that former slaves "should be removed to some place where they can be kept more apart from the respectable white people, and where, if possible constant employment can be given to them."[23]

While military officials ordered some former slaves to recross the Potomac to live in prisons and former slave pens in Alexandria and Fortress Monroe, others were left on their own. Meanwhile, a sudden snowstorm fell upon the city, followed by rain and icy cold temperatures, forcing former slaves to find shelter on frozen, or muddy, uninhabitable streets. With few options, many former slaves congregated in overcrowded tents in the center of Washington, DC, leaving them more susceptible to a smallpox outbreak.[24]

Although Union officials claimed smallpox "originated among the Negroes," medical authorities in Washington realized that the outbreak resulted from the Union army forcing former slaves to live in unsanitary camps. According to the Medical Society of Washington, building barracks to house former slaves would have prevented the rampant outbreak of smallpox in the first place. In their report on heath conditions during the war published in 1864, local physicians condemned military officials for not building barracks for freedpeople on the outskirts of town or in the city's vacant lots, forcing them instead to congregate in overcrowded camps in the center of town, which was filled with trash, excrement, and rotten food. The Medical Society did not blame the former slaves for

:ation of smallpox, but instead recognized the environmental factors
"It is generally admitted," the physicians posited, "that small-pox is
diseases due to domiciliary circumstances, and is at all times a pre-
isease. It has been stated over and over again by eminent authorities,
that there need not be a single case of small-pox in any city; if the authorities will
but take the proper steps to check it."[25] Sadly, the authorities in Washington were
too late. By 1864, the virus had managed to cross the Potomac River and make
its way into Alexandria and to other parts of the Upper South.[26]

The vast population movements, orchestrated largely by the Bureau to
develop a labor force, spurred massive migrations across the South that enabled
the virus to pick up momentum.[27] Additionally, many former slaves defined the
meaning of freedom as an ability to be mobile—whether that mobility resulted
from a desire to relocate to the North, or to find lost relatives, or to seek land
ownership and opportunity. In response to the arrival of freedpeople to Orangeburg, South Carolina, in November 1865, a Bureau agent requested that military
officials prohibit freedpeople from visiting neighboring plantations. While the
agent recognized that such a request would restrict former slaves' newly won
freedom, he promised that the mandate would only last until smallpox disap-
peared, noting that this was the only the way to prevent the further spread of the
virus.[28]

Traveling from place to place, freed slaves could not protect themselves from
unexpected contact with the virus. Describing his experience in Hilton Head,
South Carolina, in 1864, a freedman recounted the initial symptoms of a smallpox infection, "We tuck down wid feber . . . 'case we hasn't got nuttin' for keep
warm." In one colony in Hilton Head, where former slaves took refuge, smallpox killed freedpeople by "tens and twenties." A benevolent society worker
from Boston stationed on Hilton Head informed her sponsoring agency, the
New England Freedmen's Aid Association, that there was "no hospital on the
island except for wounded soldiers and white invalids." Without a government-
sponsored hospital, she explained, "we have scarcely any shelter for the
hundreds fleeing from slavery and ending their weary march here."[29]

Despite the medical and public knowledge that smallpox could be easily
transmitted through contact with an infected person, medical and governmental
officials interpreted the growing number of cases of smallpox as consequences of
the "dirty habits" and immoral behavior of former slaves, much as they had attributed epidemic disease to the vices of working-class and immigrant New
Yorkers in 1832 and 1848.[30] Some Bureau officials and Northern newspapers
claimed that freedpeople were responsible for their high mortality rates. A corre-
spondent for the *New York Times* wrote in 1866, "The mortality of the Negroes
in and near large towns and cities still continues to be very great. The small-pox
rages among them . . . dirt, debauchery, idleness, are the cases of this inordinate

mortality."[31] The *New York Herald* followed a similar course when a reporter reasoned that freedpeople continued to contract the virus because they lived in overcrowded "Negro cabins" and "dilapidated shanties."[32] While smallpox is an airborne, highly contagious virus that spreads simply by inhaling the air of a person infected with the virus, overcrowded conditions and unsanitary living dwellings certainly exacerbate the spread of smallpox. As one Bureau physician explained, unhealthy living conditions also led to other diseases that worsened smallpox infections. "While in tents many cases are reported to have been complicated with pneumonia, this being the cause assigned for most of the deaths ... one third of all cases died."[33]

Bureau authorities, nonetheless, repeatedly blamed the spread of smallpox particularly on freedpeople. "In view of the well-known filthy habits of the freedmen as a class," a Bureau official in Louisiana remarked in 1866, "the small number of deaths among them this season is somewhat remarkable."[34] A black clergyman in Georgia agreed with this rationale, and took it a step further when he blamed the incessant spread of smallpox on freedpeople's "immorality."[35] The notion that immorality led to the continual spread of the virus persisted throughout the duration of the epidemic. Military and religious officials in the Mississippi Valley led freed slaves to believe that "free love," or unmarried freedpeople living together, was the cause of two "adulterers" contracting and then ultimately dying of smallpox.[36]

Bureau leaders also explained that the proliferation of smallpox among freedpeople was because black people and white people reacted differently to disease and sickness. When smallpox escalated in Augusta, Georgia, in 1867, the physician on duty frantically wrote to his supervisor expressing his fear of contracting the virus. Attempting to alleviate the physician's fear, the supervisor assured him that his regional background and implicitly his race would prevent him from contracting the virus, "I trust you are frightened and not hurt by smallpox, keep cool and drink plenty of citric and lemonade ... I don't remember any Northerner having the disease though we all were excessively and consistently exposed last winter."[37]

Moreover, the government's reliance on a system of medical reports that quantified the number of freedpeople infected with the virus further underscored the medical fiction that only freed slaves were susceptible to smallpox. Federal authorities relied on a system of reporting that simply calculated the number of patients that were infected, the number under treatment, and then the number that died. This quantitative form of reporting on the virus provided federal officials in Washington with a largely statistical portrait of the smallpox epidemic, which, in turn, supplied federal officials with empirical proof that smallpox was an illness that only infected freed slaves. Due to these nosological interpretations of the virus, Bureau doctors continued to calculate the number of infected freedpeople, and rarely, if ever, documented the number of white Southerners infected with the virus.

Although white Southerners contracted smallpox, there was no systematic bureaucratic structure that comprehensively tabulated the number of white people who were infected and subsequently treated in their homes by local doctors or by municipal institutions and charitable hospitals. Some white Southerners were dislocated and abandoned during the war and appear in the Bureau records as "white refugees." According to the Bureau's documentation, there were exponentially fewer white people than black people who were treated by Bureau doctors—which made it appear to federal authorities that smallpox disproportionately infected freedpeople. In Georgia doctors throughout the state reported 5,611 freedpeople admitted to the hospital compared to 143 white people.[38] Similarly in Mississippi, an estimated 550 freedpeople contracted the virus in October of 1865, as opposed to 37 white refugees. In fact, from October 1865 to January 1866, the number of infected freedpeople, as reported by Bureau doctors in the field, far outweighed the number of white people on an average of 100 to 1.[39]

After a few months of treating fewer than five to seven white people, Bureau doctors began crossing out the column of white refugees on their annual reports and would only tally the number of infected freedpeople. When the chief medical surgeon in Louisiana noted a decrease in the number of white patients treated in early 1866, he crossed out the word "refugees" on the forms, and only treated freedpeople infected with smallpox (or any sickness).[40] Describing the prevalence of smallpox in Savannah, Georgia, the New York Herald assured readers that while "whites have not entirely escaped, the number of cases yet developed is quite small and of a mild type." But among the freedpeople, the paper reported, "the disease travels almost with the speed of an epidemic."[41] The New York Times reported that in 1866 and again 1867, the number of freedpeople far outweighed the number of white people infected with the virus.[42]

Extinction

Despite the arguments made by some, such as the Medical Society in Washington, DC, many federal leaders and writers for the Northern press understood the smallpox epidemic as a consequence of emancipation.[43] The fact that medical reports coming from the South stated that the epidemic affected mostly, if not exclusively, freedpeople only buttressed this perception. A reporter for the Nation in 1866 corroborated the claim when he wrote, "There has been considerable speculation as to the effect of freedom upon the physical condition of the former slave. By many it is thought that his ultimate fate will be that of the Indian, and for this opinion there seems to be some ground. That mortality and disease are largely on the increase cannot be doubted: of this fact I am assured by leading physicians, and the statistics would seem to confirm this statement."[44] A religious leader echoed the assertion in 1863 when he stated, "Like his brother the Indian of the forest, he must melt away and disappear forever from the midst of us."[45] Medical authorities, journalists, and even researchers who later studied the high rates of mortality during the postwar period, consistently used arguments about biological differences between the races as an explanation for the large number of freedpeople's deaths caused by smallpox.[46] "The emancipation was a starting point in more ways than one. Here began, not only his career as a freedman and struggle for elevation, but his physical decline," stated one physician. "It is certain this death rate is uniformly double that of the whites and in many cases three or four times as large."[47]

The leaders of the Medical Division of the Freedmen's Bureau also expected the extinction of the black race and consequently did not provide Bureau physicians in the South with adequate money and resources to build pest houses to quarantine infected former slaves or to conduct vaccination campaigns to protect freedpeople from the virus. Congressman Samuel Cox, a Democrat from Illinois, argued that former slaves were, in fact, "dying out." He also compared the high rate of mortality among emancipated slaves to that of Native Americans, and thereby cautioned members of Congress to not violate the Constitution and provide federal assistance to freedpeople since their death was inevitable.[48] Since many in Congress, particularly in 1865, believed that freed slaves were meant to go extinct, they did not allocate money toward government programs designed to provide them with medical assistance.

That said, once the word extinction was used, it shifted attention away from the corporeal reality of freedpeople dying, as well as the effects of an epidemic spreading throughout the South. By comparing the high death rate among emancipated slaves to that of Native Americans, these officials placed more of an emphasis on *explaining* the epidemic than responding to it, which morphed this biological crisis into a discourse.[49] The use of the term extinction asserted that the demise of former slaves was a foregone conclusion.[50] As the *Alabama Independent* in Birmingham warned in 1866, "Unless some organized effort is made to arrest its progress it will become atmospheric and sweep over the land."[51]

Because they viewed the smallpox epidemic in the context of extinction, federal officials saw no need to follow the standard protocols that health authorities in both the North and the South had followed for decades. Since the eighteenth century, outbreaks of smallpox, sometimes as few as two to three cases, constituted an "epidemic."[52] Definitions of epidemics did not always trace back to a particular number of infected people or to a mortality rate.[53] The decision of eighteenth-century medical and municipal officials to implore communities to

isolate those infected with smallpox to quarantined areas or for doctors to provide a range of treatments represents the community's enactment of rituals
mobilized for an epidemic.[54]

When government leaders declared an epidemic, local physicians started to
inoculate townspeople. The process of inoculation involved infecting a healthy
person with a strain of the virus with the hope that the healthy patient would
develop a mild case of smallpox, and, after a few weeks, gain an immunity toward
it.[55] The problem with this procedure was that the inoculated person, with even
a mild strain of the virus, could inadvertently spread smallpox. Although the discovery of vaccination in the late eighteenth century, which involved cowpox,
promised a lifetime of immunity, any announcement of a smallpox epidemic by
local and state governmental officials ignited political and medical debates surrounding vaccination.[56] Doctors published studies ranging from the history of
smallpox to pamphlets on medical treatment, while city and state government
officials argued over the civil procedures surrounding the enforcement of vaccination. In 1832, the federal government even established a campaign to vaccinate susceptible Native Americans to an outbreak of the virus.[57] The outbreaks
of smallpox throughout the seventeenth and eighteenth centuries, in short, did
not go unnoticed.[58]

In 1862, the appearance of "two or three cases of smallpox among the men"
prompted Brigadier-General Ulysses S. Grant to assure federal supervisors that
"every effort has been made to prevent the spread of the virus."[59] Both Grant and
Lee understood the danger of a few cases of the disease; they both immediately
reported these incidents to their headquarters, as part of the standard protocol
in combating the virus, and issued mandatory vaccinations of all troops.[60]

Yet, in the fall of 1865, when Bureau physicians began to report the increasing
cases of smallpox, neither the Freedmen's Bureau nor the medical profession
classified smallpox as an epidemic, unlike the first outbreak among Union troops.
James E. Yeatman, president of the Sanitary Commission, recognized the need
for the government to declare an epidemic when he arrived at Camp Benton,
Missouri. He explained to military authorities, "Small-pox has had its appearance at several posts and in one of our hospitals; every precaution has been taken
to prevent it from spreading, but, in order to arrest and mitigate the horrors of
this dreaded disease it is necessary that some obligatory order be issued to colo-
nels of regiments, holding them responsible for the prompt execution of the
same."[61] Military and government leaders failed to enact a similar order for the
freedpeople.[62]

Some officers in the field wrote suggestions to their supervisors on how to
prevent the virus from spreading further among the freedpeople. A military official in Greensboro, North Carolina, in the spring of 1866 hoped that there would
be "no unnecessary delay" to build a smallpox house a quarter mile from the

freedmen's camp in order "to arrest the fearful disease which is increasing every day."[63] A Union officer stationed in Louisiana that same spring "respectfully suggested that an order declaring vaccination to be a military necessity," which, he argued, "would save many lives among these poor people."[64] The *New York Times* echoed the need for vaccinations in 1866: "The Freedmen's Bureau could do as much good in seeing to the vaccination of the blacks as in any other way. Unless something is done for them, the Negro population of the South will begin to melt away in freedom."[65]

Although Union officials in the South continued to report on the devastation and deaths that smallpox caused among the freedpeople, federal authorities in Washington failed to react. The federal government's neglect of the initial outbreaks of smallpox among the freedpeople in Washington, DC, Mississippi, and Louisiana allowed the virus to expand rapidly. By early autumn of 1865, the virus reached Washington, North Carolina, and infected well over 300 freedpeople in one week. In the Sea Islands, where former Confederate doctors joined the fight to halt the virus, it killed roughly 800 freedpeople a week in November and December.[66]

Doctors across the South reported an increase in the number of smallpox cases in their communities. In Augusta, Georgia, doctors reported 40 patients infected with the virus in October 1865. Less than four months later, the number of infected freedpeople there tripled, totaling 135. Throughout the winter and early spring months, Freedmen's Bureau doctors and freedpeople remained defenseless against the epidemic. Not until May of 1866 did the outbreak begin to show signs of slowly dissipating. Bureau records indicate that the number of infected freedpeople dropped from 135 cases a week to about 40 cases.[67]

While such numbers may suggest the demise of the virus, it could also potentially indicate its strength as well. Smallpox invariably reached populations of former slaves who had already been infected with the virus during slavery or the war, and who would be immune. Yet, smallpox continued to proliferate. Although it is not possible to provide a better assessment of the population of Augusta and the percentage of people infected with smallpox, the mere fact that Bureau medical officials established a presence there and remained for eight months suggests that it was considered a medical crisis. The Bureau only established hospitals and contracted doctors across the postwar South in response to medical disasters and after quelling the crises; it often sought justifications to dismantle these systems swiftly to prevent dependence. When the surgeon-in-chief attempted to close the Freedmen's Hospital in North Carolina in February 1867, local doctors refused "to entertain" the order, arguing that it was essential for a certain number of beds "to be kept up" at all times. Officials in Washington, however, ignored these rebuttals and shut down the hospital.[68] Since smallpox can remain dormant in a person for three weeks before showing symptoms, the reports that document a decrease in the number of cases only indicate the number of patients that the physician encountered at the time of the report. These reports did not take into account those who could have contracted the virus within the past week. Six to seven weeks after federal officials ordered a hospital to be closed in western North Carolina, the virus returned in February of 1867 infecting more people than it did the first time.[69]

By 1869, the chairman of the Committee of Freedmen's Affairs estimated that smallpox had infected roughly 49,000 freedpeople throughout the postwar South from June of 1865 to December of 1867.[70] This statistic tells only part of the story. Records of Bureau physicians in the field suggest that the numbers in their specific jurisdictions were, in fact, much higher. In the Carolinas roughly 30,000 freedpeople succumbed to the virus in less than a six-month period in 1865.[71] From December of 1865 to October of 1866, when the epidemic reached its peak, Bureau physicians in Georgia, Louisiana, North Carolina, and Virginia estimated that hundreds of freedpeople a month became infected with the virus.[72] Due to the countless freedpeople in need of medical assistance, many Bureau doctors claimed to be unable to keep accurate records. "I am unable to forward the consolidated reports of the sick freedmen for the month of February," wrote a Bureau doctor from North Carolina.[73] As mentioned, the statistics regarding the number of afflicted freedpeople only represent those that Bureau doctors encountered. In rural regions and in places where the Bureau did not establish a medical presence, cases went unreported. When the smallpox epidemic hit the area surrounding Raleigh, North Carolina, in February 1866, two freedwomen "walked twenty-two miles" in search of rations and support. The unexpected cold weather combined with the outbreak of smallpox in the state capital, however, depleted the Bureau's supply reserve. After discovering that even the benevolent office had "only empty barrels and boxes," and "nothing of real service to offer," the women wept.[74]

Statistics fail to convey the great emotion and fear that the so-called pestilence incited among those living in the postwar South.[75] A Bureau official in Kentucky described smallpox as a "monster that needed to be checked"; another agent witnessing the "severity and almost malignancy of the epidemic" believed that the virus was on the rise and predicted that "before the coming summer is over it will decimate the colored population."[76] Although some freedmen and freedwomen had been vaccinated during slavery or previously infected, many freedpeople feared the virus would attack their children.[77] Children succumbed to smallpox at a higher rate than any other age group. As one Bureau official noted in 1864, "In country parishes where vaccination is not the custom, with no physician near, where the colored children are poorly fed and clad, and much exposed, they sicken, die, and are buried, without a record of their numbers."[78] The *Christian Recorder* added, "You may see a child well and hearty this morning, and in the evening you will hear of its death."[79]

Most doctors responded to the sudden and dramatic outbreak of smallpox by writing letters to their supervising officials about the need to hire more doctors and staff.[80] "Smallpox is spreading among the freedpeople," wrote a physician in Orangeburg, South Carolina, in November 1865. "I have but one surgeon and he is unable to attend to each place, besides taking care of the hospital. Could you send me a surgeon?"[81] Bureau doctors requested money and permission to build hospitals, asked questions about medical treatment and hospital management, and informed authorities in Washington that smallpox plagued the postwar South.[82] "A report has reached me," wrote a physician in 1865 in Georgetown, South Carolina, "that smallpox is raging to an alarming extent in a place about fifteen miles from here."[83] When word got to a Bureau physician that smallpox lurked in the outer perimeters of the hospital's jurisdiction, the doctor immediately vaccinated those around the hospital and then made his way on horseback to those who lived in rural areas. "Disease is coming under my notice and great affliction and suffering evidently exists among the freedmen," wrote a Bureau doctor in December 1865, "much if necessarily beyond the reach of relief from my efforts as my duties are so numerous and onerous as to make it simply and plainly an impossibility for me to visit all the sick on the surrounding plantations besides I have no horse that I can rely for use at all times when I need him."[84] Bureau doctors traveling to freedmen's communities surrounding Charleston, South Carolina, to treat the epidemic requested two separate ambulances—one to transport smallpox patients, the other for those suffering from noncontagious diseases. When supervising Bureau authorities did not send a separate wagon to carry the infected freedpeople, Bureau physicians complained that they were unable—for the past year—to contain the virus because they lacked the necessary means to remove infected patients to the smallpox ward in Charleston.[85]

Despite these letters, federal authorities failed to perceive smallpox as a problem that demanded immediate action. Chief of the Medical Division Caleb Horner issued numerous circulars to physicians on other medical issues relating to the treatment of the freedpeople and the operations of the Bureau hospitals, but neglected to inform Bureau physicians of the protocol on how to respond to the smallpox epidemic. O. O. Howard, the leader of the Freedmen's Bureau, who consistently sympathized with the plight of the freedpeople, omitted the mention of the outbreak in his reports to Congress.[86] Reports from assistant commissioners, who forwarded statements from Bureau doctors in the South to the secretary of war, also ignored the epidemic.[87] As a reporter for the *New York Herald* observed in Savannah, Georgia, in May 1866, "limited precautions against contagious disease" have yet to be taken in the South.[88]

Since federal authorities failed to mobilize a national, "organized effort," to arrest the spread of smallpox, many Bureau physicians, most of whom lacked the support of their colleagues in neighboring districts, independently attempted to

slow down the proliferation of the virus through quarantine. Taking money from
their meager hospital budgets, Bureau doctors rented or built temporary smallpox asylums to quarantine afflicted freedpeople. In many freedmen's communities, they used former army tents as pest houses or as quarantine facilities.[89]
These makeshift provisions, however, failed. The army tents, according to Bureau
doctors, "were in a miserable condition," and only aided the spread of the virus.
Physicians during this period did not attempt to provide elaborate forms of medical treatment, but only to remove infected bedding, blankets, and clothing to a
quarantined area. In Charlotte, North Carolina, physicians feared the virus so ter-
ribly that immediately after discovering a smallpox-infected patient in the hospital, Bureau officials ordered the hospital to be burned to the ground—destroying
the only site of medical intervention in the region.[90]

Without a workable, efficient, and general medical system, Bureau doctors
were unable to monitor the changing health conditions in their regions. As one
doctor explained in Georgetown, South Carolina, "The visiting of patients
steadily on the increase and the prescribing for others at my office requires no
small amount of time daily. Add to these my charge of the smallpox patients is
now numbering fifteen, and you will perceive that my duties are not very light."[91]
As the responsibilities of doctors increased, the virus continued to spread in the
Carolinas, Georgia, and Louisiana, infecting well over 30 to 40 people a week.[92]
Bureau physicians frequently distributed clean clothing, blankets, and even bedding to freedpeople but many Bureau hospitals lacked these rudimentary supplies. "We are indeed 'roughing it,' this winter," wrote a benevolent reformer
stationed in Norfolk, Virginia, in 1866. "The poor blacks will suffer during this
hard winter. They can hardly feed, much less clothe themselves. Government
deserting us makes this time hard."[93] "I am entirely confident," wrote a Bureau
physician in Charleston, South Carolina, in January 1866, "that the fatality
among my smallpox patients is greatly increased by the lack of necessary bedding to protect them from the cold . . . There is no bedding of any kind at my
command and all that the patients have is such as they take with them from their
homes, and some of them have none to take."[94]

Without a federal protocol to follow, Bureau doctors were left on their own to
determine how to combat the outbreak of smallpox in their particular jurisdictions. As a result, some virtually ignored outbreaks of smallpox and were even
unwittingly responsible for the virus's continued spread. Other Bureau officials
failed to respond or even to report the presence of the smallpox in their regions.
One Bureau physician mentioned the appearance of smallpox in his district
because "smallpox got in the way of the planting" in South Carolina in 1866.[95]
The chief surgeon in Georgia did not respond to the outbreak of smallpox in
1865, because he did not view the reported cases of the virus in his jurisdiction
as his part of his responsibility.[96]

Smallpox erupted in a settlement on the south bank of the Trent River near New Bern, North Carolina, in 1866, according to military authorities, because the superintendent in charge of the region "exercised arbitrary and despotic power." A delegation of freedmen from the settlement approached military officials and charged that the superintendent inflicted "oppression and outrages" among those living in the community. The military subsequently investigated the charges and discovered that freedpeople became infected with smallpox because of the superintendent's corrupt behavior. In one case, the military authorities learned, the superintendent "arrested a man for debt, shut him up in the black house—the prison—for months, while his wife and children, reduced to abject destitution, died with the smallpox, and took him from the prison under guard and compelled him to bury his last child in the cradle in which it died."[97]

The neglect of infected freedpeople by some Bureau officials and doctors contributed to the spread of smallpox throughout 1866 and early 1867. Neighboring doctors, agents from other Bureau divisions, and freedpeople in the community wrote letters of complaint to supervising officials about how some Bureau doctors left patients unattended or allowed their hospitals to become filthy and vulnerable to the virus. The unsanitary conditions of the smallpox hospital in Columbia, South Carolina, in the fall of 1866, prompted a group of former slaves to inform military officials of the indifferent and inhumane treatment of sick patients. The delegation of freedpeople stated:

> Twenty-nine colored persons, men, women, and children, suffering from the smallpox, were crowded into one room, about twenty feet by twenty-four in size, and placed on the bare floor, with no bedding, while their only covering was the blankets that they had bought with them. These poor creatures were left in this condition several days, some of them delirious, with only one black woman to attend them, and without any nourishment but meat and bread. A number of respectable old colored people, attacked with smallpox, were thus taken from their comfortable homes and placed in this room to die of neglect.[98]

By the winter of 1866-1867, smallpox had seeped into southern Arkansas, Northern Louisiana, Texas, and other parts of the South, affecting populations that had not been exposed to the virus during the war, but had become vulnerable due to the lack of a standard policy on how to prevent the disease.[99] Even when the federal government began to receive reports from areas of the South that had not yet been hit with the virus, it had ignored these accounts.[100] Meanwhile, most Bureau officials learned of the extent to which smallpox pervaded throughout the South when schoolteachers submitted their annual records, indicating the large decrease in the number of pupils in attendance due to the epidemic.[101] Benevolent organizations established headquarters throughout the rural South—particularly in areas where there was no Bureau hospital—and, as a result, were, on many occasions, first to report on the appearance of smallpox among freedpeople in the countryside.[102] Many of these organizations arrived in the South in the final months of the war to set up schools for newly emancipated slaves but quickly discovered that medical services were desperately required. In Tennessee, for instance, benevolent associations in Chattanooga and Murfreesboro contributed supplies and medicine to establish hospitals in these regions.[103] Since benevolent organizations typically founded headquarters in all parts of the South, they would often notify either neighboring military or Bureau officials, or their sponsoring agencies, about the outbreak of smallpox among former slaves.

As smallpox continued to spread, assistant commissioners ordered Bureau doctors to return to the 1864 practice of mandatory vaccination, which was instituted by the Union army. "You must go out vigorously and vaccinate," commanded the chief surgeon in North Carolina in 1866.[104] Bureau doctors complained that mandatory vaccinating was difficult.[105] They explained that they had to "re-vaccinate" and conduct second and sometimes even third vaccinations because the initial procedure failed, or because the vaccination was administered improperly. In Tennessee, of the 1,200 vaccinations administered from December 1865 to May 1866, over 830 proved unsuccessful.[106] Yet, in many districts, Bureau doctors were without adequate supplies or the necessary staff to perform follow-up vaccinations. "I received your request," wrote the chief medical surgeon in Georgia in January 1867, "I can not furnish you any vaccine virus it is furnished by the medical purveyor but all that I have seen from that source has been useless."[107] Even after waiting weeks for small vials filled with vaccine to arrive from the North, it was often damaged or insufficient to provide for all members of a community.[108] A doctor from South Carolina lamented:

> The smallpox in this community is spreading, it can receive at my hands no check. I regret to say that the great scientific protective influence of vaccination has not yet reached me, and as a consequence I am without vaccine matter . . . The private physicians have none, the surgeon in charge of troops have none . . . I have therefore been powerless to prevent smallpox.[109]

When a shipment of medicine arrived in Christ's Church, South Carolina, the medical purveyor failed to include vaccine, "not even a scab," the physician grumbled in May 1866. The lack of vaccine forced the physician to return to the century-old practice of inoculation. Because the Bureau doctor was responsible for vaccinating well over 150 freedpeople, whom the supervising military officer only allowed the doctor to vaccinate on Saturdays when "the Negroes were idle," the physician was compelled to inoculate the freedmen as their only protection against the virus. "I am obliged to wait until tomorrow Saturday," the physician explained, and then, "I expect to take with me one of the school children whom I vaccinated a few days ago, and to transfer the fresh lymph from the mature pustule on her arm to the others on the George White plantation."[110] A procedure that likely proved to be ineffective, given the number of people in need of inoculation and only one pustule to use.

Freedpeople's Resistance

In some regions, physicians offered vaccination, but many freedpeople resisted such invasive medical treatment. When the military was in charge of the health and welfare of former slaves during the war, the Union army required mandatory vaccination in 1864. This policy failed because of freedpeople's resistance to the measure and the military's failure to enforce mandatory vaccination.[111] Describing the inability of Bureau physicians in Louisiana to implement vaccinations in 1864, one official noted, "Our efforts to induce the general vaccination have failed, in consequence of the fears of the children and the superstition of many of the parents."[112]

Although many enslaved people had been vaccinated before the war, many freedpeople during the war resisted mandatory vaccination because they resented the Union army for interfering in their health matters or considered vaccination a harmful procedure. Describing an attempt to provide vaccination to bondspeople in North Carolina in 1864, the superintendent of Negro Affairs explained that freedpeople "frequently conceal those attacked with it [smallpox] under blankets and beds, and hide them in their houses, even after dissolution had taken places, so gregarious are they, as they burrow together in their filthy cabins, so ignorant are they of the value of skillful medical treatment. This is the sum of a negro's ailments—he has a 'right smart misery' somewhere; and his *materia medica* consists of roots, herbs, and castor oil!"[113] The superintendent's assertion that freedpeople avoided vaccination and the intervention of Union doctors placed the blame on former slaves for the epidemic.

Due to the military's inability to conduct vaccinations in freedpeople's homes, some Bureau doctors went into schools and instituted mandatory vaccinations for children.[114] Doctors also required freedpeople to register at the local Bureau hospital and either get vaccinated or prove that they were vaccinated by showing their scar, but many freedpeople refused to go to the hospitals for vaccinations. With the help of the local police and other Bureau authorities, some Bureau physicians, particularly in rural regions, broke into freedpeople's homes and required immediate vaccination. In Cooke County, Georgia, former slaves—according to city officials—"refused any attention from the Doctor saying that they would manage their own affairs."[115] Due to the continual outbreak of smallpox in the state, authorities recommended that Bureau agents compel freedpeople to go to the hospital or else arrest them. When freedpeople in Orangeburg, South Carolina, resisted vaccination, Bureau authorities and local doctors arrested the former slaves. Once they were released from jail, they reported their story to the local newspaper and argued that the Bureau limited their mandatory vaccination campaign to "coloreds only." When the story reached leading Bureau administrators in the state, the Bureau officials responsible for the arrest realized that they had made a mistake by imposing such strict penalties for those who resisted vaccination.[116]

The arrests were, in many respects, an exception. Since many Bureau doctors, particularly those stationed in rural areas, lacked the resources to treat and to vaccinate all the former slaves residing in a particular area, it was feasible for freedpeople to avoid the Bureau physicians conducting mandatory vaccinations. Moreover, many local governments resented the Bureau's presence and refused to provide police support even if it meant not ending the epidemic. As a Bureau physician in Georgia explained to Caleb Horner in 1866, the head of the Medical Division, "they [local governments] refuse to take care of smallpox cases and as it appears would rather the disease spread over the city than do something."[117]

Smallpox in the North

The federal government's failure to immediately respond to the outbreak of smallpox among freedpeople starkly contrasted with the ways in which health officials in the North handled the outbreak. As the virus spread in the South, eruptions of the virus simultaneously exploded in the North, particularly in New York City.[118] From accounts of the so-called distemper in Staten Island to reports that Irish immigrants and working-class city residents infected tenement buildings, health officials continually provided residents of the city with guidelines on how to avoid infection.[119] Northern health officials required physicians, hotel-keepers, and officers of vessels to report within 24 hours every case of smallpox or other contagious disease that came to their knowledge. They also warned against overcrowded living quarters, in particular stressing that cellars, boarding houses, and closets should not be rented to strangers who might carry the virus. Municipal authorities, as well as local citizens, policed neighborhoods and streets for signs of the virus and worked tirelessly to prevent smallpox from spreading.[120]

New York City health officials attempted to determine the cause for the rapid dissemination of the virus; whereas, in the South, officials did not attempt to explore the origins of the virus. Although the surveillance measures that

Northerners employed to detect the origin of the virus and to find infected residents remains controversial, the New York City case nevertheless reveals the extent to which nineteenth-century Americans understood disease causation.[121] New York health officials recognized that smallpox could cross racial, ethnic, and class lines, whereas, the federal government operated under the outdated premise that smallpox would remain isolated among the newly freed population.

Had federal officials—like city authorities in New York in 1865–66 and even in Washington, DC, in 1862—investigated the social factors that contributed to the spread of smallpox among freedpeople, they might have found that the experience of emancipation led to dislocation and abject poverty, which facilitated the spread of smallpox among former slaves. Instead, they attributed the outbreak among former slaves to their racial background and the notion that, when freed, black people would go extinct.

Federal authorities insisted they were unable to respond to the smallpox epidemic because they lacked the manpower, resources, and facilities to do so. While the Medical Division was certainly beleaguered, the federal government did, in fact, manage to establish the necessary protocols, elicit adequate manpower, and extend their authority into the postwar South when they feared that an outbreak of cholera would infect white people and plague the nation.

An Epidemic within an Epidemic

In the midst of the smallpox epidemic in 1866, federal authorities declared a state of emergency due to the mere possibility of an attack of cholera in the postwar South. Referred to as "Asiatic Cholera" throughout the world, the federal government tracked the epidemic as originating in Asia, traveling to Russia, and spreading into Europe. They documented it making its way across the Atlantic, first appearing in Cuba and then possibly entering seaports in the Carolinas and Louisiana. Having just won the Civil War, the federal government felt empowered to take on this epidemic—despite the difficulties other governments had in preventing cholera from spreading.[122] While army doctors complained that they were unable to offer adequate care and treatment to emancipated slaves, when cholera threatened both white Northerners and Southerners federal officials managed to develop the necessary protocol and amass resources and manpower to stop the spread of the epidemic.

Stationed in the postwar South, as part of the federal government's occupation of the former Confederacy, army physicians typically avoided addressing freedpeople's health concerns. Yet fearing a possible cholera outbreak, the surgeon general assigned army doctors to work more closely with Bureau physicians to monitor the health conditions of the South. Because cholera had proven a threat to Europeans and Asians, the surgeon general took more seriously its threat to all Americans.

Although U.S. Surgeon General Joseph Barnes, who oversaw medical affairs throughout the country, failed to declare the hundreds of reported cases of smallpox as an epidemic, he took seriously the entrance of cholera into U.S. ports because it posed a greater threat to white people's health and the national economy. Once he announced the possible arrival of "Asiatic cholera" in the United States in 1866, assistant commissioners warned Bureau doctors of the epidemic and provided them with detailed instructions on how to prevent it from entering their communities.[123] Federal authorities informed army doctors stationed throughout the South that overcrowded and unsanitary living quarters exacerbated the spread of cholera.[124] They ordered homes and public streets to be whitewashed with lime, privies to be emptied, living quarters limited to no more than five to seven people per dwelling, proper ventilation to be maintained, and clean clothing to be distributed.

The news that cholera had entered the South and other parts of the country provoked the U.S. surgeon general to publish and circulate letters that he received regarding the appearance of the disease. His *Report on Epidemic Cholera in the Army of the United States, During the Year 1866* not only contained information on how to prevent the disease from invading one's territory and spreading, but, more critically, it also informed Bureau doctors and administrators that an epidemic had erupted. Nothing this sophisticated was disseminated when smallpox epidemic erupted. The mere publication of this book illustrates how organized and systematic the federal government could be in response to an epidemic. It also powerfully indicates that the surgeon general recognized the need to synthesize doctors' experience in the field and the federal government's protocol on how to respond to an epidemic in order for them to be used in future campaigns against epidemics. The report codified federal authority as it expanded efficaciously in response to the cholera epidemic.

Armed with this compilation of directives and observations, medical officials could protect their communities from an epidemic. Once federal authorities informed local doctors that cholera had entered the water supply, Bureau doctors could more carefully monitor the sanitary conditions around major waterways and exercise particular caution in the receipt of goods from other seaports, particularly Cuba, where federal officials assumed "the pestilence" had arrived.[125]

The outbreak of cholera proved that the federal government understood how to counteract disease transmission but ignored these protocols when the victims were former slaves. "In order to reduce the great amount of disease prevailing among the inmates of the camp and to prevent the appearance and spread of an epidemic," wrote a military official in Mobile, Alabama, in 1866, "the strictest sanitary regulations should be enforced by the officers every day."[126] Once the outbreak entered a region, federal authorities warned, hospitals should release their destitute patients to make room for those affected by cholera.[127] Further, Bureau authorities feared that freedpeople would spread the virus. O. O. Howard, leader of the Bureau, stated, "Bureau surveillance of the blacks were prompt and constant."[128] This statement reveals the federal government's ability to respond to black health issues, despite its later claims to be unable to prevent the spread of smallpox.

Moreover, the tenor of the federal government's reaction to the outbreak of an epidemic had dramatically changed. When describing smallpox, they used words that emphasized how overworked and limited Bureau doctors were in their arduous campaign against the virus. Yet, when discussing cholera, the surgeon general described how efficient and capable army doctors were. He wrote, "These reports were made with commendable diligence by the medical officers brought in contact with cholera during the year."[129]

By the summer of 1866, cholera had entered the port of New Orleans. Bureau physicians stationed in the region penned letters to their supervising officials in Washington, alerting them of the situation. Two weeks later, Bureau doctors in Shreveport, Louisiana, roughly 300 miles from New Orleans, diagnosed 20 freedpeople infected with the disease. And by the fall of 1866, Bureau doctors and agents in the Carolinas and Georgia were reporting on the appearance of cholera in their states.[130] Following the Bureau protocol, local doctors reported the cases to the assistant commissioner, who then forwarded their reports to Washington.[131]

By November of 1866, cholera had subsided. Federal authorities received monthly reports from Bureau doctors and assistant commissioners throughout the South documenting a decrease in the number of cases, indicating that the Bureau's precautions and warnings had prevented the virus from further spreading throughout the postwar South. An Arkansas doctor recounted in 1866, "During that portion of this period, in which the cholera has prevailed, the various hospitals and asylums under the care of the Bureau have suffered but little. Only twenty-five cases of cholera were reported."[132] Alert to the potential danger of cholera, the Freedmen's Bureau effectively helped halt the spread of the bacterial epidemic.[133]

In the winter of 1867, a year after cholera first entered the New Orleans harbor, Bureau officials continued to warn local doctors on a monthly basis about the possible threat of its return in the summer months. Federal authorities provided detailed instructions on ordering essential supplies, particularly sulfuric acid as a disinfectant; maintaining sanitary living conditions; and warding off the disease. Officials directed doctors to keep a watch for cases of cholera in their districts and to immediately contact their supervising officers at the first discovery of the bacteria.[134]

The measures adopted to counteract cholera in 1866 and again in 1867 far exceeded what federal officials provided to local doctors in their campaigns against smallpox. The assistant commissioner from New Orleans summed it up best when he stated in 1866 that Louisiana had not been entirely free from smallpox for several years, but of cholera "so much dreaded during this spring and summer, there has not been a single case."[135] A Bureau agent from Tennessee echoed this sentiment when he said in 1866, "this county has done little for the sick and poor, except provide medicines during the cholera epidemic."[136]

The Problematic Reports on Smallpox

Adding to this confusion, newspapers had reported that smallpox dissipated in the South and the health conditions of freedpeople in rural regions improved since the war. In the winter of 1865 and spring of 1866—when the virus claimed the most number of lives—reports from the *New York Times* and the *Nation* stated that the health of the "South was good." In 1865, the *New York Times* reported, "Smallpox is on the wane," in New Orleans.[137] In another article in the *Times* published in 1866, the journalist described high mortality rates among former slaves in cities and then argued that health on plantations "was as good as usual."[138] By claiming that the conditions were "good," the *Times* not only kept with the federal policy of denying the presence of disease in the South until it became undeniable, but they also perpetuated a conventional myth that the city was disease-ridden and the countryside was healthy. Bureau authorities made similar statements to migrating freedpeople. When Bureau officials met with a group of former slaves leaving Kentucky in 1865, the Bureau warned against "flocking into the towns and cities . . . Hundreds, unless they speedily move to the country," Bureau authorities stated, "will fall victims of pestilence. The smallpox is now prevalent . . . By all means seek healthy homes in the country."[139]

A few months later the *Nation* contributed to this mischaracterization by incorrectly reporting that "the sanitary condition of the freed people has far improved," and, as a result, "all Bureau hospitals have been abolished, medical attendance being part of the labor contracts of the employers."[140] Although the federal government did not "abolish all Bureau hospitals" until 1868, many assumed that employers provided medical care, and even worse, that the health of the postwar South was improving.

In the end, the smallpox epidemic reflected a number of contradictions. On the one hand, the federal government established hospitals in the South and employed physicians to respond to the medical crises that plagued emancipated slaves. On the other hand, when it came to the outbreak of smallpox, the Medical Division of the Freedmen's Bureau failed to offer adequate support. In part,

the failure resulted from the inefficiencies of the system, the inability
cians to maintain sufficient communication with federal officials, the
of transporting supplies, the dislocation and destruction that overwh
South, and the difficulty in establishing adequate quarantine measure
ministering proper vaccinations. Yet, the outbreak of cholera suggests that
despite the fact the federal government's headquarters was hundreds of miles
away from the Deep South, the federal government with the help of the army,
the support of local citizens, and the work of Bureau doctors managed to quell
an epidemic that quite literally plagued the rest of the world.

Federal officials did not respond so effectively to the smallpox epidemic,
because they believed that it was an epidemic confined to emancipated slaves.
Statistical reports that they received from physicians stationed throughout the
postwar South only buttressed this claim. The idea that only freedpeople became
infected with smallpox fueled the extinction thesis—which explains the Bureau's
failure to follow decades-long protocol on how to stop the spread of the virus.
That said, to subscribe to a theory about extinction, but at the same time conduct the operation of Bureau hospitals in the South, is inherently a contradiction. In other words, if government officials thought that freedpeople were really
going extinct, then why establish Bureau hospitals in the first place?

The reason for this contradiction lies in the fact that federal authorities understood smallpox differently from other illnesses that plagued freedpeople. The
Medical Division viewed its mission in terms of providing basic relief to freedpeople. By distributing clothing and food to emancipated slaves in response to
exposure and starvation, the Medical Division, like Northern antebellum almshouses, could facilitate the goals of free labor. Moreover, by employing physicians and building hospitals, the federal government through the aegis of the
Medical Division could fill the gap left by former slaveholders and local governments and react to outbreaks of dysentery, yellow fever, and, most of all, cholera.
But federal leaders understood smallpox differently; they narrated this epidemic
both as a result of emancipation and as a result of the inherent physiological
differences between white and black people—which explains why they did not
mobilize an aggressive campaign to prevent it from spreading.

Both during the epidemic and in the decades following it, a few physicians,
who had served in Freedmen's Hospitals, published reports on the medical conditions of the period that sharply contradicted the propaganda that the South
was a healthy locale for freedpeople, and more closely investigated why smallpox
and other illnesses spread in the region. Alexander T. Augusta, one of the few
black physicians who practiced in the Medical Division of the Freedmen Bureau,
constantly explained to supervisors in his monthly reports and letters of 1865–
67 that disease spread among the freedpeople due to lack of medical resources
and the unhealthy environments where they were forced to live. When disease

escalated in Savannah, Georgia, in 1865, where Augusta served as the assistant medical surgeon, he informed military and municipal officials that the sickness developed among the freedpeople due to the proximity in which freedpeople lived to the privy. He advocated for the privy to not only be emptied, but also fought to have the hospital and the freedpeople's living areas relocated to a more sanitary area in the city. Augusta also explained to his supervisors that smallpox continued to spread in Savannah, not because of the dirty habits of former slaves or innate physiological difference, but because municipal officials "refuse to bury dead freedmen lying in the streets and in some cases when they have died of smallpox."[141] By submitting detailed and investigative correspondence, Augusta attempted to promote and expand knowledge of why and how disease continued to infect freedpeople. His analyses and conclusions suggest his understanding of how environmental factors contributed to the onslaught of smallpox.

That roughly a hundred other Bureau physicians served in the South and failed to offer reports that investigated the conditions of the freedpeople or the causes of the virus—even those who were sympathetic to the health conditions of the freedpeople—indicates that they understood the incessant spread of smallpox, disproportionately among freedpeople, as a result of innate physiological differences, the extinction thesis, and/or the "dirty and unhealthy habits of former slaves." That Augusta continued to investigate why disease spread among freedpeople strongly suggests that he rejected the assumption that black people were inherently vulnerable to smallpox. In his reports, Augusta challenged the accuracy of the conventional wisdom of the day by considering how people—black and white—were more susceptible to disease when they were part of a dense population restricted to a confined area.

In 1888, years after serving as the director of medical affairs in Washington, DC, Robert Reyburn, one of the chief architects of Freedmen's Hospital in Washington, also debunked contemporary conventional wisdom when he published an article titled, "Types of Diseases among the Freedpeople."[142] Drawing on his experiences as a physician in Freedmen's Hospitals, Reyburn contended that sickness resulted from environmental causes. In particular, he made clear that black soldiers were not—as many assumed—inherently immune to fevers, and that the high rates of illness among former slaves resulted from lack of proper medical care. He further argued that if poor white people were in a similar situation they too would have contracted similar viruses. Reyburn desperately attempted to discredit what was considered common knowledge by emphasizing the relationship between environmental factors and disease.

Similarly, Rebecca Crumpler, the only known black female doctor employed by the Bureau, argued that the factors that caused disease could have been prevented. "There is no doubt that thousands of little ones annually die at our very doors, from diseases which could have been prevented, or cut short by timely aid.

People do not wish to feel that death ensues through neglect on their part."[143] Based on her experience at a Freedmen's Hospital in Virginia, where she encountered hundreds of freed slaves, Crumpler recognized that the most fatal threat to freedpeople's health was the lack of shelter, clothing, and nutrition. Without the fundamentals, many freedpeople, particularly freedwomen and children, became susceptible to smallpox and infected by it. Her book, *Medical Discourses*, served as a rebuttal to the prevailing idea that black people were physiologically different from white people and thereby more likely to be infected by contagious diseases, such as smallpox and cholera.

By analyzing the factors that cause illness and by advocating a prevention discourse, Crumpler's book represented a sophisticated analysis of disease causation, which was at odds with the Bureau's reaction to the smallpox epidemic. "They seem to forget there is a cause for every ailment, and that it may be in their power to remove it. My chief desire in presenting this book is to impress upon someone's mind the possibilities of prevention." Since prevention remained her main motivation for writing the book, Crumpler aimed to reach a broad reading audience beyond medical professionals "I desire that my book shall be as a primary reader in the hands of every woman."[144] By writing directly to freedwomen and their children, Crumpler identified a segment of the freed slave population that had been marked as *dependent* and thereby had become more vulnerable to sickness and disease.

wasn't just a physician, but also an author invested in providing women w/ key medical info

5

The Healing Power of Labor

Dependent, Disabled, Orphaned, Elderly, and Female Freed Slaves in the Postwar South

> Ever since I realized there waz someone callt
> a colored girl an evil woman a bitch or a nag
> i been tryin not to be that.
> —Ntozake Shange, *For Colored Girls Who Have Considered / Suicide /*
> *When the Rainbow Was Enuf* (1975)

Congregated on an abandoned lot in the northwest corner of Washington, DC, a group of former slaves attempted to sell animal bones—a good form of fertilizer—to planters passing through the capital. Wearing "rags" and living in huts made of "sticks," the freed slaves had migrated from southern Virginia to the nation's capital in the hopes of finding employment. Ordered by Bureau agents to leave the abandoned plantations where the overused land offered little chance of producing cotton, the freed slaves eventually made their way to Washington, DC. Tired, hungry, and desperate, they settled in a deserted part of the city, where they found dead horses left over from the war. The decomposed bodies of the horses no longer offered meat and nourishment, but the bones—some puncturing through the rotten flesh, others stacked in piles on the muddy ground—presented an opportunity to earn some money. As plantation laborers, they recognized the value of the bones, which could be crumbled and buried in the soil along with cottonseed, as fertilizer.

The bones needed to be dried out, however, before being sold. The freed-people salvaged discarded Union tents and laid the bones on tarps to dry in the sun. The periodic trafficking of the bones through the busier sections of the city caught the attention of Bureau health officials, who ordered the enterprise shut down in fear that such a scavenger production would exacerbate the city's already poor health conditions.[1]

Bartering bones for cash or necessities served as one of the few ways these former slaves could earn a living. Throughout the South, a number of enterprising freedpeople turned to scavenging and processing the detritus of war to survive the economic instability of Reconstruction. One family scoured the shores of South Carolina for war materials, like iron, left in the sand by the military; while others, like those in Washington, DC, collected skulls and bones, hoping to make a profit from local industries that specialized as "bone-grinders."[2]

Freedpeople often explained the economic rationale for collecting bones without mentioning the religious and spiritual issues that such practices may have raised for them. Did freedpeople define these decomposed bodies as unburied souls? Did they view the vast and overwhelming number of human and animal remains as possessing demonic power, or were they fearful of the possibility of ghosts as they dug through the dirt to pull out the corpses? In certain religions practiced by people of the African diaspora, bones symbolized taboo. Did freedpeople, in turn, struggle to accomplish this work as it connoted spiritual meanings that lurked beyond the understanding of the white Northerners and Southerners, who reported on these practices in the first place?[3]

The collecting and bartering of bones may have raised these questions and many more for the former slaves who engaged in this form of employment, but they had no choice. It was the only available work for them. So much talk of free labor, of cotton, and of the promise of rebuilding the South hung in the air during the Reconstruction era, but on the ground a different reality unfolded—a reality where dead bodies provided the only chance to survive the challenges of the postwar period.

Unlike the smallpox epidemic, federal leaders understood the troubles produced by poverty but nevertheless struggled to adequately solve these crises. Since Freedmen's Hospitals functioned like nineteenth-century almshouses, one of the ways that the Bureau responded to the destitution was to separate the "able-bodied," those who could be recruited as agricultural laborers, from the "destitute" or "dependent." According to the Bureau, dependent or destitute referred to a range of former slaves—from freedmen, who could not find adequate employment and suffered from the great crop failures of 1866–67, to freedwomen and their children displaced by the war and emancipation, to disabled, elderly, and orphaned ex-slaves.

The category of dependency was in flux and unstable. At times, it could refer to freedpeople who were temporarily unemployed, or it could also refer to those whom Bureau agents considered to be permanently removed from the labor force, such as disabled and elderly freed slaves as well as freedwomen. Since the definition of "dependency" resulted from the perspective of the Bureau labor agent, physician, or Southern planter, there was not a universally accepted understanding of the term. Despite this ambiguity, Bureau agents often defined an individual's dependency in relation to their labor potential and health.

Within the Bureau's calculations, there was, as a result, a symbiotic relationship between labor and health. Employment offered former slaves the stability to weather the chaos of the tumultuous postwar years and an income with which to pay for basic necessities. Without employment, freedpeople not only faced the uncertain Reconstruction years on shaky ground but could not afford shelter, clothing, food, and medicine to survive. Lacking the funds to pay for their fundamental needs, freedmen and women became increasingly vulnerable to disease as a consequence of spotty nutrition, exposure, and the vagaries of itinerant living. In the Bureau's response, an almost single-minded focus on freedpeople's productivity as agricultural laborers defined their health. O. O. Howard, leader of the Bureau, directed federal agents to "strive to overcome a singular false pride which shows certain almost helpless refugees willing to be supported in idleness. While we provide for the aged, inform, and sick, let us encourage, or if necessary compel, the able-bodied to labor for their own support."[4]

Causes of Dependency

Throughout the Reconstruction period, federal officials understood health and illness in terms of freedpeople's labor power. Federal leaders often claimed that "free labor" would not only transform former slaves into independent workers, who could determine their course of employment, but it would also—according to many in the North—solve the health and social problems that plagued the South. In fact, in response to the suffering and medical crises that broke out among freedpeople in contraband camps, military officials urged the government to move former slaves to plantations where they could be employed.[5] Additionally, as two leading military officials explained to President Andrew Johnson in the immediate aftermath of the war, "The best protection the freedman has in the South is the value of his labor in the market."[6] O. O. Howard, leader of the Bureau, preached the value of free labor: "In brief, all the beautiful natural order that God has imposed, making us superior, wise, and provident and them confiding, childlike, and dependent, will be destroyed as much as the peace of Eden was by allowing Eve to eat of the tree of knowledge. Fix it so that we can be the mind and they the obedient muscle, and all will be well, whether you call it *free labor* or not."[7]

The problem, however, was that for free labor to work, freedpeople needed employment opportunities. The *Freedmen's Record* reported that "the demand for labor exceeds the supply" in Alabama in 1866.[8] The war had destroyed much of the land available for cultivation and emancipation caused dramatic population shifts, so laborers were not where they were needed.[9] In Virginia, Bureau officials reported in June 1866 that the counties of York and Elizabeth were "filled with thousands belonging to other counties" and needed to get them back to their "old homes" to work before a "large mass of helpless, naked, starving people" settled into "counties that cannot support them."[10]

The antebellum expansion of the cotton crop shifted the population of enslaved peoples from the Upper South into the Mississippi Valley and the Low Country South.[11] During the Civil War, as Union troops occupied the lower corridor of the Southern theater, freed slaves migrated away from plantations to military camps, near cities, moving back to the Upper South and to the North.[12] Of the 8,000 freedpeople that lived in Alexandria, Virginia, in 1865, for example, Union officials estimated that over 5,000 of the town's residents had fled from plantations in the Deep South.[13] Freed slaves from the coast of Georgia had migrated to Savannah because it was known for its corn and cotton plantations, and wealthy estates; but in September 1865, the Bureau official in charge described it "as laid waste by the Army . . . So complete was the destitution this occasioned," he wrote "that thousands of families, white and black, in the city and on the plantation were reduced to a state of poverty, with no means of support."[14]

Since the federal government employed many freedmen as soldiers and laborers in the Union army, military officials—in the months following the Civil War—often sent regiments to cottons fields to cultivate the land. More frequently, however, Bureau and military officials entered freedmen's communities and Union camps and removed able-bodied freedmen and sent them to plantations in need of workers. Louisa Jacobs, reformer and daughter of Harriet Jacobs, described the government's efforts to create a labor force by moving freedpeople from Savannah to South Carolina in 1866. "They had been carried into the interior of South Carolina. Now they are brought and driven back into the State: out of one Egypt into another. They are looking for 'de freedom,' they say."

The process of literally "carrying off" able-bodied freedmen, however, left their families without the economic means to support themselves.[15] When the able-bodied men were taken away as woodcutters and gravediggers on Craney Island, Virginia, a Northern teacher reporting to the American Freedmen's Inquiry Commission described the condition of women, children, and disabled men that were left on the island as worthy of a "Government Poor House."[16]

Bureau officials on the ground, congressmen in Washington, DC, and even former Confederates continued to view "free labor" as the "the new order" that would revitalize the South; yet the proponents of this economic plan failed to consider what to do with those who could not find work. When the question of the viability of a free labor system in the South did enter political and economic discussions, it was often circumscribed in racist language about the inherent inability of freedpeople to work independently and to manage their own land. Critics of free labor designed cartoons that mocked emancipated slaves negotiating their business affairs, while Southern political commentators repeatedly told of freedpeople's innate need for supervision and instruction.[17] Meanwhile, the proponents of free labor couched their arguments in similarly racist language, but they described freedpeople's robust ability to handle the challenges posed by the economic transformations.[18]

Both the advocates and critics of free labor failed to consider the structural problems involved in the transition of a slave economy to a free labor economy. From shortages of available land for cultivation to limited employment opportunities both in the rising industries of the South and on the plantations, those engaged in the discussion about free labor did not explore the challenges of establishing an economic system that extended beyond merely one's willingness to work. The war, for instance, destroyed much of the land available for cultivation. Combat-damaged land had already been compromised by the soil exhaustion that had propelled Southern slaveholders in the 1830s to the 1850s to push west to expand their cotton plantations. Therefore, the plantations that the federal government occupied after the war were not as lush and fruitful as they expected; arable land was necessary to establish a free labor economy.[19]

Furthermore, federal officials ignored the ways in which the development of free labor actually created dependency in the postwar South.[20] As the Bureau continued to recruit more men to serve as laborers, many other freedpeople, defined as less than able bodied, were left in their wake. Describing one of these communities, a Bureau official from Alabama wrote, "Remote, unfriended, melancholy, slow, the widow and the fatherless, the aged and infirm, are scattered through the 'piney woods,' almost beyond the reach of work, or schools."[21] An agent from New Orleans declared in 1867, "The number of destitute aged freedpeople is increasing since they have no homes and will charge upon the Bureau."[22]

Bureau officials attempted to solve the problem by finding employment for dependents on nearby plantations. When that did not work, they transported freedpeople to other cities and states in need of laborers. When employment could still not be found for elderly, orphaned, and disabled freedpeople, for example, the Bureau tried to find kin and neighbors in the immediate community to care for them.[23] Although family and kin networks supported dependent freedpeople in the immediate aftermath of the war, low wages strained these relations. By 1866, poor earnings, compounded by crop failure, shattered much of the promise of free labor, and, in turn, worsened the condition of dependent freedpeople, who lacked resources to support themselves.

To make matters even more difficult for former slaves, O. O. Howard, leader of the Bureau, in an attempt to instill a sense of economic independence, terminated the wartime policies that provided rations to dependent freedpeople in 1866.[24] Not until later in the year, when assistant commissioners reported to Howard the illness and suffering among dependent freedpeople, did the federal government extend rations and medical support to the roughly 500,000 unemployed freedpeople.[25] This effort was neither consistent throughout the South nor sufficient. Unemployed freedpeople were to receive two-thirds the amount of the standard ration allotted to soldiers during the war, and the quality and quantity of available shelter or clean clothing were minimal at best.[26]

Bureau authorities, however, cautioned against providing relief for an extended period of time, as this would only encourage dependency among the freedpeople. In Washington, DC, a leading Bureau official chastised his subordinates for not carefully monitoring the relief provided to dependents in the nation's capital, warning that former slaves would become a burden to the government.[27] In general, Howard ordered agents to exercise great "discrimination in administering relief, so as to include none that are not absolutely necessitous and destitute."[28]

Yet, by January of 1866, Bureau agents in the field found Howard's instructions ineffective since they considered nearly all those requesting relief "absolutely necessitous and destitute." An agent in Washington, DC explained that he could not turn away those who were in search of assistance and rations.[29] Indeed, throughout the South, the number of dependent freedpeople in need of assistance far surpassed what agents on the ground could accommodate.

Finding support for unemployed freedpeople was an added responsibility for Bureau agents, who also were required to mediate labor disputes, broker contracts, and assist Northern teachers in their plans to establish schools. Depending on an individual agent's priorities, requests for relief may not have been even addressed. One agent for the freedpeople in the Sea Islands, South Carolina, Chaplain James Beecher, ignored the destitution that afflicted the hundreds of former slaves in his jurisdiction and instead devoted his time to complaining to military and government officials in Washington, DC about the mere suggestion of providing freed slaves with "40 acres and a mule."[30]

Because the federal government feared that providing rations to the dependent freedpeople would drain the national budget and incite dependency and laziness among the "able-bodied" freedpeople, the Bureau was often slow in providing relief to dependent freedpeople.[31] The Bureau, as such, operated at cross-purposes. On one level, the federal government created Freedmen's Hospitals in response to poverty and dependency, yet Bureau leaders remained deeply skeptical about the ongoing prospect of providing relief to destitute freedpeople. The Bureau was intended as a temporary measure, yet care for the elderly, for example, demanded a long-term, permanent solution. Unlike destitute freedpeople who entered a hospital on a short-term basis with the expectation of ultimately rejoining the labor force, the elderly required, as one Bureau official demanded, "some system by which the old could be cared for."[32] These problems inevitably thwarted the Bureau's work and, more important, left freedpeople without the basic necessities to survive.

Dependency among the Disabled, Elderly, Orphaned, and Female

The federal government's use of the guidelines established by the Second Confiscation Act of 1862 meant that it employed only "able-bodied men." Males between the ages of 16 and 45 were often considered able-bodied—although boys as young as 12 to 15 were sometimes organized into labor gangs. Surgeons then placed the elderly, the physically handicapped, and children into separate camps. When Army surgeons were not present, military officials evaluated formerly enslaved men based on their own criteria; such as Francis Sternberg, a Bureau agent in Lafourche Parish, Louisiana, who admitted he had neither the time nor means to investigate the applicants, so he mostly guessed.[33]

The Bureau's consistent use of the term "able-bodied" illustrates that disability and one's physicality was at the forefront of how Bureau officials understood freedpeople's fitness for agricultural labor. Bureau officials often calculated how many disabled people were in a particular region, which stemmed more from the government's efforts to obtain a profile of the labor force of a region rather than to gain an understanding about freedpeople's health. Tabulating the number of disabled people enabled the federal government to demarcate between those who could work and those who could not, and also notified officials in Washington, DC, of the number of freed slaves who could qualify for assistance. For example, from September 1, 1866, to September 1, 1867, the Bureau reported 1,400 blind freedmen; 414 "deaf and dumb"; 1,134 "idiotic or imbecile"; 552 "insane"; 251 "club footed."[34] But these numbers were often complicated and distorted. These figures represent only the number of disabled people that Bureau agents came in contact with; many more lived in various parts of the post-bellum South but did not register on the Bureau's radar. For example, Harriet Jacobs noted that in Savannah in December, 1865 there were 93 freedpeople were either blind or permanently disabled in addition to 200 more that she described as "decrepit."[35] More to the point, the Bureau did not establish a clear definition of what it meant to be categorized as "insane" or "an imbecile," or even what constituted "blindness" or "deafness." Thus, each Bureau agent made these decisions based on his own impression. In February 1867 in Virginia, for example, a Bureau agent filed a report on the number of "deaf, dumb, and blind" freedmen under his charge.[36] He noted that of the seven freedpeople with disabilities who he had encountered their conditions ranged from "good to bad to very bad"—which illustrates the extent to which the medical reporting of freed slaves' condition was subjective and ambiguous, at best.

While this process functioned idiosyncratically, it, nevertheless, aggressively recruited enslaved men and rejected single freedwomen, elderly, disabled, and orphaned former slaves. These so-called dependents were then placed in separate hospitals, dispensaries, and almshouse.[37] A reporter for the *Freedmen's Record* wrote in 1865:

> Boston is full of associations, and individual men and women, who dispense alms to poorest of the poor, standing between them and starvation, cold, and death. This charity is recognized as a necessity, and approved and supported by those who have means to spare for this purpose. Here in Washington, where the need is far greater, we have no such associations, hardly any organized benevolence which provides for the physical sufferings of the wretched and helpless. In Boston, the mass of the miserably poor are whites. They are blacks here [Washington, DC], where color is only an additional passport to poverty and degradation.[38]

In the slaveholding economy, elderly, female, and even disabled slaves had a certain value, or, at least, a place within the plantation community.[39] On antebellum plantations, elderly female slaves assisted in domestic responsibilities—rearing children, cooking, and handling a number of household responsibilities. Elderly male slaves, if skilled, continued to work at their trades, while others cultivated small vegetable gardens, assisted with the upkeep of the livestock, or lent a hand with domestic work. Even if they were not working at the capacity that slaveholders demanded, many planters allowed elderly and incapacitated slaves to remain on antebellum plantations.[40]

With the end of slavery, planters no longer allowed elderly freedpeople to live on their land. Unlike younger slaves who could immediately flee from their masters' homes at the first sound of Union gunfire, elderly slaves had little choice but to remain on the plantation. After the war, however, many planters were frustrated by the Bureau's formal contracts and meddling into their business, and retaliated by refusing to take care of elderly slaves and literally forcing them off their land. As early as 1864, when military officials began surveying land available for cotton cultivation, they found elderly slaves suffering on deserted plantations. A benevolent reformer stationed in Mt. Pleasant, South Carolina in 1866 met "one man, nearly one hundred years old" with "his wife, a very small woman, evidently grown less by continued hard labor." The Northerner "examined their bedding and found it to consist of two threadbare blankets and a wooden bedstead. I asked them how they got on in the cold nights, and the woman said they did not dare to go to bed at all, for fear they would freeze, but sat up in the fireplace all night."[41]

With nowhere to go, many elderly slaves tried to survive in abandoned barns and plantations. Author and reformer Harriet Jacobs observed in 1866 that many of the aged freedmen and women were "worn out with field labor . . . Infirm, penniless, homeless, they wander about dependent on charity for bread and shelter . . . Many of them suffer and die from want."[42] Jacobs further described meeting an elderly freedwoman in Alexandria, whom Bureau officials had brought back to headquarters, who "sadly needed" assistance, "for both limbs had been frozen so that amputation was necessary at the knee; it was pitiful to see her moving herself about on the floor without any ability ever again to stand upright . . . Yet she seemed cheerful," Jacobs explained, and "spoke of her troubles without repining."[43]

In most cases, planters considered elderly ex-slaves "too old to work," claiming that an able-bodied worker could execute a task in half the time in which an "aged man" could.[44] In the new economy of free labor, planters carefully evaluated workers purely by the cash value that they could produce in a given day, as opposed to during slavery when they thought in terms of lifetime productivity. On the outskirts of Washington, DC, a Bureau officer claimed that Ann Greshen, a 58-year-old freedwoman, was "not capable of learning enough to provide herself and consequently cannot recommend that wages be paid to her." Greshen then filed a complaint at the local Bureau office against her employer to be compensated for the wages due to her. After evaluating her claim, Bureau agents sided with the planter, stating that a woman of her age more than likely was not able to produce enough in a day. As a result, Bureau agents not only deprived her of her wages, but also took her stove to pay her employer because he provided her with room and board. Greshen had no way of earning a living within the new labor market and was subsequently left as dependent.[45]

Dependency also included children. Thousands of enslaved children were liberated from plantations, separated from their families or displaced by emancipation. Although planters entrapped many children as apprentices due to their parents' economic status, Bureau officials described those who were not part of a labor arrangement and lacked financial support as "orphans."[46] On antebellum plantations, there had been no such thing as "orphans," because children were bought and sold, and even unemployed children were considered part of the plantation community by slaveholders.[47] After the war, many of these children were defined by the federal government as too young to work and therefore dependent. A benevolent worker in Alexandria worried about the fate of "little girls" in the camp, who did not have work; she feared "for if I have nothing for them to do pretty soon, someone else will get the start of me." It is likely that she feared the little girls could be abducted in the camp and used for prostitution.[48]

The gradual displacement of women from the labor force was the most severe consequence of the development of free labor ideology in the South. Although it is difficult to calculate the exact number of destitute freedwomen, because Bureau agents were often unable to keep accurate records, agents throughout the South continually reported more freedwomen in need of assistance than freedmen. An estimated 5,274 freedwomen were in need of relief in Tennessee compared to a 1,000 freedmen; similarly in Virginia, roughly 8,867 freedwomen were provided rations compared with 3,000 freedmen.[49]

Despite the fact that black women were recognized as able-bodied during slavery and were employed by the Union army during the war to work in hospitals, to wash uniforms, or to serve as cooks, federal officials in Washington reclassified them as they devised plans to organize a labor force.[50] Certainly, many freedwomen who traveled with their husbands or other family members were employed as plantation laborers. But there were thousands of other freedwomen who were separated from their families and communities and then marked as destitute in the postwar South.[51]

Based on regulations created during the war, freedwomen and children were to receive rations and support from their husbands' and/or fathers' enlistment.[52] This policy continued after the war because Bureau agents and planters often preferred making contracts with the men who served as heads of the household. There was not a standard federal policy on how to handle the cases of freedwomen who were not part of kin networks. Federal and military authorities considered single, dependent freedwomen as immoral and licentious. A Bureau chaplain in the Mississippi Valley argued that unmarried freedwomen "promoted promiscuous intermingling."[53] As a result, Bureau officials adamantly refused to establish an official network of support for single freedwomen, believing such provisions would only encourage their unmarried status.

By negotiating contracts with men as heads of families, Bureau officials attempted to transform large groups of freedpeople of various ages and sexes into neatly circumscribed family units, who could work together or even own plots of land.[54] Marriage indirectly facilitated the goals of free labor and simultaneously made it more difficult for displaced and dependent freedwomen to find employment. Freedwomen who were part of kinship networks had the opportunity to either withdraw from the labor force and devote their time and effort to household duties and child rearing, or, depending on their location and the economic condition of the family, join the agricultural labor force with the male members of their families. These freedwomen had the structure and the support of family to endure both the crises of the emancipation and the challenges of the new free labor system.[55] As a benevolent worker in New Bern, North Carolina, explained to her membership in Boston in 1866, "Where there are men in the family, they get along quite nicely; for they work at the trades, etc., . . . but as often is the case, I find a woman with six or eight children to care for, some of them sick, perhaps, and an old grandmother perfectly unable to take care of herself."[56]

Without a family association, it was difficult for freedwomen to find employment. Many were searching for lost family members, looking for work, or following migration patterns, and, as a result, they were temporarily outside of these kin networks. An 18-year-old freedwoman, who we only know as "Hannah," was abandoned in a rural part of South Carolina because the freedpeople that she was traveling with "were not interested in her."[57] Local, state, and charitable institutions offered no support to such people, as they did for displaced white people.

Without the support of local asylums and often far removed from communal support, many unemployed freedwomen suffered alone. Living in an abandoned dump cart in Montgomery, Alabama, a freedwoman gave birth to her son. As she attempted to climb out of the cart, she fell, dropped her infant son, and was knocked unconscious. Hours later, the *Montgomery Daily Ledger* reported, hogs came along and ate the infant.[58] The *Richmond Dispatch* reported a freedwoman found dead of starvation on the streets of the city.[59] A few miles outside of Augusta, Georgia, a Bureau physician discovered a freedwoman lying in a ditch, who he later diagnosed as blind and syphilitic.[60] In Orangeburg, South Carolina, a woman was found lying on cotton bales while suffering from rheumatic fever. She was eventually discovered by a Bureau agent, who diagnosed her as destitute, unable to work, and feverish.[61] In the bustling nation's capital, the story was the same: a Bureau physician found elderly women in a hovel, starving and diseased.[62]

When freedwomen congregated in open areas or city streets in an effort to form their own kin networks, their presence alarmed municipal authorities and infuriated local white residents. The author of an article in *DeBow's Review*, a periodical read by Southern white planters, described 300 dependent freedwomen living near Bureau headquarters in Richmond, Virginia, as "idle as the dogs." These 300 "Amazonidee," he wrote, "constitute a zoological garden. They are of all colors, from ebony-black to almost pure white; and of all races, except the pure Caucasian."[63] Many white residents living in the postwar South vilified unemployed freedwomen.

Some former slaveholders manipulatively offered to keep emancipated women on their plantations, arguing that formerly enslaved women were part of their families or that the freedwomen wanted to remain as servants, which contradicted how planters responded to disabled and elderly freedpeople's need for shelter. According to a plantation mistress in Kentucky, the freedwomen "wanted to stay with us." When a Northern benevolent worker questioned the freedwomen's true intentions, the mistress retorted, "I tell my people, now they are free, and they can go if they want to, and work for themselves; but every one of them 'stick by,' and it 'pears like they can't spare me."[64]

While former slaveholders made the claim that freedwomen wanted to remain on former slave plantations, evidence suggests that many freedwomen were coerced into such labor arrangements due to their otherwise dependent status. Unlike the employment of freedmen, freedwomen—due to the nature of domestic work—were uniformly absent from the hiring process and contract negotiations. The labor arrangement between plantation owners and freedmen required the participation of Bureau agents as witnesses to ensure that freedmen, when marking an "X" next to their names, approved the terms of the contract. The employment of freedwomen on plantations did not involve formal contracts. Instead, former slaveholders approached the Bureau office to inform the agent that freedwomen remained on the plantation to work as domestics. Official contracts were not drafted by the agent in an attempt to protect the rights of the female employee. Former slaveholders simply required the Bureau's stamp of approval. For instance, a former slaveholder in Farmville, Virginia, in 1865 received permission from a local Bureau agent to keep "Rosie" as a domestic servant based purely on the mistress's account that the "colored girl prefers to stay."[65]

This could lead to clashes over female domestic laborers. A legal dispute between two former slaveholders developed in Pike County, Alabama, in 1867, for example, when a freedwoman, entered in the legal transcript as "Eliza," argued that she "never signed her hand on a written contract." Yet, both planters claimed to have had a contract with her. Eliza explained that her husband made a contract with the planter, but the planter did not make one with her. The problem arose when Eliza decided to seek other employment. Her husband's formal employer refused to pay her 50 cents a day for her work, and stipulated that he would only provide food and clothing for her, not her two children. "Dissatisfied" with her current arrangement, she secured employment at a neighboring home. Her new employer promised to feed and clothe Eliza and both her children. When Eliza's employer learned that she intended to quit, he filed a legal charge against the new employer. Eliza was not entitled to be a party in her own case or to choose her employment; that decision was to be battled out between the white planters, who behaved as if slavery had not ended and enslaved people could still be treated as property to be bought, sold, and traded. Freedwomen's domestic labor power fluctuated between something highly valuable and in demand, as this case reveals, and something that was devalued and outside the legal changes ushered in by Reconstruction.[66]

Many freedwomen decided to abandon plantation life and risk possible destitution than to continue to work under such conditions. When a freedwoman in Kentucky escaped from a plantation, the mistress in charge was so enraged that the other freedwomen would escape that she made one formerly enslaved woman "cut across both her feet with a pocket-knife, through the skin, so that blood was left in her tracks" should she try to escape.[67] When former slave-holders could not force formerly enslaved women to work as domestic servants, they reported them to local authorities and had them arrested on bogus charges. Describing her visit to a women's penitentiary in Washington, DC, a Freedmen's Aid reformer wrote in her diary about meeting many "colored women," who were "placed by their former owners for trivial offenses, the real cause being that of leaving them."[68]

Unlike single freedmen who could more easily move around the postwar South in search of employment, freedwomen were constrained by the terms of the new free labor economy and their need to protect their children. As one Bureau agent observed, "Among the dependents are many women with children, most of them are able to work but are living here on a scanty of rations in idle-ness and in rags, because they can not on account of their children and the scar-city of work get employed."[69] The agent failed to recognize that this problem developed because of the ways in which the Bureau reordered familial relations. During slavery, older enslaved women looked after the children of female la-borers. After slavery, the dislocation of many kin networks made it difficult for single freedwomen to depend on the help of elderly freedwomen, since the Bureau often relegated older freedwomen, who could have served as nannies, to refugee communities and asylums—depriving dependent freedwomen of caretakers to assist them with their children while they pursued employment.

Compounding matters, if freedwomen could not prove that they had a steady income, they risked losing their children to apprenticeship. Although these laws varied by state, many planters only needed to show Bureau officials that freedwomen were either unemployed or vagrants, and they could have their children taken away from them.[70] According to a Bureau official in Mary-land in December 1866, a "county orphans court bound out a four-month old baby, suckling at its mother's breast, on the grounds that the mother could not support the child."[71]

Due to the strict and often uncompromising ways in which the apprentice-ship laws were structured, reformer Harriet Jacobs traveled to England in hope of raising money for an orphanage, so that freed children would no longer be subjected to apprenticeship. As Jacobs explained to readers in the *Anti-Slavery Reporter*, "There are many thousands of orphans in the Southern States . . . no provision has been made except through the Freedmen's Bureau, which provides that the orphan be apprenticed till of age. It not unfrequently happens that the apprenticeship is to the former owner. As the Spirit of Slavery is not exorcised yet, the child, in many instances, in cruelly treated." Women's employment choices, in turn, were very much circumscribed by their role as mothers as they tried to protect their children from apprenticeship laws.[72] Faced with these options, many dependent women continued to migrate in search of employment and shelter.

When dependent freedwomen were able to secure employment, they were not paid as much as men. In the Mississippi Valley, for example, employers promised freedmen that they would be paid $25 a month and freedwomen $18 a month. In reality, employers paid freedmen $10 a month and freedwomen $7; the planter then deducted an additional one to two dollars for the cost of clothing. Concerned about the plight of freedwomen, a Bureau agent posited:

> Suppose she has a child—and black women do have children—what then? Suppose the rebels took off the first suit of clothing she bought, suppose fraud to have been practised toward her, or in sickness her ration charged her, or that she was compelled to pay for the rations her children ate,—what then? . . . It is sincerely to be hoped that, hereafter, labor may compete in the open market; that demand and supply shall regulate prices; and that liberty and justice, wherever practised this year, may have the advantage of their good repute among the laborers.[73]

Labor, however, did not compete in the open market, particularly for dependent freedwomen in search of employment. The Bureau privileged one model of labor: hard fieldwork of cotton cultivation, which it did not consider single freedwomen fit.[74] The decision to base the revitalization of the South around one crop simultaneously displaced single freedwomen from the labor force and exacerbated their dependent condition. Only in a few instances did federal officials attempt to provide former bondswomen with alternatives to the plantation labor force. In Washington, DC, the Bureau appointed a reformer to create a curriculum in the Campbell Hospital Industrial School for the "benefit of colored women who have grown up in ignorance of all domestic habits." The purpose of the school—as an article published in 1866 in the *Freedmen's Record* explained— was "for instruction and employment for those who can find no remunerative labor, or are so situated that they are not engaged in regular service." Freedwomen at the Campbell Hospital Industrial School were taught to "knit, darn, patch, and mend," and "were paid in clothes the value of their work at the end of the month."[75]

In North Carolina, the military attempted to circumvent the problem by suggesting to federal authorities in Washington, as early as 1864, that they "introduce a branch or any branches of labor by which they [freedwomen] could gain a livelihood." Since the state did not produce the best cotton, the military official suggested that women use osier willow, which grows well in the swamp lands of that region, to "manufacture willow baskets or palm leaf hats, or the braiding straw . . . These or similar process of light handicraft ought to be introduced among them as an essential part of the new social order to be established."[76]

While this particular military agent's suggestions would have helped alleviate some of the problems of dependency in North Carolina, many Bureau agents throughout the South did not devise employment opportunities for freedwomen because they perceived women's place to be in the home. In an address given to the freedpeople of Arlington Heights, Virginia, in 1865, a leading Bureau official instructed freedwomen to make good homes for their families, while freedmen were to labor in the fields.[77] The problem, however, was that not all freedwomen were married or part of kin networks, many lost their husbands in the war, while others were separated from their family during slavery. Moreover, these freedwomen did not have established homes but struggled to survive in shanty huts and makeshift tents. The Bureau, their ostensible safety net, failed to provide them with adequate shelter, leaving them vulnerable to disease and sickness.

Throughout the postwar period, Bureau agents and former slaveholders tried to overcome the problems of dependency by transporting freedwomen to Northern locations in need of domestic servants. In Northern Virginia, former planters, Bureau agents, and members of the Pennsylvania Abolition Society negotiated for freedwomen to be sent to Baltimore, Maryland, and Montgomery County, Pennsylvania, to serve as domestics.[78] While Northern benevolent reformers attempted to provide destitute freedwomen with an opportunity to leave the South by guaranteeing employment, it remains unclear if freedwomen wanted to leave the South and if they wanted to work as domestics. Their dependent status suggested to both well-intentioned reformers and Bureau authorities they could make the decision for formerly enslaved women.

The Bureau's Inability to Treat Dependency

The continual presence of dependent freedpeople in and around Bureau offices at times shifted officials' focus from questions about the labor force to more pressing questions about how to handle the thousands of dependent freedpeople who applied for assistance.[79] In Beaufort, South Carolina, a Northern teacher wrote, "The sick and destitute are left to shirk for themselves." Quoting a government official, the benevolent reformer wrote, "They [freedpeople] must starve and perhaps the quicker the better for them and the world. Such people will never be able to take care of themselves, and Government has become tired and will not do it any longer."[80]

By late 1866, federal authorities could no longer ignore the reports of unemployed freedpeople suffering in the postwar South and slowly began to develop a policy that would address their condition. Doctors, however, were not given special provisions to treat these dependents and had to rely on the supplies allocated for sick freedpeople to be used for those who were unemployed. It was not until 1866, when the smallpox epidemic began to dissipate, that the federal government officially legislated the Bureau to treat dependent freedpeople. While Freedmen's Hospitals functioned as asylums since their founding, they became increasingly invested in issues of dependency. Since physicians distributed rations and determined both who was able-bodied and who should be eligible to receive support, it made sense that the Medical Division expanded its efforts in assisting the destitute.[81]

Caring for dependent freedpeople was, nonetheless, an added challenge for the Medical Division. Hospitals were already overcrowded, understaffed, and without adequate resources. The predicament of dependent freedpeople posed new questions regarding the treatment of patients and the operations of the Medical Division in the South. The Medical Division assumed that afflicted freedpeople would ultimately be cured and then given the opportunity to rejoin the labor force. The same logic could have easily been applied to the destitute freedpeople, but it could not be applied to the orphaned, elderly, and disabled.[82]

As a Bureau agent from Southern Virginia explained in 1866, "The workings of the Bureau have in a great measure been in harmony," but "there have been recent cases of extreme necessity and affliction, one a deaf and dumb colored man unable to work for his support, another a woman who has fits and is physically incapable of making a living—another an aged infirm colored man who is entirely worn out by hard service, and others which have come to my notice."[83] Local offices initially handled the increasing cases of dependency by placing these freedpeople in hospitals—where Bureau physicians would then evaluate their condition and determine if they could receive rations. Based on the physical condition of the mother and children, as well as the Bureau's facilities, the family was normally kept together. When the hospital could not accommodate the family, the children were often separated from their mothers. "We greatly need a building where small children can be provided for during the sickness of parents," explained a military official in Louisiana in 1865 about the status of dependent and sick freedpeople.[84]

In general, Freedmen's Hospitals varied in the kind of support they could provide to dependent freedpeople. The hospitals' ability to help elderly, disabled, and poor ex-slaves relied on the location of the hospital, the number of dependent freedpeople in need of assistance, and the its size and resources. Larger Freedmen's Hospitals could provide rooms or parts of the hospital to be demarcated for dependent freedpeople. At L'Overture Hospital in Alexandria, Virginia, for example, the hospital included 100 beds and accommodated an average of 45 patients.[85] As a result, this particular institution could easily admit more patients to its ward and even had the resources to establish a home for old and infirm freedpeople, admitting on average 10 patients a week.[86] In hospitals consisting of fewer than 20 beds, doctors attempted to find adequate space for the dependent freedpeople by transforming abandoned hotels and schools into asylums. If suitable accommodations did not exist, physicians placed requests to have the elderly transported to a neighboring Freedmen's Hospital.[87]

Bureau authorities petitioned local and state asylums to assist in handling the increasing number of dependents, but these institutions flatly rejected freedpeople. Many of these municipal facilities expanded their operations during the war for dependent white refugees, but they refused to admit former slaves, especially in the immediate aftermath of the war. Even benevolent organizations, which presumably subscribed to more egalitarian, religious, and humanitarian philosophies, claimed that lack of adequate facilities and funds prevented them from enrolling freedpeople at their almshouses. Although many of these organizations exhausted their funds during the war, their refusal to allow freedpeople into their asylums was a de facto practice. Just as women were separated from men in almshouses and hospital wards, some black people were separated from whites in charitable institutions in 1865 and early 1866.[88]

Federal authorities in Washington tried to solve this problem by allocating funds to local Bureau agents to develop a transportation policy. If those applying for assistance proved that they had family members or had secured employment in a neighboring state, the Bureau would arrange for their transportation to that region.[89]

The transportation program was intended to take the burden of dependent people off Freedmen's Hospitals, but it was flawed in many respects. It was very expensive and relied heavily on the Bureau's inadequate bureaucratic network.[90] Proof of guaranteed employment or living arrangements was difficult for former slaves to provide, because they often struggled to be in touch with family members or had not yet secured employment in the desired destination. Letters were often lost and transportation requests denied.[91] A freedwoman in April 1866 requested that her mother, who was placed in a Freedmen's Hospital in New Orleans, Louisiana, be transported to her home in Richmond, Virginia. The woman stated that her mother "was between 60 and 70 and was very feeble in health." She further asserted that her mother "shall never be of any expense to the government if we can only get her here as my husband and myself anxiously desire to provide her comfort." After the request circulated through the various bureaucratic channels, an official in Washington finally approved the woman's request. When the official sent the funds and forms to the Louisiana hospital to transport the elderly woman to Virginia, the physician reported back to Washington authorities that the woman's mother had died the week before "after a long affliction of cancer in the breast."[92]

The Creation of Orphanages and Elderly Homes

Because many of these measures did not effectively solve the problems of dependency, authorities in Washington decided that the Medical Division would expand its efforts and construct specific institutions for dependent freed slaves. Federal officials called for the creation of separate almshouses designed specifically for destitute, elderly, orphaned, and disabled freed slaves that would serve as annexes to the hospitals. The Bureau then faced many questions: Who would run these almshouses? How would they be funded, and where would they be established? Would these asylums be temporary institutions, or would they function as reform institutions similar to Northern orphanages and homes?[93]

In preparation for asylums, assistant commissioners instructed physicians to begin allowing destitute freedpeople to enroll formally as permanent patients in hospitals. Physicians were reluctant to expand their workload, claiming that their efforts were needed more for patients suffering from dysentery, yellow fever, or contagious diseases; and that inadequate supplies, limited space, and staff shortages prevented them from treating all those requiring assistance. Admitting dependent freedpeople as permanent patients to Freedmen's Hospitals would only, from their perspective, diminish their ability to treat the sick.

Despite the doctors' protests, Bureau authorities in Washington pressured assistant commissioners to address the issue of dependency by creating separate institutions.[94] In the end, both assistant commissioners and doctors became responsible for the expansion of the Medical Division and for the care of destitute freedpeople.[95] Bureau doctors made daily reports on the medical conditions of the residents, while the assistant commissioner ordered beds and supplies, and handled transportation requests. To reach freedpeople in rural regions, assistant commissioners appointed a member of the freedpeople's community to distribute weekly rations.[96] With the assistant commissioners' financial and organizational support, the Medical Division was able to build hospitals and asylums for destitute freedpeople throughout South, including in remote rural regions. The assistant commissioner in Tennessee, for example, donated a $1,000 to help the sick and destitute freedpeople in Davidson, which is located in the outskirts of Nashville; this funding provided a template for local Bureau medical authorities to establish a hospital in the region.[97] Over 50 asylums for dependent former slaves were set up in the South, serving thousands of freedpeople from 1866 to 1870.[98] Although, the operation of 50 institutions was not adequate to respond to the needs of a population of over four million.

Federal authorities commissioned the Bureau to build a central Freedmen's Hospital and then to build subsidiary asylums around it, which would allow physicians to better supervise the institutions under their care. This plan to centralize the asylums in one location would better facilitate the transition to free labor. From the Bureau's perspective, establishing the asylum for those unable to work away from the laboring population alleviated the fear that providing support for dependent freedpeople might promote indolence among able-bodied ex-slaves.

The development of these communities began to transform the Southern landscape, indicating the end of a slave-based, plantation economy and landscape. By late 1867, the South started to resemble other free labor societies, as various communities for dependent freedpeople emerged.[99] In the Washington, DC area, the government transformed the contraband camp located north of the Potomac in Virginia, famously known as Freedmen's Village, into a refuge for elderly freedpeople. Due to the large number of elderly freedpeople in the Washington area, it was an ideal location, separate from the sharecropping plantations in Virginia, yet close enough to the nation's capital to allow doctors and Bureau officials a short commute to the village. Bureau officials easily transported dependent freedpeople from southern Virginia, North Carolina, and even parts of Louisiana to Freedmen's Village. After a few months serving as a retreat for the elderly, Freedmen's Village became a refuge for other non-able-bodied, dependent ex-slaves, particularly blind, insane, and deaf freedpeople. Bureau authorities also established a hospital and an orphanage in the village.[100] In other parts of the South, Bureau authorities built homes for the elderly, blind, and disabled, but few locations resembled the sophisticated efforts that defined Freedmen's Village.[101]

Although, in addition to Freedmen's Village in Virginia, home colonies, or home farms as they were sometimes called, developed in mostly rural areas of the South. Home colonies were essentially large plantations that were transformed into smaller farms for sharecropping. Within these colonies, Bureau authorities established schools, labor offices, and hospitals.[102] As the relief efforts of the Medical Division expanded, these home colonies became ideal settings for the Bureau to establish asylums for dependent people.[103] When Freedmen's Hospitals closed in Shreveport and St. John's Island, dependent freedpeople were sent to the Rest Home Colony in Louisiana. Similarly, when the Medical Division withdrew from Wilmington, North Carolina, elderly and orphaned freedpeople were sent to the main medical headquarters in the state at New Bern.[104]

The Bureau, however, did not systematically develop a policy for one group simply because they adopted measures for another. The creation of almshouses for elderly freedpeople did not simultaneously lead Bureau authorities to construct orphanages for children. As with most of the Bureau's operations, measures to generate institutions or policies for a particular group of freedpeople resulted from specific circumstances. Due to the overwhelming number of dependent freedwomen throughout the South, for example, The National Home for Destitute Colored Women and Children was founded.[105]

The concern for orphans in the postwar South emerged in response to the national orphan crises.[106] Despite initiatives in the North to deal with orphans, Southern charitable organizations continued to refuse to provide support to children. Madame Louise de Mortie, a freeborn woman from Virginia, moved to New Orleans to help orphans and was recognized by the Freedmen's Bureau for her contributions to the black community. Many years later, W. E. B. Du Bois also extolled the virtues of de Mortie's work with the orphans when he wrote, "She went to the orphaned colored children of New Orleans,—out of freedom into insult and oppression and into the teeth of yellow fever. She toiled and dreamed."[107]

But individual efforts alone could not ameliorate the conditions of so many young freedpeople. As a result, freedpeople often turned to Northern benevolent associations that provided considerable financial support to black orphans in the postwar South. Benevolent organizations contributed enormously to the Freedmen's Bureau's construction of orphanages, and their assistance was generally welcomed.[108] Remarking on the overall support of benevolent associations to the expansion of medical services for freedpeople, John Eaton, chaplain of the Union army, recalled years later, "Fortunately for the success of our labors among the colored people, the benevolent workers at the North began to respond with great generosity to the needs of the destitute refugees."[109]

Building on their commitment to aid freed children of color, benevolent organizations produced a network with Bureau agents in the South that allowed Southern children to enter orphanages in the North and Midwest, particularly in Brooklyn, New York, and Philadelphia.[110] Their leaders also encouraged the construction of roughly a dozen orphanages for black children and sent funds, supplies, and resources to reformers serving in the South. Commissioned by the New York Freedmen's Aid Commission, Laura Haviland, a benevolent reformer, brought a group of "orphan children," who "were picked up on the streets," and suffering from "chills and fever," to an orphan school in Michigan.[111]

Since many of the orphans required medical assistance, it made sense that Bureau physicians served as the heads of orphanages.[112] Matrons oversaw the daily operations of the orphanage and took care of the children, while doctors distributed rations, clothing, and medicine, and served as the liaison between the Bureau and the benevolent organizations. As a result, orphanages were often built close to Freedmen's Hospitals, so that Bureau physicians could easily travel from one institution to the next. Benevolent organizations not only provided financial and educational support, but also often hosted activities for the freed children on Sundays and met with families who were interested in adopting.[113]

Although it is difficult to determine the exact number of orphanages and orphans in the South, Bureau officials reported roughly 40 orphanages in operation during Reconstruction.[114] In Charleston, South Carolina, for example, there was only one orphanage from 1790 to 1850, but by the end of the war, there were 10 orphanages in the city. City officials in Charleston reported that the majority of the orphans were black.[115] In other Southern cities, the estimates of orphans range from 1,800 in North Carolina to 120 in Tennessee. The Bureau classified orphans as children from age 2 to 16, but most were clustered between ages 8 and 11. As was the case in the North, many of these orphans lived in these homes temporarily but might come back for them when they found firmer financial footing. Many of these "half-orphans" had mothers who were temporarily unable to they provide for them. Additionally, when parents became sick and were admitted to the hospital, Bureau physicians took responsibility for finding adequate living quarters for the children. While they first tried to find members of the community to take responsibility for them, they could be admitted to orphanages. If the parents died, the Bureau felt a more direct responsibility and placed children in orphanages as a refuge.[116]

In general, the increased development of orphanages, hospitals, and asylums provided a more stable and permanent solution to the problems of dependency, replacing the Bureau's idiosyncratic and often erratic policy of disseminating rations at local Bureau headquarters. These institutions, for instance, allowed freedpeople to stay in these facilities for over a week, moving beyond the Bureau's strict guidelines for length of support.[117] Freedmen's orphanages also contributed to the development of the labor force, because they provided freed children with the tools to become workers. The education programs—which included courses from reading to hygiene—attempted to prepare young freedpeople for the challenges of entering the workforce. Along with lessons, the Bureau instilled the values of hard work, discipline, and cleanliness.[118] With the exception of orphanages, the Freedmen's asylums did not teach destitute freedpeople skills in order to find employment.

In some Northern asylums, superintendents not only separated the young from the old, and the disabled from the insane, but, interestingly, they grouped individuals according to whether they were loud or quiet, talkative or shy. As a result, many Northern asylum authorities organized institutions in order to reform patients so that they could ultimately rejoin the labor force. Superintendents of these institutions engaged in a pedagogy of reform; they encouraged the importance of good hygiene and assigned patients with tasks that emphasized regularity, responsibility, and punctuality.[119] Bureau officials did not pursue a similar course. Even when Bureau authorities separated dependents by age, gender, and disability, they continued in their policies and in their practices to place these freedpeople under the same umbrella of destitution and dependency.[120]

The communities offered dependent freedpeople a safe refuge, and the Medical Division needed more institutions like them; yet, the continual lack of available land and financial resources prevented Medical Division authorities from establishing communities in other regions in the South. More to the point, the federal government viewed its role as temporary, feared that these institutions would encourage dependency, and wanted state and municipal authorities to eventually take responsibility for disabled, elderly, orphaned, and destitute freedpeople.

The Famine of 1867–68

In 1867, a drought erupted that exponentially increased the number of cases of destitution throughout the South. The once lush and fertile land that stretched from the cotton fields of South Carolina to the sugar plantations of Louisiana began to turn brown and dry up, leaving newly minted landowners and share-croppers penniless in 1867–68.[121] With little support from Bureau offices, freedpeople as well as white refugees suffered enormously from the lack of rain-fall and consequent crop failure and deaths of livestock.[122] Famine soon engulfed the South. The federal government was initially unaware of the failure of the harvest and the subsequent erosion of crops throughout the South, in large part because its agents had increasingly left the area. Once Bureau agents negotiated contracts or settled disputes between planters and freedpeople, they reported to federal offices that their services were no longer needed and they left the South.

Southern planters recognized the devastating ways in which drought and crop failure undermined efforts to regain a foothold in economic production. In the summer of 1865, while Bureau and military officials busily organized freedmen into labor gangs, white Southerners noticed how the initial signs of the drought exacerbated the condition of destitute people in the region. Julius J. Fleming told readers of the *Charleston Courier* in August 1865, "Drought con-tinues with damaging effects on late crops . . . There are some places in the dis-trict where the corn crop will not average more than three bushels to the acre, and some acres will not yield even a peck."[123] A few weeks later, he reported:

> The country has not experienced for many years a more damaging drought than the present for it still continues, only slightly relieved by light and partial showers. It has been very fatal to the rice, potato, and pea crops . . . And in fact, gathering our information from reliable sources in all parts of the state, we hesitate not to say that the present cotton crop of South Carolina will not much, if at all, exceed five thousand bales; and there will not be enough provisions, raised to supply the existing population . . . A large part of our territory was ravaged by Sherman's and Potter's armies, and the planting interest almost annihilated.[124]

Meanwhile, Bureau authorities in Washington, DC, failed to realize that an environmental disaster, such as a drought and subsequent famine, could render their hard work meaningless and place employed freedpeople into a position of dependency.[125] Compounding matters, by 1867, Bureau officials no longer defined the poor as destitute or dependent; that terminology was increasingly deployed to define elderly, disabled, orphaned, and female former slaves. Once the Bureau created asylums for these permanent dependents, federal officials argued that medical officials no longer needed to keep their hospitals in operation. By 1867, of the 42 hospitals that the Bureau opened during its two-year tenure in the South, only 20 remained in operation.[126]

The drought and subsequent famine, however, called into question the precipitous decision to disband hospitals and relief institutions that addressed cases of poverty. The drought and famine also exposed the limitations of Northern free labor ideology. Bureau officials on the ground and the federal leaders in Washington never imagined that one day freedpeople could be hard at work on their farms or plantations and exemplify the government's hopes of rebuilding the South, but a week, a month, or even a year later, when the rain stopped or when insects, which ravaged cotton fields, appeared that picture of freedpeople's prosperity crumbled. Environmental problems led working former slaves to once again be placed in a dependent position and susceptible to starvation, illness, and death.

As Bureau officials stationed throughout the South soon learned, the famine exhausted what little resources freedpeople had. As an assistant commissioner from Alabama reported in 1867, "By an issue that was known as the 'destitute ration,' relief on a large scale had been afforded to them during the preceding year; in the hope that with the maturing of the crops that system might be discontinued. But an alternate excess of frost and heat, of rain and drought, in turn severely injured every crop, creating an amount of suffering greater than that which it had been attempted to relieve."[127] A teacher in Columbia, South Carolina, reported a similar situation in 1867 in which the Bureau was unable to provide rations to freedpeople who were starving for a few weeks. "Provisions for the poor," the teacher wrote, "were wretched."[128]

Since the federal government believed it was not their responsibility to offer relief, but the responsibility of voluntary associations, they stood by and watched as Bureau agents and teachers reported on the suffering and starving of the freedpeople. As O. O. Howard explained, "It is not the intention of the Government that the Bureau shall supersede the various benevolent organizations in the work of administering relief. This must still be afforded by the benevolence of the people through their voluntary societies, no government appropriations having been made for that purposes."[129] Northern benevolent organizations, which were already stationed in the South, established the Southern Relief Commission as a way to combat the onslaught of destitution. These groups invariably, if unwittingly, took Howard's cue and led the response to the crisis. The organization, which included sponsors like the Ladies Organization of Baltimore and benevolent associations in Philadelphia and Cincinnati, sent clothing and food to the South. But they were unable to provide resources ample enough to ward off the famine and could not reach many in need in the rural parts of the South.[130]

The famine intensified as prices for seed, groceries, and other necessities increased in 1868. A Bureau agent stationed in Raleigh, North Carolina, said succinctly in May 1868, "The principal causes of the destitution are from the failure of the corn and cotton crop"; the people are "unable to buy necessary food."[131] While a handful of committed Bureau agents and doctors remained in the South and attempted to respond to the famine, the majority of support for dependent freedpeople came from local charitable organizations. A reformer in Tennessee stated in 1868, "There will be more destitution and suffering among the colored people of Tennessee this winter than last. Now this remark may seem strange but it is a fact, and a sad one too, for the freedmen. In this locality, and also around Nashville, the freedmen are not so well off today as they were a year ago at this time. The low price of cotton, and the high price of all kinds of groceries, have reduced the poor people to worse than nothing."[132] Explaining the economic problems facing the freedpeople in Okolona, Mississippi, a reformer noted in 1868, "The failure of the cotton crop, and the consequent misery" devastated "many of the families of the freedmen here . . . Corn is good, but even that, with the cotton fails to pay for the rations already consumed by the laborers, or to repay the employer the capital invested in carrying on the business of the plantation."[133]

Meanwhile, Bureau agents fell back on their strategy of transporting unemployed freedpeople, even to regions where there were no opportunities to work and they were not welcome. In Giles County, Virginia, Bureau authorities refused to provide support to newly arrived freedmen who lived in the county for less than a year. The local community provided relief to only those "who have been citizens of the county for twelve months" and then commanded those who were not from Giles County to be "ordered back to their own county."[134] As a result, what developed was a crisscrossing of freedpeople throughout the South— migrations to and from possible places of employment, journeys to cities for relief, and sojourns across the plantation South in search of kin networks who could offer shelter from the famine. One white Southerner commented on the dislocation, "The Negroes are to be pitied. The new order of things has burst upon them. Many of them leaving their former homes are wandering over the country in a state of idleness."[135] Witnessing the displacement and suffering condition of dependent freedpeople signaled to many Bureau agents freedpeople's unfitness or even unwillingness to handle the challenges of freedom.

When new Reconstruction state governments came into power in 1867, Bureau agents demonstrated the extent to which the Republican plan for

Reconstruction was working—ignoring the famine and drought in their reports to Congress. Not only did Bureau officials overlook and underestimate the dire conditions of the postwar South, but they reported to federal officials in Washington that the conditions in the South were "good," and "improving."[136] Bureau agents shifted federal attention away from the increasing problems of dependency, which would indicate that they were not doing their jobs well, and instead emphasized the success of free labor. Bureau records contain numerous examples of the problems that transpired between planters and freedpeople over labor contracts, but to discuss the continuing problem of dependency would invariably have undermined the promise of reconstructing the South.

In his 1869 report to the secretary of war, Bureau leader O. O. Howard recounted the great progress and success that his various field agents observed in 1867–1868 in the South, ignoring the cases of starvation, dislocation, and destitution caused by the famine. Decades later, in his *Autobiography*, Howard congratulated himself on a job well done in response to the famine.

> [The] extensive destitution of all classes of people, including the freedmen, became so heartrending, that for once I anticipated the action of Congress. It was one offense of which none of those who were hostile to my administration ever complained. I had abundant authority so far as the loyal refugees and freedmen were involved to feed them to the extent of our food appropriation; but we had reduced this number to narrow limits when this famine fell upon the Southern coasts. In some counties, actual starvation set in.[137]

Howard acknowledged that he had so effectively dismantled hospitals and centers for relief throughout the South during the early years of Reconstruction that there was no safety net to protect freedpeople from the onslaught of the drought and the subsequent famine. Or, he suggests that it would take an act of Congress to provide relief, which was beyond his role in providing aid to freedpeople. Either way, Howard recognized the responsibility of the government to end the famine and the role it could have played in preventing it. The Bureau's sharp regulation of relief to freedpeople meant that freed slaves received little help in handling the unexpected agricultural crisis.

Circular Movement

In an effort to solve the problems of the famine, the federal government literally placed freedpeople back in the position that led to their dependency—they set them back in motion, again in search of employment. The forced migrations and independent movements of freedpeople that crisscrossed the South throughout 1866 and 1867 redoubled their vulnerability to sickness, suffering, and disease. Constantly on the move, former slaves were increasingly susceptible to a host of illnesses, such as exposure and dysentery, and to violent epidemic outbreaks, like smallpox and even cholera. Succinctly, freedpeople's labor status shaped their health.

The federal government, meanwhile, could not take their eyes off the labor power that freedpeople's bodies could produce. Its strict understanding of who qualified as a laborer left thousands of women, children, elderly, and disabled slaves unable to pursue a meaningful life of "freedom."[138] While, at first, the government reacted to this problem by creating specific asylums, lack of funding and personnel—not to mention freedpeople's likely unwillingness to be separated from the working members of their families and kin networks—resulted in these institutions being less than capable of responding to the problems of unemployment and so-called dependency.

Unlike during the smallpox epidemic, the government did take action to counter the crises surrounding destitution, but it lacked the resources, manpower, and capability to act effectively. Officials also inaccurately framed poverty and destitution as temporary problems without recognizing how free labor ideology created dependency and produced a continuous need for institutions to house those that did not fit into the labor force.

Narrating Illness

Freedpeople's Health Claims at Reconstruction's End

I, Too, Sing America

—Langston Hughes (1932)

Her name was Jeannette Small, and she was starving to death. Her family was nowhere to be found. To make matters worse, the Bureau agent who discovered her defined her as "idiotic."[1]

Jeannette's starvation was the result of the drought of 1867–68 and the subsequent famine that plagued South Carolina; the state where she was found. By the time her condition was documented by a Bureau agent, the federal government had realized that newspaper reports of black men lining up to vote and school-children studying in neatly decorated classrooms were not the only stories emerging from the Reconstruction South. The government had responded to the situation of starving women by building asylums and homes designed especially for "destitute women."

Yet, Jeannette's case was different. The Bureau agent labeled her as "idiotic," and there was no place in the Bureau hospitals for people with mental disabilities. According to the Bureau, "insane" freedpeople could not be placed in the same room as the elderly, the poor, or the young because they were "disruptive." The problem of what do with Jeannette and with the hundreds of other "insane" freedpeople that appeared throughout the Bureau's correspondence ultimately led to the most radical transformation in the Bureau's policy and paved the way for the Bureau to withdrawal entirely from the South.

Since arriving in the South in 1865, the Bureau's goal was to transfer care of the disabled and "indigent sick" freedpeople to state and local authorities and organizations. But state governments refused to acknowledge freedpeople as citizens, thus asylums, hospitals, and overseers of the poor refused to help them. Lack of citizenship became a way for Southern state and charitable institutions to justify withholding medical and other assistance from destitute freedpeople, while continuing to support poor white residents.

In 1866, Congress passed the Civil Rights Act, which served as precursor to the Fourteenth Amendment and defined black people as citizens entitled to all the public services that white citizens enjoyed, including access to state hospitals and asylums. The creation of this bill and the ratification of this amendment theoretically established legal grounds for freedpeople, like Jeannette Small, to enter state facilities. While a portion of the new state governments succeeded in changing the policy of state-run institutions, some medical superintendents—for example, in Arkansas, Georgia, North Carolina, and Alabama—continued to illegally refuse freedpeople admission to state and local almshouses and hospitals.[2]

While federal legislation enacted change, local and state governments operated according to their own political agendas. As a result, Bureau doctors could not rely on federal or new state governments to enforce changes in policy at the local level. Instead, Bureau doctors, along with many former slaves, worked to force municipal authorities to open the doors of state and local hospitals to freedpeople on a patient-by-patient basis.

Bureau doctors and agents had to convince state and local officials that it was in the best interest of their community to enroll freedpeople into these asylums. They accomplished this by tapping into fears about unsupervised "insane" freedpeople in these communities. Recognizing that "insane" freedpeople possessed a formidable threat to the safety and sanctity of white and even black Southern communities, local and state authorities agreed to enroll mentally disabled freedpeople in state-run asylums. When Bureau doctors and agents realized that this tactic worked, they intensified these fears by planting into white Southerners' minds the threat of epidemic outbreaks that would proliferate in the summer months if sick freedpeople were not given access to state institutions that housed the "indigent sick."

Gradually, the Bureau began the process of transferring responsibility of dependent freedpeople, namely, elderly and orphaned former slaves, as well as destitute, sick, and disabled freedpeople, to the state. With each patient transferred out of a Bureau facility, the closer the Bureau came to dismantling its systems of care and leaving the Reconstruction South. By 1872, with the exception of Freedmen's Hospital in Washington, DC, the Bureau had managed to successfully transfer authority over many freedpeople to state governments and close all the hospitals, almshouses, and asylums they had established in the 1860s.[3]

Whether Jeannette Small went to the insane asylum in Charleston or to a facility in Milledgeville, Georgia, where many mentally disabled freedpeople were frequently sent, or if she was ever claimed by family and friends, something had radically changed by 1868. State governments for the first time in their history recognized freedpeople as citizens.

On a federal level, a major transformation had also unfolded in the province of freedpeople's health. The creation of the U.S. pension system enabled Civil War black veterans and their families to begin the process of receiving financial support for medical injuries and health problems caused by the war. Although pensions were restricted to families whose sons, fathers, and brothers served in the Union army, the program offered freedpeople the ability to define their own health conditions and to turn to the federal government for support for medical services.[4] Freedpeople detailed a wide range of illnesses, from gastrointestinal issues to broken arms and legs, to the physicians who had to provide a patient's medical analysis with the pension application.

The doctor's role in this exchange should not undermine the broader transformation that had taken place. During the 1860s, freedpeople's health was merely quantified, as Bureau and Union army doctors tabulated the number of sick freedpeople in a particular region or the number of former slaves infected with a particular virus. Only in select correspondence between Bureau agents and physicians do the names of some sick freedpeople even appear. The vast and overwhelming majority of records are simply statistical statements. The creation of the pension application replaced these quantitative reports with individual patient files that included the patient's medical history, a physical exam, a description of the ailment, and, sometimes, testimony from family members, friends, or employers detailing the illness. Included was an outline of a human body, on which the physician could annotate more clearly the site of the illness or injury.[5] For the first time, freedpeople had a chance to articulate matters concerning their own health to the federal government.

By the 1870s the changing political climate increasingly shaped freedpeople's ability to articulate their health concerns and seek treatment. On the state level, they could qualify for access to state-run facilities. On a federal level, they could qualify for pensions. Both changes slowly empowered freedpeople to articulate their health conditions to government authorities and to receive support from the state.

Instances of Insanity

Before state and municipal medical authorities accepted black patients into the same hospitals that treated white patients, Bureau doctors and the federal government first had to recognize mentally disabled freedpeople as a category of dependents that required federal intervention. In a two-page report to the chief medical officer in Washington in the fall of 1866, Dr. L. A. Edwards, a Bureau physician in North Carolina, inquired what to do with insane freedmen and wanted to know if public authorities were responsible for these and other dependents.[6] Among Bureau doctors and officials, as well as others in the nineteenth century, the term "insane" had a range of different meanings. For some, insanity was synonymous with "idiotic," "dumb," or "imbecile."[7] For other medical professionals, like a physician in Georgia, insanity meant "melancholy." The Bureau's wide-ranging definition of the term "insanity" was not uncommon during this period.[8] Bureau doctors were unsure how to handle the many cases of mental disability brought to their attention. Reports included "an insane freedwoman," running frantically through the streets of Charleston, South Carolina, and accounts of an "insane colored woman" disturbing the otherwise quiet life in New Bern, North Carolina.[9] Often described as violent and uncontrollable, insane freedpeople were not usually referenced by name but listed in Bureau records as "the Idiot," or, in the case of a freedwoman brought to the attention of authorities in Washington, DC, as "Dummy."[10]

Most, if not all, of these cases concerned patients who were freedwomen.[11] Unlike freedmen, who could have been placed into a labor gang and transported to a plantation, freedwomen were displaced from the labor force and migrated from town to town in search of temporary employment and shelter. It is likely that the effects of migration, surviving the aftermath of the war and epidemic outbreaks, and often living without subsistence more than likely caused many freedwomen to appear to Bureau agents as unstable.[12]

Bureau physicians and officials were unsure how to handle the relatively small, but nonetheless significant, cases of mental disability they encountered. The key issue was how to treat them, especially because one case could demand much of the doctor's time. In the North, insane patients were placed in separate asylums, where they were treated with a regimen that stressed solid work habits, religious instruction, and amusement in order to aid their return to society.[13] Bureau doctors lacked special quarters, floors, or divisions to separate mentally disabled freedpeople from other dependents or from each other; consequently their presence created major problems. As the assistant commissioner in Mississippi recounted in his annual report to federal officials in Washington in 1866:

> The surgeon also reports upon the necessity of provision for indigent insane colored persons. It has been absolutely necessary to take charge of a number, and the limited accommodations is not extended as yet to more than one room, and here there is great danger that the patients in their frenzies will injure each other. Fire cannot be allowed them without endangering the buildings, and many necessaries are needed for them which the appropriation does not allow; and as for the "refugees and freedmen's fund," it is not likely that it is large enough to meet the demands upon it which an attempt to build a hospital would make.[14]

Throughout the Bureau's correspondence and reports, doctors expressed their inability to handle cases of the "insane colored paupers." In Atlanta, Georgia, a physician explained in 1867, "By getting rid of the insane it would not only be less expensive but much less difficult to keep the hospital in good condition."[15] Bureau officials pleaded with superintendents of local insane asylums and heads of state hospitals to accept one or, at the most, two insane freedpeople into state facilities.

At first, these requests were flatly denied. In 1866, a Bureau doctor described how state authorities in Kentucky had not only refused to make "provisions for the support of its pauper freedmen" but also, "any provision on the part of the State for the care of the insane of the same class."[16] Mississippi state authorities continued to deny insane freedpeople admission to the asylum despite their knowledge of the Bureau's inability to treat those afflicted with mental disorders. Bureau authorities hoped—according to one official—"that the session of the legislature just closed [in 1866] would have acted in this matter, as well in other matters of provision for the colored people: but no relieving law was passed, and the negro, whether sane or insane must still be an object of charity on the [federal] government."[17]

Disregarding the passage of the Civil Rights Act, medical superintendents consistently broke the law by refusing to admit dependent freedpeople to state asylums. The provisional governor in Galveston, Texas, for example, informed state authorities of the recent Civil Rights Act in June 1866 and of their responsibility to abide by the federal law. "By the laws of the United States these people are citizens, and by the action of the late convention of this State they are vested with all civil and personal rights," the provisional governor wrote. "They are as fully entitled to the benefits of the law of the State for the relief of the poor and suffering is too clear to require argument." Medical authorities refused to budge.[18]

Since local governments refused to adhere to federal legislation, Bureau physicians demanded that state authorities should, at least, uphold the integrity of their own laws. In view of the fact that the language of city codes stated that asylums were open to "paupers," Bureau officials used this definition as part of their campaigns to gain destitute freedpeople admission to public facilities. Providing substantive proof that former slaves were indeed "paupers," Bureau doctors filed applications on behalf of insane and indigent freedpeople. According to state authorities and superintendents of insane asylums, however, paupers referred only to white people. Bureau doctors and agents refused to accept this and continued to demonstrate to asylum superintendents that individual freedpeople were, in fact, paupers and, according to the state laws, qualified for admission to almshouses. "I want to make application for them [insane freedmen] in the state asylum," wrote one Bureau official in Georgia in 1867, "they being paupers, and request that you will inform me if they will be received under your charge."[19]

After receiving a negative response from the superintendent of the state asylum in Georgia, he wrote a second time, declaring "all the insane are paupers, I insist that the law should apply" to these cases.[20]

Bureau physicians attempted to circumvent medical superintendents' restrictions by individually contacting local mayors and county officers for support. While such tactics worked in Virginia and Georgia, other state officials, like those in North Carolina and Louisiana in 1866, tried to derail these efforts by enacting a clause that the patients must have lived in the county for a year to qualify as paupers in need of medical assistance at the insane asylum.[21] A Bureau agent explained this otherwise unknown caveat to a physician in Salisbury, North Carolina, "the Justice of the Peace have declined to act on the grounds that they [insane freedmen] have no settlement in this county and it cannot be ascertained from which they came to this place."[22] Because of the constant migration of emancipated slaves, as well as the Bureau's restriction of freedpeople—particularly those marked as dependent and insane—to regulated communities and hospitals, it was nearly impossible for mentally afflicted freedpeople to have secured a year's residence in a community to qualify for admission to the insane asylum.[23]

In a manipulative move, Bureau doctors evoked fears about the presence of "insane freedmen" set loose in the community without supervision. "Rose, who was the subject of previous communication, is very troublesome to the citizens of this place," wrote a Bureau agent in Monticello, Florida, in June 1867. "Her insanity is fraught with danger," he explained, and "no one seems to have authority to take care of her."[24] This tactic proved successful as Bureau doctors were able to negotiate with the county to admit mentally afflicted freedpeople to county insane asylums. Mayors in places like Mitchell, Georgia, New Orleans, Louisiana, and towns in North Carolina overrode medical superintendents' rejections and forced the local asylums to admit freedpeople.[25] This tactic may have relied on racist perceptions, but it worked.[26]

Since many counties in the postwar South did not have separate insane asylums, patients were often transported to what was known as the "Central Lunatic Asylum" of a given state. "It is presumed by the middle of August [1867] all the insane patients in the Freedmen's Hospital," wrote the assistant commissioner in Georgia, "will be taken charge of by the state at the state Lunatic Asylum near Milledgeville." Later that month, the assistant commissioner wrote to the medical staff in Georgia to apply to "Inferior Court in Augusta about cases of lunacy."[27] Bureau officials successfully negotiated with officials in a number of counties in Georgia to open the Central Lunatic Asylum to freedpeople; once this happened, the Bureau then possessed the power—despite the opposition of some local counties—to get freedpeople throughout the state admitted to the asylum. Local courts, as a result, facilitated these initiatives as the state began to accommodate emancipated slaves.[28] In other cases, when Bureau officials gained no headway directly with superintendents of these institutions, letters written to or endorsed by the mayor or county official often did. In Mobile, Alabama, a letter written by the mayor in 1866 went so far as to get a freed person admitted to an institution in Louisiana.[29]

By late 1867, new state governments created by the Northern Republicans took control of the South and accepted Bureau physicians' requests to open state asylums to insane freedpeople. In order to facilitate the process of admitting black patients, Bureau physicians and local authorities created a "Certification of Insanity," which authorized the transfer of insane patients to the state mental institution. Many of the documents simply included the patient's name, age, and a short physical description; and were used to keep records of the interactions between the Bureau and the state. These certificates, nonetheless, serve as evidence of integration in public services during Reconstruction.[30]

The integration of insane asylums, however, did not lead state authorities across the postwar South to universally assume responsibility for destitute and sick freedpeople. Instead, Bureau doctors and former slaves continued to negotiate with local and state officials for support, but they began to lose the support of the federal government during this period. Since the federal government had passed legislation and instituted new state governments, it no longer felt obligated to support freedpeople. Without the help of the government, and by extension the military, to enforce these new political changes, many state governments continued to deny destitute freedpeople medical assistance.

From Fear of Smallpox to Integration

When smallpox reappeared in the postwar South in the autumn of 1866, many Bureau officials petitioned state governments for aid from local officials. When their requests were denied, Bureau physicians employed a rhetorical strategy similar to that used to gain insane patients acceptance into state asylums. By evoking *fears* about the dangers of smallpox among former slaves seeping into the white community, Bureau physicians commanded the attention of local and state officials who otherwise remained unmoved by the reemergence of the virus.

In May of 1866, a month after the passage of the Civil Rights Bill, state officials in Louisiana, for example, agreed to extend medical treatment to destitute freedpeople in cases of contagious diseases.[31] Yet when the virus began to reappear among freedpeople in Shreveport in December, the local medical superintendent illegally refused freedpeople admittance to the county pest house. The Shreveport Bureau physician explained to city officials, "the establishment of a

Pest House devolves upon the Civil authorities as in the event of their failure to do so small pox must spread among all classes of persons and that in providing for freedmen in this respect they are simply protecting the white population."[32]

New awareness of the connected fate of citizens and an emergent public health sensibility began to change the views of local administrators.[33] The fear that the virus could infect white residents, not the law or the government, impelled state officials to begin to recognize black people as citizens entitled to admission to pest homes. In general, throughout much of the postwar South, policy changes on the local level did not follow federal legislation, but unfolded in response to negotiations on the ground between Bureau physicians and municipal officials in the context of contagion. In Savannah, Georgia, reports in September 1867 of well over 30 people, both black and white, dying per day from smallpox prompted the mayor to work with the Bureau agent in command of the region to develop measures to slow down the spread of the virus. The support of the mayor proved particularly helpful because the Bureau physician in Savannah "left the city at the first alarm" of the virus. Together, the mayor and the commanding Bureau officer secured a boarding house and solicited the assistance of a doctor to treat those infected and devise a protocol to prevent further contagion.[34] One of the reasons that this effort was possible was due to the presence of new state governments, which did not exist in 1865 under Johnson's administration that limited federal support.

Bureau authorities further enlarged the fear of epidemics among many white Southerners by publicizing how the threat of epidemic outbreaks increased in warm weather. The return of smallpox, combined with the fear of a possible return of Asiatic cholera, created an unprecedented alliance between the Bureau and white Southerners.[35] By 1867, afflicted black patients were placed in the same quarters as white patients infected with smallpox. Officials in parts of Alabama, South Carolina, and Georgia no longer differentiated between black and white pest homes.[36] Although the decision to place freedpeople in pest homes could be perceived as a form of social control on the part of municipal and state governments, the rates of infection among freedpeople would have likely quadrupled (as they did among the freed slave population in 1865–66) without black patients being quarantined. On a symbolic level, enrolling freedpeople in such institutions pointed to the fact that they had slowly gained access to the benefits of citizenship.[37]

In other regions in the Reconstruction South where these fear tactics were not employed or did not prove successful, Bureau doctors were pressured by federal authorities to abandon their posts by 1867, even if they had not yet turned over the Freedmen's Hospital to the county or the state. If operations had not yet been handed over to state authorities, there were often no health care provisions

for freedpeople. Bureau doctors, who remained in the South and were committed to helping freedpeople, salvaged what minimal resources they had to
keep their hospitals operating. The federal government's devastating cuts to
their budgets ultimately forced Bureau doctors to limit the number of patients
they could treat. Consequently, Bureau doctors began to bargain with municipal
hospitals to exchange their resources for state and local officials to provide medical treatment. From hospitals beds to clean clothing to whole buildings, Bureau
doctors bartered with local medical authorities and slowly ingratiated themselves into local medical institutions. Local authorities, in turn, became more
amenable to the idea of providing medical assistance to former slaves.

These negotiations took place at the very moment when black political mobilization gained momentum in the South. Former slaves demanded that local and
county officials who had not abided by the Civil Rights Act extend medical
treatment to destitute and sick freedpeople. While black political mobilization
on the national level remained uneven until 1867, local campaigns for citizenship and access to state accommodations began as early as 1865.[38] In communities across the South, freedpeople insisted that medical provisions be included
as part of larger campaigns to gain the benefits of citizenship, from suffrage to
public education.[39] In Savannah, Georgia, a local doctor served as the mouthpiece for former slaves in the city when he contacted municipal officials and
asked for help gaining medical treatment for the freedpeople. The physician
explained that the freedpeople approached him first and asked him to serve as
their representative. He then worked out arrangements with the city and started
offering medical treatment to former slaves.[40]

In Richmond, Virginia, when political changes did not provide freedpeople
with medical assistance, they took matters into their own hands. A local black
physician representing the freedpeople approached local officials in January
1867 and requested that the county establish a "medical fund" to assist former
slaves. He proposed that the local government create a tax to be deducted from
the "workingman's wage" to pay for medical provisions for the freedpeople.[41] In
Summerville, South Carolina, a group of emancipated slaves in 1868 petitioned
the Bureau physician to keep the Bureau hospital in operation for another year.
Inspired by the freedpeople's pleas, the Bureau physician contacted local authorities to ensure that the municipal government would assume responsibility for
the freedpeople's health. Had the freedpeople not pressured the local Bureau
office, provisions on the local level may not have been made.[42]

The idiosyncratic way in which negotiations over freedpeople's admission to
state health facilities unfolded suggests that the success of Reconstruction
relied not only on the larger aims of the federal government but also, and perhaps more importantly, on the intricacies of local politics and individual situations. These piecemeal negotiations between Bureau doctors, former slaves,

and local officials accomplished two major goals: first, they fa
Bureau's ultimate transfer of authority to state institutions in 18
thereby contributed to the state's recognition that access to almsh
central benefit of citizenship; second, they opened a space for free
articulate their health concerns, contributing to their political em~~..~..~..~...
under Reconstruction.

By 1877, the federal government's effort to rebuild the South ended. While some state governments had assumed responsibility for freedpeople's medical care, other freedpeople throughout the South continued to be denied support and admission to health facilities by local and state governments. Not having access to medical services during the Reconstruction period would, for a number of black Southerners, serve as the beginning of a system of discrimination that would only worsen in the 1880s and beyond.

"Having Our Say"

By the early 1880s, many of the changes that Reconstruction had promised had slowly receded. White Southerners regained more power and began to impose a number of restrictions that limited freedpeople's political, economic, and social gains. From the unlawful creation of voting restrictions that prevented freedpeople from participating in elections, to the widespread economic abuses that bankrupted black sharecroppers, to the white-hooded vigilantes who terrified and lynched black people at nightfall, white Southerners undermined the revolutionary gains made by freedpeople. In spite of this, there was a glimmer of change on the federal level.[43]

The creation of the pension system for Union soldiers expanded in 1890, offering more freedpeople the opportunity to articulate their medical conditions to the federal government and receive financial compensation. During the Civil War and the immediate postwar decades, soldiers and their families could apply for a pension only if the enlisted soldier's death or injury was a direct consequence of his military duty. In 1890, Congress passed a law that expanded the category of who could qualify for a pension. According to the new law, "Any veteran who could prove at least 90 days of service in the Civil War, an honorable discharge, and any disability not caused by 'vicious habits' but not necessarily caused by service in the War." This act also provided pensions to widows and dependents of veterans who were not killed during the war. In 1904, President Theodore Roosevelt issued an executive order granting pensions based on age: to any veteran over 62 years old. In 1907 and 1912 Congress passed acts granting pensions based on age and the time of service.[44]

The expansion of the pension system in 1890 meant federal officials had to consider individual symptoms and the unique conditions of each veteran's health, rather than deal with freedpeople's health collectively. To take just one example, long after the war ended, a bullet remained lodged in Joseph Abbott's body. His doctor detected that the bullet had pierced through his buttocks and was permanently wedged in his scrotum. Another doctor who weighed in on Abbott's case noted, "you can still feel the bullet." On a diagrammed illustration, the physician noted the entry point of the bullet and where it stayed for decades. Given that Abbott had been injured in the line of duty, he met the prerequisite to apply for a pension. Since the application required a medical diagnosis, Abbot's full medical history was taken. His application documents not only the bullet lodged in his scrotum, but also his heart condition (recorded as mitral valve); he suffered from hemorrhoids and rheumatism as well. If federal officials had doubted the veracity of the gunshot wound, then Abbott's claim about hemorrhoids, which were commonly reported among veterans, or his heart condition could have potentially qualified him for a pension.[45]

The expansion of pension qualifications came with a caveat. If pension applicants were not claiming injury or death, the physician who compiled the file was required to detail if the said ailments resulted from "vicious habits." In Abbott's case, the doctor assured federal authorities that Abbott's gunshot injury, hemorrhoids, heart problem, and rheumatic condition did not result from "vicious habits."

Although the government did not define "vicious habits," the nineteenth-century meaning connoted vice, depravity, and addiction to immorality.[46] The use of this term indicates that, despite the major transformations in terms of the federal government's relationship with black people's health, it continued to formulate a definition of health based on early nineteenth-century understandings that a person's health was the product of "habits." While the question of "vicious habits" was posed to both white and black veterans, the term carried deep moral connotations for black applicants whose health had historically been read through a prism of morality, hypersexuality, and inferiority.[47] The use of "vicious habits" also contradicted the medical profession's move toward more scientific explanations for the causes of sickness.

Abbott, along with other black veterans and their doctors, deftly managed to circumvent the finding of "vicious habits" causing sickness by filling their application files with copious details regarding the effects of many illnesses that commonly debilitated black veterans. Both Abbott and his physician explained how his injury and illnesses prevented him from working, thereby shifting the government's focus away from possible questions of moral and social character. By describing his desire to work, Abbott conveyed to government authorities that he embraced free labor ideology but was unable to endure grueling work conditions due to his health. Abbott and other black veteran applicants also underscored the labor that they performed as soldiers to illustrate to federal officials their military service and patriotic commitment to the nation.

Rheumatism was one common sign of the devastating effects painful wartime work had on soldiers' bodies long after the war ended. Nineteenth-century physicians used the term "rheumatism" (sometimes rheumatic fever) to encompass a wide range of illnesses, including overarching pain, aches, weakness, and fever. Some doctors believed that rheumatism resulted from exposure to cold weather, while others thought it was linked to cardiac problems.[48] Investigations of the disease's cause resulted in a number of physicians ruling out exposure as a precondition and arguing that bacteria was at the root of the illness. Yet, for many physicians, the cause, symptoms, and meaning of rheumatism remained debated well into the twentieth century.[49] In the context of late nineteenth-century pension applicants, the broad use of the term "rheumatism" worked in favor of black veterans, streamlining their symptoms into a recognizable idiom that federal officials recognized as worthy of federal compensation.[50]

In the end, Joseph Abbott was awarded a pension. Yet, many freedpeople who expressed their health claims to federal authorities were not as successful as Joseph Abbott. Throughout the late nineteenth and early twentieth centuries, hundreds of freedpeople wrote to the federal government requesting pensions for the injuries and illnesses that family members incurred during the war or for the death of their loved ones. Their applications were often unanswered or denied.[51] Approval might come after years of providing copious documentation and engaging in never-ending correspondence with pension personnel. It took seven years, for example, for Julia Allen to receive a pension from her husband's death in 1865. Her husband, Ellis Allen, suffering from remittent fever, had been admitted to Corps d'Afrique USA General Hospital in New Orleans in 1865. While in the hospital he died from what doctors defined as "Phthisis Pulmonalises," a form of tuberculosis. His pension application includes a letter of support from Henry Mudd, a Union soldier, who testified that Ellis Allen had served under Mudd's brother, the late Colonel Mudd. Mudd described Allen as "a good honest faithful boy and I am told did his duty well as a soldier." Mudd further claimed that Julia and her child were in great need of the assistance. During these years, it is unclear how Julia and her child survived the waves of economic depression and epidemic illnesses that plagued the postwar South. The federal government delayed Julia Allen's case because of what they defined as a questionable moral issue. According to the application, Julia stated that she remarried in 1869, four years after her husband's death. The federal government often interrogated female applicants about the validity of their marriages and demanded that freedwomen provide supporting evidence to validate their union. While federal officials often questioned the veracity of enslaved people's unions made before the war, they even doubted the legality of marriages made during and after the war that were sanctioned by the state.[52] Freedwomen were required to include letters from members of the community as well as an original marriage certificate. Ella Criddle, the wife of a black veteran, had pleaded unsuccessfully with federal officials to return her marriage certificate, which she had included as part of her pension application file. Even more poignant are Criddle's own words requesting relief:

> I am so in need of everything medicine food and everything why make me suffer like this when my husband suffered four his country and I his widow have to suffer for the want of nourishments and things. Do be reasonable have a heart and give a pension to an old woman who is much in need of the some for I have not many years to live and grant that you will lengthen my life a little longer that my last days may be glad ones that my husband served his country not in vain and that you will help his widow and not able to help herself.[53]

The pension system not only opened the door for freedpeople to define their health conditions to the federal government but also provided an outlet for freedwomen to articulate the ways in which the postwar period had left them in an utter state of poverty and despair. The pension system provided Criddle with a chance to describe to federal officials her suffering and, more important, to hold the government accountable to its promise to offer pensions for soldiers who had valiantly served the Union cause. While Criddle's husband had received a pension due to rheumatism and other health conditions, she was unable to collect the remaining portion of her husband's pension as a widow, due to the fact that she had been married before. From 1897 to 1919, she wrote dozens of letters, pleading with government officials for support and had furnished copious documentation of her marriage to Isaiah. Criddle's heartbreaking story of hoping to receive a pension so that her "last days may be glad ones" does, if only for the edifices of history, include a silver lining.

Criddle had formal and official recourse. There was a protocol that she could follow. There were people in power to whom she could write—the government had legislated that women, like her, many born as slaves, could, at least in theory, officially receive support from the state. A paper trail of documentation and correspondence developed behind her. This bureaucratic process alone signaled a major change: freedpeople were recognized as citizens, whose health conditions—theoretically—mattered to the federal government.

Freedmen's Hospital in Washington, DC

As former veterans and their families recorded their health conditions on the pages of pension applications, freedpeople living in and around the nation's capital expressed their medical concerns and needs to doctors at the last remaining Freedmen's Hospital, which was located in Washington, DC. Suspicions that local authorities would be unable to accommodate freedpeople, combined with Bureau doctors' perception of unfair medical treatment in municipal institutions in the city, impelled a handful of Bureau doctors to band together and maintain the hospital.[54]

In addition, federal authorities witnessed the daily need for a hospital to accommodate the needs of African-American migrants, who began arriving in Washington during the war and continued well into the 1890s. Congress decided to extend the contract for Freedmen's Hospital, in February 1872, and federal support of the hospital continued into the early twentieth century.[55]

Throughout the last decades of the nineteenth century, Freedmen's Hospital became an important institution that validated and listened carefully to freedpeople's individual medical concerns and demands. While many black people continued to turn to the hospital for food and shelter, doctors expanded their treatment of noncontagious health problems that affected individual freedpeople. Records from Freedmen's Hospital in the late nineteenth century demonstrate a range of health problems that black patients hoped doctors could cure, from one patient who had a "tongue covered with thick brown fur," to another who suffered epithelioma (which refers to a growth or tumor), to women seeking care for problems during pregnancy. Patients also articulated symptoms of illnesses such as asthma and uterine cancer that Bureau doctors ignored during Reconstruction as they focused on contagious diseases.[56]

Freedmen's Hospital doctors in DC also offered the more studied observations of freedpeople's health than any other group of physicians in the Reconstruction South. A few physicians at the DC hospital began conducting autopsies of freedpeople's bodies. While at the time a controversial medical practice (and it is unclear if family members consented to these investigations), the physicians who conducted these autopsies remained deeply committed to understanding the causes of diseases.[57] The published reports of black patient autopsies appear alongside similar reports written for white bodies, underscoring the medical examiners' efforts to understand the black body from a medical and scientific perspective.[58] The former practice of detached observation of black bodies was being slowly overtaken by careful investigation, based on what black patients articulated about their health to their doctors and what could be gleaned from the study of their bodies after death.[59] Many physicians employed at Freedmen's Hospital in DC were not the doctors of the antebellum South, who pruriently examined the black body to satisfy their interests, or doctors required to fulfill their Union contracts, but doctors who chose to serve the increasingly black community of the city. The work that these doctors performed must be understood through a more complex framework that avoids reducing all medical intervention into a tool of a dominant class or of the state.

Among the Bureau doctors who gathered in Washington and continued Freedmen's Hospital were Robert Reyburn, a leading, white administrator in the Medical Division; Alexander Augusta, a black physician from Savannah; Charles Purvis, a black physician who served throughout the South; and medical director Caleb Horner.[60] Not only did these doctors administer care, but they were also committed to training black physicians. As early as 1868, the Medical Department at Freedmen's Hospital, under the auspices of Howard University, admitted medical students. No longer would black men need to travel abroad to earn a medical degree or to face the often racist and hostile attitudes of the few elite universities that allowed black male students to matriculate in the nineteenth century. By 1907, there were more than 288 students in the program and more than 3,000 who had graduated from the medical school since its founding. "Nothing succeeds like success," penned Robert Reyburn, who served as the dean of the Medical School.[61] Freedmen's Hospital also admitted and graduated some of the country's first black female nurses.

The Medical Society in Washington even boasted about the success of the Freedmen's Hospital as an institution that provided treatment to local black residents. White doctors in DC discussed the vitality and importance of Freedmen's Hospital in the 1860s and 1870s, but often for reasons that many black patients would find offensive. Because white residents consistently commented on the unhealthy conditions of black migrants to the city, the hospital offered white residents security that sick and impoverished former slaves would be contained. Unlike in other regions, where African-American patients attempted to gain entrance into otherwise white-only hospitals, Freedmen's Hospital segregated black patients for medical treatment.[62]

Freedmen's Hospital in Washington was a living symbol of the voice that Reconstruction gave to black people for documenting their health and treating their ailments. Within the hospital, patients could be heard detailing their pain and narrating their illnesses, a marked change from the postwar years when doctors, former abolitionists, and federal officials spoke on their behalf. The radical changes that unfolded at Freedmen's Hospital in Washington, DC, reflected broader transformations throughout the nation, where freedpeople made claims on the state by articulating their health conditions and medical demands.

By the early 1870s, throughout much of the Reconstruction South, freedpeople, along with Bureau doctors, had deftly managed to convince state authorities to allow dependent freedpeople to enroll in municipal asylums and state hospitals designated for the "insane" and "indigent poor." The Civil Rights Act of 1866 combined with new state governments facilitated these changes. Bureau doctors along with freedpeople persuaded state officials in some locales to provide support in the form of vaccinations and quarantine facilities when epidemic outbreaks threatened black communities. Additionally, from the late 1860s to 1890, the pension system enabled black veterans and their families to explain to federal officials how the war devastated their health. By defining how the war led to illness, injury, and even death, freedpeople and their families requested financial compensation for the loss of their labor power or their loved ones. Many freedwomen gained a voice, as widows and wives of black veterans, to communicate to federal authorities how the postwar period, and the decades after, produced economic conditions and medical crises that made it difficult for their families to survive.

Conclusion

In the second year of the Civil War, Harriet Jacobs, an ex-slave turned author and reformer, boarded a train in Philadelphia and headed south. Like many others at the train station, Jacobs was on her way to Washington, DC, to support the war effort. Her mission was to visit freed slaves who had migrated to the capital and then to report on their condition to Northern reformers. In describing her journey to William Lloyd Garrison, the famed abolitionist and editor of *The Liberator*, she wrote, "I reached the capital without molestation." The morning after her arrival, she went to Duff Green's Row, a government refugee camp for newly emancipated slaves. "I found men, women and children all huddled together, without any distinction or regard to age or sex," she explained. "Some of them were in the most pitiable condition. Many were sick with measles, diptheria [*sic*], scarlet and typhoid fever. Some had a few filthy rags to lie on; others had nothing but the bare floor for a couch." She then described what appeared to be a hospital, yet "there was no matron" and "nothing at hand to administer to the comfort of the sick and dying." She added, "There were, some days, as many as ten deaths reported at this place in twenty-four hours." As she talked to a few of the patients and offered them clothing, blankets, and kind words, she soon realized that the military and government officials who had organized the camp probably did know how badly the freedpeople were suffering. As she explained to Garrison, "I felt that their sufferings must be unknown to the people." She went on to state that there was no one among the freedpeople "to soothe the last agonies of death." In army hospitals, chaplains and nurses comforted dying soldiers, offering them a prayer and a promise to contact their families, but, as Jacobs explained, there was no one by the sides of the sick and dying freed slaves. As she bent down to adjust a blanket or to offer a reassuring word, they looked up at her with "tearful eyes" that asked, "is this freedom?"[1]

This book has attempted to answer this question by interrogating the various economic, political, social, and medical forces that produced illness and shaped the meaning of freedom in the South. Emancipation left thousands of former slaves, like those Jacobs described at Duff Green's Row, sick and dying. Measles, fever, and diphtheria developed because of the overcrowded and unsanitary conditions at similar refugee camps, conditions that were exacerbated by the fact that freedpeople were forced to take refuge on "bare" floors and in "filthy rags."

The former bondspeople Jacobs encountered had entered into a war in which more soldiers died from disease than from battle. Many doctors in both urban and rural regions had knowledge of and experience in treating measles, typhoid fever, diphtheria, and other illnesses that plagued freed slaves, such as smallpox, dysentery, and pneumonia, but the war radically altered the scale and magnitude with which these illnesses spread. Doctors were forced to treat an increasing number of patients in hospitals where resources were scarce and approaching battles loomed over their operations.

The war produced large-scale migrations of soldiers, civilians, and freed slaves that transformed outbreaks of disease into epidemics. The freedpeople Jacobs met in Duff Green's Row more than likely migrated from the Upper South and other parts of the Confederate theater to Washington, DC, in the hope of achieving freedom. The North represented the so-called promised land and, while this remained theoretically true, in practice freedpeople were forced to live in camps that were dangerous and unhealthy. Additionally, in the time it took to reach their destination, ex-slaves often became sick because they lacked adequate clothing, food, and shelter during their journey.

Even if they did not become sick in transit, being forced to live in a confined camp made illness all the more likely, as doctors and sanitary reformers were unable to protect freedpeople against the invisible attack of germs. During the Civil War years, doctors and reformers lacked an understanding of bacteria and germ theory as the cause of disease, which rendered ineffective even their most fastidious efforts to combat its spread. Doctors argued over disease causation, methods of treatment, and the role of the physician. While the creation of the American Medical Association in 1846 attempted to resolve these conflicts, throughout the Civil War and Reconstruction, doctors continued to debate the efficacy of healing. The outbreak of cholera in 1866 further troubled doctors as some moved toward a nascent form of epidemiology to understand how cholera spread in the water, while others remained skeptical of this scientific approach and continued to draw on earlier understandings that emphasized social appearance, morality, and other subjective factors as the cause of disease transmission. When doctors treated freedpeople, however, they often failed to adopt these new scientific developments and instead blamed the spread of disease on black people's innate vulnerability to illness.

Beyond the lack of medical knowledge and the infighting among the medical community, freedpeople's illness and suffering stemmed from the simple fact that no one was prepared for the massive liberation of enslaved people. When politicians discussed the possibility that the war would lead to the destruction of slavery, they described the social, political, economic, and legal implications that this transformation would engender, failing to consider the basic questions of how freedpeople would survive. Where were former slaves to find shelter, clothing, food, and medical support? The existing social structures failed to offer any support during this period. The war shattered antebellum systems of medical care, both those organized by slaveholders and by enslaved people. Freedpeople's healing practices that sustained them during slavery offered little defense in the face of epidemic diseases and endemic poverty. On the local and state level, municipal hospitals and charitable organizations that tended to offer shelter to the dispossessed refused to enroll black patients, while on the federal level, the surgeon general was unprepared to respond to the massive disease problems that plagued the South. More to the point, before the Civil War, the federal government was a limited institution and did not recognize itself as responsible for the health and well-being of citizens.

The war had successfully dismantled the institution of slavery, but it raised a whole new set of questions about how society should be reorganized, of which public health was just one aspect. Jacobs's letter to Garrison reveals this problem. Due to the fact that there was no institutional structure to respond to the suffering and sickness of emancipated slaves, abolitionists initially attempted to fill the void. Jacobs's report of freedpeople "huddled together" in "the most pitiable condition" was published in *The Liberator*, a leading abolitionist newspaper, in an effort to raise money, clothing, and support for emancipated slaves.

As freedpeople waited in refugee camps for abolitionists to send food, clothing, and other forms of relief, military and federal authorities saw economic value in their bodies. Similar to antebellum slave pens where enslaved people were kept before they were auctioned and sold to a bidder in the Deep South, Duff Green's Row was used as a holding ground for ex-slaves, while the military and federal government determined how they would capitalize on the labor that their bodies could produce. The creation of the Medical Division of the Freedmen's Bureau sought to facilitate these efforts. The establishment of hospitals enabled military officials to separate the sick from those they deemed "able-bodied" and thereby employable. Hospitals then served as shelters for so-called dependent freedpeople, namely women, children, elderly, and the destitute. Military officials also subscribed to the free-labor theory that employment could cure the thousands of sick and dying freed slaves behind Union lines. According to their logic, if freedpeople were given employment opportunities they could become economically independent and self-supporting, and less susceptible to illness.

The creation of Freedmen's Hospitals, however, functioned at cross-purposes. While these institutions were designed to alleviate suffering and sickness, the federal government's fear that freedpeople would become dependent on the government for support limited the amount of aid given to these hospitals, which often left doctors without the adequate support, resources, and personnel to combat illness. Thus, when smallpox broke out in Washington in 1862 in a camp not too far from the barracks that Jacobs visited, the virus spread to the Upper South and other parts of Lower South and Mississippi Valley because there was no institutional structure in place to slow it down or stop it. Freedmen's Hospitals' inefficiencies and the government's refusal to create a permanent medical presence in the postwar South enabled smallpox, a virus that doctors knew how to contain and to treat, to continue to spread among freed slaves.

Since the eighteenth century, doctors understood how to contain a smallpox outbreak by using quarantine and even vaccinations and inoculations, but because of the chaos of the postwar years and the inadequacies of federal bureaucracy, doctors struggled to establish regulated areas for quarantine, let alone provide clean materials to replace infected clothing, bedding, and tents. Moreover, the massive migrations orchestrated by the federal government to develop a labor force led to additional dislocation among the freedpeople, which unintentionally led to the further spread of the virus across the postwar South. Many newspapers rationalized the outbreak of smallpox by propagating the medical fiction that smallpox only infected black people. In the meantime, members of Congress stormed the Congressional floor, claiming that the high rate of mortality among former slaves confirmed the proslavery parable that if left on their own freed slaves would go extinct. The smallpox epidemic thus resulted from specific factors connected to the exigencies of the war, freedpeople's dislocation, the limitations of free labor ideology, and the federal government's unorganized efforts to rebuild the South.

Since the Bureau first arrived in the South, the federal government had planned that it would only be a temporary institution and that state authorities would assume responsibility for freed slaves. Yet when emancipation began and freed slaves sought assistance from these institutions, the leaders of these asylums and almshouses then added the caveat that only "citizens" could be admitted. Since freed slaves were not citizens during the war and the early years of Reconstruction, they were denied admission and remained relegated to the villages, camps, and federally occupied plantations. By 1868, many Bureau doctors negotiated with state authorities to allow freed slaves who were mentally disabled to enter asylums. Once Bureau doctors made headway with this group of patients, they slowly expanded their efforts to transfer authority of all dependent freedpeople to state institutions. By allowing freedpeople to enroll in state institutions, federal officials made a critical claim about the meaning of citizenship: access to medical services became a benefit of citizenship. Before the Civil War, access to state and local asylums were open to the indigent poor and the dispossessed. That Bureau doctors eventually negotiated freedpeople's admission to state institutions powerfully reveals that access to basic relief became a benefit of citizenship.

More to the point, the broader experiences of freed slaves' political mobilization reveals the extent to which health formed a central part of freedpeople's campaigns for rights. Before the organized crusades for suffrage, freedpeople's activism focused on access to food, clothing, shelter, medicine, and burials for their family and kin. Former slaves' petitions to military officials for basic necessities and their collaboration with former abolitionists illustrate their early political recognition that access to basic health care was fundamental to their freedom. Many Northern reformers, like Jacobs, often spoke on behalf of former slaves, informing their sponsoring agencies of freedpeople's needs and requests. However, Jacobs's printed interaction with freedpeople in Washington is rare in its ability to capture the details of her visit. Often the military and even benevolent bureaucratic system did not directly encapsulate freedpeople's voices or direct requests; they simply wrote to their supervising officials about their need for medical support.

It is, therefore, necessary to imagine the various contexts in which freed slaves interacted and had conversations with military and former abolitionists to understand how freedpeople's political mobilization began with demands for basic necessities. When Jacobs wrote, "There were, some days, as many as ten deaths reported at this place in twenty-four hours," she may have known this based on her own observations but it is more than likely that freedpeople in the camp conveyed this to her. Her reference to "some days" as many as 10 die in a 24-hour period does not likely reflect the single day she spent in Duff Green's Row but is probably the result of discussions she had with former slaves, who told her of this astonishing mortality.

Freedpeople became the first to report on the death and disease that attacked their community, and they were first to track the mortality that devastated their families, friends, and community. Freed slaves, not the military or even the benevolent organizations, first realized that the war and emancipation produced enormous suffering, sickness, and death; the creation of hospitals that responded to illness and the federal mechanisms that reported on death came later. Freedpeople's observations informed military and benevolent organizations of these problems, which ultimately led to more formal, institutional responses.

The military had no vested interest in freedpeople's sickness and death and often rationalized it as an unavoidable, natural consequence of war, a phenomenon they had witnessed tearing through their own ranks. By constantly petitioning the military for support and cultivating the assistance of benevolent reformers to aid them, freed slaves ultimately made their health claims known to the government. Some freedmen, who enlisted in the army, used their status as newly minted soldiers to work through the bureaucratic channels of the military to gain support for their families but not all freedpeople knew soldiers who could petition the government on their behalf. As a result the early forms of black political mobilization unfolded on the ground, in the camps, among the sick and suffering.

Freedpeople's political mobilization for better health conditions led local, state, and, most of all, the federal government to consider the health of the emancipated population as part of their responsibility to rebuild the South. While many officials argued that the federal government should not provide support to freed slaves and fought vehemently to terminate the efforts of the Medical Division, the mere existence of this institution powerfully reveals the extent to which the federal government has had a role in addressing the health of the citizenry since the Civil War. Prior to the Civil War, local governments joined forces with physicians in response to the outbreak of epidemics, while state governments provided facilities for the poor and people with disabilities. Benevolent and charitable organizations also offered relief to those in need. For the most part, this medical assistance varied by location, and even then it was idiosyncratic.[2] The emancipation of four million slaves called into question the function of these institutions and demanded an institutional response beyond these otherwise diffused local and state measures.

The Medical Division illustrates that freed slaves were the first advocates of federal health care. They petitioned military and federal agents to help provide them with support to survive the exigencies of dislocation and war. Their actions mobilized the federal government to no longer be a limited institution and to expand its authority in ways that few imagined before the war. Many historians have explained how the emancipation of four million people led the federal government to articulate the meaning of citizenship; by examining how the federal government responded to the health conditions of emancipated slaves, this book reveals how health became embedded in the meaning of citizenship.

The presence of sick freedpeople in the South signifies many important themes in the history of the Civil War and Reconstruction. Homing in on freedpeople's health conditions shifts attention away from the definition of war as a story of military engagement and instead reveals the extent to which the war was about surviving the effects of battle. It reveals how freedpeople fought to obtain clothing, food, shelter, and medicine in order to survive a period that has been otherwise heralded as a glorious triumph. Destruction not only came in the shape of demolished buildings, bridges, homes, cities, towns, and land, but also shattered the social, political, economic, and legal structures that ordered, organized, and maintained this world. The notion of reconstruction tends to address this issue, in part, but it leaves out what it meant to survive this transition. What did it mean to live in a world where rebuilding efforts did not take place overnight? The major struggle for freedpeople during this period was waiting for change. Yet to describe freedpeople as idle risks portraying them as lacking initiative, independence, or agency, which counters the significant research that has restored freedpeople's history as individuals active, engaged, and in search of opportunity.

Nevertheless, one of the overarching objectives of this book has been to demonstrate that the many obstacles that freedpeople encountered could not have been overcome, regardless of how indefatigable or independent they were. The fact that the war produced the largest biological crisis of the nineteenth century meant that freed slaves entered into a world in which it was difficult to survive.[3] Moreover, the demands for their labor underlay virtually every federal policy drafted during this period, limiting their possibilities in freedom. The fact that the military restricted freed slaves to contraband camps cannot be overstated; this was the start of the process of emancipation that ultimately morphed into refugee lockdowns in which freedpeople were coerced to return to the plantation South as laborers. While freedpeople engaged in a grassroots movement of political organization that could be traced back to the antebellum period, power at the moment of emancipation remained in the hands of a president who believed that former slaveholders should be pardoned and be allowed to rebuild the South. So freedpeople had to wait until 1866 and 1867, when radical members of the Republican Party wrested power away from President Andrew Johnson and then began to make significant changes that led to the achievement of rights and citizenship.[4] The years of waiting for change were not simply an idle period of disappointment and delay, but an unexpectedly dark time that led to widespread sickness, mortality, and poverty.

Tracing the destruction of chattel slavery through the history of freedpeople's health provides deeper insight into the meaning of freedom, not just during Reconstruction but throughout American history. The narrative of American freedom implies triumph, celebration, and progress, but these terms leave little rhetorical room to tell the history of the thousands of freedpeople who were displaced from their homes, became sick, and died during the Civil War and Reconstruction. What does freedom mean if many people failed to survive the war and emancipation? If freedom cannot adequately articulate the ending of slavery, what can?

Thinking about the destruction of slavery as a "process of emancipation," a phrase borrowed from Latin American and Caribbean scholars, more effectively conveys the many complicated and nuanced ways that former slaves experienced the ending of slavery in the United States. This book charts how emancipation represented more of a beginning than an ending. Freedpeople's efforts to remain in good health in the face of war and massive dislocation punctuates this beginning. Freedpeople's health conditions reveal the gulf between the federal government's articulation of emancipation and the everyday lives of former slaves.[5]

On a quotidian level, the massive dislocation experienced by former slaves, who went in search of basic necessities, led to the outbreak of sickness and disease. Emancipated slaves interacted with Union army soldiers, which further intensified the spread of sickness. The diseases that infected the freedpeople, namely smallpox, fever, and cholera, were not endemic to the South but the result of specific factors caused by the war and the government's response to emancipation.

Freedpeople's health points to the disorder of the postwar period, particularly their massive displacement. Freedpeople traveled throughout the South in search of lost family members, jobs, education, and other opportunities, because the regions where they were liberated proved to be dead ends. During their journeys, they often became sick and died. Underscoring the factors that led to high mortality and sickness among freedpeople, *Sick from Freedom* argues that dislocation and disorder defined the experience of emancipation.

The archives exemplify the challenges of understanding freedpeople's experiences. Boxes labeled as containing relevant documents about freedpeople's health instead held administrative correspondence and statistical charts, with notes mostly about freedpeople's labor. Even when details about medical conditions were forthcoming, they did not offer a clear and dependable portrait of freedpeople's health. Bureau doctors did not often record health conditions in great detail but used terms such as suffering, sickness, and diseased. Even when they did reference smallpox or cholera specifically, it is unclear if they were actually seeing these illnesses or projecting their own understanding of disease onto freedpeople's bodies. Although one of the major tenets of the history of public health and medicine is to recognize the specificities of disease and not lump all illnesses into one anachronistic category, the sources are frequently not explicit about the illnesses nor do they articulate the particular aliments that affected freedpeople. While the use of the term "suffering" may appear vague and broad, it is often employed to capture a particular sentiment, mood, or tone that emanates from the documents under discussion. Despite the problematic nature of the sources and the imprecise and often unclear language employed during the nineteenth-century to discuss illness, this book reveals the extent to which epidemics, illnesses, and poverty defined the process of emancipation.

As the first book on the health conditions of emancipated slaves, this study cannot answer all of the questions that haunt this investigation but it can generate further research. How did freedpeople rationalize and explain the spread of disease? What were their religious and cultural responses to death? How did their healing practices allow many formerly enslaved people to survive the war? Did the federal government's response to freedpeople's health, especially their collection of data about disease and death in the postwar South, inform the discourse about eugenics later in the nineteenth century? How did the health policies that developed during Reconstruction influence the government's campaign to stop the spread of yellow fever in the late nineteenth century, which ultimately led to the creation of the Department of Health? How did the expansion of medical authority shape the government's response to health problems during the Spanish American War or the federal campaign against hookworm in Puerto Rico at the turn of the twentieth century? Is there a connection between Northern reformers' efforts to provide relief to emancipated slaves and the arrival of the philanthropic Rockefeller Foundation later in the twentieth century?

These questions remain unanswered, but so too do the actual medical conditions of former slaves. Much of the suffering and illness during this period did not get recorded or detailed since the army and the federal government did not systematically collect and tabulate this information during the war. Even when the federal government created the Medical Division during Reconstruction, hospitals were not established evenly throughout the South and there was not a federal system that documented freedpeople's health conditions. Any study of freedpeople's health will invariably be incomplete given the ways in which these bureaucratic structures operated and the mechanisms in place to gather information.

The prevailing logic is that Reconstruction failed due to the withdrawal of the federal government from the South in the 1870s, but as this book has demonstrated, the federal government did not solve problems that freedpeople faced in the 1860s. It had very specific ideas about the relationship between freedpeople's labor and health, which often limited their care and dictated governmental responses to medical crises, exacerbating the problems freed slaves faced. The government's organization of freedpeople into a labor force separated families, quarantined women and children to contraband camps, and summarily stripped African Americans of their cultural resources to care for their bodies.

The surviving fragments of evidence that have stood the test of time reveal the chaos and disorder of emancipation. Descriptions of the smallpox epidemic, as well as other disease outbreaks, often highlight the thousands of former slaves who made their way from plantations to cities, from refugee camps to farms, and from the South to the North. These snippets about former slaves as malnourished, sick, and dressed in ragged clothes, some depicted as half naked, exposing bruised and infected bodies, may say less about the severity of illness and the effects of emancipation and more about the conditions of slavery; those who encountered and described freedpeople were for the first time witnessing the effects of slavery. For those who had experienced slavery, such as Elizabeth Keckley, and had then witnessed the migration of former slaves to the nation's capital, these shreds of evidence reveal that sickness and disease made the road to freedom "rugged and full of thorns."[6]

Epilogue

Illness and Suffering: Unintended Consequences of Federal Reconstruction in the South and West

"We have examined the West from the perspective of Reconstruction. We have not seen Reconstruction from the perspective of the post-bellum West."

—Steven Hahn, *"Reconstruction and the American Political Tradition," Keynote Address, W.E.B. DuBois' Black Reconstruction in America 75th Anniversary Symposium (2010)*

While historians have rightly outlined the many complicated reasons why Reconstruction ended, ranging from the failure of military occupation to the financial crisis of 1873 to the election of President Hayes, Reconstruction, in many ways, did not end in 1877; instead, it drifted west. After leaving the post-war South, many of the military leaders, Bureau agents, and benevolent reformers never went back home to the North but were reassigned by the federal government to respond to the crisis of Native American resettlement.[1]

By 1865, Northern victory in the Civil War, combined with the apparent success of free labor among freedpeople in the South, offered the federal government a model for how to respond to a displaced population.[2] The Civil War had greatly expanded the reach of federal authority throughout the country by assigning U.S. Army soldiers to police the Western territories. While Army officials had established a permanent presence in the Southwest after the War of 1812 and Mexican War, the Civil War further increased this military presence. More important, the federal government came in contact with the lives of the people who populated these regions—a turning point in the expansion of federal authority. After the Civil War, Union soldiers established federal camps and fortresses throughout the continental United States from Northern Florida to California to the Pacific Northwest to the Dakotas and Montana and even to Alaska.

Similar to the ways in which the federal government and the U.S. Army transported newly emancipated slaves to regions in need of laborers, by September
1865, military authorities accelerated the process of moving Native Americans
to reservations to become agricultural laborers. While the reservation system
officially predated Reconstruction by a decade, the establishment of reservations intensified throughout the West after the Civil War. Before the war, many
Native Americans under U.S. government control were either captives of unfair
treaties or refugees from military conflict; afterward, the federal government
began using the military to incorporate them into a labor force.[3]

The federal government's idea of establishing a camp that would be powered
by free labor and placed under military control developed during Reconstruction. In the late 1860s and 1870s, skirmishes and war broke out between Indians
and white settlers in the West. At the conclusion of these battles, in the cases
where the federal army claimed victory over Native Americans, the question
arose about how to respond to the social and political status of Native Americans
displaced by war. In response to this dilemma, President Ulysses S. Grant
increased the number of reservations throughout the West. Thus, the reservation system became the government's panacea for the problem of Indian war
refugees, similar to the contraband camps and Freedmen's Villages created in
response to former slaves. Both the contraband camp and the reservation system
enabled the federal government to develop a labor force by placing people in a
regulated area, where the military could draw on their labor as needed. The
common interpretation is that the government needed to organize freedpeople
into a labor force in the South, whereas in the West, the government needed to
clear Native peoples from the land in order to develop the region. A closer examination of these processes reveals that the contraband camps and reservations
both served as holding grounds for agricultural laborers.

The demise of the Freedmen's Bureau in the late 1860s enabled the federal
government to devote money, manpower, and other resources to promote
"civilization" among Native Americans. It is not a coincidence that Congress
approved the Indian Appropriation Act on April 10, 1869, which allocated more
than two million dollars to assist in the transition of Native Americans from "nomadic life" to reservations, just as the Freedmen's Bureau began to collapse
throughout the South. By that time the government had received reports from
Freedmen's Bureau agents suggesting that Reconstruction had succeeded.[4]
According to these accounts, mortality rates had declined, many freedpeople
had been employed, suffrage had been extended to freedmen, and the care of
destitute freedpeople had been transferred to newly formed state governments.

While the presence of Native Americans had haunted the federal government
since the founding of the Republic, the tensions between the government and
Native groups heightened in the decades leading up to the Civil War as white

settlers pushed farther into the interior of the country. Battles began popping up in the West between Native Americans and the U.S. Army. In 1862 on the Minnesota frontier, the federal government broke its promise with the Santee Indians and did not pay an annuity to the Indians for land that they bought from them. Compounding matters, white settlers who lived in the region exploited the Santee by taking advantage of their dependent status on government annuities and charging them outrageous sums of money for basic necessities. In response to this unfair treatment that left hundreds of Native peoples starving and sick, four Santee Indians attacked and killed five white settlers in August 1862. This attack motivated other Santee Indians to attack neighboring white settlers, which eventually led to the Dakota War, also referred to as Little Crow's War. O. O. Howard, leader of the Freedmen's Bureau, claimed that the Santee uprising was a direct response to the Civil War. "Previously to this, Little Crow, seeing how much our garrisons had been weakened to supply the wants of the Civil War, had carefully planned a hostile rising on the part of the Indians with a view to pillage and the driving back of new settlements."[5] A bloody war ensued between the Santee and white settlers, which did not end until the U.S. Army intervened and forced the Santee to surrender. According to one report, 700 people were massacred in this war.[6] Once U.S. officials became involved, they ordered 300 Santee to be executed. In a surprise twist, President Lincoln commuted the sentences of the majority of Indians to imprisonment instead and reduced the number of those to be hanged from 300 to 38. On December 26, 1862, a week before the Emancipation Proclamation was issued, the federal government hanged 38 Santee Indians, making it the largest mass execution in U.S. history.[7]

From the end of 1862 to the conclusion of the war in April of 1865, Indian refugees of the Dakota War remained under tight military surveillance. Union victory in the South emboldened military officials to believe that they had the capacity and knowledge to handle other refugee populations throughout the country. After the Dakota War, government officials were unsure how to manage the Indians, other than to keep them under strict military control. Three years later, the Northern victory in the Civil War, combined with the apparent success of free labor among freedpeople in the South, emboldened Union and federal officials to use the Reconstruction South as a template to develop federal policy for Native American refugees in the West. In September 1865, military authorities began the process of moving the refugees of the Dakota War from the Minnesota frontier to reservations in Crow Creek and Yanktown, Dakota, to become agricultural laborers.

The federal government's development of Reconstruction programs offered a model for managing the once diverse nations of tribes and getting Native peoples to work for the benefit of the Republic. While the government had developed treaties with Native groups before the war, the passage of the Indian Appropriation

Act of March 3, 1871, meant that Congress no longer recognized Indians as part of a tribe or nation and would not make treaties with Native American groups. This Act instead defined Native peoples as individuals and as "wards." Consequently, the government placed Native peoples on reservations where they would begin to cultivate and to ultimately own their own land. This strategy gave the federal government unfettered access to land in the West. The government planned for Native Americans to become self-supporting through agricultural labor and no longer depend on hunting and fishing for their subsistence. As one agent explained in 1869, "If these Indians are encouraged and assisted in this undertaking it . . . would encourage others and do much toward promoting industry and civilization among their various tribes in this Superintendancy."[8]

Throughout the American West, military officials, working alongside agents of the Office of Indian Affairs, used military surveillance to force those opposed to agricultural production to work as farm laborers, as in the postwar South. The government also attempted to construct schools within reservations in order to educate Native peoples in Euro-American traditions and beliefs. It drew on Northern religious and benevolent groups for help with the plans of "civilizing" Native Americans through schools on reservations. President Grant even requested recommendations from Northern reformers when he appointed agents and commissioners for the Office of Indian Affairs.[9] In some cases, the same Northern reformers who worked in the South moved to the West to continue their work. For example, novelist Helen Hunt Jackson described in a letter to federal authorities how a Pennsylvania woman who had taught the freedpeople had organized a school for roughly 30–40 pupils in Southern California in the early 1880s.[10]

In fact, the same type of personnel that had labored alongside freedpeople in the rebuilding of the South was employed on reservations throughout the West. Northern reformers, the Union Army, doctors, and federal agents employed by the Freedmen's Bureau constituted the four major groups in the South. The federal government replicated this bureaucratic structure by relying on the support of Northern reformers, the military, physicians, and federal agents to work for what would become the Bureau of Indian Affairs.[11]

The most significant group to transfer to the West was the military leadership. Both the Freedmen's Bureau and the Office of Indian Affairs grew out of the War Department; O. O. Howard, the famed leader of the Freedmen's Bureau, was appointed to head the Department of the Columbia in the West in 1874 when the Bureau shut down. While in the West, Charles Erskine Scott Wood, Howard's chief secretary, often wrote with great admiration about Howard's ability to settle contentious conflicts between the federal government and Native peoples and his efficient resolutions of the thorny questions of land ownership and resettlement.[12] Howard undoubtedly drew on his experience resettling freedpeople in the South. He was not alone, as other military and federal agents transferred their skills to the West.

More important, the program of Reconstruction offered federal authorities a template for establishing a free labor economy in the West, which was, in fact, the government's original plan since the Western territories first entered the Union. Since the 1820s, the sectional crisis revolved around the question of whether a free labor or a slave labor economy would be implemented in the Western territories. Once the North won the war, the government exploited freedpeople's displacement in order to transform the Southern slave economy into a free labor economy and turned their sights on the West. By making Native American refugees into agricultural producers, the government transformed various regions in the West into free labor markets. Reservations in turn resembled a hybrid of contraband camps, which housed government refugees, and postwar plantation economies, governed by Freedmen's Bureau officials and the government, that fostered free labor.[13]

By placing freedpeople in federally restricted areas, military officials could then easily draw on this pool of workers when labor opportunities arose. Just as organizing freedpeople into a labor force became a way for the federal government to respond to the confusion and chaos that the war and emancipation sparked, it did so in response to the Indian wars and the displacement of Native Americans. As Ferdinand Andrews, editor of *The Traveler*, noted regarding the resettlement of Navajo war refugees to reservations in the 1867, "The abolition of peonage, which was finally consummated by the act of Congress of March 22, 1867 afforded the faithful Indians an opportunity to resume their pledges, which they did by embracing Gen. Carleton's order, surrendering themselves as prisoners and submitting to be transported more than 400 miles from their native valleys and mountains to a place selected for them by General Carleton, called the Basque Redondo, on the Pecos river. Here, they have been held ever since guarded and maintained as prisoners at an immense expense with continued and almost fruitless attempts under the direction of the War Dept to settle down quietly and contented by in the pursuit of agricultural and other self-supporting occupations."[14]

As in the Reconstruction South, Army officials failed to take into consideration how the sheer movement of Native Americans from one location to another would result in severe health problems. Tens of thousands suffered from starvation, others became infected with tuberculosis and smallpox, and even more died of unidentified illnesses.[15] As one federal official explained, "The fault is not with the people—the white settlers, who are only accepting the invitation of the laws to settle the country—but with the Government and the Congress, which has failed to establish any practical mode of relief and means for the settlement of the Indians."[16]

More than 1,300 Santee Indians were sent on two separate steamboats to the Crow Creek reservation in Dakota after Little Crow's War, but the voyage proved dangerous for all those involved. On one of the steamboats, soldiers confined the Santee to the bowels of the ship, where it was densely crowded and many could not even breathe. A U.S. Army official later defined the lower decks as "suffocating." The lack of fresh air, compounded by the Army not feeding the Santee for more than 10 days, led to more than 16 deaths on the ship. When the Santee finally arrived at their destination, many were suffering from fever, dysentery, and malnutrition. According to one report filed by an Army officer, roughly three to four Indians died each day; the same report estimated that more than 300 Santee had died within the first six months of resettlement on the reservation.[17]

Illness got articulated in numerous military descriptions of starvation and death among Indians recorded by the federal government. As a young Indian boy from the Soboba Indian Tribe in San Jacinto Valley, California, explained in a letter written to the President of the United States, "Many of the people are sick, and sometimes I am afraid that we are all going to die."[18]

Postbellum Southern plantations and the reservation system forced both freedpeople and Indians into a position of poverty and dependence that made each group more susceptible to sickness and death. Forced to live under federal control, neither of these groups could draw on their past experiences or cultural traditions of survival, such as cultivating their own vegetable gardens or even hunting beyond the borders of the camps.[19] In New Mexico, the Jicarillas, who numbered close to a thousand and were, as some observers noted, "the poorest of the Western tribes," complained "that they have been deprived of their hunting grounds and the means whereby they have been accustomed to sustain themselves." According to one report, "They are compelled to rely almost entirely upon government rations; and these they think are scantily supplied."[20] A federal agent working for the Office of Indian Affairs further noted, "The Jicarillas say that they must have bread to eat, and if they are not fed, they will be under the necessity of depredating upon the cattle and crops of the citizens, which they do not want to do if it can be avoided."[21]

The correspondence between officials at the Office of Indian Affairs and authorities in Washington closely resembles that between Bureau agents and federal officers regarding the distribution of basic necessities in the South. According to one military telegram in 1871, an Army officer desperately asked, "I have no arrangement by Indian Department to feed Indians at Fort Lorraine; to what extent am I to feed them?"[22] In general, supplies were not delivered on time, rations arrived late or not at all, and the government lacked the administrative structure to adequately support populations of people they placed in positions of dependence. Describing the dependent condition of Native Americans forced to resettle on reservations, one government official wrote in the early 1870s, "Prostitution, robbery, drunkenness, and murder have been common results in the last few years, where peace reigned before. Misery, disease, and death are the impending fate of these wretched creatures, if suffered longer live the life of forced vagrancy."[23]

When federal officials developed plans for developing a free labor system among Native Americans, they did not consider the possible setbacks that would thwart agricultural production. As they had in the South, the government naively assumed that by providing nominal support to Native peoples, agriculture would flourish and economic self-reliance would naturally ensue. A federal agent stationed in California in 1866, for example, commented on the prospect of developing a system of free labor in the West that eerily resembled the rhetoric of dependency that circulated throughout the Reconstruction South: "It is the policy of this department to make Indians self-sustaining. Those in California have reservations that are represented as being fertile, and producing abundant crops, and it is thought that with proper management and due economy the expense to the government of sustaining them would not be considerable; that nothing but clothing and agricultural implements need to be purchased. It is certainly very strange that it should ever become necessary to incur an indebtness in taking care of them."[24]

The construction of reservations, however, did not promote independence and economic autonomy among Indians. The land assigned to Indians was usually undesirable, drought-ridden with poor soil and little access to water. Reservations robbed Indians of drawing on traditional modes of survival and left Native peoples with no choice but to beg the Indian Agency for support. As one Native American chief explained to O. O. Howard, "Our hunting season is past. A great many of our people are sick for being hungry. We may die because you will not pay us; we may die, but if we die we will leave our bones on the ground where our great Father may see where his Dakota children died."[25] The reservation produced economic conditions that left Native groups reliant on unproductive farms and without alternate sources of income or food.

Confronted with sick and dying Native Americans, the federal government ordered Native groups to be relocated. It forced the Santee to be moved to Dakota without considering the health problems such mandatory movement would create. During the journey of less than two weeks, adequate food and clothing were not procured for the group of more than a thousand people, who were already suffering from starvation, and many consequently became sick and died.[26] O. O. Howard explained that "some 1500 of the old men, women, and children died of exposure, and those who survived were obligated to eat their horses and dogs."[27]

The government took responsibility for directing the migrations of Native people since they feared their unfettered movement in the West, just as the military had feared freedpeople's unsupervised migrations during the Civil War and

Reconstruction might cause conflict with white inhabitants. In both regions, federal officials also worried that the unsupervised movement of refugees threatened the success of a free labor economy.[28] In response to the movement of Native Americans, one military official noted, "There is no doubt that the policy which tends most strongly to entice the Indians to abandon their wild and wandering mode of life, and come on the reservations and make their permanent abode there is the best policy for the Indians and for the white people."[29]

Both freedpeople and Native Americans became sick and died as the federal government attempted to establish an agricultural economy powered by free labor in the South and in the West. In an effort to ensure the labor productivity of each group, the government began to provide medical treatment and to establish hospitals. While the federal government laid plans for a medical presence, it accumulated voluminous materials about the health conditions of both populations. Doctors recorded mortality rates, tracked the spread of infections, and reported on the types of illness and epidemics that plagued patients. A federal bureaucracy emerged that documented, monitored, and addressed Native Americans' and freedpeople's health, thereby expanding into ordinary people's lives in a way that no one had imagined before the Civil War.

NOTES

Abbreviations

AHS	Alexandria Historical Society
BRFAL	Bureau of Refugees, Freedmen, and Abandoned Lands
DU	Perkins Library, Duke University
FSSP UMD	Freedmen and Southern Society Project at the University of Maryland
HL	Houghton Library, Harvard University
HUN	Huntington Library, Pasadena, California
HSP	Historical Society of Pennsylvania
LCP	Library Company of Philadelphia
LOC	Library of Congress
LR	Letters Received
LS	Letters Sent
MHS	Massachusetts Historical Society
NARA	National Archives and Records Administration
NYAM	New York Academy of Medicine
NYPL	New York Public Library
RG	Record Group
VHS	Virginia Historical Society
VSP	Valley of the Shadow Project, University of Virginia

Introduction

1. Jos. R. Putnam to Brig. Gen. W. D. Whipple, January 30, 1865, quoted in Ira Berlin and Leslie Rowland, eds., *Families and Freedom: A Documentary History of the African-American Kinship in the Civil War Era* (New York: New Press, 1997), 77–78.
2. After Lincoln approved the enlistment of black men as soldiers, they were eventually identified as casualties. Yet, when military officials and physicians tallied the numbers of black troops who died or were injured, they often appeared in segregated lists. Casualties often meant "white" soldiers. If and when black people were identified as casualties, it was often with the adjective "black" or "Negro" placed before the noun. This rhetorical move exemplifies what historian Evelyn Brooks Higginbotham describes in her analysis of language and the implied connotations of racial making. See Evelyn Brooks Higginbotham, "African-American Women's History and the Metalanguage of Race," *Signs* 17 (Winter 1992): 251–74. For lists of black casualties, see Joseph K. Barnes, *The Medical and Surgical History of the War of the Rebellion, 1861–65*, prepared in accordance with acts of Congress, Surgeon-General's Office (Washington,

DC: GPO, 1875–88); Joseph K. Barnes, U.S. Surgeon General's Office, *Circular No. 6* (Washington, DC: GPO, November 1, 1865). J. H. Baxter, U.S. War Dept., *Statistics, Medical, and Anthropological of the Provost-Marshal-General's Bureau delivered from the Records of the Examination for Military Service in The Armies of the United States during the Late War of the Rebellion,* vol. 1 (Washington, DC: GPO, 1875). For a thorough analysis of American cultural responses to the exorbitant death tolls that the Civil War produced, see Drew Gilpin Faust, *This Republic of Suffering: Death and the American Civil War* (New York: Knopf, 2008).

3. Civil War medical historians have documented that more soldiers died from disease than battle, Paul E. Steiner, *Disease in the Civil War: Natural Biological Warfare in 1861–1865* (Springfield: Charles C. Thomas, 1968). Ira Berlin et al., *Freedom's Soldier's: The Black Military Experience* (New York: Cambridge University Press, 1992), 633–55. Frank R. Freemon, *Gangrene and Glory: Medical Care During the American Civil War* (Madison, NJ: Fairleigh Dickinson University Press, 1998), 221–28. Also see Kathryn S. Meier, "No Place for the Sick: Nature's War on Civil War Soldiers' Mental and Physical Health in the 1862 Peninsula and Shenandoah Valley Campaigns," *Journal of the Civil War Era* 1, no. 2 (June 2011): 176–206.

4. Gilbert E. Govan and James W. Livingood, "Chattanooga Under Military Occupation, 1863–1865," *Journal of Southern History* 17, no. 1 (February 1951): 23–47. In the following pages, I draw on this article in order to offer a descriptive account of Chattanooga during the American Civil War.

5. During the early years of the Civil War, there was not a military protocol to tabulate the number of former slaves who became sick or died, let alone provide a detailed explanation for individual cases of mortality. See, for example, M.K. Hogan to C.W. Horner, November 23, 1865, Raleigh, N.C., e. 2535, L.S., RG 105, NARA.

6. Govan and Livingood, "Chattanooga Under Military Occupation, 1863–1865," 47.

7. Ibid., 27.

8. Ibid., 27.

9. Ibid., 46.

10. Nell Irvin Painter has provocatively posited the notion of "soul murder" in order to explain the emotional, physical, and psychological violence that enslaved people endured in the antebellum South. Since there is very little record to archivally document these traumas, Painter turns to modern psychology to offer a conceptual frame to examine these experiences. Also, deeply concerned with the problem of the archives, Saidiya Hartman meditates on the inability of narrative to capture the experience of enslaved women, and the violence that participated in the construction of the archive and the silencing of enslaved people. Additionally, Jennifer Morgan considers the structure of the archives and the inability of these institutions to document the people who often built them. Nell Irvin Painter, "Soul Murder and Slavery: Toward a Fully Loaded Cost Accounting," in her *Southern History Across the Color Line* (Chapel Hill: University of North Carolina Press, 2002), 15–39; Saidiya Hartman, "Venus in Two Acts," *Small Axe* 12, no. 2 (June 2008): 1–14; Jennifer Morgan, "Why I Write," in *Why We Write: The Politics and Practice of Writing for Social Change,* ed. Jim Downs (New York: Routledge, 2006), 39–48.

11. See David Blight, *Race and Reunion: The Civil War in American Memory* (Cambridge, MA: Belknap Press of Harvard University Press, 2001).

12. Based on the surviving record and the methods by which government officials collected data during this period, it is impossible to obtain an accurate number of freed slaves who were sick, died, or even received medical assistance during the Civil War and Reconstruction periods. To begin with, no one during the early years of the Civil War, especially in 1862, kept an accurate count of mortality among the population of ex-slaves; there was not a protocol to allow ex-slaves to enter Union lines—let alone a system to count how many were sick and how many died. I explain this point in more detail in chapter 1. Even when the federal government created the Medical Division of the Freedmen's Bureau in 1865, this occurred after many freedpeople became sick, suffered, and died in 1863–1865. I explain this point in more detail in chapter 3. The Bureau was unable to gain an accurate

sense of how many freedpeople were sick because Bureau doctors were not systematically and uniformly stationed throughout the South. I explain this point in more detail throughout the book, especially in chapters 3 and 4. Furthermore, the surviving evidence tends to contradict itself. O. O. Howard, the Freedmen's Bureau leader, provides one estimate that over 45,000 freedmen received medical aid, but records by doctors, Bureau agents, and benevolent reformers often report much higher numbers. Additionally, reports from Howard, as well as Bureau doctors and officers stationed throughout the Reconstruction South, provide details that thousands of freedpeople received relief such as food, clothing, and shelter. Yet in the context of the Bureau's categorization of "destitution" and "sickness," there is little distinction between providing formal medical treatment in response to sickness or offering assistance in response to poverty. Consequently, statistics about relief given to destitute freedpeople should also be tabulated as part of the medical interventions that the federal government orchestrated. I explain this point in more detail in chapter 5. Oliver Otis Howard, *Autobiography of Oliver Otis Howard*, vol. 2 (New York: Baker and Taylor, 1907), 259–60. O. O. Howard, *Report of Brevet Major General O. O. Howard to the Secretary of War, October 20, 1869* (Washington, DC: GPO, 1869). For Bureau agents' and doctors' reports, see U.S. War Dept., BRFAL, *Laws in Relation to Freedmen*, 39th Cong., 2nd sess., Senate Executive Document, no. 6 (Washington, DC: GPO, 1866–67).

13. This logic persists today; historians fear that any indictment of freedom would in some way substantiate a claim put forth by slaveholders 200 years ago. The first references of emancipated slaves as sick appeared in twentieth-century accounts of the Civil War and Reconstruction. William Archibald Dunning, a historian at Columbia University, trained a cohort of graduate students, many of whom studied the Reconstruction South and portrayed freed slaves as sick in their research. For decades, this interpretation of freedpeople as incapable of self-government, the culprits of Reconstruction's demise, and diseased and dying, persisted as the leading interpretation of the period—despite the publication of W. E. B. Du Bois's landmark study, *Black Reconstruction* (1935), which portrayed freedpeople as political agents negotiating the terms of emancipation. By the 1960s, the civil rights movement had inspired scores of historians to challenge Dunning's findings—which led to the excavation of powerful documentary evidence that freed slaves were, in fact, active political agents in the reconstruction of the nation. Taking their cue from Du Bois, historians from Louis Gerteis and Eric Foner to Elsa Barkley Brown and to, most recently, Steven Hahn have persuasively shattered the Dunning School interpretation by proving how freedpeople gained political rights, battled over employment contracts, and established schools throughout the postwar South. While the interpretation of African Americans throughout U.S. history finally began to change, historians, nevertheless, seem to have treated nineteenth-century medical sources simply as products of either a racist medical system or of a bigoted historiography, or both. In their stead, this new generation of social historians promoted an image of freed slaves as autonomous individuals whose embrace of freedom miraculously came with little cost to their physical selves. These historians, thus, constructed an image of freed slaves as robust, independent, and devoid of health problems. In their defense, if these historians drew attention to the sickly and suffering condition of former slaves in the historiography, they risked undermining the emerging image of freedpeople in the 1970s as powerful, independent actors. As a result, references to freed slaves as sick and dying literally vanished from the historiography, despite the historiographical recognition that the Civil War period produced an alarming death rate that wiped out Northern and Southern infantries. That said, Du Bois included passing references to former slaves as "suffering." Also on the subject of suffering, Leon Litwack has richly documented how the aftermath of slavery led to enormous suffering among emancipated slaves. This book differs from the aforementioned by specifically focusing on illness and by examining how free labor ideology and federal policies contributed to the spread of disease during the Civil War and Reconstruction. William Archibald Dunning, *Reconstruction, Political and Economic, 1865–1877* (New York: Harper and Brothers, 1907); W. E. B. Du Bois, *Black Reconstruction* (New York: Russell and Russell,

1935); Louis Gerteis, *From Contraband to Freedman: Federal Policy Toward Southern Blacks 1861–1865* (Westport, CT: Greenwood Press, 1973); Leon Litwack, *Been in the Storm So Long: The Aftermath of Slavery* (New York: Vintage, 1979); Eric Foner, *Reconstruction: America's Unfinished Revolution, 1863–1877* (New York: Harper Collins, 1988); Elsa Barkley Brown, "To Catch a Vision of Freedom: Reconstructing Southern Black Women's Political History, 1865–1880," in *Unequal Sisters: A Multicultural Reader in U.S. Women's History*, 3rd ed., ed. Ellen DuBois and Vicki Ruiz (New York: Routledge, 2000), 124–46; Barkley Brown, "Womanist Consciousness: Maggie Lena Walker and the Independent Order of Saint Luke," *Signs: Journal of Women in Culture & Society* 14, no. 3 (Spring 1989): 610–33; Steven Hahn, *A Nation Under Our Feet: Black Political Struggles in the Rural South from Slavery to the Great Migration* (Cambridge, MA: Harvard University Press, 2005).

14. On the Crimean War, see UK, *Hansard's Parliamentary Debates*, 3rd ser., vol. 304 (1869), 721; Ed. M. Wrench, "The Lessons of the Crimean War," *The British Medical Journal* 2, no. 2012 (July 22, 1899): 205–8. On the Cuban insurrection, see Matthew Smallman-Raynor and Andrew D. Cliff, "The Spatial Dynamics of Epidemic Diseases in War and Peace: Cuba and the Insurrection against Spain, 1895–98," *Transactions of the Institute of British Geographers* 24, no. 3 (1999): 331–32. For an excellent overview of how war accelerated the high outbreak of disease during the early modern period and especially in the nineteenth century, see Clara E. Councell, "War and Infectious Disease," *Public Health Reports (1896–1970)* 56, no. 12 (March 21, 1941): 547–73. On the Russo-Turkish War, see ibid., 549.

15. Eric Foner notes how American emancipation was unique in the context of the collapse of slavery in other slave societies in the Atlantic world. Former slaves in the United States managed to be elected to Congress while political changes took longer in Jamaica and Cuba, for example. See Eric Foner, *Nothing But Freedom: Emancipation and Its Legacy* (Baton Rouge: Louisiana State University Press, 1983).

16. For a meticulous explication of the term "soundness," see Sharla Fett, *Working Cures: Healing, Health and Power on Southern Slave Plantations* (Chapel Hill: University of North Carolina Press, 2002), 15–35.

17. Bondspeople's health and bodies were sites of violence during slavery. Slaveholders punished enslaved people by using various diuretics and deprived slaves of food, clothing, shelter, and medical care. Enslaved people's health also became a site of resistance, as many enslaved people feigned violence in an effort to defy coerced labor. See Fett, *Working Cures*, 169–92.

18. The calculation that one million freedpeople received medical aid is a modest estimate. As I explain in other sections of the book, the number of freedpeople who required medical aid far exceeded the number of people who received it. Moreover, the national tallies of sick freedpeople often failed to accurately count all those in need; this system of accounting proved inadequate to capture the medical aid that doctors provided at the local and state levels. For a general statistical overview of the Bureau's work, see Paul Skeels Peirce, *The Freedmen's Bureau: A Chapter in the History of Reconstruction* (Iowa City: University, 1904), 93. Some Bureau doctors also explained that there was no system that counted the number of sick or dead freedpeople. M. K. Hogan to C. W. Horner, November 23, 1865, Raleigh, N.C., e. 2535, L.S., RG 105, NARA.

19. I profited enormously from Ann Marie Davis's stunning research on the origin and use of nosological reports by British imperial forces in nineteenth-century Japan. See Ann Marie Davis, "Bodies, Numbers, and Empires: Representing 'The Prostitute' in Modern Japan (1850–1912)" (PhD diss., University of California, Los Angeles, 2009), 6–66. For a historical analysis of statistical classifications in clinical medicine, see Ulrich Trohler, "Quantifying Experience and Beating Biases: A New Culture in Eighteenth-Century British Clinical Medicine," in *Body Counts: Medical Quantification in Historical and Sociological Perspective*, ed. Gerald Jorland, Annick Opinel, and George Weisz (Montreal: McGill-Queen's University Press, 2005), 19–50.

20. Before the advent of germ theory, see Charles E. Rosenberg, *The Cholera Years: The United States in 1832, 1849, and 1866* (Chicago: University of Chicago Press, 1962), Bruno Latour,

The Pasteurization of France (Cambridge, MA: Harvard University Press, 1988), John Warner, *The Therapeutic Perspective: Medical Practice, Knowledge, and Identity in America* (Princeton, NJ: Princeton University Press, 1997). After the discovery of the microbe and the subsequent reliance on laboratory science, see Judith Walzer Leavitt, *Typhoid Mary: Captive to the Public's Heath* (Boston: Beacon Press, 1996), Nancy Tomes, *The Gospel of Germs: Men, Women and the Microbe in American Life* (Cambridge, MA: Harvard University Press, 1999).

21. Warner, *Therapeutic Perspective.*

22. John Warner, *Against the Spirit of System: The French Impulse in Nineteenth-Century American Medicine* (Baltimore: Johns Hopkins University Press, 2003).

23. Margaret Humphreys, *Intensely Human: The Health of the Black Soldier in the American Civil War* (Baltimore: Johns Hopkins University Press, 2008).

24. Todd L. Savitt and James Harvey Young, eds., *Disease and Distinctiveness in the American South* (Knoxville: University of Tennessee Press, 1998); Ronald L. Numbers and Todd L. Savitt eds., *Science and Medicine in the Old South* (Baton Rouge: Louisiana State University Press, 1989); Steven M. Stowe, *Doctoring the South: Southern Physicians and Everyday Medicine in the Mid-Nineteenth Century* (Chapel Hill: University of North Carolina Press, 2003).

25. With few exceptions, the historiography on race and medicine centers on either the antebellum period or the late nineteenth and early twentieth centuries. There has been a gap regarding the mid-nineteenth century, which this book attempts to address. On the antebellum period, see the pioneering work of Todd Savitt, *Medicine and Slavery: The Diseases and Health Care of Blacks in Antebellum Virginia* (Champaign: University of Illinois Press, 1981); and Fett, *Working Cures.* Regarding the late nineteenth and early twentieth centuries, historians Tera W. Hunter, Samuel K. Roberts, and Keith Wailoo, among others, have insightfully documented issues relating to black health, particularly medical issues relating to tuberculosis and sickle cell. See Tera W. Hunter, *To "Joy My Freedom": Southern Black Women's Lives and Labor after the Civil War* (Cambridge, MA: Harvard University Press, 1997); Keith Wailoo, *Dying in the City of the Blues: Sickle Cell Anemia and the Politics of Face and Health* (Chapel Hill: University of North Carolina Press, 2001); Samuel K. Roberts, *Infectious Fear: Politics, Disease, and the Effects of Segregation* (Baltimore: Johns Hopkins University Press, 2009). Margaret Humphreys and Harriet Washington have both attempted to examine the gap in the historiography. Humphreys examined the health of black soldiers during the Civil War, while Harriet Washington has provided a comprehensive analysis on medical experimentation from the colonial period to the present. Humphreys, *Intensely Human*; Harriet A. Washington, *Medical Apartheid: The Dark History of Medical Experimentation on Black Americans from Colonial Times to the Present* (New York: Doubleday, 2006).

26. While the government constructed Marine Hospitals during the first decades of the nineteenth century, these institutions were limited to port cities and served mostly merchant marines. For a historical overview of these institutions, see Gautham Rao, "Sailors' Health and National Wealth," *Common-Place* 9, no. 1 (October 2008). For a comprehensive history of federal authority in the nineteenth century, see Brian Balogh, *A Government Out of Sight: The Mystery of National Authority in Nineteenth-Century America* (Cambridge: Cambridge University Press, 2009).

27. The arrival of British imperial forces in China led to government officials redefining the meaning of hygiene from a personal, individual understanding of health rooted in cosmology to a more collective, communal understanding of health rooted in science. In nineteenth-century Japan, British imperial powers constructed public health measures that led to government (and even public) surveillance of the health of sex workers. Meanwhile, the outbreak of cholera in Russia in the late nineteenth century impelled government officials to produce a range of documents from sanitary requirements to reports on diet. In general, the pandemic outbreak of Asiatic cholera in the nineteenth century drove European governments to take a more active role in health and medicine. European governments became increasingly invested in sanitation issues in response to the migrations of Muslims, who participated in the annual pilgrimage to

Mecca; European powers feared that the Hajj facilitated the spread of disease and, as a result, these governments expanded their power by developing protocols that monitored the migrations. These global developments reveal how the United States' establishment of the Medical Division of the Freedmen's Bureau, on a federal level, coincided with international transformations. See Ruth Rogaski, *Hygienic Modernity: Meanings of Health and Disease in Treaty-Port China* (Berkeley: University of California Press, 2004); Davis, "Bodies, Numbers, and Empires"; Charlotte E. Henze, *Disease, Health Care and Government in Late Imperial Russia: Life and Death on the Volga, 1823–1914* (New York: Routledge, 2011). Also see Nancy Mandelker Frieden, *Russian Physicians in an Era of Reform and Revolution, 1865–1905* (Princeton, NJ: Princeton University Press, 1981). On European powers and the Hajj, see William R. Roff, "Sanitation and Security: The Imperial Powers and the Nineteenth Century Hajj," *Arabian Studies* 6 (1982): 143–60; Michael Christopher Low, "Empire and the Hajj: Pilgrims, Plagues, and Pan-Islam Under British Surveillance, 1865–1908," *International Journal of Middle East Studies* 40 (2008): 269–90. Valeska Huber, "The Unification of the Globe by Disease? The International Sanitary Conferences on Cholera, 1851–1894," *The Historical Journal* 49, no. 2 (June 2006): 453–76.

28. These moments can also be viewed in relation to one another. Historian Susan O'Donovan in her study of Reconstruction Georgia incisively explains how slavery shaped how freedpeople in the southwest corner of the state defined the possibilities of their emancipation. Given the violent system of slavery that they lived under, they had a limited view of what freedom could offer. Freed slaves in Virginia, who experienced more autonomy as slaves, demanded more involvement in the political process than their Georgian contemporaries. See Susan Eva O'Donovan, *Becoming Free in the Cotton South* (Cambridge, MA: Harvard University Press, 2007).

29. Rebecca Scott, *Slave Emancipation in Cuba: The Transition to Free Labor* (Pittsburgh: University of Pittsburgh Press, 1985). See Laurent Dubois, *A Colony of Citizens: Revolution & Slave Emancipation in the French Caribbean, 1787–1804* (Chapel Hill: University of North Carolina Press, 2004).

30. In this instance, historians of American slavery can be criticized for unwittingly propagating yet another case of American exceptionalism in their stories about the unique nature of emancipation in the United States.

Chapter 1

1. For more on the history of Camp Nelson, see Richard D. Sears, *Camp Nelson, Kentucky: A Civil War History* (Lexington: University of Kentucky Press, 2007). Camp Nelson has become increasingly popular as a Civil War tourist destination and has received a great deal of attention by antiquarians; see W. Stephen McBride, "Camp Nelson," http://www.bjmjr.net/camp_nelson/cn_mcbride.htm (retrieved August 1, 2011). On Camp Nelson as a Civil War landscape, see http://www.campnelson.org (retrieved August 1, 2011).

2. Affidavit of John Vetter, December 16, 1864, quoted in Sears, *Camp Nelson, Kentucky*, 154–55.

3. Miller's affidavit was published in the November 28, 1864, issue of the *New York Tribune*; however, the article was found in the Consolidated Quartermaster Files, filed under "Negro" at the National Archives. It seems that the condition of women and children, and in particular, the tragedy that faced the Miller family, attracted a great deal of attention: Consolidated Quartermaster Files, Box 727, RG 92, NARA.

4. *Freedmen's Record*, April, 1865, 63, available at Massachusetts Historical Society (MHS).

5. Sharla Fett has brilliantly revealed the intricate ways in which enslaved people developed medical treatments during the antebellum period. When the war struck, bondspeople could not depend on these methods to fight off illness. In large part, as the story of the Miller family reveals, emancipated slaves lacked clothing, food, and shelter—let alone access to the ingredients that could combat illness. See Sharla M. Fett, *Working Cures: Healing, Health and Power on Southern Slave Plantations* (Chapel Hill: University of North Carolina Press, 2002).

6. According to the historians Ira Berlin and Leslie Rowland, slaves who escaped from the border states—Delaware, Maryland, Kentucky, and Missouri—often found themselves "slapped back into slavery." See Berlin and Rowland, *Families and Freedom* (New York: The New Press, 1997), 33.

7. Three of the children's names are Joseph Jr., Maria, and Calvin. The fourth child's name is not listed nor are ages given for each child. See Affidavit of Albert A. Livermore, June 26, 1865, quoted in Sears, *Camp Nelson, Kentucky*, 220–21.

8. Affidavit of John Vetter, December 16, 1864, quoted in Sears, *Camp Nelson, Kentucky*, 154–55.

9. Affidavit of Scofield, December 16, 1864, quoted in Sears, *Camp Nelson, Kentucky*, 154.

10. Hall to Resieaux, December 16, 1864, quoted in Sears, *Camp Nelson, Kentucky*, 134–35.

11. Affidavit of Albert A. Livermore, June 26, 1865, quoted in Sears, *Camp Nelson, Kentucky*, 220–21.

12. Medical historians developed the phrase "framing the disease," as a way to examine how social, political, and economic circumstances contribute to the outbreak of sickness and disease. See Charles Rosenberg and Janet Golden, eds., *Framing the Disease: Studies in Cultural History* (New Brunswick, NJ: Rutgers University, 1992).

13. Affidavit of Albert A. Livermore, June 26, 1865, quoted in Sears, *Camp Nelson, Kentucky*, 220–21.

14. Howard provides a rough estimate that over a half-million slaves were sick during the Civil War years. See O. O. Howard, *Autobiography of Oliver Otis Howard*, vol. 2 (New York: Baker and Taylor, 1907), 364. That said, as I mention in other chapters, the surviving statistical evidence is often contradictory and incomplete.

15. Civil War medical historians have documented the devastating effect that disease had on armies. For example, over one million soldiers suffered from diarrhea and dysentery alone and roughly 44,000 died from it. Yet the author who compiled this data recognizes that the actual number may in fact be much higher. See Joseph K. Barnes, Surgeon General's Office, *The Medical and Surgical History of the War of the Rebellion (1861–65)*, prepared in accordance with acts of Congress (Washington, DC: GPO, 1875–88), 2. Additionally, as Paul E. Steiner explains, "wounds also represented a type of natural bacterial warfare because nearly every wound was infected regardless of its cause by bullet, shrapnel, bayonet, or saber." See Paul E. Steiner, *Disease in the Civil War: Natural Biological Warfare in 1861–1865* (Springfield, IL: Charles C. Thomas, 1968), 11. In general, Steiner offers one of the most comprehensives accounts on the medical consequences of war; see, in particular, pages 3–49. For an insightful and illustrative account of the medical realities of the war, see Frank R. Freemon, *Gangrene and Glory: Medical Care During the American Civil War* (Madison, NJ: Fairleigh Dickinson University Press, 1998), 221–28. On black troops, see Ira Berlin et al., *Black Military Experience* (New York: Cambridge University Press, 1992), 633–55. For an excellent analysis of how the environment shaped the health of soldiers, see Kathryn S. Meier, "No Place for the Sick: Nature's War on Civil War Soldier Mental and Physical Health in the 1862 Peninsula and Shenandoah Valley Campaigns," *The Journal of the Civil War Era* 1, no. 2 (June 2011): 176–206.

16. Howard, *Autobiography*, 363–64.

17. Ibid., 183.

18. John Eaton to Levi Coffin, July 5, 1864, in *Extracts from Reports of Superintendents of the Freedmen*, compiled by Rev. Joseph Warren, D.D., second series, June 1864 (Vicksburg: Freedmen Press Print, 1864), 52, NYPL.

19. Maria R. Mann to Elisa, February 10, 1863, and Maria Mann to Miss Peabody, April 19, 1863, Maria Mann Papers, LOC, quoted in Louis Gerteis, *From Contraband to Freedman: Federal Policy Toward Southern Blacks 1861–1865* (Westport, CT: Greenwood Press, 1973), 120. Gerteis further claims that more than half of the black population died within one month in Helena, Arkansas, but their places were quickly filled by arriving contrabands, ibid., 121. Also on Mann's work, see *Report of the Western Sanitary Commission, July 1, 1863* (St. Louis, MO: Western Sanitary Commission Rooms), 24–25.

20. Major-General Benjamin Butler notes that some of the "contraband" who arrived at federal lines were sick. Benjamin F. Butler, *Autobiography and Personal Reminiscences of*

Major-General Benjamin F. Butler, Butler's Book: A Review of His Legal, Political, and Military Career (Boston: A. M. Thayer, 1892), 261.

21. Sears, *Camp Nelson, Kentucky*, 165–66.

22. Thomas J. M'Kie, "The Negro and Some of his Disease as Observed in the Vicinity of Woodlawn, S.C.," South Carolina Medical Association (Charleston: Walter, Evans, and Cogswell etc., 1881).

23. Elizabeth Keckley, *Behind the Scenes, or, Thirty years a Slave, and Four Years in the White House* (New York: G. W. Carleton, 1868), 112.

24. George E. Lankford, ed., *Memories of Arkansas Slavery Narratives from the 1930s WPA Collections*, 2nd ed. (Fayetteville: University of Arkansas Press, 2006), 403.

25. See Fett, *Working Cures*.

26. On the decline of slavery in the Upper South, see Barbara Jeanne Fields, *Slavery and Freedom on the Middle Ground: Maryland During the Nineteenth Century* (New Haven, CT: Yale University Press, 1990). On the expansion of slavery, Adam Rothman, *Slave Country: American Expansion and the Origins of the Deep South* (Cambridge, MA: Harvard University Press, 2007). On acts of resistance enacted by enslaved people in response to the domestic slave trade, see Walter Johnson, *Soul by Soul: Life Inside the Antebellum Slave Market* (Cambridge, MA: Harvard University Press, 1999). For a careful examination of the subtle acts of defiance executed by enslaved people, see Stephanie M. H. Camp, *Closer to Freedom: Enslaved Women and Everyday Resistance in the Plantation South* (Chapel Hill: University of North Carolina Press, 2004).

27. A. L. Mitchell to John Eaton, May 31, 1864, in *Extracts from Reports of Superintendents of the Freedmen*, compiled by Rev. Joseph Warren, 21.

28. *Harper's Weekly*, January 11, 1862.

29. *Freedmen's Record* 1, no. 1 (January 29, 1865): 26.

30. Brig. General C. C. Washburn to Hon. E. M. Stanton, September 6, 1862, quoted in Berlin et al., *Wartime Genesis of Free Labor: The Lower South*, 665; A.A.Q.M.B.O. Carr to Capt. F. S. Winslow, July 24, 1862, quoted in Berlin, *Wartime Genesis of Free Labor: The Lower South*, 659–60; Mansfield French to Salmon P. Chase, January 6, 1863, Abraham Lincoln Papers, LOC. L. Thomas, Adjutant General, to General Meigs, September 27, 1862, Quartermaster Correspondence Consolidated Files, Contraband Camps File, Box 399, RG 92, NARA. Also see Jim Downs, "The Other Side of Freedom: Destitution, Disease, and Dependency among Freedwomen and Their Children during and after the Civil War," in *Battle Scars: Gender and Sexuality in the American Civil War*, ed. Catherine Clinton and Nina Silber (New York: Oxford University Press, 2006), 78–103.

31. For women in Virginia and the Upper South, see Col. George H. Hall to Major James Rainsford, September 18, 1863, quoted in Berlin, *Wartime Genesis of Free Labor: The Upper South*, 578–79. Testimony of Ladies Contraband Society before the American Freedmen's Inquiry Commission, December 2, 1863, quoted in ibid., 584. For women in Arkansas, Tennessee, and Vicksburg, see James E. Yeatman, "A Report on the Condition of the Freedmen of the Mississippi, Presented to the Western Sanitary Commission" (St. Louis, MO: n.p., 1864), 2–3; and Yeatman, "Report of the Western Sanitary Commission for the Year Ending June 1, 1863" (St. Louis, MO: n.p., 1863), 24–25. For women in the Mississippi Valley, see Brig. General C. C. Washburn to Hon. E. M. Stanton, September 6, 1862, quoted in Berlin, *Wartime Genesis of Free Labor: The Lower South*, 665; A.A.Q.M.B.O. Carr to Capt. F.S. Winslow, July 24, 1862, quoted in ibid., 659–60. For women in South Carolina, see Mansfield French to Salmon P. Chase, January 6, 1863, Abraham Lincoln Papers, LOC. L.Thomas, Adjutant General, to General Meigs, September 27, 1862, Quartermaster Correspondence Consolidated Files, Contraband Camps File, Box 399, RG 92, NARA. *Harper's Weekly*, January 11, 1862. For women in North Carolina, see Mrs. C. E. McKay, *Stories of Hospital and Camp* (Philadelphia: Claxton, Remsen and Haffelfinger, 1876), 167–68; A.A.Q.M. B.O. Carr to Capt. F.S. Winslow, July 24, 1862, as quoted in Berlin, *Wartime Genesis of Free Labor: The Lower South*, 659–60; Chaplain J. B. Rogers to E. L. Stanton, September 19, 1862, enclosing James M. Alexander et al. to E. M. Stanton, September 18, 1862, quoted in ibid., 667–70. Not just freedwomen and their children suffered, but also many unemployed

freedmen suffered from the breakdown of the plantation economy and the slave community. An example of this devastation can be found in a Union official's response to a War Commission Survey about the conditions in tidewater Virginia. The officer reported that "10,000" emancipated slaves reached Union lines and were in desperate need of support from the federal government." Testimony of Capt. C. B. Wilder Before the American Freedmen's Inquiry Commission, May 9, 1863, quoted in Berlin and Rowland, *Families and Freedom*, 31–33.

32. E. D. Townsend to Quartermaster General, December 2, 1864, Quartermaster Consolidated Collections Files, Negroes File, Box 72, RG 92, NARA.

33. [Etta Waters] to My Dear Husband, July 16, 1865, as quoted in Berlin and Rowland, *Families and Freedom*, 131.

34. See, for example, Affidavit of Enoch Braston (colored), January 10, 1866, quoted in Berlin and Rowland, *Families and Freedom*, 222.

35. Lucrethia to Dar husband, December 22, 1864, quoted in Berlin and Rowland, *Families and Freedom*, 160–61; Jerry Smith to Aarron Utz, January 10, 1865, quoted in Berlin and Rowland, *Families and Freedom*, 160–61.

36. While a few historians acknowledged the problems that freed families confronted when the male members of their families enlisted, these historians, nevertheless, frame this decision within the context of a struggle or hardship that families endured without considering that the sickness and death that families experienced. See Ira Berlin et al., *Freedom's Soldiers: The Black Military Experience in the Civil War* (Cambridge: Cambridge University Press, 1998). Leslie Schwalm, "'Sweet Dreams of Freedom'": Freedwomen's Reconstruction of Life and Labor in Lowcountry South Carolina," *Journal of Women's History* 9, no. 1 (Spring 1997): 9–38.

37. Certainly, enslaved people had gained a great deal of insight and knowledge on how to survive when very little was provided to them during slavery, but emancipation posed a whole new set of questions and challenges. Many of the ways in which slaves managed to survive slavery often took decades and generations to develop. These practices and traditions were not necessarily the result of one person's invention or decision. As refugees, they often lacked access to these opportunities. For a thoughtful analysis of how enslaved people survived slavery by engaging in acts of resistance, see Camp, *Closer to Freedom*.

38. There may have been scores of women who fled from these camps and courageously hoped to make it to a safer and a better life. But since military officials did not confront these women, their experience has gone virtually undocumented. Additionally, not every enslaved woman was bound by familial commitments or part of kin networks within the refugee camps, so presumably many women probably did leave these regions. But their experiences are often not charted on military or governmental records, because federal officials often only reported on those people with whom they had contact.

39. Surgeon James Bryan to Hon. E.M. Stanton, July 27, 1863, quoted in Berlin and Rowland, *Families and Freedom*, 61.

40. Louis Gerteis also reveals the intense political battles fought among federal officials, military authorities and members of benevolent associations regarding the employment of ex-slaves during this period in the Mississippi Valley. The debate often revolved around questions of "involuntary servitude" and the problems that developed in the leasing of abandoned lands. See *From Contraband to Freedman*, 129–33. Also see Amy Dru Stanley, "Beggars Can't Be Choosers: Compulsion and Contract in Postbellum America," *The Journal of American History* 78, no. 4 (March 1992): 1265–93.

41. Maria R. Mann to Elisa, February 10, 1863, Maria Mann to Miss Peabody, April 19, 1863, Maria Mann Papers, LOC, quoted in Gerteis, *From Contraband to Freedman*, 121.

42. The discourse of describing black people as animal-like undergirds this entire description beyond just the use of the term "brute." For an astute analysis on how people of African descent were often described as animals during the nineteenth century, see Mia Bay, *The White Image in the Black Mind* (New York: Oxford University Press, 2000).

43. For more on the epidemiological relationship between population movement and disease transmission, see P. Shears and T. Lusty, "Communicable Disease Epidemiology Following

Migration: Studies from the African Famine," *International Migration Review, Special Issue: Migration and Health* 21, no. 3 (Autumn 1987): 783–95. While Shears and Lusty focus their analysis on twentieth-century Africa, their argument theoretically resonates with the challenges that faced nineteenth-century emancipated slaves in the United States; moreover, their argument offers a context to understand the deadly health consequences of migration. Within the nineteenth-century U.S. context, there has been very little research conducted on the epidemiological impact of dislocation; therefore, it became necessary for me to examine this relationship in secondary literature outside the United States. See Joseph N. S. Eisenberg, "How New Roads Affect the Transmission of Diarrheal Pathogens in Rural Ecuador," *Proceedings of the National Academy of Sciences of the United States of America* 103, no. 51 (December 19, 2006):19460–65. On the relationship between the spread of disease and environmental factors, see Joseph N. S. Eisenberg, et al., "Environmental Detriments of Infectious Disease: A Framework for Tracking Casual Links and Guiding Public Health Research," *Environmental Health Perspectives* 115, no. 8 (August 2007): 1216–23.

44. Steiner, *Disease in the Civil War*, 6. Regarding Steiner's reference to "camp followers," I think he means to subtly evoke the idea that prostitutes allegedly spread sexually transmitted diseases, which, according to his logic, exacerbated the overall spread of disease during the war. Yet, camp followers could also refer to the nurses and other women who served as laundresses and cooks who followed the army. That said, I call attention to his implication about prostitutes only to further underscore yet another group of people involved in the vast movements that took place during the war. Having seen few references to prostitution in the sources, especially prostitutes who carry and transmit disease, I withhold from making a claim about the relationship between sex and disease during this period due to the paucity of sources on this topic, but I certainly acknowledge the possibility and likelihood of sexually transmitted disease, beyond the purview of prostitution, as an important factor in the overall spread of illness. References to sexually transmitted diseases do, however, appear in the encyclopedic accountings of disease among soldiers, but very little if any explanation exists on the causes of transmissions. According to some medical charts, gonorrhea ranks just as high as typhoid fever and bronchitis as a cause of sickness among the troops, but Civil War doctors do not explain how those diseases were transmitted. The reported estimates of gonorrhea range from as high as 102,893 cases in all of the army from 1861–65 to as few as two to six cases among particular regiments after the war ended in 1870. See, for example, Barnes, *Medical and Surgical History of the War of the Rebellion (1861–65)*. For a brief example of gonorrhea mentioned in the statistical charts but not elaborated in the accompanying narrative report, see U.S. Surgeon General's Office, "A Report of the Hygiene of the United States Army with Descriptions of Military Posts," *Circular No. 8* (Washington, DC: GPO, May 1, 1875), 532–43.

45. On diseased animals during the war, especially horses, see G. Terry Sharrer, "The Great Glanders Epizootic, 1861–1866: A Civil War Legacy," *Agricultural History* 69, No. 1 (Winter 1995), 79–97. On hog cholera, see U.S. Congress, House. 50th Cong., 2nd sess., House Executive Documents, Miscellaneous Documents (Washington. DC: Government Printing Office, 1889), 235, 270. One Bureau official in New Orleans described "unsightly heaps of decomposing vegetable and animal matter"; see Vols to Parker, September 3, 1867, New Orleans, Louisiana, e. 1385, LS, Chief Medical Officer, RG 105, NARA. For an excellent analysis of the biological impact that dead animals had on the environment during the Civil War, see Jack Temple Kirby, "The American Civil War: An Environmental View," National Humanities website, http://nationalhumanitiescenter.org/tserve/nattrans/ntuseland/essays/amcwar.htm (retrieved August 9, 2010). For a stunning analysis of the environment's impact on the war, see Lisa Brady, "Devouring the Land: Sherman's 1864–1865 Campaigns," in *War and the Environment: Military Destruction in the Modern Age*, ed. Charles E. Closmann (College Station: Texas A&M University Press, 2009).

46. See James Riley, *The Eighteenth-Century Campaign to Avoid Disease* (London: Palgrave Macmillan, 1987), 144. To explain the constants shifts within the population of enslaved peoples, I am building on Ira Berlin's definition of "creolization" to acknowledge changing

health patterns on plantations. See Ira Berlin, *Many Thousands Gone: The First Two Centuries of Slavery in North America* (Cambridge, MA: Belknap Press of Harvard University Press, 2000). On the Irish famine and arrival of immigrants to Philadelphia in particular, see J. Matthew Gallman, *Receiving Erin's Children: Philadelphia, Liverpool, and the Irish Famine Migration, 1845–1855* (Chapel Hill: University of North Carolina Press, 2000). On slaveholders' response to sickness in the antebellum South, see Todd Savitt, *Medicine and Slavery: The Diseases and Health Care of Blacks in Antebellum Virginia* (Urbana: University of Illinois Press, 1981). On enslaved people's response to sickness, see Fett, *Working Cures*. On the merchant's response to sickness in the North, see Erwin H. Ackerknecht, "Anti-Contagionism between 1821 and 1867," *Bulletin of the History of Medicine* 22 (1948): 562–93; Charles E. Rosenberg, *The Cholera Years: The United States in 1832, 1849, and 1866* (Chicago: University of Chicago Press, 1962), 78–98. For a provocative account of the relationship among disease transmission, Native Americans, and trade, particularly how smallpox was used to "protect traders' interest in the upper Missouri Valley" in the early nineteenth century, see David S. Jones, *Rationalizing Epidemics: Meanings and Uses of American Indian Mortality since 1600* (Cambridge, MA: Harvard University Press, 2004), 103–10, 117. That said, I focus on how nineteenth-century doctors, civil authorities, and concerned citizens responded to health problems. I do not attempt to detail the many other ways that disease spread during this time but rather to examine the local protocols that were in place when a medical crisis exploded.

47. See U.S. Surgeon General's Office, *Circular No. 6* (Washington, DC: GPO, November 1, 1865), 127–38; Also, see the publication of the multivolume series *Medical and Surgical History of the War of the Rebellion*, particularly part 3, volume 1: Major and Surgeon, Charles Smart, *Medical History*, prepared under the direction of Surgeon General John Moore, U.S. Army (Washington, DC: GPO, 1888).

48. In 1866, the surgeon general was able to develop a national protocol to prevent the fatal spread of Asiatic cholera in the United States. *Circular No. 5* provided detailed instructions for physicians and townspeople to treat the outbreak of cholera. Joseph K. Barnes, U.S. Surgeon General's Office, "Report on Epidemic Cholera in the Army of the United States, During the Year 1866" (Washington, DC: GPO, 1867).

49. P. M. Ashburn, *A History of the Medical Department of the United States Army* (Boston: Houghton Mifflin, 1929), 70–71; Captain Louis C. Duncan, *Medical Corps, U.S. Army, The Medical Department of the United States Army in the Civil War* [Washington? no date]; Charles J. Stille, *History of the United States Sanitary Commission: Being the General Report of Its Work during the War of the Rebellion* (Philadelphia: J. B. Lippincott, 1866).

50. Ashburn, *History of the Medical Department of the United States Army*, 68.

51. Duncan, *Medical Corps, U.S. Army*, 21.

52. Ashburn, *History of the Medical Department of the United States Army*, 70; in the history of Sanitary Commission, Charles Stille supports this overall point; see Stille, *History of the United States Sanitary Commission*.

53. On hip-joint amputations during the war, see George A. Otis, U.S. Surgeon General's Office, "A Report on the Amputations at the Hip-Joint in Military Surgery," *Circular No. 7* (Washington, DC: GPO, June 30, 1867). On the general health problems at Bull Run, see Duncan, *Medical Corps, U.S. Army*, 1–23. Also see Ira M. Rutkow, *Bleeding Blue and Grey: Civil War Surgery and the Evolution of American Medicine* (New York: Random House, 2005), 6, 18–28.

54. Letter to the editor, "Origin of the U.S. Sanitary Commission," *New York Times*, September 6, 1903. Stille, *History of the United States Sanitary Commission*. For the secondary literature on the Sanitary Commission with special emphasis on the role women played in the organization, see Jeanie Attie, *Patriotic Toil: Northern Women and the American Civil War* (Ithaca, NY: Cornell University Press, 1998); Judith Ann Giesberg, *Civil War Sisterhood: The U.S. Sanitary Commission and Women's Politics in Transition* (Boston: Northeastern University Press, 2000).

55. Stille, *History of the United States Sanitary Commission*, 67.

56. Ibid., 110–11.

57. Ibid.

58. For more on how Civil War doctors understood the spread of disease see Barnes, *Circular No. 6*, 121.
59. Ibid.
60. On problems with the drinking water from "fecal contaminations" to "animal impurities," see Joseph K. Barnes, *Medical and Surgical History of the War of the Rebellion*, part 2, vol. 1, *Medical History* (Washington, DC: GPO, 1879), 598–617. On the problems of water supply in the contraband camps that often led to disease outbreaks, see C. W. Mound to Edwin B. Stanton, October 23, 1863, Quartermaster Correspondence Consolidated Files, Box 399. RG 94. NARA.
61. A. T. Augusta to R. O. Abbott. June 17, 1863, Quartermaster Correspondence Consolidated Files, Contraband Camps File, Box 99, RG 92, NARA.
62. "Health in the Camp," *Atlantic Monthly*, November 1861, 571–80.
63. Jacob Gilbert Forman, *The Western Sanitary Commission; A Sketch of Its Origin, History, Labors for the Sick and Wounded of the Western Armies, and Aid Given to the Freedmen and Union Refugees, with Incidents of Hospital Life* (St. Louis, MO: Mississippi Sanitary Fair, n.d.), 14–15. On the state of Union camps, also see, O. A. Judson to Abbott, July 18, 1863, Washington, e. 5412, Miscellaneous Records, 1861–1869, Box 7, RG 393, NARA. "Health in the Hospitals," *Atlantic Monthly*, November 1861, (45–50), 718–730. Katherine Prescott Wormeley, *The Sanitary Commission of the United States Army: A Succinct Narrative of its Works and Purpose* (New York: U.S. Sanitary Commission, 1864), 42–43. Thomas Ellis, *Leaves from the Diary of an Army Surgeon: or, Incidents of Field, Camp, and Hospital Life* (New York: Bradburn, 1863), 312.
64. Ashburn, *History of the Medical Department of the United States Army*, 68.
65. Butler, *Autobiography*, 398.
66. Ashburn, *History of the Medical Department of the United States Army*.
67. Kathleen M. Brown, *Foul Bodies: Cleanliness in Early America* (New Haven, CT: Yale University Press, 2009). Also on the American Revolution's influence on American medicine, see Harvey E. Brown, U.S. Surgeon General's Office, *The Medical Department of the United States Army from 1775 to 1873* (Washington, DC: GPO, 1873), 262.
68. For a list of physicians that documents their previous military history, see Brown, *Medical Department of the United States Army from 1775 to 1873*, 286–98. Some military physicians would have encountered treating a large number of patients in Marine hospitals. These were institutions designed to provide medical treatment to sailors in various port cities. But for the most part, few Civil War doctors had this experience and those that did were certainly not used to treating patients during the drama of war. Further, according to Brown's accounting of physicians' prior war experience, Marine hospitals do not constitute military training.
69. Doctors who worked in almshouses in large cities, like Philadelphia and New York, may have had experience treating large number of patients, but the war added a new challenge to these operations. On almshouses as training grounds for physicians, see Charles Rosenberg, "From Almshouse to Hospital: The Shaping of Philadelphia General Hospital," *Milbank Memorial Fund Quarterly* 60, no. 1 (1982): 108–54. Also, see Glenna R. Schroeder-Lein, *The Encyclopedia of Civil War Medicine* (Armonk, NY: M.E. Sharpe, 2008).
70. Many nineteenth-century physicians subscribed to Galen's idea, which was built on the Ancient Greek notion that the body was controlled by four humors—black bile, blood, yellow bile, and phlegm; an imbalance of these caused disease. It was, therefore, the physician's responsibility to ensure that patient regained a state of equilibrium. For a scholarly analysis on the changes of nineteenth-century medical understandings and practices, see Charles Rosenberg, "The Therapeutic Revolution: Medicine, Meaning, and Social Change in Nineteenth-Century America," *Perspectives in Biology and Medicine* 20 (1977).
71. See Rosenberg, "The Therapeutic Revolution"; John Warner, "American Physicians in London during the Age of Paris Medicine," in *The History of Medical Education in Britain*, ed. Roy Porter and Vivian Nutton (Atlanta, GA: Editions Rodopi, 1995), 341–65.
72. Ashburn, *History of the Medical Department of the United States Army*, 74.
73. See Smart, *Medical and Surgical History of the War of the Rebellion*, part 3, vol. 1, *Medical History*, 100; 95–102. For the secondary literature on the South's distinctiveness in medical history, see Todd L. Savitt and James Harvey Young, eds., *Disease and Distinctiveness in the*

American South (Knoxville: University of Tennessee Press, 1998); Ronald L. Numbers and Todd L. Savitt eds., *Science and Medicine in the Old South* (Baton Rouge: Louisiana State University Press, 1989); Steven M. Stowe, *Doctoring the South: Southern Physicians and Everyday Medicine in the Mid-Nineteenth Century* (Chapel Hill: University of North Carolina Press, 2003); Brown, *Foul Bodies*, 298.

74. Smart, *Medical and Surgical History of the War of the Rebellion*, part 3, vol. 1, *Medical History*, 100.

75. Robert Dale, James McKay, Saml. G. Howe to E. M. Stanton, June 30, 1863, "Preliminary Report of the American Freedmen's Inquiry Commission," HL. Also on climate's effect on the spread of disease, see, for example, Civil War doctors' analysis of dysentery: Barnes, *Medical and Surgical History of the War of the Rebellion*, part 2, vol. 1, *Medical History*, 427–30.

76. The four major diseases that often get associated with the South in current historiography are malaria, yellow fever, hookworm, and pellagra. During the nineteenth century, hookworm and pellagra had not yet been identified or discovered; whereas, malaria and yellow fever were, by the beginning of the twentieth century, often associated with the South. Throughout the nineteenth century, physicians also often misdiagnosed malaria and made incorrect judgments about the nature of the disease based on perceived understandings of the North and the South. See William Osler, M.D., "The Diagnosis of Malarial Fever," *The Medical News*, March 6, 1897, available at Library of the Los Angeles County Medical Association, HUN.

77. J. H. Baxter, M.D., U.S. War Dept., *Statistics, Medical, and Anthropological of the Provost-Marshal-General's Bureau delivered from the Records of the Examination for Military Service in the Armies of the United States during the Late War of the Rebellion*, vol. 1 (Washington, DC: GPO, 1875), 380.

78. Philip Tidyman, "A Sketch of the Most Remarkable Diseases of the Negroes of the Southern States," *Philadelphia Journal of the Medical and Physical Sciences* 12 (1826): 315–36, quoted in Savitt, *Medicine and Slavery*, 22.

79. For a historical overview of how the medical profession viewed black people as immune to malaria, see Savitt, *Medicine and Slavery*, 23–35. For more information on how some members of the white medical establishment understood the presence of malaria among black people, see M'Kie, "The Negro and Some of His Disease as Observed in the Vicinity of Woodlawn, S.C."

80. Margaret Humphreys has proven malaria infected black troops during the Civil War. See Margaret Humphreys, *Intensely Human: The Health of the Black Soldier in the American Civil War* (Baltimore: Johns Hopkins University Press, 2008), 45–46.

81. See J. W. Compton, May 20, 1865, "Extracts from Report of Dr. J.W. Compton," in *Statistics, Medical, and Anthropological of the Provost-Marshal-General's Bureau*, compiled by Baxter, 368. Also, see Dr. E. P. Buckner's "Report from Kentucky," June 15, 1865, 6th District, Kentucky, also in Baxter, 379–80.

82. Benjamin Apthorp Gould, *Investigations in the Military and Anthropological Statistics of American Soldiers* (New York: Published for the U.S. Sanitary Commission, by Hurd and Houghton. Cambridge, MA: Riverside Press, 1869). Josiah Nott became a leading proponent in the decades leading up to the Civil War: Josiah Clark Nott, *Types of Mankind* (Philadelphia: J. B. Lippincott, Grambo, 1854).

83. Cases of intermittent fever consistently appear in many if not all the records that document freedpeople's health during the Civil War and Reconstruction. For examples, see Register of Contrabands in Corps d'Afrique, New Orleans, 1863 (Partial List), Records of the New Orleans Field Office, State of Louisiana, 1865–68, M1483, RG 105, NARA; B.B. Wilson to T.W. Sherman, July 18, 1864, Dept. of Gulf, 1756, LR, Box 11, W559, C570. FSSP.

84. The publication of medical articles during the first half of the nineteenth century that drew distinctions between the races based on climate and physiological differences should also be contextualized within the social and political context of the abolitionist and proslavery debates. These articles provided a scientific explanation that reified differences between the North and South. Samuel A. Cartwright wrote in 1851 a widely read article titled "The Diseases and Physical Particularities of the Negro Race." Published less than a decade before the start of the Civil War, Cartwright's article argued that when slaves are well fed

and treated kindly they would not run away and fall victim to "dysaesthesia Aethiopis," a fictional mental illness. While the article is allegedly about a medical issue, Cartwright nonetheless plays into abolitionist and proslavery debates. In response to the Northern critique that the violent nature of the institution of slavery propelled slaves to run away, Cartwright argues that slaves were actually suffering from a mental disease that triggered them to run away and then offers a medical cure to solve this problem. The implicit abolitionist and proslavery context in which the article is inexplicably framed solidifies a North–South dichotomy that enables Cartwright to convince his readers of the distinct physiological qualities of black people. This medical idea gained momentum because it was published during a time when a number of people portrayed the South as a uniquely distinct place, from novelist Harriet Beecher Stowe's description of Simon Legree's plantation in *Uncle Tom's Cabin*, to journalist Frederick Law Olmstead's claim that the South lagged behind Northern industrial progress. Samuel A. Cartwright, "Report on the Diseases and Physical Peculiarities of the Negro Race," *New Orleans Medical and Surgical Journal* 7 (1850–1851).

85. B. B. Wilson to T. W. Sherman, July 18, 1864, Dept. of Gulf, 1756, LR, Box 11, W559 (1864), C570, FSSP. For an overview of health disparities between black and white enlisted men, see Ira Berlin, et al. *Freedom: A Documentary History of Emancipation, 1861–1867: The Black Military Experience* (London: Cambridge University Press, 1982), 633–55.

86. Benjamin Woodward, "Notes on a Trip through Arkansas," quoted in Humphreys, *Intensely Human*, 68.

87. Humphreys, *Intensely Human*, 67.

88. For a theoretical and historical discussion on how the creation of hospitals created epistemological shifts in medical knowledge as well how physicians see the same illness yet formulate changing and competing understandings of disease, see Michel Foucault, *The Birth of the Clinic: An Archeology of Medical Perception* (New York: Vintage, 1994). In the twentieth century, long after the introduction of advanced scientific technologies that can adequately and correctly diagnose and explain illness, physicians today continue to make judgments about illness based on subjective external variables, such as appearance, social class, and educational background. In the nineteenth century, before the advent of bacteriology and other sophisticated understandings of disease causation, medical diagnoses continually were defined by appearance and other outward characteristics, especially among people of African descent. See Rosenberg, *Cholera Years*. Physicians and scholars of medicine have furthered developed these ideas by paying particular attention to the role of patients in the construction of disease, see Rita Charon, *Narratives of Medicine: Honoring the Stories of Illness* (New York: Oxford University Press, 2008); Arthur Kleinman, *Illness Narratives: Suffering, Healing, and the Human Condition* (New York: Basic Books, 1989).

89. The records organized by the Army Department and later by the Medical Division of the Freedmen's Bureau only catalogue contagious illnesses. For example, the leading health problem reported in Georgia in 1867–1868 was syphilis. Bureau doctors copiously recorded rates of infection in adult males and adult females from January 1867 to August of 1868. I have examined more than 100 reports for this case; without listing each record, I have included the reference for the archival box that includes all the reports. See "Reports of the Surgeon," Atlanta, Georgia, e. 745, Folder 27, 36, 37 RG 105, NARA.

90. Some reformers in the United States may have been able to draw connections between insect vectors and disease causation despite the advent of scientific theory that elucidated such claims. Bruno Latour has cogently demonstrated how hygienists eventually paved the way for Louis Pasteur's late nineteenth-century discovery of germ theory and his subsequent influence on the study of microbiology around the globe. See Latour, *The Pasteurization of France* (Cambridge, MA: Harvard University Press, 1988).

91. Smart, *Medical and Surgical History of the War of the Rebellion*, part 3, vol. 1, *Medical History*, 153–56; Surgeon General's Office, *Circular No. 6*.

92. While Eaton's statement assumes a continuation of paternalism, it nonetheless underscores the idea that escaped slaves were in immediate need of food, clothing, and shelter. John Eaton, *Grant, Lincoln and the Freedmen* (New York: Longman's, Green, 1907), 19. In his

report to the Sanitary Commission, Dr. Robert Ware also raised the question of how to feed and clothe the contraband, see *Harper's Weekly*, January 11, 1862. Much of the scholarship on this issue has emphasized the political and economic aspects of emancipation and overlooked the physical and medical consequences of this critical transition. Gerteis, *From Contraband to Freedman*; Edward Magdol, *Essays on the Freedmen's Community* (Westport, CT: Greenwood Press, 1977); Donald G. Nieman, *Day of the Jubilee: The Civil War Experience of Black Southerners* (New York: Garland, 1994); Barbara J. Fields, "Who Freed the Slaves?" in *The Civil War*, ed. Geoffrey C. Ward et al. (New York: Knopf, 1990); Robert Engs, *Freedom's First Generation: Black Hampton, Virginia, 1861–1890* (Philadelphia: University of Pennsylvania Press, 1979); Cam Walker, "Cornith: The Story of a Contraband Camp," *Civil War History* 20, no. 1 (1974), 5–22; Martha Mitchell Bigelow, "Freedmen of the Mississippi Valley, 1862–1865," *Journal of Mississippi History* 26, no. 1 (1964): 28–44; W. E. B. Du Bois, *Black Reconstruction in America* (New York: Russell and Russell, 1935), 63, 80.

93. Aikman also makes the point about colonization when he asks, "Have we a right to send out the country the emancipated slaves." William Aikman, *The Future of the Colored Race in America: Being an Article in the Presbyterian Quarterly Review, July 1862* (New York: Anson D.F. Randolph, 1862).

94. Throughout the antebellum North, there were charitable institutions organized to help manumitted slaves in their transition to free lives. There were also education and employment opportunities available to newly manumitted slaves. While newly freed slaves in the North certainly struggled in their adjustment to free lives, there were laws that responded to their predicament, and the society in broad terms had created various mechanisms that attended to their status. The same organizational structures and social mores did not exist in the Civil War South. For free black life in the North, see Julie Winch, *Philadelphia's Black Elite: Activism, Accommodation, and the Struggle for Autonomy, 1787–1848* (Philadelphia: Temple University Press, 1993); Leslie Harris, *In the Shadow of Slavery: African Americans in New York City, 1626–1863* (Chicago: University of Chicago Press, 2004).

95. Howard, *Autobiography*, 165–66.

96. Ibid.

97. Henry Carey Baird, *General Washington and General Jackson, on Negro Soldiers* (Philadelphia: Henry Carey Baird, 1863).

98. Howard, *Autobiography*, 167–68. Also see George Bentley, *A History of the Freedmen's Bureau* (New York: Octagon Books, 1974), 13.

99. Howard quotes Butler directly in his autobiography; see Howard *Autobiography*, 167–69.

100. Ibid., 258, 261. Furthermore, historian Walter Johnson refers to the commodification of slave bodies during the antebellum as the "chattel principle." See Johnson, *Soul by Soul*.

101. For an eloquent linguistic analysis of the term contraband, see Barbara J. Fields, "Who Freed the Slaves?" in *The Civil War*, ed. Geoffrey Ward et al. (New York: Alfred Knopf, 1990), 178–79.

102. S. I. Wilcox to Capt. Newton Flagg, June 26, 1865, "Report of Physician in Charge of Contraband," Consolidated Quartermaster Files, Negroes File, Box 720, RG 92, NARA.

103. John Eaton to Levi Coffin, July 5, 1864, in "Extracts from Reports of Superintendents of the Freedmen," compiled by Rev. Joseph Warren, D.D., 49.

104. Col. John Eaton, Jr. General Superintendent of Refugees and Freedmen, "Colored Orphan Asylum," March 1, 1865, 1, Memphis Colored Orphan Asylum, Memphis, Tenn. NYPL.

105. Aikman, *Future of the Colored Race in America*, 11.

106. There was even one popular theory that argued that emancipation would lead to high rates of insanity among the black population, which marshaled statistical evidence to prove the point. See T. J. Morgan, LL.D., "Africans in America" (New York: The American Baptist Home Mission Society, 1898); on insanity, see Edward Jarvis, "Insanity Among the Coloured Population of the Free States" (T.K. and P.G. Collins Printers, 1844); F. Miller, "The Effects of Emancipation Upon the Mental and Physical Health of the Negro of the South" (Wilmington, N.C., 1896).

107. *Richmond Dispatch*, November 10, 1863.

108. Howard, *Autobiography*, 314.

Chapter 2

1. Laura S. Haviland, *A Woman's Life-Work; Labors and Experiences* (Chicago: Waite, 1887), 246.
2. Ibid., 246–47.
3. *First Annual Report of the National Freedman's Relief Association* (New York: February 19, 1863), MHS; *Freedmen's Record*, April, 1865, 63, MHS; see also Henry L. Stint, ed., *Dear Ones at Home: Letters from Contraband Camps* (Nashville, TN: Vanderbilt University Press, 1966).
4. Drew Faust charts how the federal government became involved in the burying of fallen soldiers during the war, but this slowly growing enterprise did not address emancipated slaves. See Faust, *This Republic of Suffering: Death and the American Civil War* (New York: Vintage, 2009).
5. Ibid.
6. There was no formal mechanism that captured or recorded the death toll among the former slave population. Therefore, there is no archival record available. On burial grounds, there are a few cemeteries for freed slaves, but those are typically part of larger contraband communities. For example, in Alexandria, Virginia, a few miles outside Washington, DC, military officials designated a plot of land to bury former slaves who died. But Alexandria and the major contraband camps in Cornith, Mississippi, and Camp Nelson, Kentucky, were the exception not the rule. Throughout the Confederate theater, both near the battlefields and distant from the points of conflict, emancipated slaves died and nothing was done to properly bury their bodies.
7. Quoted in "The Beast," episode 3, *Civil War*, videocassette, directed by Ken Burns (PBS, 1990).
8. The historiography on the Freedmen's Bureau in the last 30 years or so has primarily focused on the Bureau's political, economic, legal, and educational activities. There have only been a few scattered studies of the Bureau's work in establishing hospitals and providing medical relief. These studies have focused on specific states. See Gaines Foster, "The Limitations of Federal Health Care for Freedmen, 1860–1868," *Journal of Southern History* 48, no. 3 (August 1982): 349–72; Gail Hasson, "Health and Welfare of Freedmen in Reconstruction Alabama," *The Alabama Review* 35, no. 2 (April 1982): 94–110; Marshall Scott Legan, "Disease and Freedmen in Mississippi During Reconstruction," *Journal of History of Medicine* (July 1973): 257–67; Todd Savitt, "Politics in Medicine: The Georgia Freedmen's Bureau and the Organization of Health Care, 1865–1866," *Civil War History* 28 (1982): 45–64.
9. In many ways, my work builds directly on Nancy Hewitt's pioneering work of women activists in Rochester, New York. While Hewitt concludes with the Civil War years, this chapter picks up where Hewitt's story ends and follows many of the same women whom Hewitt identified in her book as leaders of the movement in creating better conditions for emancipated slaves. In her recently published book, *Radical Women's Reconstruction*, Carol Faulkner has smartly called attention to the role women abolitionists played in the Freedmen's Aid movement. Similar to the spirit of Faulkner's study, this chapter charts the integral role Northern white women abolitionists played in the development of federal policy. See Nancy A. Hewitt, *Women's Activism and Social Change: Rochester, New York, 1822–1872* (Ithaca, NY: Cornell University Press, 1984); Carol Faulkner, *Women's Radical Reconstruction: The Freedmen's Aid Movement* (Philadelphia: University of Pennsylvania, 2006). Also see Jeanie Attie, *Patriotic Toil: Northern Women and the American Civil War* (Ithaca, NY: Cornell University Press, 1998); Mary Farmer-Kaiser, *Freedwomen and the Freedmen's Bureau: Race, Gender, and Public Policy in the Age of Emancipation* (New York: New York University Press, 2010); Reggie L. Pearson, "'There Are Many Sick, Feeble, and Suffering Freedmen': The Freedmen's Bureau's Health-care Activities During Reconstruction in North Carolina, 1865–1868," *North Carolina Historical Review* 79, no. 2 (2002): 141–81.
10. While historians acknowledged that the Union army employed ex-slaves, they have often framed these incidents as either moments when the federal government attempted to take a stab at rebuilding the South during the war by creating a "Rehearsal for Reconstruction,"

or as the "wartime genesis of free labor" when former slaves began to be paid for their work. These interpretations place too much emphasis on the question of ex-slaves' agency and overlook the federal government's role in forcing fugitive slaves to return to the plantation South. Moreover, when historians use the term "wartime genesis of free labor," they anticipate the coming of a free labor economy to the South before the Civil War ended. Examining freedpeople's labor within the context of the war—not with an eye toward Reconstruction—reveals that freed slaves' labor power became the only way that the federal government even engaged the unexpected liberation of freed slaves in the first place. See Willie Lee Rose, *The Port Royal Experiment* (Indianapolis, IN: Bobbs-Merrill, 1964); Ira Berlin et al., *The Wartime Genesis of Free Labor: The Upper South* (New York: Cambridge University Press, 1993); Ira Berlin et al., *The Wartime Genesis of Free Labor: The Lower South* (New York: Cambridge University Press, 1990). Amy Dru Stanley's analysis of contracts during the postwar period subtly if sharply challenges this historiography on the war and is more aligned to the argument that this chapter makes. See Amy Dru Stanley, "Beggars Can't Be Choosers: Compulsion and Contract in Postbellum America," *The Journal of American History* 78, no. 4 (March 1992): 1265–93.

11. *Liberator*, February 21, 1862, 2.
12. See Berlin, *Wartime Genesis of Free Labor: The Upper South*, 16. For a cogent and detailed analysis of how freedpeople, especially formerly enslaved women from the Low Country South, resisted the military and government control over their labor, see Leslie Schwalm, " 'Sweet Dreams of Freedom': Freedwomen's Reconstruction of Life and Labor in Lowcountry South Carolina," *Journal of Women's History* 9, no. 1 (Spring 1997): 9–38.
13. See Louis Gerteis, *From Contraband to Freedman: Federal Policy Toward Southern Blacks 1861–1865* (Westport, CT: Greenwood Press, 1973), 50.
14. During the war, the money earned from freed slaves' labor flowed to the coffers of the U.S. Treasury. After the war, the Treasury Department continued to benefit from their labor in the sum of $40 million tax collected, which was the result of former slaves producing more than two million bales of cotton in 1866–67. See O. O. Howard, *Autobiography of Oliver Otis Howard*, vol. 2. (New York: Baker and Taylor, 1907), 367. In response to critics of free labor, Howard used these statistics to demonstrate the large amount of money ex-slaves made for the government.
15. William Dwight Jr. to Mother, April 5, 1863, Folder April 1863, Box No. 13 January to June 1863, Dwight Family Papers, MHS.
16. Leslie Schwalm, for example, argues that contraband women defined the course of their freedom. See Schwalm, "Sweet Dreams of Freedom," 4. Let me clarify that Schwalm's arguments for the Reconstruction period are convincing and insightful; yet, I disagree with her understanding of freedpeople's labor as a sign of agency during the Civil War period. Berlin views wartime service as a way that prepared emancipated slaves for the challenges of a postwar, free labor economy. He argues that thousands of slaves "entered the postwar world already experienced in the ways of free labor." This interpretation places too much of an emphasis on Reconstruction without paying adequate attention to idea that Union officials forced former slaves into labor during the Civil War. Berlin further claims that "Free labor emerged in the Union-occupied South as freedom was being redefined in the North." While cleverly stated, the use of passive voice here does not explain who redefined freedom in the North. Moreover, the idea that an amorphous power structure in the North defined freedom is an incorrect assertion; throughout the South, Union army officials on federally run plantations, made it very clear to ex-slaves that they defined the terms of "freedom" and forced them back to work. Berlin, *Wartime Genesis of Free Labor: The Upper South*, 2. Julie Saville's more subtle evocation of "inducing wage labor behind federal lines" aligns more with my argument, as she recognizes the role that the army played in forcing enslaved people back to the plantation. See Saville, *The Work of Reconstruction: From Slave to Wage Laborer in South Carolina, 1860–1870* (New York: Cambridge University Press, 1996), 36. Also, Amy Dru Stanley's analysis of contracts during the postbellum period powerfully reveals the ways in which the Bureau forced emancipated slaves into labor arrangements. More to the point, her argument better reflects the tension of this period. See Stanley, "Beggars Can't Be Choosers," 1283–84.

17. Howard, *Autobiography*, 390.
18. Brig. Genl. Wm. Dwight to Lt. Col. Richard B. Irwin, March 23, 1863, Folder March 1863, Box No. 13 January to June 1863, Dwight Family Papers, MHS.
19. Gerteis, *From Contraband to Freedman*, 157.
20. For an illustrative description of antebellum slave pens, see Walter Johnson, *Soul by Soul: Life Inside the Antebellum Slave Market* (Cambridge, MA: Harvard University Press, 1999), 2.
21. *Home Evangelist* 14, no. 3 (March 1863): 10, NYPL. There seems to have been a fire in a slave pen that killed many enslaved children and infants. For more information on the fire and the general mortality of those who died, while being forced to live in the slave pen in 1863–1864, see "Book of Records Containing Marriage and Deaths That Have Occurred within the Official Jurisdiction of Rev. A. Gladwin together with any Biographical and other Reminisces that may be Collected," (microfilm), Barrett Library, AHS.
22. In her cogent and insightful study of Cuba, Rebecca Scott explains how emancipation unfolded as a social process. Scott persuasively credits slaves for taking advantage of military conscription, the creation of specific laws, and the reformulation of economic conditions that slowly chipped away at the slavocracy. Rebecca Scott, *Slave Emancipation: The Transition to Free Labor, 1860–1899* (Pittsburgh: University of Pittsburgh Press, 1985). Similarly, throughout the British Caribbean, officials in London created the system of apprenticeship in order to keep former slaves tied to plantations. Slaves became free in 1834 due to the passage of the Slavery Abolition Act of 1833, but were bound to their masters for a period of seven years and paid little wages. British authorities created the Apprenticeship Law so that ex-slaves would not create problems for planters in the immediate aftermath of the collapse of slavery. See W. L. Burn, *Emancipation and Apprenticeship in the British West Indies* (London: Jonathan Cape Ltd, 1937; repr., Westport, CT: Greenwood Press, 1975). Finally, in Guadeloupe, slavery did not come to an immediate end in spite of slave insurrection but instead it took many years for the institution of slavery to dissipate. See Laurent Dubois, *A Colony of Citizens: Revolution and Slave Emancipation in the French Caribbean, 1787–1804* (Chapel Hill: University of North Carolina Press, 2004). On the general transition from slave to wage labor in the Atlantic world, see Mary Turner, ed., *From Chattel Slaves to Wage Slaves: The Dynamics of Labor Bargaining in the Americas* (Bloomington: Indiana University Press, 1995). On the social and legal process of emancipation throughout the Atlantic world, see Frederick Cooper et al., *Beyond Slavery: Explorations of Race, Labor, and Citizenship in Postemancipation Societies* (Chapel Hill: University of North Carolina Press, 2000).
23. Butler, however, was not the only military official who declared in the postwar decades that his Civil War policy held revolutionary consequences—despite the fact that during the war, it was clear that the military did not care about the welfare of the slaves. Also see Ulysses S. Grant, *Personal Memoir of Ulysses S. Grant* (New York: C. L. Webster, 1885), 177.
24. B. F. Butler to Brig. General J. W. Phelps, September 8, 1862, quoted in Gerteis, *From Contraband to Freedman*, 68.
25. See Howard, *Autobiography*, 167–68; George Bentley, *A History of the Freedmen's Bureau* (New York: Octagon Books, 1974), 13. Louis Gerteis argues that former slaves in the eastern shores of Virginia were forced to accept contracts as laborers during the Civil War years. Throughout his study of the transition of "contraband to freedman," Gerteis powerfully reveals how military officers and the federal government were only interested in the labor of emancipated slaves. See Gerteis, *From Contraband to Freedman*, 61.
26. B. F. Butler to Maj. Gen Henry W. Halleck, September 1, 1862, quoted in Gerteis, *From Contraband to Freedman*, 72.
27. See for example Benjamin F. Butler, *Autobiography and Personal Reminiscences of Major-General Benjamin F. Butler, Butler's Book: A Review of His Legal, Political, and Military Career* (Boston: A.M. Thayer, 1892), 213, 193, 124–28.
28. Ibid., 1034–35.
29. Ibid., 1034.
30. Historian Louis Gerteis makes a similar argument; he explains, "The mobilization of land and labor in the Mississippi Valley came not out of moral concern for the freedmen but as a matter of military necessity." Gerteis, *From Contraband to Freedman*, 119–20.

31. Charles A. Humphreys, *Field, Camp, Hospital, and Prison in the Civil War, 1863–1865* (Boston: Geo. H. Ellis, 1918), 1.

32. *Weekly Anglo African*, March 22, 1862.

33. Grant, *Personal Memoir of Ulysses S. Grant*, 177.

34. Ibid. General Heintzelman endorsement, Wyman to Slough, November 24, 1862, quoted in Berlin et al., *Wartime Genesis of Free Labor: The Upper South*, 277.

35. Hulbert to Lincoln, March 27, 1863, quoted in Gerteis, *From Contraband to Freedman*, 120.

36. In January of 1861, the Medical Corps simply included a Surgeon General, 30 surgeons and 83 assistant surgeons, and of these 21 resigned to "take part in the Rebellion, and three assistant surgeons were dismissed for disloyalty." See Harvey E. Brown, *The Medical Department of the United States Army from 1775 to 1873* (Washington, DC: GPO, 1873), 215, HUN. Brown provides a list of physicians that documents their previous military history, 286–98.

37. See, for example, Brig. Genl. Wm. Dwight to Lt. Col. Richard B. Irwin, 23 March 1863, folder "March 1863," Box January to June, 1863, Dwight Family Papers, MHS, William Dwight Jr. to Mother, April 5, 1863, Folder April 1863, Box No. 13 January to June 1863, Dwight Family Papers, MHS. When stationed in the Gulf in New Orleans, William criticizes the Union leadership and makes endless references to Napoleon, Caesar, and wars in Russia. Also see Brown, *The Medical Department of the United States Army from 1775 to 1873*, 262

38. *Liberator*, February 14, 1862, 26. For a fascinating analysis of the ways in which the term contraband was used in various forms of nineteenth-century cultural production. See Kate Masur, "'A Rare Phenomenon of Philological Vegetation': The Word 'Contraband' and the Meanings of Emancipation in the United States," *Journal of American History* 93, no. 4 (2007): 1–65.

39. *Weekly Anglo African*, March 1, 1862.

40. *Atlantic Monthly*, November 1861, 626–40.

41. *National Freedmen's Relief Association*, May 1863, 1.

42. *Liberator*, March 7, 1862, 39.

43. *Freedmen's Record*, April, 1865, 63.

44. *Christian Recorder*, November 6, 1862.

45. Ibid.

46. "Volunteers Wanted," *Weekly Anglo African*, March 1, 1862; *Liberator*, March 7, 1862; *Weekly Anglo African*, March 22, 1862.

47. For an excellent analysis of the ways in which Northern women began to use charitable organizations to advance political causes and how certain groups of Northern women became politically involved in the debates and campaigns of the antebellum period, see Hewitt, *Women's Activism and Social Change: Rochester, 1822–1872*.

48. Sarah Gage Journal, George Gage Papers, Manuscript Division, DU.

49. There is a distinct relationship between cleanliness and health in the nineteenth century. Often times, those who appeared dirty were often either considered sick or susceptible to illness. For a broad, comprehensive analysis of cleanliness, see Kathleen M. Brown, *Foul Bodies: Cleanliness in Early America* (New Haven, CT: Yale University Press, 2009).

50. *Freedmen's Record*, April, 1865, 63.

51. Julia Wilbur Diary, November 5–10, 1862, microfilm, AHS.

52. In regard to the reference to the slave pen, antebellum Alexandria was a major station in the interstate slave trade. Before buyers and auctioneers bid on slaves, they were often kept in a slave pen, which during the war became a holding cell for slaves who migrated to Northern Virginia.

53. Julia Wilbur Diary, November 6, 1862, AHS.

54. Julia Wilbur to Abraham Lincoln, November 7, 1862, and Capt. John C. Wyman to Brig. General John P. Slough, November 24, 1862, quoted in Berlin et al., *Wartime Genesis of Free Labor: The Upper South*, 276–77.

55. For reformers' concern for personal hygiene, see Lydia Marie Child, *Freedmen's Book* (Boston: Ticknor and Fields, 1865). For military understanding of a clean environment see, Robert Reyburn, *Type of Disease among Freed People of the United States* (Washington, DC:

Gibson Bros., 1891; New York Academy of Medicine [NYAM]). Also see, Kipps to Robinson, October 12, 1866, Alabama, Office of Staff Officers, Surgeon, LS, vol. 1 (31), September 7, 1865–July 21, 1865, M809, Roll 8, RG 105, NARA. Also see Bentley, *History of the Freedmen's Bureau*, 27. Kathleen Brown provides a brilliant discussion of how authors of medical advice books warned of carbolic acid in the air and extolled the value of fresh air. These discussions in the 1830s formed as a precursor to late-nineteenth century discussions on ventilation. See her *Foul Bodies*, 234–37. For general nineteenth-century understandings of etiology, see K. Codell Carter, *The Rise of Causal Concepts of Disease: Case Histories* (Burlington, VT: Ashgate, 2003).

56. B. B. French to Hon. Edwin M. Stanton, February 13, 1862, quoted in Berlin et al., *Wartime Genesis of Free Labor: The Upper South*, 262–63; *Nation*, August 15, 1872.

57. Julia Wilbur to Abraham Lincoln, November 7, 1862, and Capt. John C. Wyman to Brig. General John P. Slough, November 24, 1862, quoted in Berlin et al., *The Wartime Genesis of Free Labor: The Upper South*, 276–77.

58. Captain John C. Wyman to Brig. Genl. John P. Slough, Oct. 21, 1862, quoted in Berlin et al., *Wartime Genesis of Free Labor: The Upper South*, 268–69.

59. Quoted in Berlin et al., *Wartime Genesis of Free Labor: The Upper South*, 278–79.

60. Stanley, "Beggars Can't Be Choosers," 1283–84.

61. *Weekly Anglo African*, March 22, 1862.

62. Michael B. Katz, *In the Shadow of the Poor House: A Social History of Welfare in America* (New York: Basic Books, 1986); David J. Rothman, *The Discovery of the Asylum: Social Order and Disorder in the New Republic* (Boston: Little, Brown, 1971).

63. Gerteis, *From Contraband to Freedman*.

64. Benjamin F. Butler, *Autobiography and Personal Reminiscences of Major-General Benjamin F. Butler, Butler's Book: A Review of His Legal, Political, and Military Career* (Boston: A. M. Thayer, 1892), 394–413.

65. Historian Louis S. Gerteis argues that Butler reversed his contraband policy that he developed at Fortress Monroe in Virginia when he arrived in New Orleans. Gerteis further argues that Butler "employed those blacks he found useful and excluded the rest, 'leaving them subject to the ordinary laws of the community.'" See Gerteis, *From Contraband to Freedman*, 67.

66. James Parton, *General Butler in New Orleans, History of the Administration of the Department of the Gulf in the year 1862: With an Account of the Capture of New Orleans, and a Sketch of the Previous Career of the General, Civil and Military* (New York: Mason Brothers, 1864), 307, Dubois, *Reconstruction*, 67–71.

67. Parton, *General Butler in New Orleans*, 304, 307.

68. Nathanial Prentiss Banks to James Henry Lane, 1864, in "Letter from Major General N.P. Banks, 1864," results of subject search on term "civil war" in online catalogue of The American Civil War: Letters and Diaries Database, Butler Library, Columbia University (accessed October 23, 2003). In Richmond, Virginia, the situation was similar, an estimated 2,000 white people all were receiving rations; whereas, only 200 black people were eligible for rations. The black population was estimated at nearly the same as the white population. See J. T. Trowbridge, *The South: A Tour of Its Battle-fields and Ruined Cities, A Journey Through the Desolated States, and Talks With the People* (Hartford, CT: L Stebbins, 1867), 160–63.

69. Butler to Stanton, May 25, 1862, quoted in Armstead L. Robinson, "Worser dan Jeff Davis: The Coming of Free Labor During the Civil War, 1861–1865," in *Essays on the Postbellum Southern Economy*, ed. Thavolia Glymph and John J. Kushma (College Station: University of Texas, 1985), 23.

70. For more on the American Freedmen's Aid Inquiry Commission, see Bentley, *History of the Freedmen's Bureau*, 25.

71. Robert Dale Owen, J. McKay, Samuel G. Howe to Hon. Edwin M. Stanton, June 30, 1863, *Preliminary Report of the American Freedmen's Inquiry Commission*, HL.

72. Robert Dale Owen, J. McKay, Samuel G. Howe to Hon. Edwin M. Stanton May 15, 1864, *Final Report of the American Freedmen's Inquiry Commission to the Secretary of War*, "Chapter III—The Future in the United States of the African Race," HL.

73. Bentley, *History of the Freedmen's Bureau*, 26.
74. James E. Yeatman et al. to President Lincoln, November 6, 1863, Gilder Lehrman Collection, New York, Digital History, 1545.11; Also see Ira Berlin et al., *Slaves No More: Three Essays on Emancipation and the Civil War* (Cambridge: Cambridge University Press, 1992), 132.
75. Yeatman, "A Report on the Conditions of the Freedmen of Mississippi," presented to the Western Sanitary Commission, December 17, 1863, quoted in Gerteis, *From Contraband to Freedman*, 130.
76. Ibid., 131.
77. See Gerteis, *From Contraband to Freedman*, 128–33.
78. Harriet A. Jacobs, "Life Among the Contrabands," *Liberator*, September 5, 1862, 3.
79. Quotes in *Freedoms Record*: February 1865; April 1865; May 1865, 78–79; July 1865, 108–09; September 1865, 1–2; October 1865, 158–62, July 1866, 133–34. L. P. Brockett, *Heroines of the Rebellion: or, Woman's Work in the Civil War; A Record of Heroism, Patriotism and Patience* (Philadelphia: Hubbard, 1888), 147, 157, 164, 186; and Swint, *Dear Ones at Home: Letters From Contraband Camps*, 148–49, 5, 19, 23, 24, 29–33, 135–36.
80. The Results of Emancipation in the United States of America, by a Committee of the American Freedmen's Union Commission (New York, c. 1867), 28–31, LOC. There is a rich literature that charts freedpeople's eagerness to learn to read and to write despite their arduous work schedules that often precluded them from attending school during the day or even on a regular basis. See Robert C. Morris, *Reading, 'Riting, and Reconstruction: The Education of Freedmen in the South, 1861–1870* (Chicago: University of Chicago Press, 1981); and Jim Downs, "Uplift, Violence, and Service: Black Women Educators in the Reconstruction South," *The Southern Historian* 24 (Spring 2003): 29–39.
81. This bureaucratic structure provided the blueprint for federal medical care during Reconstruction. As historian Peter Hall argues, benevolent organizations often provided the infrastructure and model for federal organizations and programs. In the case of the Freedmen's Bureau, he persuasively demonstrates the ways in which O. O. Howard and other architects of the Bureau were greatly influenced by not only the mission of these organizations but also their bureaucratic and organizational structure. Peter Hall, "Religion and the Organizational Revolution in the United States," in *Sacred Companies*, ed. N. J. Demerath et al. (New York: Oxford University Press, 1998), 99–116.
82. Howard, *Autobiography*, 194–201, Brockett, *Heroines of Rebellion*, 186; Yeatman, *Report on the Conditions of the Freedmen of Mississippi*, 16.
83. Howard, *Autobiography*, 194–201.
84. Cong. Globe, 38th Cong., 1st sess., 569, 572, 741, quoted in Michael Anthony Cooke, "The Health of Blacks During Reconstruction," (PhD diss., University of Maryland, 1983), 74.
85. Cong. Globe, 38th Cong., 1st sess., 709.
86. Ibid.
87. Ibid.
88. For more on Sumner's motivations, see Gerteis, *From Contraband to Freedmen*, 184. Also see Bentley, *History of the Freedmen's Bureau*.
89. Gerteis, *From Contraband to Freedmen*, 184.
90. See, for example, Berlin et al., *Wartime Genesis of Free Labor: The Lower South* and *Wartime Genesis of Free Labor: The Upper South*.
91. Willie Lee Rose's classic tome, *Rehearsal for Reconstruction*, unwittingly has led to this blurring of lines between the Civil War years and the Reconstruction period since Rose identified a unique moment when the government employed freed slaves as part of an "experiment" in the Sea Islands that dot the coasts of South Carolina and Georgia. Many historians have seen wartime labor as a prelude to the creation of a free labor economy in the South, when, in fact, these were two distinct episodes, in which the federal government operated under different motivations for organizing freed slaves into a labor force. See Willie Lee Rose, *The Port Royal Experiment* (Indianapolis, IN: Bobbs-Merrill, 1964).
92. For an excellent analysis of the clash between benevolent reformers and Bureau and military authorities, see Faulkner, *Women's Radical Reconstruction*. Also see Jean Fagan Yellin, *Harriet Jacobs: A Life* (New York: Basic Civitas Books, 2004).

Chapter 3

1. *Harper's Weekly*, May 5, 1860.
2. As president of the New York State Medical Society, D. B. St. John Roosa bemoaned the lack of attention paid to ventilation and proper sanitation in nineteenth-century hospitals. He further argued that hospital boards of directors, who designed hospitals, often excluded doctors from taking part in conversations about the organization and construction of hospitals. See D. B. St. John Roosa, M.D., President of the Society, "The Relations of the Medical Profession to the State" (New York: Published by the Order of the Society, 1879), 16. Also see Kathleen M. Brown, *Foul Bodies: Cleanliness in Early America* (New Haven, CT: Yale University Press, 2009), 234–37. On the disastrous and deadly conditions of army hospitals, see Paul E. Steiner, *Disease in the Civil War: Natural Biological Warfare in 1861–1865* (Springfield, IL: Charles C. Thomas, 1968); Frank R. Freemon, *Gangrene and Glory: Medical Care During the American Civil War* (Madison, NJ: Fairleigh Dickinson University Press, 1998).
3. Edwin M. Knights Jr., M.D., "The History of Bellevue Hospital," *History Magazine*, December–January 2000; W. Gill Wylie, M.D., *Hospitals: Their History, Organization, and Construction* (New York: D. Appleton, 1877), 180; Charles Rosenberg, "From Almshouse to Hospital: The Shaping of Philadelphia General Hospital," *Milbank Memorial Fund Quarterly* 60, no. 1 (1982): 108–54.
4. David Rothman's *The Discovery of the Asylum* was one of the first and most important books on the history of the asylum as an institution that imposed social order. Seth Rockman's *Scraping By* moves beyond the discourse of social control, and instead offers a more complicated and nuanced interpretation of the ways in which workers at various times used the asylum to their benefit. See Rothman, *The Discovery of the Asylum: Social Order And Disorder in the New Republic* (New York: Little, Brown, 1971); Seth Rockman, *Scraping By: Wage Labor, Slavery, and Survival in Early Baltimore* (Baltimore: Johns Hopkins University Press, 2008).
5. On Vanderwhost, see Robert Lebby to Asst. Surgeon T. Turner, August 9, 1865, Charleston, South Carolina, e. 3135, LS, RG 105, NARA.
6. Wylie, M.D., *Hospitals: Their History, Organization, and Construction*, 165–68. See Rothman, *Discovery of the Asylum*; and Rockman, *Scraping By*.
7. On relief in the Civil War South, see W. Martin Hope and Jason H. Silverman, *Relief and Recovery in Post-Civil War South Carolina: A Death by Inches* (Lewiston, NY: Edwin Mellen Press, 1997). Furthermore, Stephanie McCurry reveals the extent to which relief was not even available to many Southerners, particularly poor white women. Lacking basic necessities, many of these women engaged in bread riots in order to feed their families and mounted political campaigns as soldiers' wives to gain support. Stephanie McCurry, *Confederate Reckoning: Power and Politics in the Civil War South* (Cambridge, MA: Harvard University Press, 2010).
8. Griswold to Hayden, October 31, 1865, Chief Medical Officer, Annual Report, e. 1393, Chief Medical Officer (Misc), Box 40, RG 105, NARA. *New York Times*, January 27, 1866; U.S. War Department, BRFAL, *Laws in Relation to Freedmen*, U.S. Senate 39th Cong., 2nd sess., Senate Executive Document, no. 6 (Washington, DC: GPO, 1866–67), 79–81.
9. Pelzer to Mr. A. Fairly, March 13, 1866, Charleston, SC; Pelzer to H. Baer, March 15, 1866; Pelzer to Circular Letter, all in e. 3132, LS, vol. 1, RG 105, NARA. Local authorities did not agree to take infected freedpeople to Stewart City Hospital until September, six months after the initial letter from the Bureau.
10. Augusta to Lawton, May 17, 1866, Georgia, Savannah Lincoln Hospital, LS, vol. 1, December 1865–January 1868, M1903, Roll 85, RG 105, NARA.
11. Williams to D. B. M. Wilson, September 7, 1866, Mobile, AL, Offices of Staff Officers, Surgeon, LS, vol. 1 (31), September 7, 1865–July 21, 1865, M1901, Roll 8, RG 105, NARA.
12. For South Carolina, see J. S. Caulfield to W. R. Dewitt, September 10, 1865, South Carolina, Chief Medical Officer, e. 2979, LR. For Georgia, see Augusta to Caleb Horner, June 2, 1866, Georgia, Savannah Lincoln Hospital, LS, vol. 1, December 1865–January 1868, M1901, Roll 85. For Alabama, A. M. Ryan to Shrokly, April 30, 1868, Alabama, Records of

the Assistant Commissioner for the State of Alabama, Reports of the Operation of the Sub-district, M809, Roll 18, Frame 67–68. For North Carolina, see Hillebrandt to Kinston, June 18, 1866, North Carolina, e. 2535, LS, Box 37, all in RG 105, NARA. For Arkansas, Missouri, and Indian Territory, see War Dept., *Laws in Relation to Freedmen*, 28.

13. Hill to Thomas, December 3, 1864, Surgeon General's Office, Washington, DC, e. 2040, LR, Box 35, RG 105, NARA.

14. 39th Cong., 1st sess., House of Representatives, House Executive Documents, no. 11; See also John Eaton, *Grant, Lincoln and the Freedmen* (New York: Longmans, Green, 1907).

15. The six army medical units were established in New Orleans, Charleston, Sea Islands, Alexandria, Mississippi Valley, and New Berne, North Carolina. M. K. Hogan to C. W. Horner, November 23, 1865, New Berne, NC, e. 2468, Box 14, RG 105, NARA.

16. War Dept., *Laws in Relation to Freedmen*, 16.

17. M.K. Hogan to C.W. Horner, November 23, 1865, Raleigh, N.C., e. 2535, L.S., RG 105, NARA.

18. Ibid.

19. Ibid.

20. Testimony of Col. Geo. H. Hanks before the American Freedmen's Inquiry Commission, quoted in Ira Berlin et al., *The Wartime Genesis of Free Labor: The Lower South* (Cambridge: Cambridge University Press, 1990), 520.

21. *Second Report of a Committee of Representatives of New York Yearly Meeting of Friends Upon the Conditions and Wants of the Colored Refugees, 1863*, From Slavery to Freedom: The African-American Pamphlet Collection, 1824–1909, Abraham Lincoln Papers, LOC.

22. F. M. Minteur to W. W. Smith, December 18, 1865, e. 2979, Chief Medical Officer, LR, 1865–1866, RG 105, NARA. While Strawberry Ferry is not rural, the plantation remained outside of the purview of the Medical Division in Charleston. Emancipated slaves, who did not live near Bureau hospitals, were left on their own to combat the epidemic.

23. For example, see War Dept., *Laws in Relation to Freedmen*, 153–54.

24. "Agreement between Baskerville and Betty, a Negro Family," December 25, 1865, "Agreement between Mason and Baskerville, December 25, 1865," "Agreement of Hands with R. Baskerville for the year 1866" Signed November 24, 1865, Mss1B2924a 1669–1685, "Agreement, 1867 & 1868," "Hands Agreement, 1868," Baskerville Family Papers; "Contracts," Allen Family Papers, Buckingham Country, VA, January 1866–January 1868, Mss1AL546c, microfilm; "Isaac Claiborne, January 17, 1866, Amelia County," Harvie Family Papers, Mss1H2636c2844, "Amelia Burton," Harvie Family Papers, Mss1H2636a2841, all VHS.

25. "Agreement Between Charles J. Haskell and Freedmen and Freedwomen on Alston Plantation," July 21, 1865, Section 24, Mssic1118a 731–32, and January 1, 1866, Section 43, Mss1c1118a8881, Cabell Family Papers, VHS.

26. Grady McWhiney, ed., *Reconstruction and the Freedmen* (Chicago: McNally, 1963), 52.

27. Johnson ignored the fact that Marine Hospitals were the precedent to Bureau hospitals. More to the point, Johnson denied the effort to increase the roll of the Bureau, See "Bills and Resolutions," Cong. Globe, 39th Cong., 1st Sess. 129 (1866).

28. For more on Johnson's response to the Bureau, see Hans L. Trefousse, "Andrew Johnson and the Freedmen's Bureau," in *The Freedmen's Bureau and Reconstruction: Reconsiderations*, ed. Paul A. Cimbala and Randall M. Miller (New York: Fordham University Press, 1999), 29–45.

29. For military reports on the condition of freedpeople, see, M. K. Hogan to C. W. Horner, November 23, 1865, North Carolina, e. 2468, Box 14; A.A. Lawrence to H. N. Howard, October 31, 1866, Freedmen's Village, Washington, DC, Subordinate Field Officers, Annual Reports 1865–1868, 6; C. Tripp to S. Helenaville, September 23, 1865, South Carolina, e. 2979, LR, Box 37; Augusta to Lawton, May 17, 1866, Georgia, Savannah Lincoln Hospital, LS, vol. 1, December 1865–January 1868, all in RG 105, NARA. Eaton, *Grant, Lincoln and the Freedmen*, 30–33. For civilian reports, W. C. Adams to Robert Burns, April 6, 1866, Georgia, Mss1B9468a17, Burrus Family Papers, VHS; L. P. Brockett, *Heroines of the Rebellion: or, Woman's Work in the Civil War; A Record of Heroism, Patriotism and Patience* (Philadelphia: Hubbard, 1888), 140, 159, 164, 186. J. T. Trowbridge, *South: A Tour of Its*

Battlefields and Ruined Cities, A Journey Through the Desolated States, and Talks with the People (Hartford, CT: L. Stebbins, 1866); Lois Bryan Adams, *Letter from Washington, 1863–1865*, edited and with an introduction by Evelyn Leasher (Detroit: Wayne State University Press, 1999). Eliza Frances Andrews, *The Wartime Journal of a Georgia Girl, 1864–1865* (New York: D. Appleton, 1908); Spencer Bidwell King, Jr., ed. (Macon, GA: Ardivan Press, 1960); Grady McWhiney, ed., *Reconstruction and the Freedmen* (Chicago: McNally, 1963), 29–32.

30. S. N.Clark to W. W. Rogerts, October 6, 1866, Washington, DC, A-9931, DC A/G 520, LS, v. 53, pp. 22–23, letter 49, FSSP.

31. Eaton, *Grant, Lincoln and the Freedmen*, 105.

32. On May 12, 1865, Maj. Gen. Oliver Otis Howard was assigned as the Commissioner. 39th Cong., 1st sess. House of Representatives, House Executive Documents, no. 11, 11–12.

33. Ibid.

34. For John Eaton's role in assisting Howard organize the Bureau, see Eaton, *Grant, Lincoln and the Freedmen*, 236–51.

35. Hill to Thomas, December 3, 1864, Surgeon General's Office, Washington, DC, e. 2040, LR, Box 35, RG 105, NARA; 39th Cong., 1st sess., House of Representatives, House Executive Documents, No. 11; Eaton, *Grant, Lincoln and the Freedmen*, 237; Howard, *Autobiography*, 258–59.

36. Howard, *Autobiography*, 218.

37. Ibid., 312.

38. David Rothman makes the connection between the creation of asylums and social order in his classic study, *The Discovery of the Asylum: Social Order and Disorder in the New Republic* (New York: Little, Brown, 1971). For a more theoretical discussion on the relationship between institutions and surveillance, see Foucault's discussion of panopticism. Michel Foucault: *The Birth of the Clinic: An Archeology of Medical Perception* (New York: Vintage, 1994).

39. Howard quoted his first circular verbatim in his autobiography. See Howard, *Autobiography*, 212–13.

40. Ibid. For a penetrating analysis of compulsive labor among the freedpeople during this period, see Amy Dru Stanley, "Beggars Can't Be Choosers: Compulsion and Contract in Postbellum America," *The Journal of American History* 78, no. 4 (March 1992): 1265–93.

41. Howard, *Autobiography*, 214.

42. Howard, *Autobiography*, 226.

43. War Dept., *Laws in Relation to Freedmen*, 16.

44. It is also important to note that throughout the nineteenth century, the notion of preventive medicine was not widely accepted. Physicians were called in response to a problem instead of being consulted before a potential medical crisis could erupt. For more on physicians' frustration with the state not adopting preventive measures, see D. B. St. John Roosa, M.D., President of the Society "The Relations of the Medical Profession to the State" (New York: Published by the Order of the Society, 1879), 16.

45. Eaton, *Grant, Lincoln and the Freedmen*, 160.

46. On almshouses as training grounds for physicians, see Charles Rosenberg, "From Almshouse to Hospital," 108–54.

47. Rebecca Crumpler, *A Book of Medical Discourses* (Boston: Cashman, Keating, 1883), 2.

48. On smallpox, see W. H. Elridge to DeWitt, September 25, 1865; I. M. Carr to C. W. Horner, September 28, 1865, Georgetown, SC; S. C. Brown to R. Libby, November 21, 1865, Charleston, SC; F. L. Frosh to Saxton, November 20, 1865, Charleston, SC; C. H. Brownley to DeWitt, December 11, 1865, James Island, SC, all can be found in e. 2979, LR, RG 105, NARA. On clean water, see A. T. Augusta to R. O. Abbott, June 17, 1863, Quartermaster Correspondence Consolidated Files, Contraband Camps 1863 File, Box 99, RG 92, NARA.

49. W. F. Spurgin to C. H. Howard, April 9, 1866, District of Columbia, A-9753, 456 Letter, Box 2, #1232, FSSP; Hogan to Cilley, January 17, 1866, North Carolina, e. 2535, LS, p. 18, RG 105, NARA; War Dept., *Laws in Relation to Freedmen*, 12.

50. Lawton to O. O. Kinsman, September 19, 1865, Offices of Staff Officers, Surgeon-in-Chief, LS and Register of LR, vol. 52, September 1865–July 1867, M1903, Roll 26, RG 105, NARA.

51. *Freedmen's Record*, January 1866, 3–4.
52. Wilcox to Capt. Newtown Flagg, June 26, 1865, Quartermaster Report, December 1864–1865, Quartermaster Consolidated Collection, Negroes File, Box 720, RG 82, NARA.
53. Griswold to Hayden, October 31, 1865, Chief Medical Officer, Annual Report, e. 1393, Chief Medical Officer (Misc), Box 40, RG 105, NARA; War Dept., *Laws in Relation to Freedmen*, 109.
54. Emmanuel Ezekiel to Radzinsky, September 10, 1866, Orangeburg, SC, e. 3314, LS and Special Orders Received, RG 105, NARA. In February 1866, Congress passed a bill that enabled the federal government to occupy no more than 3 million acres of land in Florida, Mississippi, and Arkansas for the use of hospitals and asylums, but in South Carolina, it seems such a policy was not adopted. See *Harper's Weekly*, "Domestic Intelligence," February 10, 1866, 83.
55. War Dept., *Laws in Relation to Freedmen*, 111.
56. *Freedmen's Record*, January 1866, 3–4.
57. For more on the Johnson's first presidential veto and the extension of the Freedmen's Bureau, see LaWanda Cox and John H. Cox, eds., *Reconstruction, the Negro, and the New South* (Columbia: University of South Carolina Press, 1973), 31–32. Unlike the massive project undertaken by the federal government to properly bury Union soldiers, a similar program did not exist for freedpeople. Instead, burials and the creation of cemeteries depended upon the decisions made by individual Bureau leaders. Moreover, there is little archival data about where freedpeople were buried during the Reconstruction era. A recent archival excavation of a plot of land in Alexandria, Virginia, on which a gas station was built in the late twentieth century, led to the discovery of a Freedmen's Cemetery. As a result of this finding, I was then able to locate some of the burial records of the freedpeople in Alexandria from the Civil War years. See Gladwin, "Book of Records Containing Marriage and Deaths That Have Occurred within the Official Jurisdiction of Rev. A. Gladwin together with any Biographical and other Reminisces that may be Collected" (microfilm), Barrett Library, VHS. For more on the federal government's efforts to bury enlisted men, see Drew Gilpin Faust, *This Republic of Suffering: Death and the American Civil War* (New York: Vintage, 2009).
58. Gardner to Campbell, April 30, 1866, and Campbell to Whittlesey, April 30, 1866, both in Raleigh, NC, e. 2536, LS, RG 105, NARA.
59. Robert Lebby to W. R. Dewitt, Chief Surgeon, November 4, 1865, Charleston, SC, Roper Hospital, e. 3135, LS, RG 105, NARA.
60. Ibid. Edward Pierce, *Atlantic Monthly*, "The Freedmen at Port Royal," September 1863, 291–315. Also see Jim Downs, "The Other Side of Freedom: Destitution, Disease, and Dependency among Freedwomen and Their Children during and after the Civil War," in *Battle Scars: Gender and Sexuality in the American Civil War*, ed. Catherine Clinton and Nina Silber (New York: Oxford University Press, 2006), 78–103.
61. On postmortem in Alabama, see Kipp to R. H. Beumty, H. Hood (in Selma), J. Schetz (Montgomery), C. Miller (Demopolis), November 28, 1865, Alabama, Officers of the State Offices, Surgeon, LS, vol. 1 (31), 50, September 7, 1865–July 21, 1865, M1900, Roll 8, RG 105, NARA. On the need for freedpeople's burials to be entirely separate from the other citizens in North Carolina, see Campbell to Whittlesey, April 30, 1866, North Carolina, e. 2535, LS, RG 105, NARA. H. N. Hubbard to Mayor Eldridge. April 28, 1868, Washington, DC, M1902, Roll 20, RG 105, NARA. On body snatching, see A. A. Lawrence to H. N. Howard, January 11, 1866, Washington, DC, M1902, Roll 20, RG 105, NARA.
62. Pelzer to E. L. Deanes, February 19, 1868, Charleston, SC, e. 3162, LS, RG 105, NARA.
63. Holman to C. A. Cilley, September 4, 1865, North Carolina, e. 2535, LS, p. 114 (ledger), RG 105, NARA; M. K. Hogan to C. W. Horner, November 23, 1865, North Carolina, e. 2468, Box 14, RG 105, NARA.
64. W. F. Spurgin to Torrey Turner, September 1, 1865, Local Superintendent for Washington and Georgetown Correspondence, vol. 1 (77), LS, July 15, 1865–September 10, 1867, M1902, Roll 13, RG 105, NARA. Henry Saunders to Griswold, February 12, 1866, Louisiana, e. 1393, LR, Box 40, RG 105, NARA.

65. Lawton to Tillson, September 29, 1865, Georgia, Endorsements, Chief Medical Officer; and Lawton to C. W. Horner, September 29, 1865, Georgia, Offices of the Staff Officers, Surgeon in Chief, vol. 52, LS and Register of LR, September 1865–July 1867, M1903, Roll 26, RG 105, NARA.

66. A. J. Swartzwelden to Major Grove, September 11, 1865, Memphis, TN, e. 3556, LS, Box 73, RG 105, NARA.

67. Dewitt to Lt. Col. A. K. Smith, January 20, 1866, South Carolina, Chief Medical Surgeon, e. 2979, LR, Box 37, RG 105, NARA; John David Smith, "'The Work It Did Not Do Because It Could Not': Georgia and the 'New' Freedmen's Bureau Historiography," *Georgia Historical Quarterly* 352, no. 2 (Summer 1998): 343–44.

68. Barnes to Hogan, September 29, 1865, North Carolina, e. 2536, p. 8, LS, RG 105, NARA.

69. Swartzwelden to Grove, September 11, 1865, Tennessee, e. 3556, LR, Box 73; J. V. De Hanne to Clement, June 21, 1867, Atlanta, GA, Offices of the Staff Officers, Surgeon-in-Chief, LS and Register of LR, vol. 52, September 1865–July 1867, M1903, Roll 26; Kipps to Horner, November 15, 1865, Mobile, AL, Offices of the Staff Officers, Surgeon-in-Chief, LS, vol. 1 (31), 41–46, September 7, 1865–July 21, 1865, all in RG 105, NARA.

70. Swartzwelden to J. E. Smith, September 4, 1865, Memphis, TN, e. 3556, LS, Box 73, RG 105, NARA.

71. Eaton, *Grant, Lincoln and the Freedmen*, 22, 32.

72. D. Markay to Lieut. J. M. Lee, September 30, 1867, Louisiana, e. 1393, Annual Report, Chief Medical Report, p. 10, (Misc.), Box 40, RG 105, NARA.

73. Asa Teal to Eliphalet Whittlesey, October 6, 1865, Reports of Operation, N.C., Assistant Commissioner Records, quoted in Reggie Pearson, "'There Are Many Sick, Feeble, And Suffering Freedmen': The Freedmen's Bureau's Health-Care Activities During Reconstruction In North Carolina, 1865–1868," *North Carolina Historical Review* 79, no. 2 (2002): 147.

74. War Dept., *Laws in Relation to Freedmen*, 99.

75. DeWitt to Caleb Horner, December 11, 1865, South Carolina, e. 2977, LS, vol. 1, 106–07, RG 105, NARA.

76. Charles Rosenberg, "Social Class and Medical Care in Nineteenth-Century America: The Rise and Fall of the Dispensary," *Journal of the History of Medicine and Allied Sciences* 29, no. 1 (1974): 32–54.

77. Lawton to Lewis, October 4, 1865, Georgia, Offices of the Staff Officers, Surgeon-in-Chief, LS and Register of LR, vol. 52, September 1865–July 1867, M1903, Roll 26, RG 105, NARA.

78. Higgs to Corner, April 8, 1867, Offices of the Staff Officers, Surgeon-in-Chief, Endorsements Sent and Received, p. 29, M1902, Roll 13, RG 105 NARA. Ibid., April 20, 1867, p. 30.

79. War Dept., *Laws in Relation to Freedmen*.

80. On toxic smells, see Brown, *Foul Bodies*, 183–89.

81. G. A. Wheeler, A.A. Surgeon to Captain A.A. Lawrence, February 14, 1867, Freedmen's Village, LR, M1902, Roll 20, Frame 349–50, RG 105, NARA. For a brilliant discussion on the relationship between laundering and cleanliness, see Brown, *Foul Bodies*.

82. J. W. Lawton to Surgeon B. McClin, September 15, 1865, Offices of Staff Officers, Surgeon-in-Chief, LS and Register of LR, vol. 52, September 1865–July 1867, M1903, Roll 26, RG 105, NARA.

83. C. A. Ciley to Hogan, January 24, 1866, Salisbury, NC, e. 2535, LS, p. 18; ibid., January 13, 1866 both in RG 105, NARA.

84. W. F. Spurgin to Torrey Turner, September 1, 1865, Local Superintendent for Washington and Georgetown Correspondence, LS, vol. 1 (77), July 15, 1865–September 10, 1867, M1902, Roll 13, RG 105, NARA. Henry Saunders to Griswold, Louisiana, February 12, 1866, e. 1393, LR, Box 40, RG 105, NARA.

85. S. D. Radzinksky to Happersett, October 6, 1866, Orangeburg, SC, Hogendabler to Happersett, December 24, 1866, Hogendabler to Happersett, Hamburg, SC, Chief Medical Surgeon, all in e. 2979, LR, Box 37, RG 105, NARA.

86. B. Burgh Smith to W. R. DeWitt, October 14, 1865, Charleston, SC, e. 3249, LS, vol. 1; ibid., November 4, 1865; ibid., March 13, 1865; Beckett to George Wright, March 22, 1867;

Beckett to Hogan, May 21, 1867; Beckett to Wright, August 29, 1867, all in e.3249, LS, vol. 1, RG 105, NARA.

87. List of Employees in the Refugees and Freedmen's Hospital at Atlanta For the Year Ending January 1866, Reports of the Surgeon in Charge, Atlanta, GA, e. 745, Folder 26, RG 105, NARA; DeHanne to T. R. Clement, June 9, 1867, Office of Staff Officers, Surgeon-in-Chief, LS and Register of LR, vol. 52, September 1865–July 1867, M1903, Roll 26, RG 105, NARA.

88. Lawton to Horner, September 29, 1865, Offices of the Staff Officers, LS and Received, vol., 52, M1902, Roll 26, RG 105, NARA.

89. Pease to Griswold, September 9, 1865, Louisiana, Chief Medical Officer, e. 1393, LR, Box 40, RG 105, NARA.

90. Hogan to Yeomans, November 30, 1866, New Berne, NC, e.2536, LS, vol. 2, RG 105, NARA.

91. Hogan to R. B. Matlock, March 9, 1867, North Carolina, e. 2536, LS, vol. 2, RG 105, NARA.

92. B. Burgh Smith to W. R. DeWitt, October 14, 1865, Charleston, SC, e. 3249, LS, vol. 1, RG 105, NARA; I. L. Beckett to R. K. Scott, January 15, 1867, e. 3249, LS, vol. 1, RG 105, NARA.

93. Alexandria had well over 13 hospitals, whereas, in the entire state of Louisiana, there were less than a dozen. Hospitals Vertical File, AHS; E. Griswold to Hayden, October 31, 1865, Chief Medical Officer, Annual Report, e. 1393, Chief Medical Officer (Misc), Box 40, RG 105, NARA.

94. C. H. Howard to O. O. Howard, October 22, 1866, Annual Reports, e. 9926, DC AC, 449 LS, Vol. 7, p. 112–22. FSSP.

95. A. T. Augusta to J. W. Lawton, August 9, 1866; August 14, 1866; August 21, 1866; September 1, 1866; A. T. Augusta to A.A. Schell, August 18, 1866; Augusta to Capt. Watson, August 21, 1866, all in Georgia, Savannah Lincoln Hospital, LS, M1903, Roll 85, RG 105, NARA.

96. War Dept., *Laws in Relation to Freedmen*.

97. Ibid.

98. J. S. Caulfield to W. R. Dewitt, September 10, 1865, South Carolina, Chief Medical Officer, e. 2979, LR, Box 37, RG 105, NARA. (Although this document is from Georgia, it was found in the South Carolina box—which could be the result of an error in the archival collection or it could be that the Bureau officer, at that moment, had authority over both regions.)

99. Wilcox to Capt. Newtown Flagg, June 26, 1865, Quartermaster Report, December 1864–1865, Quartermaster Consolidated Collection, Negroes File, Box 720, RG 82, NARA.

100. *New York Herald*, February 17, 1866. For an overview of the 1866 veto, see Cox and Cox, *Reconstruction, the Negro, and the New South*, 31–77

101. Monthly Statement of Hospital Funds and Rations Return, Augusta, GA, Freedmen's Hospital, vol. 162, October 1865–May 1868, M1903, Roll 49; Clark to Howard, April 15, 1868, Washington DC, Subordinate Field Officers, Freedmen's Village, M1902, Roll 21; J. C. O'Neal to Howard, December 31, 1867, Subordinate Field Officers, LR, vol. 85, M1902, Roll 20; Hogan to Day, January 8, 1867, North Carolina, e. 2536, LS, vol. 2. Diet tables—Caleb Horner to Griswold, September 20, 1865, Louisiana, e. 1393, LR, Box 40, all in RG 105, NARA.

102. Augusta to Sickles, January 5, 1866, Georgia, Savannah Lincoln Hospital, LS, vol. 1, December 1865–January 1868, M1903, Roll 85, RG 105, NARA.

103. Kipp to Sawyer, October 11, 1865, Alabama, Officers of the State Offices, Surgeon, LS, vol. 1 (31), September 7, 1865–July 21, 1865, M1900, Roll 8, RG 105, NARA.

104. War Dept., *Laws in Relation to Freedmen*, 81–82.

105. G. A. Wheeler, A. A. Surgeon to Captain A. A. Lawrence, February 14, 1867, Freedmen's Village, LR, M1902, Roll 20, Frame 349–50, RG 105, NARA.

106. Charles J. Stille, *History of the United States Sanitary Commission: Being the General Report of its Work during the War of the Rebellion* (Philadelphia: J. B. Lippincott, 1866); Jacob Gilbert Forman, The Western Sanitary Commission, "A Sketch of Its Origin, History, Labors for the Sick and Wounded of the Western Armies, and Aid Given to the Freedmen and Union

Refugees, with Incidents of Hospital Life" (St. Louis, MO: Published for the Mississippi Sanitary Fair), 14–15; P. M. Ashburn, *A History of the Medical Department of the United States Army* (Boston: Houghton Mifflin, 1929). Captain Louis C. Duncan, *Medical Corps, U.S. Army, The Medical Department of the United States Army in the Civil War* [Washington? n.d.], 20–1. On the subject of ventilation, I also profited enormously from a paper on ventilation that Margaret Humphreys presented at the Society of Civil War Historians, Second Biennial Meeting, June 2010, "Out of Harm's Way? The Satterlee General Hospital of Philadelphia." I also want to move beyond the strict idea that the principles underlying the subject of microbiology did not circulate until Pasteur's discovery. Instead, I support Bruno Latour's argument that Pasteur built on existing ideas and principles that were known among hygienists. See Bruno Latour, *The Pasteurization of France* (Cambridge, MA: Harvard University Press, 1988); Elan Daniel Lewis, *Review of Pasteurization of France, Yale Journal of Biology and Medicine* 62, no. 1 (January–February 1989): 47–48.

107. Ward to ?, July 11, 1866, North Carolina, e. 2535, LS, Box 37. Also see, Kipps to Robinson, October 12, 1866, Alabama, Office of Staff Officers, Surgeon, LS, vol. 1. (31), September 7, 1865–July 21, 1865, Roll 8; Hogan to Ward, July 11, 1866, North Carolina, e. 2535, LS, p. 55. Also see, C. A. Ciley to Hogan, January 24, 1866, Salisbury, NC, e. 2535, LS, p. 18, all in RG 105, NARA.

108. Historian David Rosner documents that it was not until the late nineteenth century that hospitals were forced to begin charging patients. See Rosner, *A Once Charitable Enterprise: Hospitals and Health Care in Brooklyn and New York, 1885–1915* (New York: Cambridge University Press, 1982), 62.

109. James Yeatman, *A Report on the Condition of the Freedmen of the Mississippi* (St. Louis, MO: n.p., 1864), 7.

110. Thomas Conway, "The Freedmen of Louisiana: Final Report of the Bureau of Free Labor, Department of the Gulf. To Major General R.S. Canby" (Printed at the New Orleans Times Book and Job Office, 1865), 31.

111. Howard, *Circular No. 5*, quoted in Eaton, *Grant, Lincoln and the Freedmen*, 238–40.

112. W. F. Spurgin to Torrey Turner, September 1, 1865, Local Superintendent for Washington and Georgetown Correspondence, LS, vol. 1 (77), July 15, 1865–September 10, 1867, M1902, Roll 13, RG 105, NARA.

113. Steedman and Fullerton, "The Freedmen's Bureau: Reports of Generals Steedman and Fullerton on the Condition of the Freedmen's Bureau in the Southern States," May 8, 1866, 2. From Slavery to Freedom: The African-American Pamphlet Collection, 1824–1909, LOC.

114. Robert Harrison, "Welfare and Employment Policies of the Freedmen's Bureau in the District of Columbia," *Journal of Southern History* 72, no. 1 (February 2006):75–110.

115. Headquarters, BRFAL, State of Texas, Office Surgeon in Chief, October 31, 1866, Senate Executive Documents for the Second Session of the 39th Congress of the U.S.A, 1866–67 (Washington, DC: GPO, 1867), 153–54.

116. Ibid., 153.

117. Report of C. H. Howard, April 1, 1867, Records of the Field and Officers for the District of Columbia, 1865–1870, p. 48, M1902, Roll 1, RG 105, NARA.

118. Charles J. Trips to Major General Wagner, January 5, 1867, Montgomery, AL, M1900, Roll 18, Frame 474, RG 105, NARA.

119. For example, see, George McComber to General Robinson, July 7, 1866, North Carolina, e. 2535, LS, RG 105, NARA.

120. Eliphalet Whittlesey to D. W. Hand, July 13, 1865, North Carolina, quoted in Pearson, "There Are Many Sick, Feeble, And Suffering Freedmen," 148.

121. Hogan to Yeomans, December 8, 1866, New Berne, NC, e. 2536, LS, vol. 2, RG 105, NARA.

122. D. Markay to Lieut. J. M. Lee, September 30, 1867, Louisiana, e. 1393, Annual Report, Chief Medical Report, p. 10, (Misc), Box 40, RG 105, NARA.

123. For example, many freedpeople were employed to work at Freedmen's Village in Arlington, VA. Superintendent Field Offices, Freedmen's Village, Reports 1865–68, M1902, Roll 21, Frame 70, RG 105, NARA.

124. Augusta to J. V. DeHanne, May 2, 1867, Georgia, Savannah Lincoln Hospital, LS, December 1865–January 1868, M1903, Roll 85, Frame 961, RG 105, NARA.

125. Hogan to Day, January 8, 1867, North Carolina, e.2536, LS, vol. 2, RG 105, NARA.
126. War Dept., *Laws in Relation to Freedmen*, 28.
127. Howard commissioned the establishment of vegetable gardens in conjunction with hospitals in his order of March 15, 1866, See War Dept., *Laws in Relation to Freedmen*, 108.
128. Doctors in North Carolina, for example, struggled to implement the garden project. Hogan to Newtown, February 20, 1867, March 13, 1867, Raleigh, NC; Hogan to Barthoff, February 28, 1867, Raleigh, NC; Hogan to Day, Wilmington, NC; Hogan to Bell, March 13, 1867, Salisbury, NC; Hogan to Edwards, April 4, 1867, Wilmington, NC, all in e. 2536, LS, vol. 2, RG 105, NARA.
129. Augusta to Horner, July 1866, and August 7, 1866, Georgia, Savannah Lincoln Hospital, LS, vol. 1, December 1865–January 1868, M1903, Roll 85, RG 105. NARA.
130. J. V. DeHanne to M. F. Barres, January 19, 1867, Georgia, LR, M1903, Roll 49, RG 105, NARA.
131. For an insightful analysis of the conflict between Bureau agents and Northern benevolent associations, see Carol Faulkner, *Women's Radical Reconstruction* (Philadelphia: University of Pennsylvania Press, 2004).
132. Eaton, *Grant, Lincoln and the Freedmen*, 130–31, 144. See War Dept., *Laws in Relation to Freedmen*, 12.
133. *Second Annual Report of the New England Freedmen's Aid Society* (Boston: Published at the Office of the Society, 1864), 35, MHS.
134. Harriet Jacobs received aid from Northern reform organizations to support her work among the freedpeople. In many of her letters from 1865 to 1866, she describes providing assistance to Bureau hospitals. See Jean Fagan Yellin et al., *The Harriet Jacobs Family Papers, Volume Two* (Chapel Hill: University of North Carolina Press, 2008), 642–63. Throughout the benevolent records, there are numerous examples of Northern reformers supporting Bureau relief efforts. See *Freedmen's Record*, volumes 1–4, 1863–1868; also see Henry Lee Swint, ed., *Dear Ones At Home: Letters from Contraband Camps* (Nashville, TN: Vanderbilt University Press, 1966).
135. Lawton to C. Horner, September 29, 1865, Offices of Staff Officers, Surgeon-in-Chief, LS and Register of LR, vol. 52, September 1865–July 1867, M1903, Roll 26, RG 105, NARA.
136. Abby Howland Woolsey to Harriet Gilman, March 9, 1865, in *Letters of a Family During the War for the Union 1861–1865*, vol. 2 (New Haven, CT: Tuttle, Morehouse & Taylor, 1899).
137. Historian Steven Hahn coherently charts how kin networks survived slavery, Reconstruction, and Jim Crow; Elsa Barkley Brown cogently explains how freedpeople conceptualized family units differently from white prevailing notions of family—these kin networks, Barkley Brown argues, fundamentally reconstituted the political and economic reconstruction of the South. Dylan Penningroth further advances the centrality of kin networks in his incisive analysis of how freedpeople relied on kin connections to claim property. Steven Hahn, *A Nation Under Our Feet: Black Political Struggles in the Rural South from Slavery to the Great Migration* (Cambridge, MA: Harvard University Press, 2005); Elsa Barkley Brown, "To Catch a Vision of Freedom: Reconstructing Southern Black Women's Political History, 1865–1880," in *Unequal Sisters: A Multicultural Reader in U.S. Women's History*, 3rd ed., ed. Ellen DuBois and Vicki Ruiz (New York: Routledge, 2000), 124–46; Barkley Brown, "Womanist Consciousness: Maggie Lena Walker and the Independent Order of Saint Luke," *Signs: Journal of Women in Culture & Society* 14, no. 3 (Spring 1989): 610–33; Dylan C. Penningroth, *The Claims of Kinfolk: African-American Property and Community in the Nineteenth-Century South* (Chapel Hill: University of North Carolina Press, 2003).
138. *Freedmen's Record*, May 1868, 81.
139. Ibid., 78–9.
140. Julie Winch, *Philadelphia's Black Elite: Activism, Accommodation, and the Struggle for Autonomy, 1787–1848* (Philadelphia: Temple University Press, 1993). Leslie Harris, *In the Shadow of Slavery: African-Americans in New York City, 1626–1863* (Chicago: University of Chicago Press, 2004).
141. Steedman and Fullerton, "The Freedmen's Bureau," LOC.
142. Griswold to Hayden, October 31, 1865, Chief Medical Officer, Annual Report, e. 1393, Chief Medical Officer (Misc), Box 40, RG 105, NARA.

143. Senate Executive Documents for the Second Session of the 39th Congress of the U.S.A, 1866–67. War Dept., *Laws in Relation to Freedmen*.

144. Ward to Fleming, July 11, 1866; Lt. C. M. Dodge to Fleming; July 11, 1866; and McComber to Maj. General Robinson, August 21, 1866, all in Plymouth, NC, e. 2536, LS, RG 105, NARA.

145. *Second Freedmen's Bureau Bill*, Section 3, "An Act To Amend An Act Entitled 'An act to establish a Bureau for the relief of Freedmen and Refugees,' and for other purposes," H.R. 613, 39th Cong., 1st Session, LOC.

146. In his study of the Republican Party's support of black suffrage after the Civil War, Wang Xi suggests that Republicans aggressively fought for voting rights for freedpeople as a way to increase their own party membership in the South. See Wang Xi, *The Trial of Democracy: Black Suffrage and Northern Republican, 1860–1910* (Athens: University of Georgia Press, 1997). Building on his argument, I attempt to reveal the ulterior motives of the Republican Party in their fight for the extension of the Bureau in the South. While on the surface, they argued it was for the relief and medical support of newly emancipated slaves, they also had an economic and political investment in freedpeople's labor power.

147. Swartzwelden to Warren, March 31, 1868, Chief Medical Officer, e. 1385 LS, p. 317; Griswold to T. W. Conway, August 15, 1865, e. 1385, LS, p. 85; Griswold to T. W. Conway, October 18, 1865, e. 2536, all in e.1385, RG 105, NARA. Planters also cut down the amount of time for emancipated slaves to recover from illness and forced them to return to the fields. See F.M. Minter to W.W. Smith, December 1865, South Carolina, e. 2979, Box 38, Chief Medical Officer, LR, RG 105, NARA.

Chapter 4

1. Hogan to J. K. Fleming, February 12, 1866, Scrapbook of Letters Received; Fleming to Hogan, April 4, 1866; Horner to Hogan, April 11, 1866, all in e. 2788, Scrapbook of LR, RG 105, NARA.

2. *Second Report of a Committee of Representatives of New York Yearly Meeting of Friends Upon the Conditions and Wants of the Colored Refugees*, From Slavery to Freedom: The African-American Pamphlet Collection, 1824–1909, LOC; Jean Fagan Yellin et al., *The Harriet Jacobs Family Papers, Volume Two* (Chapel Hill: University of North Carolina Press, 2008), 642–63; L. P. Brockett, *Woman's Work in the Civil War: A Record of Heroism, Patriotism and Patience, 1820–1893* (Philadelphia: Hubbard Brothers, 1888), 193–94.

3. *New York Times*, March 26, 1865.

4. I have examined thousands of records regarding the smallpox epidemic and have found few sources that comment on what the epidemic meant for freedpeople.

5. Historian of science David S. Jones insightfully warns that historians cannot witness how historical actors experienced epidemics. David S. Jones, *Rationalizing Epidemics: Meanings and Uses of American Indian Mortality since 1600* (Cambridge, MA: Harvard University Press, 2004), 12–13.

6. According to historian Charles Rosenberg, despite the fact that smallpox had been known as a contagious disease for centuries, many people nevertheless subscribed to the idea that personal behavior made one susceptible to smallpox infection. See Charles E. Rosenberg, "What Is an Epidemic: AIDS in Historical Perspective" *Daedalus* 118, no. 2, *Living with AIDS* (Spring 1989): 6–7.

7. Beyond the de facto measures, there was also a public health rationale for these practices. Since the eighteenth century in the United States (and even earlier in Europe), townspeople, medical authorities, and municipal officials often quarantined smallpox patients to isolated regions to prevent the further spread of the disease. Donald R. Hopkins, *Princes and Peasants: Smallpox in History* (Chicago: University of Chicago Press, 1983).

8. Xi Wang cogently argues that Republicans supported black enfranchisement in order to expand their party's base in the South. See Xi Wang, *The Trial of Democracy: Black Suffrage and Northern Republicans, 1860–1910* (Athens: University of Georgia Press, 1997).

9. Sharla Fett, *Working Cures: Health, Healing, and Power on Southern Slave Plantations* (Chapel Hill: University of North Carolina Press, 2002), 40. Also see, for example, John Thornton,

Africa and Africans in the Making of the Atlantic World, 1400–1800 (Cambridge: Cambridge University Press, 1998), 243, 265, 267.

10. In his autobiography, O. O. Howard brushes over the devastation and death caused by the smallpox epidemic by claiming that the government promptly responded to epidemic outbreaks and quelled them—which was unfortunately not the case. See Howard, *Autobiography*, 295–96.

11. Despite the current medical understanding that smallpox is a virus and not a disease, throughout the nineteenth-century Bureau records, doctors and other military officials refer to it as a "disease." They also use the terms "scourge," "distemper," and "affliction." I often use the term "virus" when I am trying to explain a particular point about smallpox transmission. When I describe it as a "disease," it is often due to the sources that I am drawing from or the historical context that I am attempting to develop.

12. U.S. War Dept., Record and Pension Office, War Records Office, et al. *The War of the Rebellion: A Compilation of the Official Records of the Union and Confederate Armies*, series 1, vol. 7 (Washington, DC: GPO, 1894), 810. For a history of smallpox and its origins, see Hopkins, *Princes and Peasants*, 14. Hopkins argues that the first dated account of smallpox appears as early as 1570–1085 BCE. Also see, Elizabeth Fenn, *Pox Americana: The Great Smallpox Epidemic of 1775–82* (New York: Hill and Wang, 2001).

13. My study offers the first analysis of the smallpox epidemic and the health conditions of ex-slaves after the war. In her study *Intensely Human*, Margaret Humphreys has convincingly documented the health conditions of black soldiers during this period, but her focus remains on the military experience—which represents a fraction of the ex-slave population. See Humphreys, *Intensely Human: The Health of the Black Soldier in the American Civil* (Baltimore: Johns Hopkins University Press, 2008).

14. War Dept., *War of the Rebellion: A Compilation of the Official Records of the Union and Confederate Armies*, series 1, vol. 9, 466, 507, 643; and ibid., series 1, vol. 1, 147, 655.

15. Smallpox is caused by a virus known as *variola*. There is a distinction between major variola and minor variola. On contracting smallpox, see Hopkins, *Princes and Peasants*, 3, 7. On freedpeople contracting the virus, see War Dept., *War of the Rebellion: A Compilation of the Official Records of the Union and Confederate Armies*, series 1, vol. 17, 517; Elizabeth Leslie Rous Comstock, "Letter from Elizabeth Leslie Rous Comstock, October 12, 1862," 132, *The American Civil War: Letters and Diaries*, database online (Alexander Street Press, 2003). Julia Ellen LeGrand Waitz, *The Journal of Julia LeGrand, New Orleans, 1862–1863*, ed. by Kate Mason Rowland and Agnes E. Croxall (Richmond, VA: Everett Waddey, 1911), 172.

16. Hopkins, *Princes and Peasants*, 4.

17. Steedman and Fullerton, "The Freedmen's Bureau: Reports of Generals Steedman and Fullerton on the Condition of the Freedmen's Bureau in the Southern States," May 8, 1866, p. 2, From Slavery to Freedom: The African-American Pamphlet Collection, 1824–1909, LOC.

18. While the epidemic in Washington, DC, marks the earliest reference that I have uncovered to smallpox during this period, the question remains how did smallpox even make it to Washington? I am not exactly sure if it was already present in DC or the mid-Atlantic region and then spread due to the movement of troops, the emancipation of slaves, or the displacement of civilians. My hunch is that it came from the West. Historian David S. Jones has meticulously documented the presence of smallpox in the West, particularly in the Ohio and Missouri River frontiers throughout the early nineteenth century. He also notes that traders along the Missouri River sent smallpox-infected furs to New York in 1837. While the traders claimed that smallpox did not break out in New York, this example, nevertheless, reveals the commercial traffic between the West and the East that would have provided pathways for the virus to travel during the Civil War. Moreover, the organization of troops from the West and the movement between the West and the Atlantic seaboard caused by the war could have further opened up pathways for smallpox outbreaks. See Jones, *Rationalizing Epidemics*, 1, 75.

19. During the nineteenth century, many Americans burned tar to clear the air and to ward off infection. The severity of the epidemic likely caused former slaves to take extreme measures and cover their bodies with tar. On nineteenth-century reactions to smallpox,

see Rosenberg, "What Is an Epidemic: AIDS in Historical Perspective," 6–7. Frances Harding Casstevens, *George W. Alexander and Castle Thunder: A Confederate Prison and its Commandant* (Jefferson, NC: McFarland, 2004), 86.

20. *Washington Evening Star*, January 11, 1862; *Weekly Anglo African*, January 18, 1862 and February 1, 1862; *Washington during the Civil War: The Diary of Horatio Nelson Taft, 1861–1865*, January 8, 1862, January 9, 1862, January 15, 1862, LOC; Abby Woolsey to Gerogeanna Muiron Bacon and Elizabeth Newton Howland, January 7, 1862 in *Letters of a Family during the War for the Union 1861–1865*, vol. 1, 246, LOC. Jane Eliza Woolsey to Georgeanna Muirson Bacon and Eliza Newton Howland, January, 1862, ibid., 247. Clare Pierce Wood to Amos Wood, Wood Family Letters, South Hadley Historical Society, The American Civil War: Letters and Diaries online, University of Chicago Database, 2003.

21. *Washington during the Civil War: The Diary of Horatio Nelson Taft, 1861–1865*, January 8, 1862, January 9, 1862, January 15, 1862, LOC.

22. Various letters of Jno. Rogers, Sanitary Dept., Dept. of Metropolitan Police to Army, quoted in Kate Masur, "Reconstructing the Nation's Capital: The Politics of Race and Citizenship, 1862–1878" (PhD diss., University of Michigan, 2001), 40.

23. B. B. French to Hon. Edwin M. Stanton, February 13, 1862, quoted in Berlin et al., *Wartime Genesis of Free Labor: In the Upper South*, 262–63.

24. *Washington during the Civil War: The Diary of Horatio Nelson Taft, 1861–1865*, January 15, 1862, LOC; Slave Pen Vertical File, AHS; Berlin et al., *Wartime Genesis of Free Labor in the Upper South*, 254–59; *Alexandria Gazette*, May 20, 1864; C. C. Bitting Memoir, December 30, 1865, AHS; Julia Wilbur Diary, November 10, 1862, AHS.

25. Medical Society of the District of Columbia, *Report on the Sanitary Condition of the Cities of Washington and Georgetown* (Washington, DC: Gibson Brothers, 1864), 4–6, NYPL.

26. Albert Gladwin, *Book of Records Containing Marriage and Deaths that Occurred within the Official Jurisdiction of Rev. Albert Gladwin Together with Any Biographical or Other Reminisces, 1865*, Barrett Library, AHS. Ibid., "Coffins and Other Funeral Expenses," January 1, 1864. Due to the unevenness in the surviving record, it is impossible to provide an epidemiological map of the virus.

27. See, for example, the migrations of former slaves, who moved from the coast of South Carolina during the war, where the Bureau established hospitals, to the interior of the state, where the government lacked medical presence in 1865. Pelzer to Mr. A. Fairly, March 13, 1866, Charleston, SC, e. 3132, LS, vol. 1; Pelzer to H. Baer, March 15, 1866, e. 3132, LS, vol. 1; 17; Pelzer to Circular Letter, e. 3132, LS, vol. 1; South Carolina Chief Medical Report, LS, all in RG 105, NARA.

28. E. A. Klien to Major H. W. Smith, November 2, 1865, Orangeburg, SC, e. 2979, RG 105, NARA.

29. *Daily Record*, New England Freedmen's Aid Society, "Mrs. Pillsbury's Letter Concerning the 'Freedmen's Rest' at Hilton Head," MHS.

30. This is also common in discussions of the urban poor in the North. See, for example, John H. Griscom, *The Sanitary Condition of the Laboring Population of New York* (New York: Harper and Brothers, 1845). Also see Charles Rosenberg, *The Cholera Years: The United States in 1832, 1849, and 1866* (Chicago: Chicago University Press, 1962).

31. *New York Times*, January 22, 1866.

32. *New York Herald*, February 16, 1864.

33. M. K. Hogan to C.W. Horner, November 23, 1865, Raleigh, N.C., e. 2535, L.S., RG 105, NARA. For a general overview on smallpox transmission, see Hopkins, *Princes and Peasants*, 14.

34. U.S. War Dept., BRFAL, *Laws in Relation to Freedmen*, 39th Cong., 2nd sess, Senate Executive Document, no. 6 (Washington, DC: GPO, 1866–67), 80.

35. Bishop M. F. Jamison, *Autobiography and Work of Bishop M. F. Jamison, D.D. ("Uncle Joe") Editor, Publisher, and Church Extension Secretary; a Narration of His Whole Career from the Cradle to the Bishopric of the Colored M. E. Church in America* (Nashville, TN: Smith and Lamar, 1912).

36. John Eaton, *Grant, Lincoln and the Freedmen* (Longmans, Green, 1907), 35–36. Many nineteenth-century Americans often believed that sexually promiscuity predisposed

people to disease, a concept that has reemerged in the wake of the HIV epidemic. See Rosenberg, "What Is an Epidemic: AIDS in Historical Perspective," 1–17.

37. J. V. DeHanne to M. F. Barres, February 23, 1867, Augusta, GA, LR October 1856–May 1868, M1903, Roll 49, RG 105, NARA. Also see M.K. Hogan to C.W. Horner, November 23, 1865, Raleigh, N.C., e. 2535, L.S., RG 105, NARA. I offer a more sustained analysis of how nineteenth-century Americans associated etiology with region in chapter 1.

38. War Dept., *Laws in Relation to Freedmen*.

39. *Report of Sick and Wounded Refugees and Freedmen in Mississippi*, for the week ending Saturday, October 21, 1865, 14 Refugees, 260 Freedmen; October 28, 1865, 3 Refugees, 201 Freedmen; November 11, 1865, 1 Refugee, 111 Freedmen; November 18, 1865, 0 Refugees, 79 Freedmen; November 25, 1865, 0 Refugees, 67 Freedmen; December 2, 1865, 4 Refugees, 149 Freedmen; December 9, 1865, 4 Refugees, 389 Freedmen, December 16, 1865, 4 Refugees, 371 Freedmen; December 23, 1865, 3 Refugees, 300 Freedmen; December 30, 1865, 2 Refugees, 325 Freedmen; Weekly Reports, Mississippi, e. 2018, box 32a, RG 105, NARA.

40. *Report of the Sick and Wounded Refugees and Freedmen in Hospitals in District of Louisiana*, for the week ending, May 4, 1867, e. 1396, Chief Medical Officer, Weekly Reports, Unentered, 1865–1866, RG 105, NARA.

41. *New York Herald*, February 16, 1865.

42. *New York Times*, "Mortality Among the Negro," January 22, 1866.

43. I want to mark a critical distinction between the period of emancipation and the early nineteenth century. While ideas about black people as physiologically and mentally inferior circulated through medical and even political discourse in the early to mid-1800s, the process of emancipation provided a stage for this racist illogic to gain momentum and to take on new meaning. Unlike the early nineteenth century, when these ideas existed only in theory, buttressed by the medical fictions produced by loose and uninformed readings of the 1840 census, the 1860s, by direct contrast, did result with thousands of emancipated slaves dying from smallpox, starvation, exposure, among other ailments. Consequently, when journalists, scientists, doctors, politicians, and ordinary white Americans discussed black inferiority, they could then point to the problems that emancipation engendered. Yet, they did not consider structural poverty, medical neglect, and lack of basic necessities as the cause of illness and death among the ex-slave population. Instead, they rehearsed the skewed medical logic of the prewar years combined with their observations about the discontents resulting from emancipation in the 1860s in order to define black people as inferior. For an incisive analysis of early nineteenth-century ideas about black inferiority spanning from the writings of Dr. Josiah Nott to the publication of the 1840 census, see Harriet Washington, *Medical Apartheid: The Dark History of Medical Experimentation on Black Americans from Colonial Times to the Present* (New York: Doubleday, 2006), pp. 143–56.

44. *Nation*, August 15, 1872.

45. J. M. Sturtevant, "The Destiny of the African Race in the United States," *Continental Monthly* 2 (May 1863): 602, 605, 608–9, quoted in George Fredrickson, *Black Image in the White Mind: The Debate on Afro-American Character and Destiny, 1817–1914* (New York: Harper and Row, 1971), 159.

46. J. R. Hayes, *Negrophobia "On The Brain" In White Men, Or, An Essay Upon the Origin and Progress, Both Mental and Physical, of the Negro Race and the Use to Be Made of Him by the Politicians in the United States* (Washington, DC: Powell, Ginck, 1869).

47. J. T. Walton, "The Comparative Mortality of the White and Colored Races in the South," *Charlotte Medical Journal* 10 (1897): 291–94.

48. Cong., Globe, 38th Cong., 1st sess., 709. Samuel Cox, *Eight Years in Congress, from 1857 to 1865* (New York: D. Appleton, 1865), 353. Historian David S. Jones argues that if the government had subscribed to the extinction thesis, they would not have felt obligated to develop federal policies for Native Americans or black people. See Jones, *Rationalizing Epidemics*, 139.

49. Furthermore, it is critical to mark an important distinction between high mortality rates caused by an epidemic and the discourse about extinction. In other words, there is a discourse about an epidemic and then there are actual bodies that suffered from the epidemic, and at times, these phenomena overlap, but it is necessary to try to untangle their intricate

knots as the problems of language and of racial ideology can lead us to a place where we forget that people were actually dying. Within contemporary historiography, the use of the term "extinction" immediately sets off an alarm about racial inferiority based on a medical fiction that asserts hierarchies among the various races. The only reason why extinction even became a viable concept that punctuated observations about mortality rates in the nineteenth century (and earlier) was due to the fact that so many people were, in fact, dying. Of course, these claims about the large number of people dying could have been exaggerated, but the debate rarely questioned the fact that so many people were dying or doubted the extent to which smallpox plagued emancipated slaves. Those who wrote about the epidemic knew smallpox infected tens of thousands of freedpeople and left thousands more dead. What they debated was the meaning and the outcome of this high mortality, not the fact that people were actually dying. The extinction thesis thus developed in response to their anxiety and concerns about the outcome of the high death rates among emancipated slaves; this rhetoric should not undermine the material reality of the epidemic. After they developed the rationale that emancipation exacerbated the epidemic, they then used the rhetoric surrounding extinction to justify their political actions.

50. This move on the part of the federal government contradicts Charles Rosenberg's analysis of the mid-nineteenth century as a turning point in medical knowledge and practice. Rosenberg cogently argues that in response to the cholera epidemics in 1866, the medical community turned to a more sophisticated analysis of disease causation. Rosenberg may, in fact, be absolutely correct in terms of white people, but when it came to the diagnosis and treatment of black people, the medical community seemed to fall back on earlier ideas about disease causation. See Rosenberg, *The Cholera Years*.

51. Republished in *New York Times*, February 3, 1866.

52. Benjamin Rush, "The New Method of Inoculating for the Small Pox," delivered in a lecture at the University of Philadelphia, February 20, 1781 (Philadelphia: Charles Cist in Market-Street, 1781), microform, LCP; *Philadelphia Dispensary, A Comparative View of the Natural Small-pox, Inoculated Small-Pox, and Vaccination in Their Effects of Individuals And Society* (Philadelphia: Jane Aitken, 1803); Providence, RI, "At a town-council holden in and for the town of Providence, this second day of August, A.D. 1799 it is voted and resolved, that three hundred copies of the first five sections of the act, entitled, 'An act to prevent the spreading of the small-pox, and other contagious sickness in this state,' be printed, and that all vessels coming from foreign ports, or from places where infectious diseases are prevalent, shall be immediately furnished, with one of said copies..." [Providence: s.n., 1799], microform, LCP.

53. As historian Charles Rosenberg astutely argues, an epidemic is "highly visible and, unlike some aspects of humankind's biological history, does not proceed with imperceptible effect until retrospectively 'discovered' by historians and demographers"; "What Is an Epidemic: AIDS in Historical Perspective," 1.

54. I profited enormously from what Charles Rosenberg eloquently summons as the "dramaturgic form" that epidemics take. Ibid., 2.

55. The history of inoculation can be traced to an African-born slave, Onesimus, who introduced this age-old African practice to his master, the famed Puritan minister Cotton Mather. Despite much controversy, Mather introduced inoculation to eighteenth-century Bostonians.

56. Later in the eighteenth century, Dr. Edward Jenner, a British physician, attempted to circumvent this problem by demonstrating the efficacy and safety of vaccination. Hopkins argues that recent studies indicate that Jenner's vaccination was cowpox with a strain of smallpox included. Some scientists, Hopkins claims, suggest that the vaccine was actually horse pox. On Jenner, see Elizabeth Fenn, *Pox Americana: The Great Smallpox Epidemic of 1775–82* (New York: Hill and Wang, 2001); and Hopkins, *Princes and Peasants*, 8. Also see Benjamin Waterhouse, "A Prospect of Exterminating the Small-pox: Being the History of the Variolæ Vaccinæ, or Kine-pox, Commonly Called the Cow-Pox; As It Has Appeared in England: With an Account of a Series of Inoculations Performed For The Kine-Pox, in Massachusetts" (London: Cambridge Press, 1800), LCP. One of the best-known controversies surrounding the inoculation crises is the smallpox epidemic in Boston in 1721. See Margot Minardi, "The Boston Inoculation Controversy of 1721–1722: An Incident in the History of Race," *The William and*

Mary Quarterly (2004): 47–76; Maxine Van De Wetering, "A Reconsideration of the Inoculation Controversy," *The New England Quarterly* 58, no. 1 (1985): 46–67. Also see Sarah Stidstone Gronim, "Imagining Inoculation: Smallpox, the Body, and Social Relations of Healing in the Eighteenth Century," *Bulletin of the History of Medicine* 80 (2006): 247–68.

57. Historian David Jones explains that Congress passed an act that called for vaccination of the Indians on May 5, 1832. According to Jones, the program ultimately proved unsuccessful and there was a second effort in 1838. The point, however, is that the Indian vaccination campaign provided an antecedent to the outbreak among former slaves, but the federal government failed to adopt similar measures when Bureau authorities and the Northern press reported on the epidemic among the freedpeople. See Jones, *Rationalizing Epidemics*, 113–14.

58. J. M. Toner, M.D, "A Paper on the Propriety and Necessity of Compulsory Vaccination," extracted from the Transactions of the American Medical Association (Philadelphia: Collins Printer, 1865) LCP; "A Series of Letters and Other Documents Relating to the Late Epidemic or Yellow Fever; Comprising The Correspondence of the Mayor of the City," The Board of Health, the Executive of the State of Maryland, and the Reports of the Faculty and District Medical Society of Baltimore, Second Dispensary (Baltimore: William Warner, 1820), LCP. Also see Fenn, *Pox Americana*; James Colgrove, "Between Persuasion and Compulsion: Smallpox Control in Brooklyn and New York, 1894–1902," *Bulletin of the History of Medicine* 78, no. 2 (2004): 349–78.

59. War Dept., *War of the Rebellion: A Compilation of the Official Records of the Union and Confederate Armies*, series 1, vol. 7, 675; ibid., series 1, vol. 8, 58.

60. ibid., series 1, vol.19 (part II), 679.

61. ibid., series 1, vol. 8, 487.

62. ibid., series 1, vol. 19 (part II), 679.

63. S.A. Bell, March 18, 1866, e. 2535, LS, RG 105, NARA.

64. *Report of the Board of Education for Freedmen, Department of the Gulf, for the year 1864*, Daniel Murray Collection, LOC.

65. *New York Times*, February 12, 1866.

66. W. H. Elridge to DeWitt, September 25, 1865; I. M. Carr to C. W. Horner, September 28, 1865, Georgetown, SC; S. C. Brown to R. Libby, November 21, 1865, Charleston, SC; F. L. Frosh to Saxton, November 20, 1865, Charleston, SC; C. H. Brownley to DeWitt, December 11, 1865, James Island, SC, all in e. 2979, LR, RG 105, NARA.

67. For an increase in Georgia see *Report of Refugees and Freedmen in Smallpox Hospital* for Week Ending October 7, 1865, 38 patients; October 14, 1865, 40 patients; October 21, 1865, 43 patients; October 28, 1865, 48 patients; November 11, 1865, 53 patients; December 2, 1865, 65 patients; January 13, 1866, 73 patients; January 20, 1866, 93 patients; February 3, 1866, 109 patients; February 10, 1866, 121 patients; February 17, 1866, 137 patients; February 26, 1866, 139 patients; March 24, 1866, 89 patients; March 31, 1866, 64 patients, April 7, 1866, 45 patients; April 28, 1866, 37 patients. By May of 1866, the number of reported patients in Augusta, Georgia, drops to 31 patients. Register of Patients at Smallpox Hospital and Weekly Reports of Sick and Wounded, vol. 1. (163), Roll 49, RG 105, NARA. One of the major problems of obtaining an accurate population estimate for this region, or any region in the South, during the immediate aftermath of the war is the vast dislocation that emancipation engendered. Historians have not been as attentive to the changing demographics that the war and emancipation wrought. Therefore, it is quite difficult to obtain the number of freedpeople living in this region. Moreover, throughout this book, I emphasize that the numbers that have survived are often incomplete and inaccurate; as a result, I am reluctant to substantiate an argument based on empirical evidence alone.

68. F. Smith to Barholf, February 6, 1867; F. Smith to Yeamans, February 7, 1867; Smith to Fleming, February 11, 1867, all in North Carolina, e. 2536, LS, vol. 2, RG 105, NARA.

69. Hogan to Fleming, January 22, 1867; Hogan to O. O. Howard, J.K. Barnes, and S. Thomas, March 1, 1867, all in North Carolina, e. 2536, LS, vol. 2, RG 105, NARA. For other examples of a hospital closing in the midst of the epidemic, see Swartzwelden to Flood, January 3, 1868, Shreveport, LA, e. 1397, Box 46, RG 105, NARA; Edward Williams to A. F. Hayden, May 29, 1866, Shreveport, LA, e. 1393, L.R box 40, LR, RG 105.

70. T. D. Eliot, *Report of Hon. T. D. Elliot*, Chairman of the Committee of Freedmen's Affairs, The U.S. House of Representatives, March 10, 1868 (Washington, DC: GPO, 1869).

71. War Dept., *Laws in Relation to Freedmen*, 110–11; Georgia, Savannah Lincoln Hospital, LS, vol. 1, December 1865–January 1868, Roll 85, RG 105, NARA.

72. For Louisiana, see War Dept., *Laws in Relation to Freedmen*, 79–80: there were an estimated 10,000 freedpeople who received treatment; this does not include those in home colonies. In Virginia, 23,000 freedpeople were treated for smallpox, ibid., 37; in Georgia, an estimated 5,600 freedpeople received medical treatment, see Augusta to Horner, June 2, 1866, Savannah, Lincoln Hospital, LS, vol. 1 (354), December 1865–January 1868, M1903, Roll 85, RG 105 NARA. For North Carolina see, M.K. Hogan to C.W. Horner, November 23, 1865, Raleigh, N.C., e. 2535, L.S., RG 105, NARA.

73. Hogan to Edwards, March 19, 1867, North Carolina, e. 2536, vol. 2, RG 105, NARA.

74. *Freedmen's Journal*, March 1866, 57.

75. This is to say nothing of the alienation that many of those infected with smallpox likely suffered. See Monroe A. Majors, *Noted Negro Women: Their Triumphs and Activities* (Chicago: Donohue & Henneberry, 1893), 53.

76. *Report of the Board of Education for Freedmen, Department of the Gulf, for the Year 1864*. Daniel Murray Collection, LOC.

77. The fact that various slaveholders did, in fact, vaccinate or inoculate their slaves before the war, but the virus still managed to spread so violently across the South, reveals the strength and magnitude of the epidemic. On vaccination of enslaved people before the war, see Todd Lee Savitt, *Medicine and Slavery: The Diseases and Health Care of Blacks in Antebellum Virginia* (Urbana: University of Illinois Press, 1978), 220.

78. *Report of the Board of Education for Freedmen, Department of the Gulf, for the Year 1864*, Daniel Murray Collection, LOC.

79. *Christian Recorder*, July 5, 1862.

80. Lawton to Col. Boucher, October 20, 1865, Hawkins View, GA, Office of Staff Officers, Surgeon in Chief, LS and Register of LR, September 1865–July 1867, vol. 52, M1903, Roll 26, RG 105, NARA; Clark to Dalton, April 13, 1867, and May 29, 1867, ibid.

81. E. A. Korlau to H. W. Smith, November 2, 1865, Orangeburg, SC, e. 2979, Chief Medical Officer, LR, 1865–1866, Box 38, RG 105, NARA.

82. A. P. Dolnizimple to W. R. DeWitt, September 7, 1865, Hilton Head, SC, e. 2979, Chief Medical Officer, Unregistered LR, 1865–1866, Box 38, RG 105, NARA. C. H. Brownley to W. R. DeWitt, September 28, 1865, James Island, SC, e. 2979, Chief Medical Officer, Unregistered LR, Box 38, 1865–1866, RG 105, NARA.

83. Clay to DeWitt, December 20, 1865, Georgetown, SC, e. 2979, Chief Medical Officer, LR, 1865–1866, Box 38, RG 105, NARA.

84. Ibid.

85. Pelzer to Major H. W. Smith, February 15, 1866; Pelzer to Taylor, April 2, 1867; Charleston, SC, e. 3132, LS, RG 105, NARA. Also see, John E. Fallon to DeWitt, May 25, 1866, South Carolina, e.2979, Chief Medical Surgeon, LR, Box 37, RG 105, NA; Augusta to Lawton, January 26, 1866, Georgia, Savannah Lincoln Hospital, LS, vol. 1, December 1865–January 1868, M1903, Roll 85, RG 105, NARA; B. Burgh Smith to W. R. DeWitt, October 14, 1865, Charleston, SC, e. 3249, LS, vol. 1 of 1. RG 105, NARA. Sometimes even securing one horse was not enough. Due to the rural landscape, doctors often crossed deep rivers to reach freedpeople, but needed a horse on the other side because there were no ferries to carry horses over the river. Crossing the Stono River in South Carolina proved particularly challenging for one Bureau doctor, who requested that the federal government supply him, I. L. Beckett to R. K. Scott, January 15, 1867, e. 3249, LS, vol. 1, RG 105, NARA.

86. O. O. Howard, *Report of Brevet Major General O. O. Howard to the Secretary of War* (Washington: GPO, 1869).

87. War Dept., *Laws in Relation to Freedmen*.

88. *New York Herald*, March 18, 1865.

89. Fleming to Hogan, April 4, 1866, North Carolina, e. 2788, Scrapbook of LR, RG 105, NARA.

90. Hogan to Matlock, March 25, 1867, Charlotte, NC, e. 2536, LS, vol. 2, RG 105, NARA. In South Carolina, the lack of bedding led to the further spread of the virus. A. Cay Roberts to W.R. DeWitt, January 15, 1865, Georgetown, South Carolina, e.2979, Chief Medical Surgeon, LR, RG 105, NARA.

91. Robert H. Clay to DeWitt, December 20, 1865, Georgetown, SC, e. 2979, Chief Medical Officer, LR, 1865–1866, Box 38, RG 105, NARA.

92. M. K. Hogan to C. W. Horner, November 23, 1865, North Carolina, LS, e. 2468, Box 14; Bishop to Griswold, September 9, 1865, Louisiana, e. 1393, Box 40, both in RG 105, NARA. War Dept., *Laws in Relation to Freedmen.*

93. *Freedmen's Record,* January 1866, 5. Also see *Second Report of a Committee of Representatives of New York Yearly Meeting of Friends Upon the Conditions and Wants of the Colored Refugees,* LOC.

94. Robert H. Clay to W. R. DeWitt, January 16, 1866, Georgetown, SC, e. 2979, Chief Medical Officer, LR, 1865–1866, Box 37, RG 105, NARA.

95. F. W. Liedtke to Major H. W. Smith, April 30, 1866, Moncks Corner, SC, Reports of Conditions and Operations, Records of the Assistant Commissioner for the State of South Carolina, July 1865–January 1866, M869, Roll 34, RG 105, NARA.

96. Lawton to Augusta, November 21, 1865, quoted in Todd Savitt, "Politics in Medicine: The Georgia Freedmen's Bureau and the Organization of Health Care, 1865–1866," *Civil War History* 28, no. 1 (1982): 45–64.

97. *Reports of Generals Steedman and Fullerton on the Condition of the Freedmen's Bureau in the Southern States,* 5–6, LOC.

98. Beverly Nash, a black political leader during Reconstruction, published an article about the neglect of smallpox patients in South Carolina, which military officials mention in their report to federal leaders. See *Reports of Generals Steedman and Fullerton on the Condition of the Freedmen's Bureau in the Southern States,"* LOC. On Nash, see Eric Foner, *Freedom's Lawmakers: A Directory of Black Officeholders During Reconstruction* (New York: Oxford University Press, 1993). Also on Bureau doctors' neglect of smallpox patients, see M. K. Hogan to C. W. Horner, November 23, 1865, Raleigh, NC, e. 2535, L.S., RG 105, NARA.

99. Subordinate Field Offices, Devalls Bluff, AR, LS and Received, October 1865–1868, M1901, Roll 8, RG 105, NARA; W. B. Pease to J. T. Kirkman, March 6, 1867, Houston, TX, Records of the Assistant Commissioner for the State of Texas, Reports of Operations of Conditions, M821, Frame 130, RG 105, NARA. For the further outbreak of smallpox in Louisiana in 1867, see "Weekly Reports of Sick and Wounded, 1867–1868," January 5, 1867, January 12, 1867, January 19, 1867, January 26, 1867, February 2, 1867, February 9, 1867, February 16, 1867, February 23, 1867, March 2, 1867, March 9, 1867, March 16, 1867, March 23, 1867, March 30, 1867, April 6, 1867, April 13, 1867, April 20, 1867, April 27, 1867, May 4, 1867, May 11, 1867, May 18, 1867, May 25, 1867, June 1, 1867, June 8, 1867, June 15, 1867, June 22, 1867, June 29, 1867, July 6, 1867, July 13, 1867, July 20, 1867, July 27, 1867," Shreveport, LA, all in e. 1396, Box 43, RG 105. For narrative descriptions of the epidemic in various Southern locales at the end of 1866, see War Dept., *Laws in Relation to Freedmen.*

100. War Dept., *Laws in Relation to Freedmen,* 26, 66.

101. Ibid., 105. Teachers reported the epidemic throughout reports to their sponsoring organizations. See, for example, *Freedmen's Record,* February 1865, 19.

102. *Freedmen's Record,* January 1866, 5.

103. 39th Cong., 2nd sess., Senate Executive Document, no. 6, 134.

104. Fleming to Hogan, February 12, 1866, North Carolina, e. 2788, Scrapbook of LR, RG 105, NARA.

105. Ibid.

106. In Tennessee, Bureau officials established hospitals in Chattanooga, Murfreesboro, Nashville, and Memphis in December 1865 and closed them by June 1866. See War Dept., *Laws in Relation to Freedmen,* 134.

107. J. V. Devanne to M. F. Barres, January 19, 1867, Augusta, GA, LR, October 1856–May 1868, M1903, Roll 49, Frame 649–50, RG 105, NARA.

108. Augusta to Lawton, March 14, 1866, Savannah Lincoln Hospital, LS, vol. 1, December 1865–January 1868, M1903, Roll 85, RG 105, NARA.

109. Roberts to DeWitt, December 20, 1865, Georgetown, SC, e. 2979, Chief Medical Officer, LR, 1865–1866, Box 38, RG 105, NARA.

110 John E. Fallon to DeWitt, May 25, 1866, South Carolina, Chief Medical Surgeon, e.2979, LR, Box 37, RG 105, NARA.

111. Robert Reyburn to John Eaton, August 22, 1865, "Report on the Condition of the Government Farm at St. Mary's County," Maryland, A-9862, DC AC, 457 Un Rg LR, Box 22, FSSP. Also on some freedpeople's resistance to go to hospitals, see M.K. Hogan to C.W. Horner, November 23, 1865, Raleigh, N.C., e. 2535, L.S., RG 105, NARA.

112. *Report of the Board of Education for Freedmen, Department of the Gulf, for the Year 1864.* Daniel Murray Collection, LOC.

113. Horace James, *Annual Report of the Superintendent of Negro Affairs in North Carolina, 1864* (Boston: W. F. Brown and Co. Printers), 16.

114. *Report of the Board of Education for Freedmen, Department of the Gulf, for the Year 1864.* Daniel Murray Collection, LOC. As early as 1813, Congress established the National Vaccine Agency as part of the Act to Encourage Vaccination, which predated federal efforts to vaccinate Indians in 1832. The act was repealed in 1822 because a shipment of smallpox, not cowpox, was sent to a region to vaccinate the vulnerable population and accidentally killed ten people. Not until the 1880s or 1890s did state governments require mandatory vaccinations in schools. National Congress of Mothers, *Report of the Proceedings of the Second Annual Convention of the National Congress of Mothers.* Held in the City of Washington, D.C., May 2nd–7th, 1898, 243. Also see Hopkins, *Princes and Peasants,* 267–68.

115. R. S. Taylor to Gen. Davis Tillson, January 25, 1866, quoted in Savitt, "Politics in Medicine," 57.

116. Henry Root to W.R. Dewitt, June 19, 1860, e. 2979, Chief Medical Surgeon, LR, RG 105, NARA.

117. Augusta to Horner, June 2, 1866, Georgia, Savannah Lincoln Hospital, LS, vol. 1 (354), December 1865–January 1868, M1903, Roll 85, RG 105, NARA.

118. *New York Times,* October 3, 1865.

119. *New York Times,* March 14, 1865, "The Senate Investigating Committee, Concerning the Duties of the Health Warden"; ibid., January 29, 1865; ibid., February 3, 1865.

120. *New York Times,* May 20, 1866, and April 29, 1865.

121. See Rosenberg, *Cholera Years*; Riley, *Eighteenth-Century Campaign to Avoid Disease,* 144. On medical surveillance in the late nineteenth century, see Colgrove, "Between Persuasion and Compulsion," 349–78.

122. For recent scholarship on how European powers during the nineteenth century dealt with the spread of cholera into European colonies and the Continent by Muslim colonial subjects making the annual pilgrimage to Mecca see, for example, Daniel Brower, "Russian Roads to Mecca: Religious Tolerance and Muslim Pilgrimage in the Russian Empire," *Slavic Review* 55, no. 3 (1996): 567–84; Michael Christopher Low, "Empire and the Hajj: Pilgrims, Plagues, and Pan-Islam under British Surveillance, 1865–1908," *International Journal of Middle East Studies* 40 (2008): 269–90; and William R. Roff, "Sanitation and Security: The Imperial Powers and the Nineteenth Century Hajj," *Arabian Studies* 6 (1982): 143–60. Also see C. A. Bayly, *The Birth of the Modern World, 1780–1914: Global Connections and Comparison* (New York: Oxford University Press, 2004).

123. Surgeon General's Office, *Report on Epidemic Cholera in the Army of the United States, During the Year 1866* (Washington, DC: GPO, 1867).

124. Ibid.; Surgeon General's Office, *Report on Epidemic Cholera and Yellow Fever in the Army of the United States, During the Year 1867* (Washington, DC: GPO, 1868); Surgeon General's Office, *Circular No. 3,* vi, 17.

125. Surgeon General's Office, *Report on Epidemic Cholera in the Army of the United States, During the Year 1866* (Washington, DC: GPO, 1867); *Annual Report of the Resident Physician of the City of New York for 1865: Presented to the Board of Commissioners of Health at Their Meeting, January 4, 1866* (New York: Edmund Jones, 1866); John Chapman, "Diarrhea and Cholera: Their Origin, Proximate Cause, and Cure, Through the Agency of the Nervous System: By Means of Ice" (Philadelphia: J. B. Lippincott, 1866), LCP.

126. Kipps to Robinson, October 12, 1866, Alabama, Office of Staff Officers, Surgeon, LS, vol. 1 (31), September 7, 1865–July 21, M1900, Roll 8, RG 105, NARA.

127. War Dept., *Laws in Relation to Freedmen*, 108.

128. Howard, *Autobiography*, 295–96.

129. Surgeon General's Office, *Report on Epidemic Cholera and Yellow Fever in the Army of the United States, During the Year 1867*, 1.

130. War Dept., *Laws in Relation to Freedmen*, 80; Augusta to Lawton, September 8, 1866, Georgia, Savannah Lincoln Hospital, LS, vol. 1, December 1865–January 1868, M1903, Roll 85, RG 105, NARA.

131. Surgeon General's Office, *Report on Epidemic Cholera in the Army of the United States, During the Year 1866*.

132. War Dept., *Laws in Relation to Freedmen*, 27.

133. J. V. DeHanne to M. F. Barres, January 11, 1867, Augusta, GA, LR, October 1856–May 1868, M1903, Roll 49, RG 105, NARA; Kipps to Horner, June 16, 1866, Office of Staff Officers, Surgeon, Alabama, LS, vol. 1 (31), September 7, 1865–July 21, 1865, 1900, Roll 8, RG 105, NARA; Horner to Hogan, April 11, 1866, North Carolina, e. 2788, Scrapbook of LR, RG 105, NARA.

134. DeHanne to Barres, August 22, 1867, September 2, 1867, and January 11, 1867, Augusta, GA, LR, October 1856–May 1868, M1903, Roll 49, RG 105, NARA; DeHanne to Surgeon Edwards, May 28, 1867, and DeHanne to Sibley, May 27, 1867 both in Georgia, Office of Staff Officers, Surgeon in Chief, LS and Register of LR, September 1865–July 1867, vol. 52, 1903, Roll 26, RG 105, NARA.

135. War Dept., *Laws in Relation to Freedmen*, 108.

136. Ibid., 134.

137. *New York Times*, March 26, 1865.

138. *New York Times*, January 22, 1866.

139. The push to "move to the country" was also a ploy to secure a labor force on cotton plantations. I. W. Brinckerhoff, *Advice to Freedmen* and J. B. Waterbury, *Friendly Counsels for Freedmen* (New York: AMS Press, 1980), reprint of freedmen's textbooks, originally published by American Tract Society, NY [1864–1865?].

140. *Nation*, May 11, 1866.

141. A. T. Augusta to R. O. Abbott, June 17, 1863; Augusta to J. W. Lawton, August 9, August 14, August 21, 1866, all in Quartermaster Correspondence Consolidated Files, Contraband Camps 1863 File, Box 99, RG 92, NARA. Augusta to Asst. Surg. Schell, August 18, 1866; Augusta to Capt. Watson, August 21, 1866; Augusta to J. W. Lawton, September 1, 1866, all in Georgia, LS, M1903, Roll 85, RG 105, NARA.

142. Robert Reyburn, *Types of Disease among Freed People of the United States* (Washington, DC: Gibson Bros., 1891), NYAM.

143. Rebecca Crumpler, *A Book of Medical Discourses* (Boston: Cashman, Keating, 1883), 4.

144. Ibid., 3–4.

Chapter 5

1. S. N. Clark to W. W. Rodgers, October 6, 1866, Washington, D.C., DC AIG 520 (LS) v. 53, 23–24, letter 49, A-9931, FSSP.

2. David Blight has brilliantly explained how the bones left from the Civil War made many Americans feel they had finally possessed a historic landscape similar to ancient European ruins. Blight also includes a number of illustrative examples of tours of battlefields that included bones as relics as well as the scavenger economies that grew out of bartering and buying of bones during the postwar years. See David Blight, *Race and Reunion: The Civil War in American Memory* (Cambridge, MA: Belknap Press of Harvard University Press, 2001), 155–56.

3. Throughout the Atlantic world, people of African descent subscribed to intricate theories about bones, bodies, sorcery, and witchcraft. With the main exception of Margaret Washington's *A Peculiar People: Slave Religion and Community-Culture Among the Gullahs* (New York: New York University Press, 1988) and Sharla Fett's *Working Cures: Healing, Health,*

and Power on Southern Plantations (Chapel Hill: University of North Carolina Press, 2002) many of these ideas have been dismissed as superstition in the U.S. context. Scholars working in the Caribbean and Latin America, as well as historians of the slave trade, have been much better attuned to the importance and centrality of these ideas in the lives of people in both the past and present. For a brilliant analysis of the meaning of death in Jamaica, see Vincent Brown, *The Reaper's Garden: Death and Power in the World of Atlantic Slavery* (Cambridge, MA: Harvard University Press, 2010). See, for example, Paul Farmer's analysis of sorcery: *AIDS and Accusation: Haiti and the Geography of Blame* (Berkeley: University of California Press, 1992), 193–207. Also see Karen E. Richman, *Migration and Voudou* (Gainesville: University Press of Florida, 2005); Elizabeth McAlister, *Rara* (Berkeley: University of California Press, 2002). For scholarly studies that have mapped the perseverance of African traditions in the New World, see Michael Gomez, *Exchanging Our Country Marks: The Transformation of African Identities in the Colonial and Antebellum South* (Chapel Hill: University of North Carolina Press, 1998); John Thornton, *Africa and Africans in the Making of the Atlantic World, 1400–1800* (New York: Cambridge University Press, 1998); Stephanie Smallwood, *Saltwater Slavery: A Middle Passage from Africa to American Diaspora* (Cambridge, MA: Harvard University Press, 2007).

4. O. O. Howard, *Autobiography of Oliver Otis Howard*, vol. 2 (New York: Baker and Taylor, 1907), 221.

5. See Louis S. Gerteis, *From Contraband to Freedmen: Federal Policy Toward Southern Blacks 1861–1865* (Westport, CT: Greenwood Press, 1973), 130.

6. Appointed by President Johnson to inspect the South after the war, generals Steedman and Fullerton conducted a study of the South that suggested that free labor would solve the freedmen's problems and, moreover, that the power of free labor was so great that the Freedmen's Bureau was unnecessary. The report was widely circulated and published in many newspapers and journals. Steedman and Fullerton, "The Freedmen's Bureau: Reports of Generals Steedman and Fullerton on the Condition of the Freedmen's Bureau in the Southern States," May 8, 1866, From Slavery to Freedom: The African-American Pamphlet Collection, 1824–1909, LOC.

7. Howard, *Autobiography*, 313, 246.

8. *Freedmen's Record*, February 1866, 21.

9. Throughout the postwar South, the development of the labor force depended on the availability of agricultural resources, and, at times, the vexed history of slavery, which ultimately shaped labor relations. For detailed and smart analyses of how these developments transpired in specific locations throughout the South, see (in historiographical order) on Maryland, Barbara Jeanne Fields, *Slavery and Freedom on the Middle Ground: Maryland During the Nineteenth Century* (New Haven, CT: Yale University Press, 1985); on South Carolina, Julie Saville, *The Work of Reconstruction: From Slave to Wage Laborer in South Carolina, 1860–1870* (New York: Cambridge University Press, 1996); on Louisiana, John C. Rodrigue, *Reconstruction in the Cane Fields: From Slavery to Free Labor in Louisiana's Sugar Parishes, 1862–1880* (Baton Rouge: Louisiana State University Press, 2001); on Georgia, Susan O'Donovan, *Becoming Free in the Cotton South* (Cambridge, MA: Harvard University Press, 2007). In this chapter, I examine the lives of people who were left outside of these systems of wage labor.

10. *Circular No. 75*, Headquarters, Superintendent of 9th District, Orders and Circulars—5th District File, Virginia Assistant Commissioner, ser. 3801, A8407, FSSP; Harriet Jacobs, *The Freedmen*, February 1866 quoted in quoted in Jean Fagan Yellin, *The Harriet Jacobs Family Papers, Volume II* (Chapel Hill: University of North Carolina Press, 2008), 655–56.

11. For more on the shifts of the slave population, see Walter Johnson, *Soul by Soul: Life in the Antebellum Slave Market* (Cambridge, MA: Harvard University Press, 1999); Adam Rothman, *Slave Country: American Expansion and the Origins of the Deep South* (Cambridge, MA: Harvard University Press, 2005); Steven Deyle, *Carry Me Back: The Domestic Slave Trade in American Life* (New York: Oxford University Press, 2005).

12. For a thorough study of Union occupation and its discontents, see Steven Ash, *When the Yankees Came: Conflict and Chaos in the Occupied South, 1861–1865* (Chapel Hill: University of North Carolina Press, 1995).

13. S. P. Lee to W. W. Rogers, October 30, 1866, Alexandria, VA, 3878 (Misc) box 6C, A10039, FSSP.
14. A. P. Ketchum to Bvt. Maj. Genl. R. Saxton, September 1, 1865, Records of the Assistant Commissioner for the State of South Carolina, Reports of Conditions and Operations, M869 Roll 34, RG 105, NARA.
15. Letter from Louisa Matilda Jacobs, before March of 1866, quoted in Jean Fagan Yellin, *The Harriet Jacobs Family Papers, Volume II* (Chapel Hill: University of North Carolina Press, 2008), 660–61. Also, on the forced dislocation of emancipated slaves, see Edward E. Howard to Capt. Bryant, January 26, 1867, John Emory Bryant Papers, DU.

    As the government employed freedmen, the military stipulated that dependent freedpeople, in general, were to earn rations, gain shelter, and receive medical care through the support of able-bodied freedmen, yet the government failed to fulfill their promise. Capt. Murray Davis AAG to Col. James A. Hardie, December 3, 1864, D-8 1864, letters Received, ser.15, RG 159 [J-2] FSSP. Also see John Eaton, *Grant, Lincoln and the Freedmen* (New York: Longmans, Green, 1907), 58.
16. Lucy Chase before the American Freedmen's Inquiry Commission [May 10, 1863], quoted in Ira Berlin et al., *Wartime Genesis of Free Labor: The Upper South* (Cambridge: Cambridge University Press, 1993), 150–54. For a more in-depth explanation of how the recruitment of freedmen left thousands of freedwomen destitute, see Jim Downs, "The Other Side of Freedom: Destitution, Disease, and Dependency among Freedwomen and Their Children during and after the Civil War," in *Battle Scars: Gender and Sexuality in the American Civil War*, ed. Catherine Clinton and Nina Silber (New York: Oxford University Press, 2006), 78–103.
17. Some Confederates supported "free labor" because the Freedmen's Bureau, according to their logic, fulfilled the parental role that they as slaveholders had upheld. As long as the Bureau could maintain what they defined as a "Negro Nursery," then free labor was a fair endeavor. Furthermore, these few Confederates recognized that they themselves lacked the finances, resources, and manpower to reconstruct the South and to control former slaves, so they applauded free labor as a mechanism that would ultimately return their power and authority. See George Fitzhugh, "Agricultural, Commercial, Industrial Progress and Resources," *Debow's Review* 2, no. 4 (October 1866): 346–55.
18. "What Shall We [Do] With The Freedmen, Now That They Have No Masters to Take Care of Them?" *Freedmen's Record*, July 7, 1865, 108–9.
19. There is not yet a comprehensive analysis of the environmental consequences of the Civil War. Jack Kirby's preliminary essay provides the most important overview. See Jack Temple Kirby, "The American Civil War: An Environmental View," National Humanities Website, "The Uses of the Land: Perspectives on Stewardship," http://nationalhumanitiescenter. org/tserve/nattrans/ntuseland/essays/amcwar.htm (retrieved August 9, 2010). That said, there is a growing historiography on the environmental history of the South. See Lisa Brady, "Devouring the Land: Sherman's 1864–1865 Campaigns," in *War and the Environment: Military Destruction in the Modern Age*, ed. Charles E. Closmann (College Station: Texas A&M University Press, 2009); Kathryn S. Meier, "No Place for the Sick: Nature's War on Civil War Soldiers Mental and Physical Health in the 1862 Peninsula and Shenandoah Valley Campaigns," *The Journal of the Civil War Era* 1, no. 2 (June 2011): 176–206. For an insightful analysis of one plantation's environment history, with particular attention paid to land use and agricultural production, see Lynn A. Nelson, *Pharsalia: An Environmental Biography of a Southern Plantation, 1780–1880* (Athens: University of Georgia Press, 2007).
20. Eric Foner has astutely outlined the ambiguity of free labor. See Eric Foner, *Reconstruction: America's Unfinished Revolution* (New York: Harper and Row, 1988).
21. Quoted in War Dept., *Laws in Relation to Freedmen*, 20.
22. E. H. Harris to Captain Sterling, May 4, 1867, New Orleans, e. 1385, Chief Medical Officer, LS, p. 195, RG 105, NARA.
23. In his memoir about serving as a Bureau official, John Eaton describes how he would place dependent freedpeople in the homes of local communities. See Eaton, *Grant, Lincoln and the Freedmen*, Chapters 2-6; Howard, *Autobiography*, 204.

24. L. A. Edwards to War Department of BRFAL, North Carolina, e. 2535, Chief Medical Officer, September 28, 1866, LS, RG 105, NARA.

25. 500,000 dependent freedpeople is an estimate based on calculations provided in Howard, *Autobiography*, 214, 364. In the *American Freedmen*, General O. O. Howard published his report on the number of rations and stated that roughly seven million rations were provided to freedpeople from June 1865 to May 1866. See *American Freedmen*, which is included in the *Pennsylvania Freedmen's Bulletin*, September 1866, 91, LCP. As I explain in chapter 3, it is difficult to ascertain an exact number of freedpeople who received relief because accurate records were not kept, and the number varied depending on the fluctuations in the economy and kin folk arrangements.

26. New England Freedmen's Aid Society, Annual Report, 1864, 70–75, LCP.

27. W. F. Spurgin to Torrey Turner, September 1, 1865, Subordinate Field Offices, Local Superintendent for Washington and Georgetown, LS, vol. 1 (77), July 15, 1865–September 10, M1902, Roll 13, RG 105, NARA.

28. 40th Cong., 2nd sess., House of Representatives, House Executive Documents, no. 30, p. 7. Also see Eaton, *Grant, Lincoln and the Freedmen*, 238–39. Also see Amy Dru Stanley, "Beggars Can't Be Choosers: Compulsion and Contract in Postbellum America," *The Journal of American History* 78, no. 4 (March 1992):1283–84.

29. S. N. Clark, AAG to Eaton, August 21, 1865, Washington, DC, AC, 457 Unregulated Letters, Box 8. FSSP.

30. Beecher to Rice, January 31, 1866, February 7, 1866, and April 1866; Beecher to Bing, February 6, 1866, James Chaplain Beecher Papers, Manuscript Department, William R. Perkins Library, DU.

31. Appendix to the Cong. Globe, 39th Cong., 1st sess., House of Representatives, 79. Steedman and Fullerton, "The Freedmen's Bureau: Reports of Generals Steedman and Fullerton on the condition of the Freedmen's Bureau in the Southern States," 79, LOC.

32. Ward to Hogan, July 11, 1866, Plymouth, NC, e.2535, LS, RG 105, NARA.

33. See Howard White, *The Freedmen's Bureau in Louisiana* (Baton Rouge: Louisiana State University Press, 1970), 74–75.

34. *The American Annual Cyclopedia and Register of Important Events of the Year 1867, Volume VII* (New York: D. Appleton and Company, 1868), 323.

35. "Letter from Harriet Jacobs," December 24, 1865, quoted in Jean Fagan Yellin, *The Harriet Jacobs Family Papers, Volume II* (Chapel Hill: University of North Carolina Press, 2008), 651

36. "Report of Disabled Freedmen in the 9th District," February 25, 1867, VSP (accessed June 22, 2008).

37. See Lori Ginzberg, *Women and the Work of Benevolence: Morality, Politics, and Class in the Nineteenth Century* (New Haven, CT: Yale University Press, 1990); Theda Skocpol, *Protecting Soldiers and Mothers: The Political Origins of Social Policy in the United States* (Cambridge, MA: Harvard University Press, 1992).

38. *Freedmen's Record*, February 1865. Also see, Reports Relating to the Condition of Freedmen, "Report of Indigent and Destitute Freed People in the Parish of West Feliciana State of Louisiana, applying for relief, from the 1st day of April 1868 to the 30th day of April 1868," Records of the Assistant Commissioner for the State of Louisiana, 1865–1869, M1027, Roll 33, RG 105, NARA.

39. In the antebellum South, many so-called dependent people were part of the labor force. Women worked as domestics and reared children, while many elderly, skilled workers continued their trade, and others were personal servants, drivers, and gardeners. Moreover, female slaves were a large portion of the workforce. For an excellent overview on the breakdown of labor relations and work performed by enslaved men and women, see O'Donovan, *Becoming Free in the Cotton South*. For a haunting analysis of domestic labor within the plantation household, see Thavolia Glymph, *Out of the House of Bondage: The Transformation of the Plantation Household* (New York: Cambridge University Press, 2008).

40. On elderly women rearing children during the antebellum period, see Marie Jenkins Schwartz, *Birthing a Slave: Motherhood and Medicine in the Antebellum South* (Cambridge,

MA: Harvard University Press, 2006). On the role of elderly women as healers, see Fett, *Working Cures.*

41. *Friends' Intelligencer*, March 24, 1866, 41; Norreddin Cowen to Abraham Lincoln, January 24, 1864, Abraham Lincoln Papers, LOC.

42. *Anti-Slavery Reporter*, March 2, 1886, 57–58.

43. "Anecdote and Incidents of a Visit to Freedmen," *Freedmen's Record*, October 1865.

44. New England Freedmen's Aid Society, Annual Report, 1864, 70–75, LCP, 61; Hogan to Ward, July 11, 1866, Plymouth, NC, e.2535, LS, RG 105, NARA. Reports Relating to the Freedmen, "Report of the Indigent and Destitute Freedpeople in the Parish of St. Landry of Louisiana," Records of the Assistant Commissioner for the State of Louisiana, May 1868, 1865–1869, M1027, Roll 33, RG 105, NARA.

45. Clark to H. N. Howard, April 15, 1868, Washington, DC, Subordinate Field Officers, Freedmen's Village, Reports 1865–1868, M1902, Roll 21, Frame 188, RG 105, NARA.

46. For discussion about orphans in South Carolina, see Pelzer to Hogan, January 16, 1868, Charleston, South Carolina, e. 3132, LS. RG 105, NARA. Ibid., February 18, 1868, Charleston, South Carolina, e. 3132, LS. RG 105, NARA. Also at Fort Monroe, Virginia, in 1867, military officials tabulated that of the population of over 5,000 freed slaves the majority were under the age of 20. An estimated 1,031 were six years and under; roughly 1,228 were seven to 14 years old; an estimated 840 were between the ages of 15 and 20. See E.P. Williams to S.C. Armstrong, Fort Monroe, VA, 3798, AC, Box 17, W-414, A 7724, FSSP.

47. This is not to suggest that there were not orphans in the South before the war. There certainly were, but the vast majority were white and had the support of local and state almshouses and charitable institutions. There is the possibility that children born of free black people could have become orphaned. Moreover, it seems that kin networks on both plantations and within free black communities in the South would have protected children who were not living in the same household as their biological parents, foreclosing any identification of them as orphans. On kin networks, see Elsa Barkley Brown, "To Catch a Vision of Freedom: Reconstructing Southern Black Women's Political History, 1865–1880," in *Unequal Sisters: A Multicultural Reader in U.S. Women's History*, ed. Ellen DuBois and Vicki Ruiz, 3rd ed. (New York: Routledge, 2000), 124–46; Barkley Brown, "Womanist Consciousness: Maggie Lena Walker and the Independent Order of Saint Luke," *Signs: Journal of Women in Culture & Society* 14, no. 3 (Spring 1989): 610–33; Steven Hahn, *A Nation Under Our Feet: Black Political Struggles in the Rural South from Slavery to the Great Migration* (Cambridge, MA: Harvard University Press, 2005); Dylan C. Penningroth, *The Claims of Kinfolk: African-American Property and Community in the Nineteenth-Century South* (Chapel Hill: University of North Carolina Press, 2003). On postwar black urban life, see Harold Rabinowitz, *Race Relations in the Urban South, 1865–1890* (Urbana: University of Illinois Press, 1980), 128.

48. Julia A Wilbur to Anna M.C. Barnes, 2 October 1863, quoted in Jean Fagan Yellin, *The Harriet Jacobs Family Papers, Volume II* (Chapel Hill: University of North Carolina Press, 2008), 513. In a careful analysis of families during Reconstruction, Kidada Williams argues that the trauma sparked by violence of the knight riders led to the social disorganization of the black family. Based on Williams's valuable findings, I would argue that many of these orphans reported during the postwar period could also be children who escaped from their homes and families after a violent attack. See Williams, *They Left Great Marks on Me: African American Testimonies of Racial Violence from Emancipation to World War* (New York: New York University Press, 2012).

49. The statistics for Tennessee were tallied by the chief medical surgeon in Tennessee and include reports from hospitals in Chattanooga, Nashville, and Memphis as well as hospitals in Kentucky. Many times, Bureau chief medical officers oversaw the operations in their home state and a neighboring state. War Dept., *Laws in Relation to Freedmen*, 133. These numbers are compared with the 1,900 freedmen in Tennessee who received medical assistance and the 3,000 men who received assistance in Virginia. It is important to note, however, that many of these men were likely elderly, disabled, or physically handicapped. In these larger annual reports, Bureau agents did not break down the lists of dependent freedpeople according to physicality or age; they divided by gender. The

agents' correspondence, however, fills in the details. In these documents, agents would often describe masses of dependent freedpeople as women, elderly, disabled, and children. With this in mind, it is very likely that these men that are mentioned are not able-bodied and dependent for the same reasons as the women.

50. Vincent Coyler to Hon. Rob. Dale Owen, May 25, 1863, quoted in Berlin et al., *Wartime Genesis of Free Labor: The Upper South*, 127.

51. In 2006, when I published the article "The Other Side of Freedom," on the impoverished and medical conditions of formerly enslaved women in the Reconstruction, I was desperately pushing against a historiographical image of robust freedwomen and men that dominated the historiography. Moreover, historians (with the exception of Elsa Barkley Brown) who claimed to offer a gendered analysis of Reconstruction often reproduced the major themes and issues that other non-gender historians had made. By 2010, a deluge of books on gender and Reconstruction have appeared that grapple with the troubled meaning of freedom for former bondswomen and that have cogently unpacked the gender asymmetries at work within federal policy. To learn more about this exciting work, see (in historiographical order) O'Donovan, *Becoming Free in the Cotton South*; Glymph, *Out of the House of Bondage*; Hannah Rosen, *Terror in the Heart of Freedom: Citizenship, Sexual Violence, and the Meaning of Race in the Postemancipation South* (Chapel Hill: University of North Carolina Press, 2008); and Farmer-Kaiser, *Freedwomen and the Freedmen's Bureau*. Also see Barkley Brown, "To Catch a Vision of Freedom," and her "Womanist Consciousness."

52. According to General Order 46, "the family of each colored soldier so enlisted and mustered so long as he shall remain in the service and behave well, shall be furnished suitable subsistence, under the direction of the Superintendent of Negro Affairs, or their Assistants; and each soldier shall be furnished with a certificate of subsistence for his family, as soon as he is mustered." This rule applied to not only soldiers but also to those employed as laborers, Berlin et al., *Wartime Genesis of Free Labor: The Upper South*, 105. As the government employed formerly enslaved men, the military stipulated that dependent freedpeople, in general, were to earn rations, gain shelter, and receive medical care through the support of able-bodied freedmen. Capt. Murray Davis AAG to Col. James A. Hardie, 3 Dec 1864, D-8 1864, letters Received, ser.15, RG 159 [J-2].

53. Eaton, *Grant, Lincoln and the Freedmen*, 34.

54. As historian Jacqueline Jones notes, many freedwomen withdrew from the labor force during Reconstruction. But it is important to realize that these women were part of kin networks and had the financial support of male laborers. Jones, *Labor of Love, Labor of Sorrow: Black Women, Work, and the Family from Slavery to the Present* (New York: Vintage, 1985), 43–76.

55. Address Given at Arlington Cemetery, Daniel A. P. Murray Collection, 1807–1919, LOC; Eaton, *Grant, Lincoln and the Freedmen*, 34.

56. *Freedmen's Record*, January 1, 1866.

57. Daniel Freedmen and W. H. Redish to General Scott, October 12, 1866, Orangeburg, SC, e. 3314. LS, Letters, General Orders, and Special Orders Received and Endorsements Sent and Received, RG 105, NARA. Steve Hahn cogently demonstrates how kin networks benefited African Americans politically and socially, but economically the story is a bit more different, see his, *A Nation Under Our Feet*. Susan E. O'Donovan, however, presents a chilling example of how a mother abandoned her child due to the postwar crisis and confusion. O'Donovan's book probes the complicated and often taboo ways that some, if only a few, families broke apart during Reconstruction. See O'Donovan, *Becoming Free in the Cotton South*.

58. *Montgomery Daily Ledger*, 3, October 12–13, 1865, quoted in Howard N. Rabinowitz, *Race Relations in the Urban South, 1865–1900* (Urbana: University of Illinois Press, 1980), 131.

59. *Richmond Dispatch*, October 4, 1865, October 17, 1865, quoted in Rabinowitz, *Race Relations in the Urban South, 1865–1900*, 131.

60. J. Rebuis to Surgeon J. W. Lawton, August 13, 1866, Augusta, GA, LR, M1903, Roll 49, RG 105, NARA.

61. Henry Root to W. R. Dewitt, September 21, 1865, Orangeburg, SC, e. 2979, Chief Medical Officer, LR, 1865–66, RG 105, NARA.

62. H. N. Howard to O. H. Howard, September 11, 1867, Washington, DC, Subordinate Field Offices and Subassistant Commissioner (SubDistrict 1) Register of LR, M1902, Roll 20, RG 105, NARA. On the gendered dimensions of emancipation, see Downs, "The Other Side of Freedom."

63. Fitzhugh, "Agricultural, Commercial, Industrial Progress and Resources."

64. M. Waterbury, *Seven Years Among the Freedmen* (Chicago: T.R. Arnold, 1891), Manuscript Division, Perkins Library, DU.

65. A.V. Wright to Mrs. Tatum, August 26, 1865, Burke Family Papers, Mss1B9177a13-17, section 3, VHS.

66. See Magistrate Court Held at Union Church, Pike County, Alabama. February 25, 1867, Records for the Assistant Commissioner for the State of Alabama, Miscellaneous Papers, M809, Roll 23, RG 105, Freedmen's Bureau Online (retrieved December 8, 2010).

67. Laura S. Haviland, *A Woman's Life-Work: Labor and Experiences of Laura Haviland* (Chicago: C.V. Waite, 1887), 309.

68. Ibid., 380. For more on violence committed against freedwomen by their employer, see Lawanda Cox and John H. Cox, *Reconstruction, the Negro, and the New South* (Columbia: University of South Carolina Press, 1973), 4; Catherine Clinton, "Reconstructing Freedwomen" in *Divided Houses: Gender and the Civil War* (New York: Oxford University Press), 306. Thavolia Glymph offers a breathless account of the violently contested relationships that unfolded between enslaved women and plantation mistresses during the antebellum and Civil War years. See Glymph, *Out of the House of Bondage.*

69. A. A. Lawrence to H. N. Howard, October 31, 1866, Freedmen's Village and Virginia, Subordinate Field Offices, Reports 1865–1868, M1902, Roll 21, RG 105, NARA. Building on Deborah Gray White's analysis that many enslaved women did not run away because they, unlike enslaved men, had to consider the welfare of their children, a similar situation develops in the postwar period. See White, *"Aren't I A Woman?": Female Slaves in the Plantation South* (New York: Norton, 1985).

70. Apprenticeship laws varied by state. For an excellent overview on apprenticeship, see Rebecca Scott, "The Battle Over the Child: Child Apprenticeship and the Freedmen's Bureau in North Carolina," *Prologue* 10, no. 2 (1978): 101–13; and Mary Farmer-Kaiser, *Freedwomen and the Freedmen's Bureau: Race, Gender, and Public Policy in the Age of Emancipation* (New York: New York University Press, 2010), 96–140.

71. W. L. Vanderlip, to W.W. Rogers, AAAG, Annapolis, MD, December 13, 1866, A 9831, DC AC, 456 LR, Box 3, #1315, FSSP.

72. *Anti-Slavery Reporter*, March 2, 1886, 57–58.

73. Eaton, *Grant, Lincoln and the Freedmen*, 160–61.

74. Dr. Brown, for example, in Virginia, removed women from fieldwork. After he recognized that this was the cause of their dependency, he allowed them to return to the fields. See Lucy Chase before the American Freedmen's Inquiry Commission, [May 10, 1863], quoted in Berlin et al., *Wartime Genesis of Free Labor: The Upper South*, 150–54.

75 *Freedmen's Record*, June 1866, 111.

76 New England Freedmen's Aid Society, Annual Report, 1864, 70–75, LCP.

77. "Addresses and Ceremonies at the New Year's Festival to the Freedmen on Arlington Heights," LOC; Eaton, *Autobiography*, 34.

78. Harvey Terry to Jane Boustead (Agent), May 9, 1865; Oliver to Esteemed Friend, July 1, 1865; Tabitha J. Stokes to Jane Boustead, April 29, 1865, Pennsylvania Abolition Society Correspondence, 1865 File, HSP.

79 L. A. Edwards to Office of the Chief Medical Officer, September 28, 1866, North Carolina, e. 2535, LS, p. 65; Report of the Surgeon-in-Chief to Chief Medical Officer [Hogan to Horner], August 23, 1866, e. 2539, Box 29, both in RG 105, NARA. War Dept., *Laws in Relation to Freedmen*, 136.

80. *The Freedmen's Record*, May 1868, 81.

81. Howard, *Autobiography*, 170–71. This was in line with nineteenth-century thinking on the function of hospitals. See David Rosner, *A Once Charitable Enterprise: Hospitals and Health Care in Brooklyn and New York, 1885–1915* (New York: Cambridge University Press, 1982).

82. By "disabled," I am referring to physically handicapped, deaf, or blind freedpeople. These cases often develop in response to the Bureau officials' questions about how to classify people with disabilities who cannot be employed as laborers. Amelia Steward to O. O. Howard, June 30, 1867, Washington, DC, A9947, FSSP; Mrs. S. E. Draper to O. O. Howard, August 22, 1865, Washington, DC, 457 Unreg. Lr Box 8, A DC/AC FSSP. William Stone to Bvt. Lt. Col. H.W. Smith, August 7, 1866, South Carolina, M. 869, Roll 14, Freedmen's Bureau Online (Retrieved January 19, 2004). Rogers to W.F. Spurgin, December 11, 1866, Washington, DC, M1902, Roll 13, p. 103, RG 105, NARA; Beebe to Rogers, December 14, 1866, Washington, DC, M1902, Roll 13, p. 112, RG 105, NARA.

83. C. S. Schaeffer to Bvt. Brig. Genl. O. Brown, August 25, 1866, *The Reports of Charles S. Schaeffer from the Virginia Counties of Montgomery and Pulaski, with Additional Information on the Counties of Floyd, Giles, Craig, Whythe, and Roanoke, 1866–1868*; edited by Linda Killen, VHS.

84. Thomas W. Conway, "Final Report of the Bureau of Free Labor, Department of the Gulf to Major General E.R.S. Canby" (New Orleans, 1865), MHS.

85. S. P. Lee to W. W. Rogers, October 30, 1866, Alexandria, VA, 3878 (Misc) box 6C, A10039, FSSP.

86. Ibid., October 9, 1866.

87. E. H. Harris to Captain Sterling, May 4, 1867, New Orleans, Chief Medical Officer, e. 1385, LS, p. 195, RG 105, NARA.

88. For a fascinating social history of gender divisions in public institutions, see Jennifer Manion, "Women's Crime and Prison Reform in Early Pennsylvania, 1786–1829" (PhD diss., Rutgers University, 2008).

89. In some states, like Alabama, the Bureau would require the state to fund the transportation cost. See War Dept., *Laws in Relation to Freedmen*, 9–112.

90. Howard mentions in his autobiography that the transportation cost more than $1,300,000 to fund. See Howard, *Autobiography*, 331.

91. Hogan to Edwards, April 3, 1867, and Hogan to Yeoman, November 30, 1866, both in North Carolina, e. 2536, LS, vol. 2, RG 105, NARA.

92. Maria Holmes to Lt. Merrill, Richmond, VA, April 13, 1866, endorsements especially, W.B. Armstrong, April 25, 1866, VA Richmond, 4239 B51, A8158, FSSP.

93. Maj. General John A. Dix to Hon. Edwin M. Stanton, December 13, 1862, and Excerpts from Vincent Colyer to Hon. Rob. Dale Owen, May 25, 1863, quoted in Berlin, *Wartime Genesis of Free Labor: The Upper South*, 127, 139.

94. Howard, *Autobiography*, 222; War Dept., *Laws in Relation to Freedmen*, 94. To see how these institutions were funded, see *Laws in Relation to Freedmen*, 8, and Howard, *Autobiography*, 371–72. According to Howard, freedpeople produced more than two million bales of cotton, which generated over $40 million in taxes that was paid to the Treasury Department; see his *Autobiography*, 367.

95. War Dept., *Laws in Relation to Freedmen*, 5.

96. Ibid., 6–8.

97. Ibid., 134.

98. Eaton, *Autobiography*, 201–2; Reyburn, *Fifty Years in the Practice of Medicine and Surgery, 1856–1906*, 21; Howard, *Report of Brevet Major General O. O. Howard to the Secretary of War* (Washington, DC: GPO, 1869), 6–7.

99. Similarly, in the urban North such policies developed as immigrants swelled city's populations and industrial change revolutionized class and social relations. Parts of cities became refuge centers for those that did not fit into the labor force. In New York City, for example, nineteenth-century city officials demarcated the area located north of the city's main financial and commercial center as the designated space for those unable to work. There was an old-age home, an orphanage, an insane asylum, and a home for destitute women. See Pliny Earle, *History, Description and Statistics of the Bloomingdale Asylum for the Insane* (New York: Egbert, Hovey & King, Printers, 1848). For an overview of poor houses in English history, see Deborah E. B. Weiner, *Architecture and Social Reform in Late-Victorian London* (New York: St. Martin's Press, 1994). For a general overview of the relationship among architecture, social discipline, and treatments of patients, see Carla Yanni,

The Architecture of Madness: Insane Asylums in the United States (Minneapolis: University of Minnesota Press, 2007). For a theoretical discussion on the intersection of power and medical treatment, see Michel Foucault, *Discipline and Punish: The Birth of the Prison* (New York: Vintage, 1995) and his *The Birth of the Clinic: An Archeology of Medical Perception* (New York: Vintage, 1994).

100. Joseph P. Reidy " 'Coming from the Shadow of the Past': The Transition from Slavery to Freedom at Freedmen's Village, 1863–1900," *The Virginia Magazine of History and Biography* 95, no. 4 (1987): 403.

101. S. P. Lee to W. W. Rogers, October 9, 1866, VA Alex 3878 (Misc) box 6C, A10039, FSSP. E. H. Harris to Capt. Sterling, May 4, 1867, Louisiana, e. 1385, Chief Medical Officer, LS, p. 198, RG 105, NARA; Hogan to Day, October 20, 1866, North Carolina, e. 2536, LS, vol. 2, p. 21. RG 105, NARA. The construction of the Old Aged Homes for elderly freedpeople is remarkable during the time, considering that most federal benefits were only allotted to veterans who served in the war. Theda Skocpol argues how the United States, unlike Europe, offered benefits only for those who earned them. The provisions made for the elderly freedpeople suggests the ways in which the Bureau was a progressive institution ahead of its time. Indeed, the history of welfare programs in the United States has a very long and complicated political, legal, economic, and social history. The construction of asylums for the elderly suggests that some of the work of the Bureau can be understood as an antecedent, not an origin, to the creation of twentieth-century welfare programs. Skocpol, *Protecting Soldiers and Mothers*.

102. Appendix to the Cong. Globe, 39th Cong., 1st sess., House, 79; S. P. Lee to W.W. Rogers, October 9, 1866, VA Alex 3878 (Misc) box 6C, A10039 FSSP; Howard, *Autobiography*, 219, 246, and 258–59. Also see Michael F. Knight, "The Rost Home Colony, St. Charles Parish, Louisiana," *Prologue* 3, no. 3 (2001): NARA Online (Retrieved June 13, 2002).

103. Thomas W. Conway, "Final Report of the Bureau of Free Labor, Department of the Gulf to Major General E.R.S. Canby" (New Orleans, 1865). MHS; J. E. Thomas to Abraham Lincoln, January 1, 1865, Abraham Lincoln Papers, LOC; War Dept., *Laws in Relation to Freedmen*, 6.

104. Hogan to Day, October 20, 1866, Wilmington, NC, e. 2536, LS, vol. 2, p. 21, RG 105, NARA.

105. On National Home for Destitute Colored Women and Children, see Jean Fagan Yellin, *The Harriet Jacobs Family Papers, Volume II* (Chapel Hill: University of North Carolina Press, 2008), 513. In Charleston, a similar home was founded. See George Pelzer to Joseph Yates, November 18, 1867, South Carolina, e. 3132, LS, RG105, NARA. In the North, Homes for Destitute Women proliferated in response to the collapse of the household economy, while almshouses or "poor houses," as they were often called, developed in response to the reorganization of labor relations in the early nineteenth century. See Christine Stansell, *City of Women: Sex and Class in New York, 1789–1860* (Urbana: University of Illinois Press, 1987). On the emergence of asylums in response to the market revolution, see Raymond A. Mohl, *Poverty in New York, 1783–1825* (New York: Oxford University Press, 1971), 81–121.

106. On the presence of orphans in the Reconstruction South, see S. P. Lee to W. W. Rogers, October 9, 1866, VA Alex 3878 (Misc) box 6C, A10039, FSSP. Thomas W. Conway, "Final Report of the Bureau of Free Labor, Department of the Gulf to Major General E.R.S. Canby" (New Orleans, 1865), MHS. Also see Howard White, *The Freedmen's Bureau in Louisiana* (Baton Rouge: Louisiana State University Press, 1970), 79. On the national orphan crisis, see Skocpol, *Protecting Soldiers and Mothers*; Donald R. Shaffer, *After the Glory: The Struggles of Black Civil War Veterans* (Lawrence: University of Kansas, 2004); James Marten, *The Children's Civil War* (Chapel Hill: University of North Carolina Press, 1998). Timothy A. Hasci insightfully ties the proliferation of orphanages in nineteenth-century America to a number of social factors, including the cholera epidemic in 1849 and the aftermath of the Civil War in 1865. See Timothy A. Hasci, *Second Home: Orphan Asylums and Poor Families in America* (Cambridge, MA: Harvard University Press, 1997).

107. Howard, *Autobiography*, 261. W. E. B. Du Bois, *Darkwater: Voices from Within the Veil* (New York: Harcourt, Brace, and Howe, 1920), 178.

108. See Howard, *Autobiography*, 260–61. Some of these Northern benevolent organizations founded orphanages for free children of color in the North as early as 1820; see Leslie Harris, *In the Shadow of Slavery: African Americans in New York City 1626–1863* (Chicago: University of Chicago Press).

109. Eaton, *Grant, Lincoln and the Freedmen*, 36.

110. Hogan to Day, October 20, 1866, North Carolina, e. 2536, LS, vol. 2, p. 21; Griswold to Femo, August 29, 1865, Louisiana, e. 1385, LS, p. 67, both in RG 105, NARA; Harriet Jacobs, "An Appeal: Savannah Orphans Asylum," *Anti-Slavery Reporter*, March 2, 1868. Also see White, *The Freedmen's Bureau in Louisiana*, 79–83.

111. Haviland, *A Woman's Life-Work*, 377.

112. Howard, *Autobiography*, 219.

113. W. Martin Hope and Jason H. Silverman, *Relief and Recovery in Post–Civil War South Carolina: A Death by Inches* (Lewiston, NY: Edwin Mellen Press, 1997).

114. War Dept., *Laws in Relation to Freedmen*; also see Paul Skeels Peirce, *The Freedmen's Bureau: A Chapter in the History of Reconstruction* (Iowa City: University, 1904); Bentley, *History of the Freedmen's Bureau*.

115. 5,000 orphans were black, 3,000 orphans were white. See Hope and Silverman, *Relief and Recovery in Post–Civil War South Carolina*.

116. E. P. Williams to S. C. Armstrong, July 10, 1867, Ft. Monroe, Assistant Commissioner, VA, A 7724, W-414, Box 17, FSSP; W. L. Vanderlap to W. W. Rogers, December 13, 1866, A9831, DC AC, 456 LR Box 3, # 1315, A 9831, FSSP; "Report of Indigent and Destitute Freed People in the Parish of St. Landry State of Louisiana, applying for Relief from the first day of May 1868 to the thirty first day of May 1868," Records of the Assistant Commissioner for the State of Louisiana, Reports Relating to the Condition of Freedmen, 1865–1869, M1027, Roll 33, Freedmen's Bureau Online (retrieved January 1, 2010); Thomas W. Conway, "Final Report of the Bureau of Free Labor, Department of the Gulf to Major General E.R.S. Canby," (New Orleans, 1865), MHS.

117. Weekly records indicate the number of freedpeople who entered a hospital in a particular week with the number who were discharged after two or three weeks. By comparing the numbers in both columns over a two to three month period, it is clear that many freedpeople stayed at a hospital for, at least, a week or more.

118. The notion of cleanliness was very important to Northern reformers who assisted former slaves in their transition from slavery to freedom. In her open letter to the freedpeople, in the immediate aftermath of slavery, erstwhile abolitionist Lydia Marie Child praised the merits of cleanliness and argued that their "dirty cabins" and "slovenly dress" will suggest to their critics that they are unable to take care of themselves. See Child, *The Freedmen's Book* (Boston: Ticknor and Fields, 1865), 270. For a brilliant overview on the history of cleanliness, see Brown, *Foul Bodies*. For a general overview of freedpeople's education, see Robert Charles Morris, *Reading, 'Riting, and Reconstruction: The Education of Freedmen in the South, 1861–1870* (Chicago: University of Chicago Press, 1981); Heather Ann Williams, *Self-Taught: African-American Education in Slavery and Freedom* (Chapel Hill: University of North Carolina, 2005); Jim Downs, "Uplift, Violence, and Service: The Experience of Black Women Teachers in the South During Reconstruction," *The Southern Historian* 24 (Spring 2003): 29–39.

119. David J. Rothman, *The Discovery of the Asylum: Social Order and Disorder in the New Republic* (Boston: Little Brown, 1971). Seth Rockman has brilliantly revised the literature on almshouses by providing a "richer interpretative model that moves beyond the traditional narratives that characterize the history of these institutions as examples of elite benevolence, social discipline, and pauper agency." See Seth Rockman, *Scraping By: Wage Labor, Slavery, and Survival in Early Baltimore* (Baltimore: Johns Hopkins University Press), 197.

120. See, for example, "Addresses and Ceremonies at the New Year's Festival to the Freedmen, on Arlington Heights," Daniel A. P. Murray Collections, 1818–1907, LOC.

121. "Facts about the Famine," March 7, 1867, Three Centuries of Broadsides and Other Printed Ephemera, LOC.

122. *Reports of State Committees, Relief for Confederates, Ladies Southern Relief Association of Maryland* (Baltimore: Kelly and Piet, 1866), LCP.

123. John Hammond Moore, ed., *The Juhl Letters to the Charleston Courier: A View of the South, 1865–1871* (Athens: University of Georgia Press, 1974), 33.

124. Ibid., 42.

125. War Dept., *Laws in Relation to the Freedmen*.

126. Howard often prided himself on the number of hospitals, personnel, and relief that he disbanded. For example, he argued that there were 141 commissioned officers, 412 civilian agents, and 348 clerks, but he decreased that to 15 commissioned officers, 71 civilian agents, and 72 clerks. Such shortages prevented the Bureau from promptly ending the famine. See Howard, *Autobiography*, 361–62. Also, see *Report of Brevet Maj-General Wagner Swayne, Assistant Commissioner for Alabama, For the Year Ending September 30, 1867*, 9, From Slavery to Freedom: The African-American Pamphlet Collection, 1824–1909, LOC; Howard, *Autobiography*, 214, 222, and 370–71.

127. *Report of Brevet Maj-General Wagner Swayne, Assistant Commissioner for Alabama, For the Year Ending September 30, 1867*, 4, LOC. *American Freedmen*, January 1868, LOC.

128. Miss Chole Merrick, Columbia, SC, *American Freedmen*, December 1867, February 1868, 349, LCP.

129. Howard, *Autobiography*, 220.

130. Southern Commission Relief Papers, NYHS. "Facts about the Famine," March 7, 1867, Three Centuries of Broadsides and Other Printed Ephemera, LOC; *Report of Brevet Maj-General Wagner Swayne, Assistant Commissioner for Alabama, For the Year Ending September 30, 1867*, 9, LOC.

131. Issac Rosebraus to Andrew Geedis, May 26, 1868, Raleigh, e. 2468, Reports of Destitution, August–October 1867–January 1868, Box 14, RG 105, NARA.

132. *Pennsylvania Freedmen's Bulletin*, February 1868, 10, LCP.

133. Ibid., 8.

134. A. S. Firy to Lieutenant H. L. Hunt, April 12, 1866, Reports of Charles S. Schaeffer, VHS.

135. Hammond Moore, *Juhl Letters to the Charleston Courier*, 20.

136. War Dept., *Laws in Relation to Freedmen*.

137. Howard, *Autobiography*, 350.

138. Theoretically, the marking of freedwomen as dependent represents a critical watershed moment in the vexed historical development of racial ideology. Jennifer Morgan has brilliantly demonstrated how the representations of enslaved women provided the foundation for British North American travel writers and slaveholders to define all people of African descent as innately inferior and different from "white" people, while Kathleen M. Brown has persuasively argued how the creation of specific taxes on black women's labor codified racial difference in the early Chesapeake. Building on this foundational work, I submit that the marking of freedwomen as destitute further fuels the development of racial ideology by stripping women of their labor power that they possessed as enslaved people, and then defining them as dependent on the state for support. The political fiction produced by policymakers in the twentieth century about black women as unwilling or even unable to work (read: the racist caricature of the "welfare queen") begins during Reconstruction. Similar to Morgan's work that reveals that the negative representations surrounding African women became a way to define all people of African descent as inferior, the marking of freedwomen as unable to work became a heuristic or metonymy for the ways in which those in power defined all people of African descent from the mid-nineteenth century to the present as dependent. Similar to Brown's work that exposes how the state's marking of women of African descent as different from white women and thereby in need of specific legislation that addresses their particular legal and economic status, the federal government's creation of specific asylums, relief programs, and even its establishment of the Bureau itself subsequently codified freedwomen as dependent subjects in need of economic support from the state. Hence, the epigraph that begins this chapter explains the problematic category of "women." See Jennifer L. Morgan, *Laboring Women: Reproduction and Gender in New World Slavery* (Philadelphia: University of Pennsylvania Press, 2004); and Kathleen M. Brown, *Good Wives, Nasty Wenches and Anxious Patriarchs: Gender, Race and Power in Colonial Virginia* (Chapel Hill: University of North Carolina Press, 1996). Also see

Evelyn Brooks Higginbotham, "African-American Women's History and the Metalanguage of Race," *Signs* 17 (Winter 1992): 251–74. For broader analyses of the ideological development of racism, see Barbara J. Fields, "Whiteness, Racism, and Identity," *International Labor and Working-Class History* 60 (Fall 2001): 48–56. Barbara J. Fields, "Of Rogues and Geldings," *The American Historical Review* 108, no. 5 (December, 2003): 1397–1405; Barbara Jeanne Fields, "Slavery, Race, and Ideology in the United States of America," *New Left Review* 181 (May–June 1990): 95–118; Barbara Jeanne Fields, "Ideology and Race in American History," in *Region, Race and Reconstruction: Essays in Honor of C. Vann Woodward*, ed. J. Morgan Kousser and James M. McPherson (New York: Oxford University Press, 1982), 143–77. Building on Fields's formulations, Martha Hodes astutely argues, "power lies within the ability of legal, economic, and social authorities to assign and reassign racial categories to oppressive ends." See Hodes, "The Mercurial Nature and Abiding Power of Race: A Transnational Family Story," *American Historical Review* 108, no. 1 (February 2003).

Chapter 6

1. On Jeannette Small see Pelzer to Hogan, January 16, 1868, Charleston, SC, LS, e. 3132, September 1867–1869, RG 105, NARA. The archive includes other women who are portrayed as mentally disabled, such as the case of Bettie Bell. See Beebe to Rogers, December 14, 1866, Subordinate Field Offices, Local Superintendent for Washington and Georgetown Correspondences, LS, vol. 1 (77), July 15, 1865–September 10, 1867, M1902, Roll 13, RG 105, NARA.

2. For Georgia, see Augusta to Caleb Horner, June 2, 1866, Georgia, Savannah Lincoln Hospital, LS, vol. 1 (354), December 1865–January 1868, M1901, Roll 85, RG 105, NARA. For North Carolina, see Hillebrandt to Kinston, June 18, 1866, North Carolina, e. 2535, LS, Box 37, RG 105, NARA. For Arkansas, Missouri, and Indian Territory, see War Dept., *Laws in Relation to Freedmen*, 28. For Alabama, A. M. Ryan to Shrokly, April 30, 1868, Alabama, Records of the Assistant Commissioner for the State of Alabama, Reports of the Operation of the Subdistrict, M809, Roll 18, Frame 67–68, RG 105, NARA. For Louisiana, see A. C. Swartzwelder, May 22, 1868, Annual Report, e. 1393, Chief Medical Officer, Box 40, RG 105, NARA.

3. While state authorities took over control of freedpeople's health in the late 1860s, the political demise of Reconstruction in the late 1870s led to the dissolution of these efforts. For example, state authorities assumed control of the Freedmen's Bureau in Alabama in 1868. While the Freedmen's Hospital, which was located in Talladega, remained active in the late 1860s and early 1870s, by 1875 state authorities disbanded the institution. Due to the federal government's withdrawal from the South, there was no overarching authority that could refill the gap left, once again, by the state's refusal to support black people in the late 1870s to 1890s. Historians Tera W. Hunter, Samuel K. Roberts, and Keith Wailoo, among others, have adequately documented the ensuing tragedy surrounding black health during the final decades of the nineteenth century. On Atlanta, see Tera W. Hunter, *"To 'Joy My Freedom": Southern Black Women's Lives and Labor after the Civil War* (Cambridge, MA: Harvard University Press, 1997). On Memphis, see Keith Wailoo, *Dying in the City of the Blues: Sickle Cell Anemia and the Politics of Face and Health* (Chapel Hill: University of North Carolina Press, 2001). On Baltimore, see Samuel K. Roberts, *Infectious Fear: Politics, Disease, and the Effects of Segregation* (Baltimore: Johns Hopkins University Press, 2009). On Freedmen's Hospital in Alabama, see Thomas McAdory Owen, *History of Alabama and Dictionary of Alabama Biography*, vol. 1 (Chicago: S. J. Clarke Publishing, 1921), 631.

4. Indeed, black veterans represent a small percentage of the population of freed slaves, but the point here is not to suggest that freedpeople's health across the South changed because of the creation of the pension system but, rather, to underscore a gradual change in who gets to narrate black people's health.

5. Overall, the pension records, more than the Bureau archives, offered the most surprising and detailed accounts of freedpeople's health.

6. L. A. Edwards to War Dept. of BRFAL of the Chief Medical Officer, September 28, 1866, North Carolina, e. 2535, LS, RG 105, NA.

7. Vanderburgh to Mayor Clark, Freedmen's Village, April 1, 1868, Washington, DC, , Subordinate Field Officers, Freedmen's Village, Reports 1865–1868, M1902, Roll 21, Frame 182, RG 105, NARA.

8. Edward Jarvis, M.D., *Insanity and Insane Asylums* (Louisville, KY: Prentice and Weissinger, 1841), 10.

9. A. G. Brady to J. K. Fleming, June 1, 1866, New Berne, NC, e. 2535, LS, RG 105, NARA. It is important to note that the treatment of insane patients in the South during this period remained problematic. There were a few institutions dedicated to the care of mentally challenged patients, and these asylums often lacked basic resources, such as adequate food and shelter, to accommodate the number of patients that they served. Peter McCandless has provided an illustrative history of an asylum in South Carolina. See his *Moonlight, Magnolias, and Madness: Insanity in South Carolina from the Colonial Period to the Progressive Era* (Chapel Hill: University of North Carolina Press, 1996). Kirby Randolph has written an important dissertation on the care of mentally disabled freedpeople in Virginia, which, as of this writing, she is revising for publication. Randolph's forthcoming book, along with McCandless's study, will provide an important context to understand the history of mental disabilities in various corridors of the South. Kirby Ann Randolph, "Central Lunatic Asylum for the Colored Insane: A History of African Americans with Mental Disabilities, 1844–1885 (Virginia)" (PhD diss., University of Pennsylvania, 2003).

10. Pelzer to Hogan, January 16, 1868, Charleston, SC, e. 3132, LS, September 1867–1869; Beebe to Rogers, December 14, 1866, Subordinate Field Offices, Local Superintendent for Washington and Georgetown Correspondences, LS, vol. 1 (77), July 15, 1865–September 10, 1867, M1902, Roll 13, both in RG 105, NARA.

11. In Georgia, see J. V. DeHanne to Greese, June 18, 1867, Office of Staff Officers, Surgeon-in-Chief, LS and Register of LR, vol. 52, September 1865–July 1867, M1903, Roll 26; In South Carolina, see Pelzer to Hogan, January 16, 1868, Charleston, SC, LS, e. 3132, September 1867–1869; Pelzer to Lockwood, May, 28, 1868, Charleston, SC, LS, e. 3132, September 1867–1869; in North Carolina, see Chase to C. A. Cilley, June 21, 1866, Raleigh, NC, e. 2535, LS, p. 52; in Washington, DC, see Register of Patients in Female Ward of Lincoln Hospital, July 1, 1866–March 22, 1867, Consolidated Weekly Reports of Sick and Wounded Freedmen, Roll 19, M1902, all in RG 105, NARA.

12. I am building here on historian Lynette Jackson's brilliant argument about the ways in which colonial officials marked African female migrants as insane due to the violent dislocation that they experienced. See Lynette Jackson, *Surfacing Up: Psychiatry and Social Order in Colonial Zimbabwe, 1908–1968* (Ithaca, NY: Cornell University Press, 2005).

13. See Jarvis, M.D., *Insanity and Insane Asylums*, 13–25; David Rothman, *The Discovery of the Asylum: Social Order and Disorder in the New Republic* (Boston: Little, Brown, 1971). In his comprehensive study of an insane asylum in South Carolina, Peter McCandless challenges Rothman's interpretation of the asylum as simply an institution that served a disciplinary function for the rest of society. He cogently reveals how South Carolinian doctors and reformers explored innovative therapeutic remedies as treatment for insane patients. See McCandless, *Moonlight, Magnolias, and Madness*.

14. War Dept., *Laws in Relation to Freedmen*, 99.

15. J. V. DeHanne to N. D'Abiguy, June 14, 1867, Office of Staff Officers, Surgeon-in-Chief, LS and Register of LR, vol. 52, September 1865–July 1867, M1903, Roll 26, RG 105, NARA.

16. War Dept., *Laws in Relation to Freedmen*, 66.

17. Ibid., 99.

18. Laws in Relation to Freedmen, U.S. Senate 39th Cong., 2nd Sess., Senate Executive Document, No. 6, 154.

19. J. V. DeVanne to Dr. C. F. Greene, Superintendent of the State Lunatic Asylum, June 10, 1867, Office of Staff Officers, Surgeon-in-Chief, LS and Register of LR, vol. 52, September 1865–July 1867, M1903, Roll 26, RG 105, NARA.

20. Ibid., June 13, 1867.

21. On Virginia, see Randolph, "Central Lunatic Asylum for the Colored Insane." On Louisiana, see A. C. Swartzwelder, May 22, 1868, Annual Report, e. 1393, Chief Medical Officer, Box 40, RG 105, NARA.

22. S. A. Bell to Hogan, September 24, 1866, Salisbury, NC; Edie to Headquarters for Instruction, September 24, 1866, both in e. 2535, LS, RG 105, NARA.

23. For more on the North Carolina laws, see War Dept., *Laws in Relation to Freedmen*, 109. For an example of how destitute freedpeople were placed into government communities, see Joseph P. Reidy "Coming from the Shadow of the Past: The Transition from Slavery to Freedom at Freedmen's Village, 1863–1900," *The Virginia Magazine of History and Biography* 95, no. 4 (Oct. 1987): 403–28.

24. A. M. Gauwell to A. Jackson, June 18, 1867, Florida, LS, RG 105, NARA.

25. For Louisiana, see War Dept., *Laws in Relation to Freedmen*, 81. For Mitchell, GA, see Clark to J. V. DeHanne, May 25, 1867, Office of Staff Officers, Surgeon-in-Chief, LS and Register of LR, vol. 52, September 1865–July 1867, M1903, Roll 26, RG 105, NARA. For Raleigh, NC, see Chase to Mayor of Raleigh, August 13, 1866, Raleigh, NC, e. 2535, LS, p. 58, RG 105, NARA. For Charlotte, NC, P. P. Midlim, July 4, 1868, Salisbury (Western District), Misc., Box 59, RG 105, NARA.

26. In many respects, some medical officials recognized insanity during the nineteenth century as a "natural malady" related to emancipation. See Edward Jarvis, *Insanity Among the Coloured Population of the Free States* (Philadelphia: T.K & P.G. Collins Printers, 1844); Jarvis, *Insanity and Insane Asylums*; and Jarvis, "Status of the Negro," *DeBow's Review* (1867): 587–88. Parts of Jarvis's *Insanity Among the Coloured Population* were reproduced in *Medical Journal of Boston; Southern Literary Messenger* of Richmond, Virginia, in June 1843; *Hunt's Merchant Magazine*, of New York, May 1843; and in Dr. Stribbling's *Report of the Western Lunatic Asylum of Virginia*.

27. J. V. DeHanne to M. F. Barres, June 5, 1867, Austaga, GA, LR, October 1865–May 1868, Roll 49, M1903, Frame 698; ibid., July 30, 1867, both in RG 105, NARA.

28. J. V. DeHanne to N. D'Abiguy, June 14, 1867, Office of Staff Officers, Surgeon-in-Chief, LS and Register of LR, vol. 52, September 1865–July 1867, M1903,Roll 26, RG 105, NARA.

29. Chief Medical Report of 1867, e.1393, Louisiana, Box 40, RG 109, NARA.

30. Pelzer to Lockwood, May 28, 1868; and Pelzer to Chatburn, March 5, 1868, both in Charleston, SC, e. 3132, September 1867–1869, RG 105, NARA.

31. May 29, 1866, Shreveport, LA, e. 1393, LR, Box 40, RG 109, NARA.

32. Ibid., December 28, 1866.

33. Charles E. Rosenberg, *The Cholera Years: The United States in 1832, 1849, and 1866.* (Chicago: University of Chicago Press, 1962).

34. Emma Spaulding Bryant to John Emory Bryant, September 29, 1867, Folder 2, Emma Spaulding Bryant Letters, DU.

35. For a brief account on the measures enacted to prevent the further spread of an epidemic in 1867 that brought white and black citizens together, see "In Memoriam of the Lamented Dead," (Memphis, TN: Young and Brothers, 1874), 28–31, LCP.

36. Kipp to C. W. Horner, June 5, 1867, Huntsville, AL, p. 171; Kipp to C. W. Horner, June 5, 1866, Montgomery, AL, Office of the Staff Officers, Surgeon, LS, vol. 1 (31), September 7, 1865–July 21, 1865, Roll 8, Target 5, RG 105, NARA.

37. For Louisiana, see War Dept., *Laws in Relation to Freedmen*, 81. For Mitchell, GA, see Clark to J. V. DeHanne, May 25, 1867, Office of Staff Officers, Surgeon-in-Chief, LS and Register of LR, vol. 52, September 1865–July 1867, M1903, Roll 26, RG 105, NARA. For Raleigh, NC, see Chase to Mayor of Raleigh, August 13, 1866, Raleigh, NC, e. 2535, LS, p. 58, RG 105, NARA. For Charlotte, NC, P. P. Midlim, July 4, 1868, p. 58, Salisbury (Western District), Misc., Box 59, RG 105, NARA. The acceptance of freedpeople into local asylums and state institutions also marked a critical moment in the history of discrimination and public services. Harold N. Rabinowitz argues that segregation existed between whites and blacks in urban centers for decades before the full-sweep of Jim Crow in the early twentieth century, while C. Vann Woodward argues that segregation was not the default practice that organized the South. Based on my findings, I am much more in agreement with Woodward, as state institutions did not segregate black from white patients for a brief period, namely from 1868–1877. See Rabinowitz, *Race*

Relations in the Urban South 1865–1900 (Urbana: University of Illinois Press, 1980). C. Vann Woodward, *The Strange Career of Jim Crow* (New York: Oxford University Press, 1966).

38. On black political mobilization as uneven until 1867, see Eric Foner, *Reconstruction: America's Unfinished Revolution* (New York: Harper and Row, 1988).

39. S. N. Clark to Eaton, August 21, 1865, Washington, DC, Assistant Commissioner, 457 Unreg. LR, Box 8, FSSP.

40. J. S. Caulfield to W.R. Dewitt, September 10, 1865, South Carolina, e. 2979, Chief Medical Officer, LR, Box 37, RG 105, NARA. (Although this document is from GA, it was found in the SC box.)

41. David Shelton Watson to City Officials, January 31, 1867, Mss1J8586b287, Joynes Family Papers, VHS.

42. Ahern to Neive, January 29, 1868, Summerville, SC, e. 2254, Letters and Special Orders Received, vol. 1, RG 105, NARA.

43. As an example of federal change, Hannah Rosen brilliantly charts how the federal government provided freedwomen an opportunity to testify against white Southerners who raped and sexually assaulted them. The history of this period is vast and richly detailed; for the most authoritative interpretations on the post-Reconstruction decades, see C. V. Woodward, *Origins of the New South, 1877–1913* (Baton Rouge: Louisiana State University Press, 1951); Woodward, *Strange Career of Jim Crow*; Glenda Gilmore, *Gender and Jim Crow: Women and the Politics of White Supremacy in North Carolina, 1896–1920* (Chapel Hill: University of North Carolina Press, 1996); Hannah Rosen, *Terror in the Heart of Freedom: Citizenship, Sexual Violence, and the Meaning of Race in the Postemancipation South* (Chapel Hill: University of North Carolina Press, 2008).

44. Michael Hait, "Civil War Pension Application Files—A Rich Source of Detail," *Examiner*, http://www.examiner.com/african-american-genealogy-in-national/civil-war-pension-application-files-a-rich-source-of-detail (retrieved December 20, 2010).

45. Pension File of John Abbott, C 35, USCI, Application # 294085, Cert # 179683, RG15.

46. *Oxford English Dictionary Online*, s.v. "vicious," http://www.oed.com/ (accessed December 22, 2010).

47. On the complicated and often discriminatory ways that those in power evaluated black people's bodies in the nineteenth century, see Harriet Washington, *Medical Apartheid: The Dark History of Medical Experimentation on Black Americans from Colonial Times to the Present* (New York: Doubleday, 2006), especially 143–56; Margaret Humphreys, *Intensely Human: The Health of the Black Soldier in the American Civil* (Baltimore: Johns Hopkins University Press, 2008).

48. On exposure as an early explanation of rheumatism, see Alfred Mantle, "The Etiology of Rheumatism Considered from a Bacterial Point of View," *The British Medical Journal* 1, no. 1382 (June 25, 1887): 1381–84. On the connections between cardiac disease and rheumatism, see Peter C. English, "The Emergence of Rheumatic Fever in the Nineteenth Century," *The Milbank Quarterly* 67, supp. 1, Framing Disease: The Creation and Negotiation of Explanatory Schemes (1989): 3–49.

49. On how the medical profession battled internally with the meaning and treatment of rheumatism in the United States and the UK, see W. B. Cheadle et al., "Acute Rheumatism [With Discussion]," *The British Medical Journal* 1, no. 1828 (January 11, 1896): 65–74; Mantle, "The Etiology of Rheumatism Considered from a Bacterial Point of View"; Dr. Isaac Newton, "Epidemic Muscular Rheumatism," *The British Medical Journal* 2, no. 1760 (September 22, 1894): 651–52; Carrie A. Benham, "The Nursing of Rheumatism," *The American Journal of Nursing* 24, no. 9 (June 1924): 699–705.

50. Despite its elastic and quite flexible meanings, symptoms of rheumatism did not veer into the province of sexually related diseases or socially and morally inflected diseases, such as smallpox, and other illnesses often associated with "vicious habits." Additionally, during the late nineteenth century, many in the medical community often associated rheumatism with manual laborers, in large part due to its early etiology related to exposure and the emphasis on outdoor climates. This connotation further worked in black veterans' favor, as it showed that they were unable to work. On the connections to labor see William Anderson, "Cerebral Rheumatism," *The British Medical Journal* 1, no. 542 (May 20, 1871): 528–30.

51. For a comprehensive analysis of black veterans applying for pensions, see Donald R. Shaffer, *After the Glory: The Struggles of Black Civil War Veterans* (Lawrence: University of Kansas Press, 2004).

52. For an excellent discussion on black veterans, marriage, and pension applications, see Shaffer, *After the Glory*, 110–17.

53. Ella Criddle to Hon. GM Saltzgaber, August 11, 1919, Chicago, IL, Isiah Criddle, Widow no. 722, no. 733, Pension Files, RG 15, NARA.

54. Laura C. Holloway, *Howard: The Christian Hero* (New York: Funk and Wagnalls, 1885), 157. Howard, *Autobiography*, 260–61.

55. Bills and Resolutions, House of Representatives, 42nd Cong., 2nd sess., Read twice, referred to the Committee on Freedmen's Affairs, and ordered to be printed. Mr. Cobb, on leave, introduced the following bill: A Bill Abolishing the Bureau of Refugees, Freedmen and Abandoned Lands, and providing for the continuance of the Freedmen's Hospital in the District of Columbia, LOC, Also see, S 1303, 41st Cong., 3rd sess. (February 4, 1871); *Statutes at Large*, 43rd Cong., 1st sess., 938–941. Throughout the twentieth century, the federal government under the aegis of the Interior Department overlooked the operations of the hospital with the support of the District of Columbia, which shouldered part of the financial responsibility for the care of patients. While authority of Freedmen's Hospital remained complicated and confusing throughout the twentieth century, it continues today as part of Howard University Hospital—which assumed control in 1967. See HR 1502, 40th Cong., 3rd sess. (December 14, 1868). Also see Robert E. Lester ed., "Records of the Freedmen's Hospital, 1872–1910," LexisNexis Academic and Library Solutions, 2004.

56. On pregnancy and OB/GYN-related issues, see 1: 0448; 2: 0218; 3: 0038; 1: 0312, 0534, 0878; 3: 0460; 4: 0282; 5: 0564, 0865; On infants, see 1: 0448; 2: 0218; 3: 0038; On Uterine Cancer, 2: 0057; On asthma, see 2: 0675 in Robert E. Lester ed., "Records of the Freedmen's Hospital, 1872–1910," LexisNexis Academic and Library Solutions, 2004. On brown fur on the tongue, see U.S. Army Medical Museum, *Catalogue of the Medical and Microscopical Sections of the United States Army Medical Museum*, prepared under the direction of the Surgeon General, U.S. Army [Washington, DC: GPO, 1867], no. 756, p. 53; On epithelioma, see ibid, no. 741, p. 18.

57. In an effort to create a cure for vesicovaginal fistulas, J. Marion Sims abusively experimented on the bodies of three enslaved women without using anesthesia during the antebellum period. During the early twentieth century, doctors in rural Alabama conducted an experiment on untreated cases of syphilis among black men. See Washington, *Medical Apartheid*; Vanessa Gamble, "Under the Shadow of Tuskegee: African Americans and Health Care," *American Journal of Public Health* 87, no. 11 (1997): 1773–78; Jim Jones, *Bad Blood: The Tuskegee Syphilis Experiment* (New York: Free Press, 1993); Susan Reverby, *Examining Tuskegee: The Infamous Syphilis Study and Its Legacy* (Chapel Hill: University of North Carolina Press, 2009).

58. While Freedmen's Hospital in Washington, DC, was exceptional, only miles away in neighboring Baltimore the relationship between black patients and hospitals was much more troublesome. For an informed analysis of the interplay between white doctors at Johns Hopkins University and the black community of Baltimore, as well as the racist ways white physicians deployed a negative and quite derogatory profile of black health during the late nineteenth and early twentieth centuries, see Samuel Kelton Roberts, Jr., *Infectious Fear: Politics, Disease, and the Health Effects of Segregation* (Baltimore: Johns Hopkins University Press, 2009).

59. Despite claims of racism and malpractice, it is important to recognize that a core group of physicians at Freedmen's Hospital remained deeply committed to helping black patients. For complaints filed against the hospital, see Lester "Records of the Freedmen's Hospital, 1872–1910," LexisNexis Academic and Library Solutions, 2004, 3: 0854, 2: 0675, 2: 0075, 0675, 0905; 3: 0018.

60. Robert Reyburn, *Fifty Years in the Practice of Medicine and Surgery, 1856–1906* (Washington, DC: Beresford Press, 1907); also see Robert Reyburn, March 25, 1867, November 24, 1873, Army Medical Board, Medical Autobiography, Adjutant General's Office, Medical Officers and Physicians, RG 94, NARA. On Purvis, see William J. Simmons, *Men of Mark: Eminent, Progressive and Rising* (Cleveland, OH: Rewell Publishing, 1891).

61. Reyburn, *Fifty Years in the Practice of Medicine and Surgery*, 21–23.
62. Ibid.

Conclusion

1. Harriet A. Jacobs, "Life Among The Contrabands," *The Liberator*, September 5, 1862, 3.
2. Before the Civil War, the government did not establish hospitals, dispensaries, asylums, and orphanages for people who lacked familial support or the assistance of cultural and ethnic institutions. Although the government constructed Marine Hospitals during the first decades of the nineteenth century, these institutions were limited to port cities and served mostly merchant marines. For a historical overview of these institutions, see Gautham Rao, "Sailors' Health and National Wealth," *Common-Place* 9, no. 1 (October 2008). For a comprehensive history of federal authority in the nineteenth-century, see Brian Balogh, *A Government Out of Sight: The Mystery of National Authority in Nineteenth-Century America* (Cambridge: Cambridge University Press, 2009).
3. While Leon Litwack has richly documented freedpeople's struggles and hardships after slavery, this book attempts to focus on the specific struggle of freedpeople's health. It also investigates the structural issues—namely free labor ideology, the limitations of the federal government, and the disease produced by the war—that led to this suffering. Leon Litwack, *Been in the Storm So Long: The Aftermath of Slavery* (New York: Vintage, 1980).
4. On Reconstruction politics, see Eric Foner, *Reconstruction: America's Unfinished Revolution* (New York: Harper and Row, 1988).
5. Gregory P. Downs and James Downs, "Was Freedom Enough?" *New York Times*, November 11, 2011. (Retrieved November 12, 2011.)
6. Elizabeth Keckley, *Behind the Scenes: Thirty Years a Slave, and Four Years in the White House* (New York: Oxford University Press, 1988), 112.

Epilogue

1. Legal Historian Sarah Barringer Gordon challenges Eric Foner's claim that 1877 marks the collapse of Reconstruction. She argues that a second reconstruction occurred in the West in the campaign against polygamy in late-nineteenth-century Utah. See Sarah Barringer Gordon, *The Mormon Question: Polygamy and Constitutional Conflict in Nineteenth-Century America* (Chapel Hill: University of North Carolina Press, 2002), 14, 242. Moreover, historian Elliot West calls for a "Greater Reconstruction," which focuses on an exploration of how "western expansion and the Civil War raised similar questions and led to twinned crisis." See Elliot West, *The Last Indian War: The Nez Perce Story* (New York: Oxford University Press, 2009), xx.
2. Richard White has brilliantly argued that the West "served as the kindergarten for the American State." While this is certainly true, I am fascinated by the ways in which the South and West, which have been typically seen as two separate entities, actually shared some common features during Reconstruction. As I explain, there was a coming together of similar federal policies, military personal, benevolent reformers, and, most of all, bodies of knowledge that attempted to transform displaced people in both the South and the West into agricultural producers. This effort, in both situations, often led to sickness, which government officials in both regions of the country needed to respond to. Furthermore, historians of late have been calling for scholars to recognize the connections between the South and the West during Reconstruction. See Richard White, *"It's Your Misfortune and None of My Own": A History of the American West* (Norman: University of Oklahoma Press, 1991), 58; West, *The Last Indian War*, xix; Steven Hahn, "Reconstruction and the American Political Tradition," Keynote Address, W.E.B. DuBois' Black Reconstruction in America 75th Anniversary Symposium, November 10, 2010.
3. While one can certainly draw a comparison to the government's forced removal of Native Americans from Georgia to Oklahoma, in what has become famously defined as the "Trail of Tears," my sense is that this was a different occurrence based on the government's effort to create a reservation system powered by free labor in the West in the late 1860s. In the

1830s, the government was simply concerned with removing Native peoples from the land without even gesturing toward how they would survive in the newly settled region. By the late 1860s, something had changed: Reconstruction in the South had provided a blueprint on how to address the dislocation that a marginalized group of people endured. The government consequently developed ways, which ultimately proved ineffective, in responding to Native people's conditions. Although the government and military's efforts did not thwart the alarming mortality, sickness, and starvation that plagued Native peoples, their efforts represent a change from the Trail of Tears. Additionally, for a sophisticated analysis of federal policy that responded to Native Americans in the West and the last Indian War, see West, *The Last Indian War*.

4. Laws in Relation to Freedmen, U.S. Sen. 39th Cong., 2nd Sess., Senate Executive Doc. No. 6.
5. Howard, *My Life and Experiences Among Our Hostile Indians*, 110.
6. Howard, 113.
7. For more on the Dakota War, see Ruth Landes, *Southwestern Journal of Anthropology* 15, no. 1 (Spring 1959): 43–52. By placing Native Americans and the history of the West, I want to underscore the connection between the liberation of slaves and the hanging of 38 Santee, which marked the largest mass execution.
8. John A. Burbank to Hon. E. S. Parker, 9 July 1869, Frame 363, Letters Received by the Office of Indian Affairs, 1824–1880; Dakota Superintendency, 1861–1880, 1861–1867. Roll #251, NA.
9. On the role of the Quakers in the West working among Native people, see Louis Fisher, "Indian Religious Freedom: To Litigate or Legislate?" *American Indian Law Review* 26, no. 1 (2001/2002): 6–7.
10. Report on the Condition and Needs of the Mission Indians of California made by Special Agents Helen Jackson and Abbot Kinney to the Commissioner of Indian Affairs (Washington, DC: GPO, 1883), 17.
11. During the nineteenth century, the federal government organized the Office of Indian Affairs, under the Officer of the Interior. Throughout the archival records, military officials often casually refer to it as "The Indian Agency." In 1947, it became its own entity as the Bureau of Indian Affairs.
12. "Proceedings of a council between Moses of the Spokane and other Indians and Brigadier General O. O. Howard," September 7–8, 1878, WD Box 153 (7); O. O. Howard to the Assistant Adjutant General Military Division of the Pacific, September 14, 1878, WD BOX 153 (8); O. O. Howard to Messrs. G. W. Parish, M. Becker, September 26, 1878, WD Box 153 (10), Charles E. S. Wood Papers, HUN.
13. On the centrality of free labor ideology in nineteenth-century American political discourse, see Eric Foner, *Free Labor, Free Soil, Free Men: The ideology of the Republican Party before the Civil War* (New York: Oxford University Press, 1971). Foner also underscores how the development of a free labor economy necessitated the maintenance of a dependent labor class. See Foner, *Nothing But Freedom: Emancipation and Its Legacy* (Baton Rouge: Louisiana State University Press, 1983).
14. Ferdinand Andrews, "Indians in New Mexico and Arizona," Andrews Manuscript Collection ("Indians Mohave"), HUN.
15. See Report of Colonel Robert J. Stevens, Special Commissioner to Make and Investigation and Report Upon Indians in California (Washington, DC: GPO, 1868), 8; Report on the Condition and Needs of the Mission Indians of California made by Special Agents Helen Jackson and Abbot Kinney to the Commissioner of Indian Affairs (Washington, DC: GPO, 1883) 17, 24; Ferdinand Andrews, 1867, "Indians in New Mexico and Arizona," *The Traveler*, 1867, Andrews Papers Manuscript Collection, vol. 2, pp. 17–18 (listed under "Indians Mohave"), Manuscript Collection, HUN. Usher L. Burdick and Eugene D. Hart, "Jacob Horner and the Indian Campaigns of 1876 and 1877 (The Sioux and Nez Perce)" (Baltimore: Wirth Brothers, 1942), 16–17. For an excellent analysis of Native American health, see David S. Jones, *Rationalizing Epidemics: Meanings and Uses of American Indian Mortality since 1600* (Cambridge, MA: Harvard University Press, 2004).
16. Report of Chas. A Wetmore, Special U.S. Commissioner of Mission Indians of Southern California, 9 January 1875 (Washington, DC: GPO, 1875), 5.

17. Yankton Dakota, September 11, 1865, Extract from the testimony of John Williamson taken at the Lawkton, September 9, 1865, before Hon. A.W. Hubbard, Letters Received by the Office of Indian Affairs, 1824–1880; Dakota Superintendency, 1861–1880, 1861–1867. M234, Roll 250, NARA.
18. Report on the Condition and Needs of the Mission Indians of California made by Special Agents Helen Jackson and Abbot Kinney to the Commissioner of Indian Affairs (Washington: Government Printing Office, 1883), 17.
19. W. T Gentry to Bvt. Majr. Gen. Geo. Hartstuff, June 24, 1869, Frame 472, Letters Received by the Office of Indian Affairs, 1824–1880; Dakota Superintendency, 1861–1880, 1861–1867. M234, Roll 251, NARA.
20. Ferdinand Andrews, 1867, "Indians in New Mexico and Arizona," *The Traveler*, 1867, Andrews Papers Manuscript Collection, vol. 2 (listed under "Indians Mohave"), HUN.
21. Ibid.
22. Military Telegram, January 20, 1871, Frame 0050, Letters Received by the Office of the Adjutant General Main Series, 1871–1880, 1871. M666, Roll 2, NARA.
23. Report of Chas. A Wetmore, Special U.S. Commissioner of Mission Indians of Southern California, January 9, 1875 (Washington, DC: GPO, 1875).
24. D. N. Cooley to Robert J. Stevens, Esq., August 3, 1866, Report of Colonel Robert J. Stevens, Special Commissioner to Make and Investigation and Report Upon Indians in California (Washington, DC: GPO, 1868), 3, HUN.
25. O. O. Howard, *My Life and Experiences among Our Hostile Indians* (Hartford, CT: A.D. Worthington and Company, 1907), 105–6.
26. Yankton Dakota, 11 September 1865. "Extract from the testimony of John Williamson taken at the Lawkton, September 9, 1865, before Hon. A.W. Hubbard, Letters Received by the Office of Indian Affairs, 1824–1880; Dakota Superintendency, 1861–1880, 1861–1867. M234, Roll 250, NARA.
27. O. O. Howard, *My Life and Experiences among our Hostile Indians*, 109.
28. For another example of how the U.S. Army monitored the movement of Native Americans, and how Indians then needed to wait to get approval to migrate to another location, which often resulted with them starving and becoming sick, see the following case in Nebraska. The agent writes, "Bull Run with 79 lodges of Southern Cheyennes is here and wishes provision to go south . . . to Arkansas with his people to their reservation. He says he came to avoid trouble that Tall Bull got into, and as that trouble is over, he wants to return peacefully with his people. As far as I am informed these Indians have behaved well since they came north. They will wait here for an answer. Man_afraid:of_his_horses is also here with about 60 lodges. Red Cloud expected to-day. All report great scarcity of game and beg for provisions." F. F. Flint to Adjutant General of the US. Army, January 28, 1871, Frame 0067, Letters Received by the Office of the Adjutant General, Main Series, 1871–1880, Delano to W. W. Belknap, March 3, 1871, Frame 140; C. C. Auger to War and Indian Dept., March 17, 1871, Frame 0144; Letters Received by the Office of the Adjutant General, Main Series, 1871–1880, 1871. M666, Roll 2, NARA.
29. Report of the Secretary of the Interior, September 7, 1865, Office of Superintendent of Indian Affairs, Washington, Superintendency (Washington, DC: GPO, 1865), 236.

BIBLIOGRAPHY

Archival Collections and Documents

ALEXANDRIA HISTORICAL SOCIETY (AHS)

"Book of Records Containing Marriage and Deaths That Have Occurred within the Official Jurisdiction of Rev. A. Gladwin together with any Biographical and other Reminisces that may be Collected" (microfilm) Barrett Library.
Julia Wilbur Diary
Slave Pen Vertical File

DUKE UNIVERSITY (DU)

Emma Spaulding Bryant Letters
James Chaplain Beecher Papers
George Gage Papers

HOUGHTON LIBRARY, HARVARD UNIVERSITY (HL)

Owen, Robert Dale, et al. "Preliminary Report of the American Freedmen's Inquiry Commission." New York, 1863.
———. *Final Report of the American Freedmen's Inquiry Commission to the Secretary of War*, "CHAPTER III—The Future in the United States of the African Race." New York, 1864.

HISTORICAL SOCIETY OF PENNSYLVANIA (HSP)

Pennsylvania Abolition Society Correspondence

HUNTINGTON LIBRARY (HUN)

Andrews Manuscript Collection
Duncan, Captain Louis C. *Medical Corps, U.S. Army, The Medical Department of the United States Army in the Civil War* [Washington? n.d.]
Library of the Los Angeles County Medical Association
Charles E. S. Wood Papers

LIBRARY COMPANY OF PHILADELPHIA (LCP)

"At a town-council holden in and for the town of Providence, this second day of August, A.D. 1799. It is voted and resolved, that three hundred copies of the first five sections of the act, entitled, "An act to prevent the spreading of the small-pox, and other contagious sickness in this state." be printed, and that all vessels coming from foreign ports, or from places where infectious diseases are prevalent, shall be immediately furnished, with one of said copies . . . [Providence: s.n., 1799]. Microform.

Chapman, John. "Diarrhea and Cholera: Their Origin, Proximate Cause, and Cure, Through the Agency of the Nervous System: By Means of Ice." Philadelphia: J. B. Lippincott, 1866.

"In Memoriam of the Lamented Dead." Memphis, TN: Young and Brothers, 1874.

Ladies Southern Relief Association of Maryland.

"Reports of State Committees, Relief for Confederates." Baltimore: Kelly and Piet, 1866.

New England Freedmen's Aid Society, Annual Report, 1864.

Pennsylvania Freedmen's Bulletin

Rush, Benjamin. "The New Method of Inoculating for the Small Pox." Delivered at a lecture at the University of Philadelphia, February 20th, 1781. Philadelphia: Charles Cist in Market-Street, 1781.

"A Series of Letters and Other Documents Relating to the Late Epidemic or Yellow Fever; Comprising the Correspondence of the Mayor of the City." The Board of Health, the Executive of the State of Maryland, and the Reports of the Faculty and District Medical Society of Baltimore, Second Dispensary. Baltimore: William Warner, 1820.

Toner, J. M. M.D. "A Paper on the Propriety and Necessity of Compulsory Vaccination." Extracted from the Transactions of the American Medical Association. Philadelphia: Collins Printer, 1865.

Waterhouse, Benjamin. "A Prospect of Exterminating the Small-pox: Being the History of the Variolæ Vaccinæ, or Kine-pox, Commonly called the Cow-Pox; as it has appeared in England: with an account of a series of inoculations performed for the kine-pox, in Massachusetts." London: Cambridge Press, 1800.

LIBRARY OF CONGRESS (LOC)

Abraham Lincoln Papers

Address Given at Arlington Cemetery

"Addresses and Ceremonies at the New Year's Festival to the Freedmen on Arlington Heights; and statistics and statements of the educational collection of the colored people in the southern states, and other facts."

Bills and Resolutions, House of Representatives, 42nd Congress, 2nd Session, Read twice, referred to the Committee on Freedmen's Affairs, and ordered to be printed. Mr. Cobb, on leave, introduced the following bill: A Bill Abolishing the Bureau of Refugees, Freedmen and Abandoned Lands, and providing for the continuance of the Freedmen's Hospital in the District of Columbia.

Daniel Murray A. P. Collection

From Slavery to Freedom: The African-American Pamphlet Collection, 1824–1909.

Letters of a Family during the War for the Union 1861–1865.

"Facts about the Famine." Three Centuries of Broadsides and Other Printed Ephemera.

"Report of the Board of Education for Freedmen, Department of the Gulf, for the Year 1864."

"Report of Brevet Maj-General Wagner Swayne, Assistant Commissioner for Alabama."

The Results of Emancipation in the United States of America, by a Committee of the American Freedmen's Union Commission. New York, c. 1867.

"Second Report of a Committee of Representatives of New York Yearly Meeting of Friends Upon the Conditions and Wants of the Colored Refugees."

Steedman and Fullerton, "The Freedmen's Bureau: Reports of Generals Steedman and Fullerton on the Condition of the Freedmen's Bureau in the Southern States."

The Diary of Horatio Nelson Taft, 1861–1865.

MASSACHUSETTS HISTORICAL SOCIETY (MHS)

Conway, Thomas W. "Final Report of the Bureau of Free Labor, Department of the Gulf to Major General E.R.S. Canby," New Orleans, 1865

Dwight Family Papers

First Annual Report of the National Freedman's Relief Association. New York: February 19, 1863.

Freedmen's Record

Second Annual Report of the New England Freedmen's Aid Society. Boston: Published at the Office of the Society, 1864.

NATIONAL ARCHIVES AND RECORDS ADMINISTRATION (NARA)

RG 15, Record Group 15: Records of the United States Government

RG 46, Record Group 46: Records of the United States Senate

RG 92, Record Group 92: Records of the Quartermaster General

RG 105, Record Group 105: Records of the Bureau of Refugees, Freedmen, and Abandoned Lands

RG 393, Record Group 393: Records of United States Army Continental Commands, 1821–1920

NEW-YORK HISTORICAL SOCIETY (NYHS)

Southern Famine Relief Commission Papers

NEW YORK PUBLIC LIBRARY (NYPL)

Eaton, Col. John, Jr. General Superintendent of Refugees and Freedmen. "Colored Orphan Asylum." p.1, Memphis Colored Orphan Asylum, Memphis, Tenn., March 1, 1865.

Eaton, John. *Extracts from Reports of Superintendents of the Freedmen.* Compiled by Rev. Joseph Warren, D.D. Second series—June 1864. Vicksburg: Freedmen Press Print, 1864.

Home Evangelist

Medical Society of the District of Columbia. *Report on the Sanitary Condition of the Cities of Washington and Georgetown.* Washington, DC: Gibson Brothers, 1864.

Miller, F. "The Effects of Emancipation Upon the Mental and Physical Health of the Negro of the South."

The Results of Emancipation in the United States of America, by a Committee of the American Freedmen's Union Commission.

UNIVERSITY OF MARYLAND

Freedmen and Southern Society Project

VIRGINIA HISTORICAL SOCIETY (VHS)

Allen Family Papers

Baskerville Family Papers

Burke Family Papers

Burrus Family Papers

Cabell Family Papers

Harvie Family Papers

Joynes Family Papers

Emma Mordecai Diary

The Reports of Charles S. Schaeffer from the Virginia Counties of Montgomery and Pulaski, with Additional Information on the Counties of Floyd, Giles, Craig, Whythe, and Roanoke, 1866–1868. Edited by Linda Killen.

References

Ackerknecht, Erwin H. "Anti-Contagionism between 1821 and 1867." *Bulletin of the History of Medicine* 22 (1948): 562–93.

Adams, Lois Bryan. *Letter from Washington, 1861–1865*. Edited by Evelyn Leasher. Detroit: Wayne State University Press, 1999.

Aikman, William. *The Future of the Colored Race in America: Being an Article in the Presbyterian Quarterly Review, July 1862*. New York: Anson D. F. Randolph, 1862.

Alcott, Louisa M. *Hospital Sketches and Camp and Fireside Stories*. Boston: Roberts Brothers, 1892.

Alexander, Roberta Sue. *North Carolina Faces the Freedmen: Race Relations During Presidential Reconstruction*. Durham, NC: Duke University Press, 1985.

Anderson, William. "Cerebral Rheumatism." *The British Medical Journal* 1, no. 542 (May 20, 1871): 528–30.

Andrews, Eliza Frances. *The Wartime Journal of a Georgia Girl, 1864–1865*. New York: D. Appleton, 1908.

Annual Report of the Resident Physician of the City of New York for 1865: Presented to the Board of Commissioners of Health at Their Meeting, January 4, 1866. New York: Edmund Jones, 1866.

Arnold, David. *Colonizing the Body: State Medicine and Epidemic Disease in Nineteenth Century India*. Berkeley: University of California Press, 1993.

Ash, Steven. *When the Yankees Came: Conflict and Chaos in the Occupied South, 1861–1865*. Chapel Hill: University of North Carolina Press, 1995.

Ashburn, P. M. *A History of the Medical Department of the United States Army*. Boston: Houghton Mifflin, 1929.

Attie, Jeanie. *Patriotic Toil: Northern Women and the American Civil War*. Ithaca, NY: Cornell University Press, 1998.

Baird, Henry Carey. *General Washington and General Jackson, on Negro Soldiers*. Philadelphia: Henry Carey Baird, 1863.

Balogh, Brian. *A Government Out of Sight: The Mystery of National Authority in Nineteenth-Century America*. Cambridge: Cambridge University Press, 2009.

Bankole, Katherine. *Slavery and Medicine: Enslavement and Medical Practices in Antebellum Louisiana*. New York: Garland Publishing, 1998.

Barkley Brown, Elsa. "To Catch a Vision of Freedom: Reconstructing Southern Black Women's Political History, 1865–1880." In *Unequal Sisters: A Multicultural Reader in U.S. Women's History*. 3rd. ed. Edited by Ellen DuBois and Vicki Ruiz, 124–46. New York: Routledge, 2000.

Barkley Brown, Elsa. "Womanist Consciousness: Maggie Lena Walker and the Independent Order of Saint Luke." *Signs: Journal of Women in Culture & Society* 14, no. 3 (Spring 1989): 610–33.

Baxter, J. H. See U.S. War Dept.

Bay, Mia. *The White Image in the Black Mind*. New York: Oxford University Press, 2000.

Bayly, C. A. *The Birth of the Modern World, 1780–1914: Global Connections and Comparison*. New York: Oxford University Press, 2004.

Benham, Carrie A. "The Nursing of Rheumatism." *The American Journal of Nursing* 24, no. 9 (June 1924).

Bentley, George. *A History of the Freedmen's Bureau*. New York: Octagon Books, 1974.

Berlin, Ira. *Many Thousands Gone: The First Two Centuries of Slavery in North America*. Cambridge, MA: Belknap Press of Harvard University Press, 2000.

Berlin, Ira, Barbara Fields, Steven Miller, and Joseph Reidy. *Slaves No More: Three Essays on Emancipation and the Civil War*. New York: Cambridge University Press, 1992.

Berlin, Ira, Thavolia Glymph, Steven Miller, Joseph Reidy, Leslie Rowland, and Julie Saville. *The Wartime Genesis of Free Labor: The Lower South*. New York: Cambridge University Press, 1990.

Berlin, Ira, Steven Miller, Joseph Reidy, and Leslie Rowland. *The Wartime Genesis of Free Labor: The Upper South*. New York: Cambridge University Press, 1993.

Berlin, Ira, Joseph Reidy, and Leslie Rowland. Joseph Reidy, and Leslie Rowland. *Freedom: A Documentary History of Emancipation, 1861–1867: The Black Military Experience*. London: Cambridge University Press, 1982.

Berlin, Ira, Joseph Reidy, and Leslie Rowland. *Freedom's Soldiers: The Black Military Experience*. New York: Cambridge University Press, 1998.

Berlin, Ira, and Leslie Rowland, eds. *Families and Freedom: A Documentary History of the African-American Kinship in the Civil War Era*. New York: New Press, 1997.

Bigelow, Martha Mitchell. "Freedmen of the Mississippi Valley, 1862–1865." *Civil War History* 8 (March 1962): 38–47.

Blight, David. *Race and Reunion: The Civil War in American Memory.* Cambridge, MA: Belknap Press of Harvard University Press, 2001.

Brady, Lisa. "Devouring the Land: Sherman's 1864–1865 Campaigns." In *War and the Environment: Military Destruction in the Modern Age*, edited by Charles E. Closmann, 49–67. College Station: Texas A&M University Press, 2009.

Brinckerhoff, I. W. *Advice to Freedmen*, and *Friendly Counsels for Freedmen* by J. B. Waterbury. New York: AMS Press, 1980. Reprint of freedmen's textbooks, originally published by American Tract Society, NY [1864–1865?]

Brockett, L. P. *The Camp, The Battlefield, and The Hospital; or Lights and Shadows of the Great Rebellion.* Philadelphia: National Publishing, 1866.

Brockett, L. P. et al. *Heroines of the Rebellion; or, Woman's Work in the Civil War. A Record of Heroism, Patriotism, and Patience.* Philadelphia: Hubbard Brothers, 1888.

Brower, Daniel. "Russian Roads to Mecca: Religious Tolerance and Muslim Pilgrimage in the Russian Empire." *Slavic Review* 55, no. 3 (1996): 567–84.

Brown, Harvey E. *The Medical Department of the United States Army from 1775 to 1873.* Washington, DC: GPO, 1873.

Brown, Kathleen M. *Foul Bodies: Cleanliness in Early America.* New Haven, CT: Yale University Press, 2009.

Brown, Kathleen M. *Good Wives, Nasty Wenches and Anxious Patriarchs: Gender, Race and Power in Colonial Virginia.* Chapel Hill: University of North Carolina Press, 1996.

Brown, Vincent. *The Reaper's Garden: Death and Power in the World of Atlantic Slavery.* Cambridge, MA: Harvard University Press, 2010.

Brungardt, John R. *Civil War Nurse: The Diary and Letters of Hannah Ropes.* Knoxville: University of Tennessee Press, 1980.

Bucklin, Sophronia. *Hospital Camp: A Woman's Record of Thrilling Incidents Among the Wounded in the Late War.* Philadelphia: John E. Potter, 1869.

Burn, W. L. *Emancipation and Apprenticeship in the British West Indies.* Westport, CT: Greenwood Press Publishers, 1975. First published by Jonathan Cape Ltd., 1937.

Butler, Benjamin F. *Autobiography and Personal Reminiscences of Major-General Benjamin F. Butler, Butler's Book: A Review of His Legal, Political, and Military Career.* Boston: A. M. Thayer, 1892.

Burdick, Usher L., and Eugene D. Hart. *Jacob Horner and the Indian Campaigns of 1876 and 1877 (The Sioux and Nez Perce).* Baltimore: Wirth Brothers, 1942.

Camp, Stephanie M. H. *Closer to Freedom: Enslaved Women and Everyday Resistance in the Plantation South.* Chapel Hill: University of North Carolina Press, 2004.

Carter, K. Codell. *The Rise of Causal Concepts of Disease: Case Histories.* Burlington, VT: Ashgate, 2003.

Cartwright, Samuel A. "Report on the Diseases and Physical Peculiarities of the Negro Race." *New Orleans Medical and Surgical Journal* 7 (1850–1851).

Casstevens, Frances Harding. *George W. Alexander and Castle Thunder: A Confederate Prison and its Commandant.* Jefferson, NC: McFarland, 2004.

Charon, Rita. *Narratives of Medicine: Honoring the Stories of Illness.* New York: Oxford University Press, 2008.

Cheadle, W. B., et al. "Acute Rheumatism [With Discussion]." *The British Medical Journal* 1, no. 1828 (January 11, 1896).

Child, Lydia Marie. *Freedmen's Book.* Boston: Ticknor and Fields, 1865.

Cimbala, Paul A., and Randall M. Miller, eds. *The Freedmen's Bureau and Reconstruction: Reconsiderations.* New York: Fordham University Press, 1999.

Clinton, Catherine. *Harriet Tubman: The Road to Freedom.* Boston: Little, Brown, 2004.

Clinton, Catherine, and Nina Silber, eds. *Battle Scars: Gender and Sexuality in the American Civil War.* New York: Oxford University, 2006.

Clinton, Catherine, and Nina Silber, eds. *Divided Houses: Gender and the Civil War.* New York: Oxford University Press, 1992.

Colgrove, James. "Between Persuasion and Compulsion: Smallpox Control in Brooklyn and New York, 1894–1902." *Bulletin of the History of Medicine* 78, no. 2 (2004): 349–78.

Conway, Thomas. "The Freedmen of Louisiana: Final Report of the Bureau of Free Labor, Department of the Gulf. To Major General R.S. Canby." Printed at the New Orleans Times Book and Job Office, 1865.

Cooke, Michael Anthony. "The Health of Blacks During Reconstruction, 1862–1870." PhD diss., University of Maryland, 1983.

Cooper, Frederick, Thomas C. Holt, and Rebecca J. Scott. *Beyond Slavery: Explorations of Race, Labor, and Citizenship in Postemancipation Societies.* Chapel Hill: University of North Carolina Press, 2000.

Councell, Clara E. "War and Infectious Disease." *Public Health Reports (1896–1970)* 56, no. 12 (Mar. 21, 1941): 547–73.

Cox, Lawanda, and John H. Cox, eds. *Reconstruction, the Negro, and the New South.* Columbia: University of South Carolina Press, 1973.

Cox, Samuel. *Eight Years in Congress, from 1857 to 1865.* New York: D. Appleton, 1865.

Crumpler, Rebecca. *A Book of Medical Discourses.* Boston: Cashman, Keating, 1883.

Currie, James T. *Enclave: Vicksburg and Her Plantations, 1863–1870.* Jackson: University Press of Mississippi, 1980.

Davis, Ann Marie. "Bodies, Numbers, and Empires: Representing "The Prostitute" in Modern Japan (1850–1912)." PhD diss., University of California, Los Angeles, 2009.

Davis, Ronald L. F. *Good and Faithful Labor: From Slavery to Sharecropping in the Natchez District, 1860–1890.* Westport: Greenwood Press, 1982.

Demerath, N. J., ed. *Sacred Companies: Organizational Aspects of Religion and Religious Aspects of Organizations.* New York: Oxford University Press, 1998.

Dennett, John Richard. *The South As It Is, 1865–1866.* Edited by Henry M. Christman. New York: Viking Press, 1965.

Deyle, Steven. *Carry Me Back: The Domestic Slave Trade in American Life.* New York: Oxford University Press, 2005.

Downs, Gregory P., and James Downs. "Was Freedom Enough?" *New York Times,* November 11, 2011.

Downs, Jim. "The Other Side of Freedom: Destitution, Disease, and Dependency among Freedwomen and Their Children during and after the Civil War." In *Battle Scars: Gender and Sexuality in the American Civil War,* edited by Catherine Clinton and Nina Silber, 78–103 (New York: Oxford University Press, 2006).

Downs, Jim. "Uplift, Violence, and Service: Black Women Educators in the Reconstruction South." *The Southern Historian* 24 (Spring 2003): 29–39.

Dubois, Laurent. *A Colony of Citizens: Revolution & Slave Emancipation in the French Caribbean, 1787–1804.* Chapel Hill: University of North Carolina Press, 2004.

Du Bois, W. E. B. *Black Reconstruction in America.* New York: Russell and Russell, 1935.

Du Bois, W. E. B. *Darkwater: Voices from Within the Veil.* New York: Harcourt, Brace, and Howe, 1920.

Dunning, William Archibald. *Reconstruction, Political and Economic, 1865–1877.* New York: Harper and Brothers, 1907.

Earle, Pliny. *History, Description and Statistics of the Bloomingdale Asylum for the Insane.* New York: Egbert, Hovey and King, Printers, 1848.

Eaton, John. *Extracts from Reports of Superintendents of the Freedmen.* Compiled by Rev. Joseph Warren, D.D. Second series—June 1864. Vicksburg, MS: Freedmen Press Print, 1864.

Eaton, John. *Grant Lincoln and the Freedmen.* New York: Longman's, Green, 1907.

Eisenberg, Joseph N. S. "How New Roads Affect the Transmission of Diarrheal Pathogens in Rural Ecuador." *Proceedings of the National Academy of Sciences of the United States of America* 103, no. 51 (December 19, 2006): 19460–65.

Eisenberg, Joseph, N. S. MA Desai, K. Levy, S. J. Bates, S. Liang, K. Naumoff, and J. C. Scott, eds. "Environmental Detriments of Infectious Disease: A Framework for Tracking Casual Links and Guiding Public Health Research." *Environmental Health Perspectives* 115, no. 8 (August 2007): 1216–23.

Elliot, T. D. *See* U.S. Congress. House.

Ellis, Thomas. *Leaves from the Diary of an Army Surgeon: or, Incidents of Field, Camp, and Hospital Life*. New York: Bradburn, 1863.

English, Peter C. "The Emergence of Rheumatic Fever in the Nineteenth Century." *The Milbank Quarterly* 67, supp. 1 (1989): 33–49.

Engs, Robert. *Freedom's First Generation: Black Hampton, Virginia, 1861–1890*. Philadelphia: University of Pennsylvania Press, 1979.

Farmer, Paul. *AIDS and Accusation: Haiti and the Geography of Blame*. Berkeley: University of California Press, 1992.

Farmer-Kaiser, Mary. *Freedwomen and the Freedmen's Bureau: Race, Gender, and Public Policy in the Age of Emancipation*. New York: New York University Press, 2010.

Faulkner, Carol. *Women's Radical Reconstruction: The Freedmen's Aid Movement*. Philadelphia: University of Pennsylvania, 2006.

Faust, Drew Gilpin. *Mothers of Invention: Women of the Slaveholding South in the American Civil War*. Chapel Hill: University of North Carolina Press, 1996.

Faust, Drew Gilpin. *This Republic of Suffering: Death and the American Civil War*. New York: Vintage, 2009.

Fenn, Elizabeth. *Pox Americana: The Great Smallpox Epidemic of 1775–82*. New York: Hill and Wang, 2001.

Fett, Sharla. *Working Cures: Healing, Health, and Power on Southern Slave Plantations*. Chapel Hill: University of North Carolina Press, 2002.

Fields, Barbara J. "Ideology and Race in American History." In *Region, Race and Reconstruction: Essays in Honor of C. Vann Woodward*, edited by J. Morgan Kousser and James M. McPherson, 143–177. New York: Oxford University Press, 1982.

Fields, Barbara J. "Of Rogues and Geldings." *The American Historical Review* 108, no. 5 (December 2003): 1397–1405.

Fields, Barbara J. *Slavery and Freedom on the Middle Ground: Maryland During the Nineteenth Century*. New Haven, CT: Yale University Press, 1985.

Fields, Barbara J. Fields, Barbara J. "Slavery, Race, and Ideology in the United States of America." *New Left Review* 181 (May–June 1990): 95–118.

Fields, Barbara J. "Whiteness, Racism, and Identity." *International Labor and Working-Class History* 60 (Fall 2001): 48–56.

Fields, Barbara J. "Who Freed the Slaves?" In *The Civil War*, edited by Geoffrey C. Ward. New York: Knopf, 1990.

Finley, Randy. " 'In War's Wake': Health Care and Arkansas Freedmen, 1863–1888." *Arkansas Historical Quarterly* 2, no. 2 (Summer 1992): 135–63.

Fisher, Louis. "Indian Religious Freedom: To Litigate or Legislate?" *American Indian Law Review* 26, no. 1 (2001–2002): 1–39.

Fitzhugh, George. "Agricultural, Commercial, Industrial Progress and Resources." *Debow's Review* 2, no. 4 (October 1866).

Foner, Eric. *Free Labor, Free Soil, Free Men: The Ideology of the Republican Party before the Civil War*. New York: Oxford University Press, 1971.

Foner, Eric. *Freedom's Lawmakers: A Directory of Black Officeholders During Reconstruction*. New York: Oxford University Press, 1993.

Foner, Eric. *Nothing But Freedom: Emancipation and Its Legacy*. Baton Rouge: Louisiana State University Press, 1983.

Foner, Eric. *Reconstruction: America's Unfinished Business, 1863–1877*. New York: Harper and Row, 1988.

Foner, Philip S., and George E. Walker, eds. *Proceedings of the Black State Conventions*. Philadelphia: Temple University Press, 1980.

Forman, Jacob Gilbert. *The Western Sanitary Commission; A Sketch of Its Origin, History, Labors for the Sick and Wounded of the Western Armies, and Aid Given to the Freedmen and Union Refugees, with Incidents of Hospital Life*. St. Louis, MO: Published for the Mississippi Sanitary Fair, 1864.

Foucault, Michel. *The Birth of the Clinic: An Archeology of Medical Perception*. New York: Vintage, 1994.

Foucault, Michel. *Discipline and Punish: The Birth of the Prison*. New York: Vintage, 1995.

Fredrickson, George. *The Black Image in the White Mind: The Debate on Afro-American Character and Destiny, 1817–1914*. New York: Harper and Row, 1971.

Freemon, Frank R. *Gangrene and Glory: Medical Care During the American Civil War*. Madison, NJ: Fairleigh Dickinson University Press, 1998.

Frieden, Nancy Mandelker. *Russian Physicians in an Era of Reform and Revolution, 1865–1905*. Princeton, NJ: Princeton University Press, 1981.

Gallman, J. Matthew. *The Civil War Chronicle*. New York: Crown Publishers, 2000.

Gallman, J. Matthew. *Receiving Erin's Children: Philadelphia, Liverpool, and the Irish Famine Migration, 1845–1855*. Chapel Hill: University of North Carolina Press, 2000.

Gamble, Vanessa Northington. *Making a Place for Ourselves: The Black Hospital Movement, 1920–1945*. New York: Oxford University Press, 1995.

Gamble, Vanessa Northington. "Under the Shadow of Tuskegee: African Americans and Health Care." *American Journal of Public Health* 87, no. 11 (1997): 1773–78.

Gerteis, Louis S. *From Contraband to Freedmen: Federal Policy Toward Southern Blacks 1861–1865*. Westport, CT: Greenwood Press, 1973.

Giesberg, Judith Ann. *Civil War Sisterhood: The U.S. Sanitary Commission and Women's Politics in Transition*. Boston: Northeastern University Press, 2000.

Ginzberg, Lori. *Women and the Work of Benevolence: Morality, Politics, and Class in the Nineteenth Century*. New Haven, CT: Yale University Press, 1990.

Glymph, Thavolia. *Out of the House of Bondage: The Transformation of the Plantation Household*. Cambridge: Cambridge University Press, 2008.

Glymph, Thavolia, and John Kushma, eds. *Essays on the Postbellum Southern Economy*. College Station: University of Texas at Austin, 1985.

Gomez, Michael. *Exchanging Our Country Marks: The Transformation of African Identities in the Colonial and Antebellum South*. Chapel Hill: University of North Carolina Press, 1998.

Gordon, Sarah Barringer. *The Mormon Question: Polygamy and Constitutional Conflict in Nineteenth-Century America*. Chapel Hill: University of North Carolina Press, 2002.

Gould, Benjamin Apthorp. *Investigations in the Military and Anthropological Statistics of American Soldiers*. New York: Published for the U.S. Sanitary Commission, by Hurd and Houghton. Cambridge: Riverside Press, 1869.

Govan, Gilbert E., and James W. Livingood. "Chattanooga Under Military Occupation, 1863–1865." *Journal of Southern History* 17, no. 1 (February 1951): 23–47.

Grant, Ulysses S. *Personal Memoir of Ulysses S. Grant*. New York: C. L. Webster, 1885.

Greenbie, Marjorie. *Lincoln's Daughters of Mercy*. New York: G. P. Putnam's Sons, 1944.

Greiner, James M., Janet L. Coryell, and James R. Smither. *A Surgeon's Civil War: The Letters and Diary of Daniel M. Holt, M.D.* Kent, OH: Kent State University Press, 1994.

Griffin, Farah J. *Beloved Sisters and Loving Friends, Letters from Rebecca Primus of Royal Oak, Maryland, and Addie Brown of Hartford, Connecticut, 1854–1868*. New York: Knopf, 1999.

Griscom, John H. *The Sanitary Condition of the Laboring Population of New York*. New York: Harper and Brothers, 1845.

Gronim, Sarah Stidstone. "Imagining Inoculation: Smallpox, the Body, and Social Relations of Healing in the Eighteenth Century." *Bulletin of the History of Medicine* 80, (2006): 247–68.

Hahn, Steven. *A Nation Under Our Feet: Black Political Struggles in the Rural South from Slavery to the Great Migration*. Cambridge, MA: Harvard University Press, 2005.

Hahn, Steven. "Reconstruction and the American Political Tradition." Keynote address, W.E.B. DuBois' Black Reconstruction in America 75th Anniversary Symposium, November 10, 2010.

Hait, Michael. "Civil War Pension Application Files—A Rich Source of Detail." *Examiner.com.*

Hancock, Cornelia. *Letters of a Civil War Nurse*. Edited by Henrietta Stratton Jaquette. Lincoln: University of Nebraska Press, 1998.

Harris, Leslie. *In the Shadow of Slavery: African Americans in New York City, 1626–1863*. Chicago: University of Chicago Press, 2004.

Harrison, Robert. "Welfare and Employment Policies of the Freedmen's Bureau in the District of Columbia." *Journal of Southern History* 72, no. 1 (February 2006): 75–110.

Hartman, Saidiya. *Scenes of Subjection: Terror, Slavery, and Self-Making in Nineteenth-century America*. New York: Oxford University Press, 1987.

Hartman, Saidiya. "Venus in Two Acts." *Small Axe* 26 (2008): 1–14.

Hasci, Timothy A. *Second Home: Orphan Asylums and Poor Families in America*. Cambridge, MA: Harvard University Press, 1997.

Hasson, Gail. "Health and Welfare of Freedmen in Reconstruction Alabama." *The Alabama Review* 35, no. 2 (April 1982): 94–110.

Haviland, Laura S. *A Woman's Life-Work; Labors and Experiences*. Chicago: Waite, 1887.

Hayes, J. R. *Negrophobia "On the Brain" in White Men, or, An Essay upon the Origin and Progress, both Mental and Physical, of the Negro Race and the Use to Be Made of Him by the Politicians in the United States*. Washington, DC: Powell, Ginck, 1869.

Henze, Charlotte E., *Disease, Health Care and Government in Late Imperial Russia: Life and Death on the Volga, 1823–1914*. New York: Routledge, 2011.

Herberger, Charles F., ed. *A Yankee at Arms: The Diary of Lieutenant Augustus D. Ayling, 29th Massachusetts Volunteers*. Knoxville: University of Tennessee Press, 1999.

Hewitt, Nancy. *Women's Activism and Social Change: Rochester, 1822–1872*. Ithaca, NY: Cornell University Press, 1984.

Higginbotham, Evelyn Brooks. "African-American Women's History and the Metalanguage of Race." *Signs* 17 (Winter 1992): 251–74.

Hodes, Martha. "The Mercurial Nature and Abiding Power of Race: A Transnational Family Story." *American Historical Review* 108, no. 1 (February 2003): 84–118.

Holloway, Laura C. *Howard: The Christian Hero*. New York: Funk and Wagnalls, 1885.

Holt, Thomas. *Black Over White: Negro Political Leadership in South Carolina During Reconstruction*. Urbana: University of Illinois Press, 1977.

Holt, Thomas, et al. *A Special Mission: The Story of the Freedmen's Hospital, 1862–1962*. Washington, DC: Howard University, 1975.

Hope, W. Martin, and Jason H. Silverman. *Relief and Recovery in Post-Civil War South Carolina: A Death by Inches*. Lewiston, NY: Edwin Mellen Press, 1997.

Hopkins, Donald R. *Princes and Peasants: Smallpox in History*. Chicago: University of Chicago Press, 1983.

Howard, Oliver Otis. *Autobiography of Oliver Otis Howard*. Vol. 2. New York: Baker and Taylor, 1907.

Howard, Oliver Otis. *My Life and Experiences among Our Hostile Indians*. Hartford, CT: A.D. Worthington, 1907.

Howard, Oliver Otis. *Report of Brevet Major General O. O. Howard to the Secretary of War, October 20, 1869*. Washington, DC: GPO, 1869.

Huber, Valeska. "The Unification of the Globe by Disease? The International Sanitary Conferences on Cholera, 1851–1894." *The Historical Journal* 49, no. 2 (June 2006): 453–76.

Humphreys, Charles A. *Field, Camp, Hospital, and Prison in the Civil War, 1863–1865*. Boston: Geo. H. Ellis, 1918.

Humphreys, Margaret. *Intensely Human: The Health of the Black Soldier in the American Civil War*. Baltimore: Johns Hopkins University Press, 2008.

Humphreys, Margaret. *Malaria: Poverty, Race, and Public Health in the United States*. Baltimore: Johns Hopkins University Press, 2001.

Humphreys, Margaret. *Yellow Fever and the South*. New Brunswick, NJ: Rutgers University Press, 1992.

Hunter, Tera. *To 'Joy My Freedom: Southern Black Women's Lives and Labors after the Civil War*. Cambridge, MA: Harvard University Press, 1997.

Jackson, Helen, and Abbot Kinney. *Report on the Condition and Needs of the Mission Indians of California made by Special Agents Helen Jackson and Abbot Kinney to the Commissioner of Indian Affairs*. Washington, DC: GPO, 1883.

Jackson, Lynette. *Surfacing Up: Psychiatry and Social Order in Colonial Zimbabwe, 1908–1968.* Ithaca, NY: Cornell University Press, 2005.

James, Horace. *Annual Report of the Superintendent of Negro Affairs in North Carolina.* Boston: W.F. Brown, 1864.

Jamison, Bishop M. F. *Autobiography and Work of Bishop M.F. Jamison, D.D. ("Uncle Joe") Editor, Publisher, and Church Extension Secretary; a Narration of His Whole Career from the Cradle to the Bishopric of the Colored M.E. Church in America.* Nashville, TN: Smith and Lamar, 1912.

Jarvis, Edward. *Insanity Among the Coloured Population of the Free States.* T.K. and P.G. Collins Printers, 1844.

Jarvis, Edward. *Insanity and Insane Asylums.* Louisville, KY: Prentice and Weissinger, 1841.

Johnson, Walter. *Soul by Soul: Life Inside the Antebellum Slave Market.* Cambridge, MA: Harvard University Press, 1999.

Jones, David S. *Rationalizing Epidemics: Meanings and Uses of American Indian Mortality since 1600.* Cambridge, MA: Harvard University Press, 2004.

Jones, Jacqueline. *Labor of Love, Labor of Sorrow: Black Women, Work, and the Family from Slavery to the Present.* New York: Vintage, 1985.

Jones, Jacqueline. *Soldiers of Light and Love: Northern Teachers and Georgia Blacks, 1865–1873.* Chapel Hill: University of North Carolina Press, 1980.

Jones, Jim. *Bad Blood: The Tuskegee Syphilis Experiment.* New York: Free Press, 1993.

Jordan, Ervin L. Jr. *Black Confederates and Afro-Yankees in Civil War Virginia.* Charlottesville: University Press of Virginia, 1995.

Jorland, Gerard, et al. *Body Counts: Medical Quantification in Historical and Sociological Perspective.* Montreal: McGill-Queen's University Press, 2005.

Katz, Michael B. *In the Shadow of the Poor House: A Social History of Welfare in America.* New York: Basic Books, 1986.

Keckley, Elizabeth. *Behind the Scenes, Or, Thirty Years a Slave, and Four Years in the White House.* Edited by Henry Louis Gates, Jr. New York: Oxford University Press, 1988.

Kennett, Lee. *Sherman: A Soldier's Life.* New York: Harper Collins, 2001.

Kipple, Kenneth F., and Virginia Himmelsteib King. *Another Dimension to the Black Diaspora: Diet, Disease, and Racism.* Cambridge: Cambridge University Press, 1981.

Kirby, Jack Temple. "The American Civil War: An Environmental View." National Humanities website, http://nationalhumanitiescenter.org/.

Kleinman, Arthur. *Illness Narratives: Suffering, Healing, and the Human Condition.* New York: Basic Books, 1989.

Knight, Michael F. "The Rost Home Colony, St. Charles Parish, Louisiana," *Prologue,* vol. 3, no. 3 (2001): National Archives website, http://www.archives.gov/.

Lankford, George, ed. *Memories of Arkansas Slavery Narratives from the 1930s WPA Collections.* 2nd ed. Fayetteville: University of Arkansas Press, 2006.

Latour, Bruno, *The Pasteurization of France.* Cambridge, MA: Harvard University Press, 1988.

Leavitt, Judith Walzer. *Typhoid Mary: Captive to the Public's Heath.* Boston: Beacon Press, 1996.

Legan, Marshall Scott. "Disease and Freedmen in Mississippi During Reconstruction." *Journal of History of Medicine* (July 1973): 257–67.

LeGrand-Waitz, Julia Ellen. *The Journal of Julia LeGrand, New Orleans, 1862–1863.* Edited by Kate Mason Rowland and Agnes E. Croxall. Richmond, VA: Everett Waddey, 1911.

Lester, Robert E., ed. "Records of the Freedmen's Hospital, 1872–1910." LexisNexis Academic and Library Solutions, 2004.

Letterman, Jonathan. *Medical Recollections of the Army of the Potomac.* New York: D. Appleton, 1866.

Levine, Bruce. *Half Slave and Half Free: The Roots of the Civil War.* New York: Hill and Wang, 1992.

Litwack, Leon. *Been in the Storm So Long: The Aftermath of Slavery.* New York: Vintage, 1980.

Livermore, Mary A. *My Story of the War: A Woman's Narrative of Four Years Personal Experience.* Hartford, CT: A.D. Worthington, 1890.

Low, Michael Christopher. "Empire and the Hajj: Pilgrims, Plagues, and Pan-Islam under British Surveillance, 1865–1908." *International Journal of Middle East Studies* 40 (2008): 269–90.

Lowenfels, Walter, ed. *Walt Whitman's Civil War*. New York: Alfred A. Knopf, 1960.

Magdol, Edward, *Essays on the Freedmen's Community*. Westport, CT: Greenwood Press, 1977.

Majors, Monroe A. *Noted Negro Women: Their Triumphs and Activities*. Chicago: Donohue and Henneberry, 1893.

Manion, Jennifer. "Women's Crime and Prison Reform in Early Pennsylvania, 1786–1829." PhD diss., Rutgers University, 2008.

Manning, Chandra. *What This Cruel War Was Over: Soldiers, Slavery, and the Civil War*. New York: Vintage, 2008.

Mantle, Alfred. "The Etiology of Rheumatism Considered from a Bacterial Point of View." *The British Medical Journal* 1, no. 1382 (June 25, 1887): 1381–84.

Marten, James. *The Children's Civil War*. Chapel Hill: University of North Carolina Press, 1998.

Masur, Kate. "'A Rare Phenomenon of Philological Vegetation': The Word 'Contraband' and the Meanings of Emancipation in the United States," *Journal of American History* 93, no. 4 (2007): 1–65.

Masur, Kate. "Reconstructing the Nation's Capital: The Politics of Race and Citizenship, 1862–1878." PhD diss., University of Michigan, 2001.

McAdory, Thomas O. *History of Alabama and Dictionary of Alabama Biography*. Vol. 1. Chicago: S.J. Clarke Publishing Company, 1921.

McAlister, Elizabeth. *Rara*. Berkeley: University of California Press, 2002.

McCandless, Peter. *Moonlight, Magnolias, and Madness: Insanity in South Carolina from the Colonial Period to the Progressive Era*. Chapel Hill: University of North Carolina Press, 1996.

McCurry, Stephanie. *Confederate Reckoning: Power and Politics in the Civil War South*. Cambridge, MA: Harvard University Press, 2010.

McGuire, Judith. *Diary of a Southern Refugee During the War: By a Lady of Virginia, Richmond*. J. W. Randolph and English, 1889.

McKay, C. E. *Stories of Hospital and Camp Life*. Philadelphia: Claxton, Remsen, and Haffelfinger, 1876.

McPherson, James. *Ordeal by Fire: The Civil War and Reconstruction*. New York: Alfred A. Knopf, 1982.

McWhiney, Grady, ed. *Reconstruction and the Freedmen*. Chicago: McNally and Company, 1963.

Meier, Kathryn S. "No Place for the Sick: Nature's War on Civil War Soldiers Mental and Physical Health in the 1862 Peninsula and Shenandoah Valley Campaigns." *The Journal of the Civil War Era* 1, no. 2 (June 2011): 176–206.

Minardi, Margot. "The Boston Inoculation Controversy of 1721–1722: An Incident in the History of Race." *William and Mary Quarterly* (2004): 47–76.

M'Kie, Thomas J. "The Negro and Some of His Disease as Observed in the Vicinity of Woodlawn, S.C." South Carolina Medical Association. Charleston, SC: Walter, Evans, and Cogswell, 1881.

Mohl, Raymond A. *Poverty in New York, 1783–1825*. New York: Oxford University Press, 1971.

Moore, John Hammond, ed. *The Juhl Letters to the Charleston Courier: A View of the South, 1865–1871*. Athens: University of Georgia Press, 1974.

Morgan, Jennifer L. *Laboring Women: Reproduction and Gender in New World Slavery*. Philadelphia: University of Pennsylvania Press, 2004.

Morgan, Jennifer L. "Why I Write." In *Why We Write: The Politics and Practice of Writing for Social Change*, edited by Jim Downs, 39–48. New York: Routledge, 2006.

Morgan, T. J., LL.D. "Africans in America." New York: The American Baptist Home Mission Society, 1898.

Morris, Robert C. *Reading, 'Riting, and Reconstruction: The Education of Freedmen in the South, 1861–1870*. Chicago: University of Chicago Press, 1981.

Mutschler, Ben. "The Province of Affliction: Illness in New England, 1690–1820." PhD diss., Columbia University, 2000.

National Congress of Mothers. "Report of the Proceedings of the Second Annual Convention of the National Congress of Mothers." Held in the City of Washington, DC, May 2–7, 1898.

Nelson, Lynn A. *Pharsalia: An Environmental Biography of a Southern Plantation, 1780–1880.* Athens: University of Georgia Press, 2007.

Newton, Isaac. "Epidemic Muscular Rheumatism." *The British Medical Journal* 2, no. 1760 (September 22, 1894).

Nieman, Donald G. *Day of the Jubilee: The Civil War Experience of Black Southerners.* New York: Garland, 1994.

Nott, Josiah Clark. *Types of Mankind.* Philadelphia: J. B. Lippincott, Grambo, 1854.

Numbers, Ronald L., and Todd L. Savitt, eds. *Science and Medicine in the Old South.* Baton Rouge: Louisiana State University Press, 1989.

O'Connor, Erin. *Raw Material: Producing Pathology in Victorian Culture.* Durham, NC: Duke University Press, 2000.

O'Donovan, Susan E. *Becoming Free in the Cotton South.* Cambridge, MA: Harvard University Press, 2007.

Otis, George A. *See* U.S. Surgeon General's Office.

Painter, Nell Irvin. *Exodusters: Black Migration to Kansas after Reconstruction.* New York: Knopf, 1977.

Painter, Nell Irvin. *Southern History Across the Color Line.* Chapel Hill: University of North Carolina Press, 2002.

Parton, James. *General Butler in New Orleans, History of the Administration of the Department of the Gulf in the Year 1862: With an Account of the Capture of New Orleans, and a Sketch of the Previous Career of the General, Civil and Military.* New York: Mason Brothers, 1864.

Pearson, Reggie L. "'There Are Many Sick, Feeble, and Suffering Freedmen': The Freedmen's Bureau's Health-care Activities During Reconstruction in North Carolina, 1865–1868." *North Carolina Historical Review* 79, no. 2 (2002): 141–81.

Peirce, Paul Skeels. *The Freedmen's Bureau: A Chapter in the History of Reconstruction.* Iowa City: University, 1904.

Penningroth, Dylan C. *The Claims of Kinfolk: African-American Property and Community in the Nineteenth-Century South.* Chapel Hill: University of North Carolina Press, 2003.

Philadelphia Dispensary. *A Comparative View of the Natural Small-pox, Inoculated Small-pox, and Vaccination in Their Effects of Individuals and Society.* Philadelphia: Jane Aitken, 1803.

Porter, Roy, and Vivian Nutton, eds. *The History of Medical Education in Britain.* Atlanta, GA: Editions Rodopi, 1995.

Prokipowicz, Gerald, J. *All for the Regiment: The Army of the Ohio, 1861–62.* Chapel Hill: University of North Carolina Press, 2001.

Rabinowitz, Harold. *Race Relations in the Urban South, 1865–1890.* Urbana: University of Illinois Press, 1980.

Randolph, Kirby. "Central Lunatic Asylum for the Colored Insane: A History of African Americans with Mental Disabilities, 1844–1885 (Virginia)." PhD diss., University of Pennsylvania, 2003.

Ranger, Terence, and Paul Slack, eds. *Epidemics and Ideas: Essays on the Historical Perception of Pestilence.* Cambridge: Cambridge University Press, 1992.

Rao, Gautham. "Sailors' Health and National Wealth." *Common-Place* 9, no. 1 (October 2008).

Raphael, Alan. "Health and Medical Care of Black People in the United States During Reconstruction." PhD diss., University of Chicago, 1972.

Reed, William Howell. *Hospital Life in the Army of the Potomac.* Boston: William V. Spencer, 1866.

Reid, Whitelaw. *After the War: A Tour of the Southern States, 1865–1866.* Edited by C. Vann Woodward. New York: Harper and Row, 1965.

Reidy, Joseph P. "Coming From the Shadow of the Past": The Transition from Slavery to Freedom at Freedmen's Village, 1863–1900." *Virginia Magazine of History and Biography* 95, no. 4 (October 1987): 403–28.

Reverby, Susan. *Examining Tuskegee: The Infamous Syphilis Study and Its Legacy.* Chapel Hill: University of North Carolina Press, 2009.

Reyburn, Robert. *Fifty Years in the Practice of Medicine and Surgery, 1856–1906.* Washington, DC: Beresford Press, 1907.

Robert Reyburn, *Type of Disease among Freed People of the United States.* Washington, DC, Gibson Bros. 1891. New York Academy of Medicine (NYAM).

Richardson, Joe M. *Christian Reconstruction: The American Missionary Association and Southern Blacks, 1861–1890.* Athens: University of Georgia Press, 1986.

Richman, Karen E. *Migration and Voudou.* Gainesville: University Press of Florida, 2005.

Riley, James. *The Eighteenth-Century Campaign to Avoid Disease.* New York: Palgrave Macmillan, 1987.

Ripley, Peter. *Slaves and Freedmen in Civil War Louisiana.* Baton Rouge: Louisiana State University Press, 1976.

Rogaski, Ruth. *Hygienic Modernity: Meanings of Health and Disease in Treaty-Port China.* Berkeley: University of California Press, 2004.

Roberts, Samuel Kelton, Jr. *Infectious Fear: Politics, Disease, and the Health Effects of Segregation.* Baltimore: Johns Hopkins University Press, 2009.

Rockman, Seth. *Scraping By: Wage Labor, Slavery, and Survival in Early Baltimore.* Baltimore: Johns Hopkins University Press, 2008.

Roff, William R. "Sanitation and Security: The Imperial Powers and the Nineteenth Century Hajj." *Arabian Studies* 6 (1982): 143–60.

Roper, John Herbert. *Repairing the "March of Mars": The Civil War Diaries of John Samuel Apperson, Hospital Steward in the Stonewall Brigade, 1861–1865.* Macon, GA: Mercer University Press, 2001.

Rose, Willie Lee. *Rehearsal for Reconstruction: The Port Royal Experiment.* New York: Bobbs-Merrill Company, 1964.

Rosen, Hannah. *Terror in the Heart of Freedom: Citizenship, Sexual Violence, and the Meaning of Race in the Postemancipation South.* Chapel Hill: University of North Carolina Press, 2008.

Rosenberg, Charles. *The Cholera Years: The United States in 1832, 1849, and 1866.* Chicago: University of Chicago Press, 1987.

Rosenberg, Charles. "From Almshouse to Hospital: The Shaping of Philadelphia General Hospital." *Milbank Memorial Fund Quarterly* 60, no. 1 (1982):108–54.

Rosenberg, Charles. "Social Class and Medical Care in Nineteenth-Century America: The Rise and Fall of the Dispensary." *Journal of the History of Medicine and Allied Sciences* 29, no. 1 (1974): 32–54.

Rosenberg, Charles. "The Therapeutic Revolution: Medicine, Meaning, and Social Change in Nineteenth-Century America." *Perspectives in Biology and Medicine* 20 (1977): 485–506.

Rosenberg, Charles. "What Is an Epidemic: AIDS in Historical Perspective." *Daedalus* 118, no. 2 (Spring 1989): 1–17.

Rosenberg, Charles, and Janet Golden, eds. *Framing the Disease: Studies in Cultural History.* New Brunswick, NJ: Rutgers University Press, 1992.

Rosner, David. *A Once Charitable Enterprise: Hospitals and Health Care in Brooklyn and New York, 1885–1915.* Cambridge: Cambridge University Press, 1982.

Rothman, Adam. *Slave Country: American Expansion and the Origins of the Deep South.* Cambridge, MA: Harvard University Press, 2007.

Rothman, David J. *The Discovery of the Asylum: Social Order and Disorder in the New Republic.* Boston: Little, Brown, 1971.

Rutkow, Ira M. *Bleeding Blue and Grey: Civil War Surgery and the Evolution of American Medicine.* New York: Random House, 2005.

St. John Roosa, D.B.M.D. *The Relations of the Medical Profession to the State.* New York: Published by the Order of the Society, 1879.

Saville, Julie. *The Work of Reconstruction: From Slave to Wage Laborer in South Carolina, 1860–1870.* New York: Cambridge University Press, 1996.

Savitt, Todd. *Medicine and Slavery: The Diseases and Health Care of Blacks in Antebellum Virginia.* Urbana: University of Illinois Press, 1978.

Savitt, Todd. "Politics in Medicine: The Georgia Freedmen's Bureau and the Organization of Health Care, 1865–1866." *Civil War History* 28 (1982): 45–64.

Savitt, Todd, and James Harvey Young, eds. *Disease and Distinctiveness in the American South.* Knoxville: University of Tennessee Press, 1988.

Schroeder-Lein, Glenna R. *The Encyclopedia of Civil War Medicine.* Armonk, NY: M. E. Sharpe, 2008.

Schultz, Jane E. *Women at the Front: Hospital Workers in Civil War America.* Chapel Hill: University of North Carolina Press, 2007.

Schwalm, Leslie. " 'Sweet Dreams of Freedom'": Freedwomen's Reconstruction of Life and Labor in Lowcountry South Carolina." *Journal of Women's History* 9, no. 1 (Spring 1997): 9–38.

Schwartz, Marie Jenkins. *Birthing a Slave: Motherhood and Medicine in the Antebellum South.* Cambridge, MA: Harvard University Press, 2006.

Scott, Rebecca. "The Battle Over the Child: Child Apprenticeship and the Freedmen's Bureau in North Carolina." *Prologue* 10, no. 2 (1978): 101–13.

Scott, Rebecca. *Degrees of Freedom: Louisiana and Cuba after Slavery.* Cambridge, MA: Harvard University Press, 2005.

Scott, Rebecca. *Slave Emancipation: The Transition to Free Labor, 1860–1899.* Pittsburgh: University of Pittsburgh Press, 1985.

Sears, Richard D., ed. *Camp Nelson, Kentucky: A Civil War History.* Lexington: University of Kentucky Press, 2002.

"Second Report of a Committee of Representatives of New York Yearly Meeting of Friends Upon the Conditions and Wants of the Colored Refugees." 1863.

Shaffer, Donald R. *After the Glory: The Struggles of Black Civil War Veterans.* Lawrence: University of Kansas, 2004.

Sharrer, G. Terry. "The Great Glanders Epizootic, 1861–1866: A Civil War Legacy." *Agricultural History* 69, no. 1 (Winter 1995): 79–97.

Shears, P., and T. Lusty. "Communicable Disease Epidemiology Following Migration: Studies from the African Famine." *International Migration Review* 21, no. 3, Special Issue: Migration and Health (Autumn 1987): 783–95.

Simmons, William J. *Men of Mark: Eminent, Progressive and Rising.* Cleveland, OH: Rewell Publishing, 1891.

Skocpol, Theda. *Protecting Soldiers and Mothers: The Political Origins of Social Policy in the United States.* Cambridge, MA: Harvard University Press, 1992.

Smallman-Raynor, Matthew, and Andrew D. Cliff. "The Spatial Dynamics of Epidemic Diseases in War and Peace: Cuba and the Insurrection against Spain, 1895–98." *Transactions of the Institute of British Geographers,* New Series, 24, no. 3 (1999): 331–32.

Smallwood, Stephanie. *Saltwater Slavery: A Middle Passage from Africa to American Diaspora.* Cambridge, MA: Harvard University Press, 2007.

Smart, Charles, Major and Surgeon. *The Medical and Surgical History of the War of the Rebellion.* Part 3, vol. 1. *Medical History.* Washington, DC: GPO, 1888.

Smith, Jean Edward. *Grant.* New York: Simon and Schuster, 2001.

Stanley, Amy Dru. "Beggars Can't Be Choosers: Compulsion and Contract in Postbellum America." *Journal of American History* 78, no. 4 (March 1992): 1265–93.

Stansell, Christine. *City of Women: Sex and Class in New York, 1789–1860.* Urbana: University of Illinois Press, 1987.

Steiner, Paul E. *Disease in the Civil War: Natural Biological Warfare, 1861–1865.* Springfield, IL: Charles C. Thomas, 1968.

Stille, Chrales J. *History of the United States Sanitary Commission: Being the General Report of Its Work during the War of the Rebellion.* Philadelphia: J. B. Lippincott, 1866.

Stint, Henry L., ed. *Dear Ones at Home: Letters from Contraband Camps.* Nashville, TN: Vanderbilt University Press, 1966.

Stowe, Steven M. *Doctoring the South: Southern Physicians and Everyday Medicine in the Mid-Nineteenth Century.* Chapel Hill: University of North Carolina Press, 2003.

Thornton, John. *Africa and Africans in the Making of the Atlantic World, 1400–1800.* Cambridge: Cambridge University Press, 1998.

Tidwell, William A. *April '65: Confederate Covert Action in the American Civil War*. Kent, OH: Kent State University Press, 1995.

Tomes, Nancy. *The Gospel of Germs: Men, Women and the Microbe in American Life*. Cambridge, MA: Harvard University Press, 1999.

Trowbridge, J. T. *The South: A Tour of Its Battle-fields and Ruined Cities, A Journey Through the Desolated States, and Talks With the People*. Hartford, CT: L. Stebbins, 1867.

Turner, Mary, ed. *From Chattel Slaves to Wage Slaves: The Dynamics of Labor Bargaining in the Americas*. Bloomington: Indiana University Press, 1995.

United Kingdom. *Hansard's Parliamentary Debates*. 3rd ser., vol. 304. 1869.

U.S. Army Medical Museum. *Catalogue of the Medical and Microscopical Sections of the United States Army Medical Museum*. Washington, DC: GPO, 1867.

U.S. Bureau of Indian Affairs. *Report of Chas. A Wetmore, Special U.S. Commissioner of Mission Indians of Southern California, January 9, 1875*. Washington, DC: GPO, 1875.

U.S. Congress. House. 39th Cong., 1st sess., House Executive Documents, No. 11.

U.S. Congress. House. 39th Cong., 1st sess., House Executive Documents, H.R. 613.

U.S. Congress. House. 40th Cong., 2nd sess., House Executive Documents, no. 30.

U.S. Congress. House. 40th Cong., 2nd sess. Committee of Freedmen's Affairs. *Report of Chairman of the Committee of Freedmen's Affairs*. March 10, 1868, by Chairman T. D. Elliot. Washington, DC: GPO, 1869.

U.S. Congress. House. 50th Cong., 2nd sess., House Executive Documents, Miscellaneous Documents. Washington: GPO, 1889.

U.S. Congress. Senate. 39th Cong., 1st sess. *Reports of Assistant Commissioners of the Freedmen's Bureau*, Senate Executive Document 27, 1865–66.

U.S. Dept. of the Interior. *Report of the Secretary of the Interior, September 7, 1865, Office of Superintendent of Indian Affairs, Washington, Superintendency*. Washington, DC: GPO, 1865.

U.S. Surgeon General's Office. *The Medical Department of the United States Army from 1775 to 1873*, by Harvey E. Brown. Washington, DC: GPO, 1873.

U.S. Surgeon General's Office. *Medical and Surgical History of the War of the Rebellion*. Part 2. vol. 1, by Joseph K. Barnes. *Medical History*. Washington, DC: GPO, 1879.

U.S. Surgeon General's Office. *Medical and Surgical History of the War of the Rebellion*. Part 3, vol. 1, by Major and Surgeon Charles Smart. *Medical History*. Washington, DC: GPO, 1888.

U.S. Surgeon General's Office. *The Medical and Surgical History of the War of the Rebellion, 1861–65*, by Joseph K. Barnes. Washington, DC: GPO, 1875–88.

U.S. Surgeon General's Office. "A Report on the Amputations at the Hip-Joint in Military Surgery," by George A. Otis. *Circular No. 7*. Washington DC: GPO, June 30, 1867.

U.S. Surgeon General's Office. "A Report of the Hygiene of the United States Army with Descriptions of Military Posts." *Circular No. 8*. Washington, DC: GPO, May 1, 1875.

U.S. Surgeon General's Office. *Report on Epidemic Cholera and Yellow Fever in the Army of the United States, During the Year 1867*. Washington, DC: GPO, 1868.

U.S. War Dept. *Report of Brevet Major General O. O. Howard to the Secretary of War, October 20, 1869*. Washington, DC: GPO, 1869.

U.S. War Dept. *Statistics, Medical, and Anthropological of the Provost-Marshal-General's Bureau delivered from the Records of the Examination for Military Service in The Armies of the United States during the Late War of the Rebellion*. Vol. 1. Compiled by J.H. Baxter, A.M., M.D. Washington, DC: GPO, 1875.

U.S. War Dept. *The War of the Rebellion: A Compilation of the Official Records of the Union and Confederate Armies*. Series 1: vols. 1–53; series 2: vols. 1–8; series 3: vols. 1–5; series 4: vols. 1–4. Washington, DC: GPO, 1880–1901.

U.S. War Dept. BRFAL. *Laws in Relation to Freedmen*. 39th Cong., 2nd sess. Senate Executive Document, no. 6. Washington, DC: GPO, 1866–67.

Wailoo, Keith. *Dying in the City of the Blues: Sickle Cell Anemia and the Politics of Face and Health*. Chapel Hill: University of North Carolina Press, 2001.

Walker, Cam. "Cornith: The Story of a Contraband Camp." *Civil War History* 20 (1974): 5–22.

Walton, J. T. "The Comparative Mortality of the White and Colored Races in the South." *Charlotte Medical Journal* 10 (1897): 291–94.

Ward, Andrew. *The Slaves' War: The Civil War in the Words of Former Slaves.* Boston: Houghton Mifflin, 2008.

Warner, John. *Against the Spirit of System: The French Impulse in Nineteenth-Century American Medicine.* Baltimore: Johns Hopkins University Press, 2003.

Warner, John. "American Physicians in London During the Age of Paris Medicine." In *The History of Medical Education in Britain*, edited by Roy Porter and Vivian Nutton, 341–65. Atlanta, GA: Editions Rodopi, 1995.

Warner, John. *The Therapeutic Perspective: Medical Practice, Knowledge, and Identity in America.* Princeton, NJ: Princeton University Press, 1997.

Van De Wetering, Maxine. "A Reconsideration of the Inoculation Controversy." *The New England Quarterly* 58, no. 1 (1985): 46–67.

Washington, Harriet. *Medical Apartheid: The Dark History of Medical Experimentation on Black Americans from Colonial Times to the Present.* New York: Doubleday, 2008.

Washington, Margaret. *A Peculiar People: Slave Religion and Community-Culture Among the Gullahs.* New York: New York University Press, 1988.

Waterbury, M. *Seven Years Among the Freedmen.* Chicago: T. R. Arnold, 1891.

Weiner, Deborah E. B. *Architecture and Social Reform in late-Victorian London.* New York: St. Martin's Press, 1994.

Welsh, Jack D. *Medical Histories of the Union Generals.* Kent, OH: Kent State University Press, 1996.

West, Elliot. *The Last Indian War: The Nez Perce Story.* New York: Oxford University Press, 2009.

Wheelock, Julia. *The Boys in White: The Experience of A Hospital Agent In and Around Washington.* New York: Lange and Hillman, 1870.

White, Deborah Gray. *"Aren't I a Woman?": Female Slaves in the Plantation South.* New York: Norton, 1985.

White, Howard. *The Freedmen's Bureau in Louisiana.* Baton Rouge: Louisiana State University Press, 1970.

White, Richard. *"It's Your Misfortune and None of My Own": A History of the American West.* Norman: University of Oklahoma Press, 1991.

Whitman, Walt. *The Wound Dresser. The 1897 Text.* Edited by Richard M. Bucke. New York: Bodley Press, 1949.

Williams, Heather Ann. *Self-Taught: African-American Education in Slavery and Freedom.* Chapel Hill: University of North Carolina Press, 2005.

Williams, Kidada. *They Left Great Marks on Me: African American Testimonies of Racial Violence from Emancipation to World War.* New York: New York University Press, 2012.

Winch, Julie. *Philadelphia's Black Elite: Activism, Accommodation, and the Struggle for Autonomy, 1787–1848.* Philadelphia: Temple University Press, 1993.

Woods, Robert, and John Woodward. *Urban Disease and Mortality in Nineteenth Century England.* New York: St. Martin's Press, 1984.

Woodward, C. Vann. *The Strange Career of Jim Crow.* New York: Oxford University Press, 1966.

Wormeley, Katherine Prescott. *The Sanitary Commission of the United States Army: A Succinct Narrative of its Works and Purpose.* New York: U.S. Sanitary Commission, 1864.

Wrench, Ed M. "The Lessons of the Crimean War." *The British Medical Journal* 2, no. 2012 (July 22, 1899): 205–8.

Wylie, W. Gill, M.D. *Hospitals: Their History, Organization, and Construction.* New York: D. Appleton, 1877.

Xi, Wang. *The Trial of Democracy: Black Suffrage and Northern Republican, 1860–1910.* Athens: University of Georgia Press, 1997.

Yanni, Carla. *The Architecture of Madness: Insane Asylums in the United States.* Minneapolis: University of Minnesota Press, 2007.

Yeatman, James E. "Report of the Western Sanitary Commission for the Year Ending June 1, 1863." St. Louis, MO: n.p., 1863.

Yeatman, James E. "A Report on the Condition of the Freedmen of the Mississippi, Presented to the Western Sanitary Commission." St. Louis, MO: n.p., 1864.

Yellin, Jean Fagan. *Harriet Jacobs: A Life*. New York: Basic Civitas Books, 2004.

Yellin, Jean Fagan, ed. *The Harriet Jacobs Family Papers, Volume Two*. Chapel Hill: University of North Carolina Press, 2008.

INDEX

CPSIA information can be obtained
at www.ICGtesting.com
Printed in the USA
BVHW060545231222
654809BV00002B/5